THE
STAGE
MANAGEMENT
HANDBOOK

Daniel A. Ionazzi

BETTER
WAY
BOOKS

Other fine Betterway Books are available from your local bookstore or direct from the publisher.

07   06   05   04   13   12   11   10

Library of Congress Cataloging-in-Publication Data

Ionazzi, Daniel A.
    The stage management handbook/Daniel A. Ionazzi.
        p.   cm.
    Includes bibliographical references and index.
    ISBN 1-55870-235-0 (pbk.)
    1. Stage management.   I. Title.
PN2085.I5   1992
792'.068—dc20

                                        91-43215
                                        CIP

Cover design by Rick Britton
Typography by Blackhawk Typesetting

Figures 2, 3, 8, 9, 10, 11, 12, 25, 26, 27, and 28 are from the Center Theatre Group/Mark Taper Forum production of *Julius Caesar*, Cari Norton, Production Stage Manager.

To my parents

Acknowledgments

My thanks to Cari Norton, Roy Conli, the Center Theater Group/Mark Taper Forum, Michael Pule, Yvonne Ghareeb, Actors' Equity Association, Michael McLain, Bridget Kelly, Victoria Zakrzewsi, Amy Kolar, and the Department of Theater at UCLA.

I would also like to thank all the brilliant stage managers whom I have had the good fortune to work with throughout my career.

Contents

Introduction

Stage Management is more art than science. While this book will try to give you some of the tools and techniques to perfect your stage management skills, it is a fact that some people have the talent and temperament to be stage managers and others simply do not. Before discussing what a stage manager does and how to become a good stage manager, I would like to define what a stage manager is in order to have a basic foundation from which to begin.

Most people have a sense of what a stage manager is but are usually surprised to learn their perception is rather narrow. The stage manager should certainly have a knowledge of the varied components that go into the creation of a piece of theater. The physical scenery, props, costumes, lights, and sound are obvious elements requiring the attention of the stage manager, but a stage manager must be part director, playwright, designer, and producer. A stage manager will also find himself in the position of confidant, counselor, and confessor.

Actors' Equity Association (the professional union that represents stage managers) defines the duties and obligations of a stage manager as follows:

DEFINITION OF THE DUTIES AND OBLIGATIONS OF A STAGE MANAGER

A Stage Manager under Actors' Equity Contract is, or shall be obligated to perform at least the following duties for the Production to which he is engaged, and by performing them is hereby defined as the Stage Manager:

1. He shall be responsible for the calling of all rehearsals, whether before or after opening.

2. He shall assemble and maintain the Prompt Book, which is defined as the accurate playing text and stage business, together with such cue sheets, plots, daily records, etc., as are necessary for the actual technical and artistic operation of the production.

3. He shall work with the Director and the heads of all other departments, during rehearsal and after opening, schedule rehearsal and outside calls in accordance with Equity's regulations.

4. Assume active responsibility for the form and discipline of rehearsal and performance, and be the executive instrument in the technical running of each performance.

5. Maintain the artistic intentions of the Director and the Producer after opening, to the best of his ability, including calling correctional rehearsals of the company when necessary, and preparation of the Understudies, Replacements, Extras and Supers, when and if the Director and/or the Producer declines this prerogative. Therefore, if an Actor finds him/herself unable to satisfactorily work out an artistic difference of opinion with the Stage Manager regarding the intentions of the Director and Producer, the Actor has the option of seeking clarification from the Director or Producer.

6. Keep such records as are necessary to advise the Producer on matters of attendance, time, welfare benefits, or other matters relating to the rights of Equity members. The Stage Manager and Assistant Stage Manager are prohibited from the making of payrolls or any distribution of salaries.

7. Maintain discipline, as provided in the Equity Constitution, By-Laws and Rules where required, appealable in every case to Equity.

8. Stage Manager duties do not include shifting scenery, running lights, operating the Box Office, et cetera.

9. The Council shall have the power from time to time to define the meaning of the words "Stage Manager" and may alter, change or modify the meaning of Stage Manager as hereinabove defined.

10. The Stage Manager and Assistant Stage Manager are prohibited from handling contracts, having riders signed or initialed, or any other function which normally comes under the duties of the General Manager or Company Manager.

11. The Stage Manager and Assistant Stage Manager are prohibited from participating in the ordering of food for the company.

12. The Stage Manager and Assistant Stage Manager are prohibited from signing the closing notice of the company or the individual notice of any Actor's termination.

Notice that the opening statement says a stage manager is "… obligated to perform at least the following duties … ." You will be called upon and find it necessary to perform numerous other tasks. In a non-union situation, you may even be asked to perform many of the duties that Equity expressly forbids. This book assumes, for purposes of clarity, that the stage manager is working under an agreement with Actors' Equity Association.

There is no one job description for a stage manager that applies to every production. Because every production is different, every stage management position is different. Your own production experience and working environment will no doubt inspire numerous ideas and incidents I may not mention. If you can recognize these differences early enough in the production process, you have one of the important characteristics of a good stage manager and are on your way to success.

Perhaps the most encompassing definition I have ever heard came from a young stage management hopeful. After a forty-five minute discussion of the duties and responsibilities of a stage manager, I asked if she felt she had a good understanding of what I expected. She replied:

"Sure. Totally responsible for totally everything."

She was right. In fact, I believe a good stage manager will embrace this definition above all others because it not only describes the job, it describes the character of the person. Good stage managers *want* responsibility. The rest of this book details many of the tasks I expect a stage manager to undertake if he or she is to be successful. The other key to success is *character*. The variables lie in a variety of character traits that most good stage managers appear to share. Among the most important, consider the following:

A stage manager is a LEADER, who is SELF-MOTIVATED and EVEN-TEMPERED, with the ability to ANTICIPATE and ADAPT to constantly changing conditions. Stage managers are DEDICATED to and RESPON-SIBLE for every aspect of their productions without losing their SENSE OF HUMOR. They provide an EFFICIENT and ORGANIZED work environment while remaining EMPATHETIC to the people and the process. And finally, as I stated in the opening sentence of this book, stage management is art. A stage manager is as CREATIVE as any other member of the production.

It is very difficult to measure your success as a stage manager. This is partly because, unlike most management positions in business, stage managers do not have the clear guideposts of profit and loss to measure their success. Your success as a stage manager cannot be measured in quantitative terms alone. You must also measure the quality of the creative process, which is very subjective. You will constantly look for a balance between costs and benefits. Will the artistic merits of the production be significantly enhanced by the costs of extra rehearsals or the construction of rehearsal props and costumes? Is money always the solution to a problem? These are two of the most important questions you will need to answer in order to serve the producer or producing organization. As you begin the work of a stage manager, you will face challenge upon challenge cleverly disguised as problems.

You must never think of problems as negative, no matter how many times they come up. This will only depress you. Having a problem does not mean *you* have a problem. You should expect problems and take great pleasure in identifying them and implementing their solutions. No one can anticipate all the problems a production will encounter because each production is unique, and there is no past experience from which to learn. I hope to provide you with the techniques to identify the problems before they become impediments and give you methods for solving them that will not curtail the creative process.

There are three phases in the process of mounting and performing a show. Part I of this book takes you through the pre-production phase; Part II covers the rehearsal process; and Part III discusses the performance phase. This book is organized along one timeline, but you should expect many of the events and activities to occur simultaneously or even in some other order. In Part IV, you will find some insights into the organizational structure of some theaters and aspects of human behavior in these organizations. Many stage managers of long-running commercial productions believe that 10% of their work (once the show is up and running) is related to issues addressed in Parts I, II, and III. The other 90% is associated with the issues covered in Part IV. I hope a significant number of you have the opportunity to discover whether these stage managers are right.

PART I

Pre-Production

The pre-production phase consists of two components: (1) Research and (2) Planning and Organization. Research is conducted to study the material and environment of the production in order to accumulate an essential knowledge and understanding of the play and the organization that will bring it to life. Planning and organization create a framework of this information to guide you through the production process. While this is a crucial part of the process, most organizations allow very little time for stage managers to lay the foundation for a successful and efficient process. The Actors' Equity Association Agreement and Rules Governing Employment Under the Production Contract require the stage manager to be engaged at least two weeks prior to the beginning of rehearsals. The LORT (League of Resident Theaters) agreement requires only one week. This time should be considered an essential part of the process of producing a play and should be expanded whenever possible. Remember that without the time to research and organize your production, you will not be effectively able to provide the type of service and environment that will result in a quality performance.

1

Research

The research that you do now will help a great deal in your ability to anticipate future needs of the production. No two productions are the same. No two theaters are the same. Even producing the same show again at the same theater will be a very different experience, requiring a number of new solutions to the different challenges put forth by a new production. There are two fundamental sources of information to examine at this point: the script and the production environment.

THE SCRIPT

The script provides a significant amount of information regarding the design requirements of the production, casting needs, and criteria for planning the rehearsal schedule. It raises a variety of issues and questions that will help you anticipate directorial needs or challenges of the play. As with everything else you do during the pre-production phase, it will benefit you and the entire production if you know the script backwards and forwards.

To start, you should read the script for pure enjoyment. Even if you think you know the script from some past production you worked on or from seeing the play produced recently, *read the script*. Your recollection is most likely of the production and not the script. You owe it to your current production to come in with an understanding of the author's intent and not the interpretation of another group of theater artists. Your production should be original and not carry the baggage of past productions.

I know of one stage manager who thought he could save an enormous amount of time by resurrecting an old prompt book for a production of one of Shakespeare's history plays. A few days into rehearsal, the director requested time during the next day to rehearse a specific scene. The stage manager had no recollection of the scene but made a note of the director's request. At the end of the day when the stage manager was preparing the rehearsal schedule for the next day, he searched and searched his prompt book for the scene without success. As it turned out, this scene was one of several that had been cut or altered in some way in the stage manager's old prompt book based on another director's vision of the play. Unless you know the intent of the producer is to reconstruct a past production, start fresh.

After your initial read, prepare yourself for a series of detailed readings of the script. You should look for and make note of anything and everything that will have an impact on rehearsal or on the production. It is best if you focus each of these readings on gathering information or questions on a particular component of the production. This information will be used by you as well as other members of the production team. There are several forms that can be used to organize this information. You will find these forms in the Appendix.

Design Requirements

One reading should focus on the design requirements of the script. Look for anything that is an integral part of the dramatic action of the play. This information may be found in both the dialogue and the stage directions provided by the playwright. Please note that many published scripts include stage directions based on the stage manager's notes from the original production. These stage directions do not necessarily reflect the author's intent but are the outcome of the original production. You will need to make a judgment call on some of these issues as to their significance to the text. When in doubt, include them in your notes for discussion. I am not suggesting for a moment that you are to design the production in any way. In fact, you will, in most cases, join the production after the design process has begun. The intent of developing these preliminary design requirement lists is to familiarize yourself with the needs of the script and to serve as a check-and-balance system for the design function.

It is best to generate a separate list of preliminary design requirements for each design area. The Appendix provides samples of these forms for your use. At minimum, you will need a list of preliminary design requirements for each of the following:

- Scenery
- Lights
- Sound
- Costumes
- Properties

These lists should then be distributed to the individual designers and their assistants, and each list will form the basis of the running plot for that area. The lists will also serve to initiate a dialogue that will result in timely solutions to the design requirements of the script.

Theaters are organized in a variety of ways that may influence the division of responsibilities and the specific needs for this kind of information. Makeup requirements may be handled by a makeup department and even a makeup designer. In this case, a separate list should be created for this area. In other theaters, makeup will be the responsibility of the costume designer, and makeup requirements can be included with the costume list. Part IV of this text includes a discussion of theater organization.

The list of preliminary design requirements you generate is a point of departure for further conversation. After discussions with the director and designers, some items may be eliminated, others added, and some may have additional requirements placed upon them. This should be viewed as a normal part of the production process. These changes should be made to

---

ACTING AREA — The area of the stage where the play is performed. Also called the Playing Area.

CENTER STAGE — The middle area of the performance space.

STAGE DIRECTIONS — Instructions indicating the movement, blocking, or stage business of the performers or other descriptions of the physical setting or atmosphere of the play.

STAGE LEFT — When facing the audience, the area of the stage on an actor's left.

STAGE RIGHT — When facing the audience, the area of the stage on an actor's right.

your lists and redistributed to the appropriate parties to keep everyone up to speed.

SCENERY

Figure 1 is an example of how I organize my notes on the scenic requirements of a script. It is important in the organization of this material to include the location in the script where the item may be found, for easy reference by the designers and others. This should include act and scene numbers, if available, and, most important, the page number of the script. You may also feel that a general description of the set for each scene as indicated in the text is helpful, but please consult with the director and scene designer before including this description. Some directors and designers specifically avoid such descriptions so as not to be influenced and consequently limited in their creativity. However, a note that indicates the time of year, an interior or exterior, a specific location, day or night, etc., will prove very useful in future discussions.

In identifying scenery requirements, take note of dialogue that references location, directs action, or describes environment. For example, one character may simply say to another, "Open the window and let in some fresh air." Unless this action is to take place offstage or some other information is available to the contrary, the author is suggesting there be a window as part of the set. This scenic item should be included on your list. In addition, and most important, note that this window must be *practical* (i.e., it must open and close). This information should be indicated in the note column. Another play may include the line, "It's much warmer here by the fire." If the action of this scene takes place in an 18th century French château, you might assume that this fire is in a fireplace. This scenic element would also be included on your list of scenic requirements.

PRACTICAL — Any prop or piece of scenery that is usable.

Many of the items you list as scenic requirements will appear on stage in the final design, but others may not. This is a natural result of a unique group of theater artists presenting their interpretation of the script. However, their appearance on your scenic requirements list at the very least brought them to the attention of the design team for discussion and resolution. Such resolution might include altering the text to remove a specific reference or the inclusion of a particular item in the design. In any case, the production was served by this process.

LIGHTS AND SOUND

The preliminary lighting and sound requirements for a production are developed in the same manner as the scenic requirements. Once again you are looking for specific references in the script that will have some impact on the lighting or sound design of the show. The action of turning a light on or off will certainly warrant the consideration of the lighting designer. The use of a radio or other practical sound source on stage will require the attention of the sound designer.

These lists, like all others, should also include act, scene, and page numbers of the effect for fast and efficient reference. In addition, you should include a general description of the scene that is consistent with the description provided on the preliminary scene design requirements.

Often design references will affect more than one area of design. In the previous scenic requirement example, an open window may be an invitation to a sound designer to provide street sounds as background for the scene. The special effects department may also choose to provide the expected fresh air in the form of a light breeze through the window. Since this breeze is not visible on its own, the scenic designer might provide a curtain to blow in the breeze. Depending on the organizational structure of the theater, the curtain may be an item for the prop department, in which case it would appear on the property requirements list with a note stipulating that the curtain must be attached to the set in a manner that would allow it to move in the breeze.

In the second example, the fire in the 18th century French fireplace will no doubt need the services of the lighting designer to provide the warm glow of light that typically emanates from a fireplace. The prop department might need to provide the typical accoutrements associated with a fireplace. The identification and coordination of this preliminary information are the essence of the research function.

Costumes and Properties

> **PROPS or PROPERTIES —**
> All objects, except for scenery, used during a play. Categorized into hand props and set props or set dressing.

Listing the preliminary costume and property requirements for a production has an additional use that will prove very helpful as you prepare to begin rehearsal. These lists will provide a starting point for determining which items will be necessary as rehearsal props or costumes. Because many of these items will have a significant impact on the development of character and stage business, they should be made available to the actors as early in the rehearsal process as possible. This will be discussed in more detail later in this section.

You will notice on the form in the Appendix that in addition to the standard information you should include for all the design elements, there is a column for "character" on the costume requirements form and "use" on the property requirements form. Both of these design requirement lists will eventually translate nicely into preset plots for the prop and wardrobe crews and for your own performance checklists.

Special Effects and Makeup

Special effects and makeup items should appear on separate lists if these functions are staffed separately, or be included on the lists of one of the other design components based on the organization of the producing theater and the needs of the production.

Scheduling Information

One of the most valuable pieces of information you can gather during this research period relates to the use of the actors' time. Once rehearsals begin, it is incumbent upon the stage manager to get the most work out of an actor's allotted rehearsal time. A production may require the actor to attend staging rehearsals; dance rehearsals; voice, diction, or dialect work sessions; in addition to costume fittings, photo calls, interviews, and more. It is the stage manager's responsibility to see that each of these activities can occur without hindering the others or violating the Equity work regulations. Rehearsal schedules are discussed in detail in Part II.

CALL — The notification to cast and crew of rehearsal or performance. Also the countdown to curtain provided by stage management, usually half-hour call, fifteen minute call, five minute call, and places.

FRENCH SCENE — Scene that begins and ends with an actor's entrance or exit.

To begin the scheduling process requires the stage manager to break the show down into scenes or even further, into small workable segments, which can each stand alone as a single dramatic action. Some plays come with very well-defined scenes already indicated. These segments may work as they are, but in most cases you will want to break the script down even further. Other plays will require a little work on your part to determine logical segments of the script for the purpose of rehearsing and scheduling. Read through the script again with this specific task in mind.

One practical formula for breaking the show down is to define *French scenes*. A French scene is a continuous portion of the script in which the characters on stage remain constant. At any point at which someone enters or exits, a new French scene begins. There may be several French scenes in any formal scene indicated in the script. In those plays in which the same characters are on stage for a large portion of the script or for an entire act, another method will need to be devised. Remember, the purpose of this research is to make the scheduling of rehearsals more efficient. Consult with the director for a method that will accommodate the way in which he or she wishes to rehearse the play.

Scene Breakdowns

You will want to organize the information so that you can determine at a glance which actors should be called to rehearse a specific scene. The actual format will again depend on your specific production. Figure 2 illustrates a scene breakdown. Note: For actors who play multiple roles, this form also indicates the character or function in each scene. A small cast dramatic play will be less complicated and may be served very well by some other format. Do what works for you.

Entrances and Exits

Another useful format in some situations is to provide a list of entrances and exits for each character in the play. This information may be listed by the act and scene numbers used in the script if available or by page number. An example is illustrated in Figure 3. Scene breakdowns and entrance and exit information will also provide valuable information that will enable you to determine the feasibility of double casting and understudy assignments from within the original cast.

Directorial Information

Now is also the time to gather the answers to a wide variety of questions that will come up during the rehearsal process. I call this *directorial information*. Many of these questions will require consultation with the director to be sure that you are passing on information that is in keeping with his or her views of the play. The director may also request specific background information that will be useful for the company. This information may be in the form of books, works of art, music, etc.

Some of the questions may relate to historical data such as dates, places, and events of historical references in the script. A page of "Facts and Figures" will be very handy when these questions arise during rehearsals. This will not only be seen as very helpful, but will keep the rehearsal from bogging down in the inevitable debate over the facts of such events. You should consider distributing this information at the first reading. You may wish to obtain appropriate reference materials from the library and check them out to the cast and production staff during rehearsals.

Make a note of any item in the script that you may be able to provide additional information about. A reference to a public figure such as an artist, a politician, or an athlete should signal to you the need for some biographical data on the person and his or her work or activities.

Customs and manners of some periods may require expert help. A very good stage manager I know would, with the director's permission, arrange for experts on appropriate topics to meet with cast members and provide very helpful background information on customs and manners of specific societies or cultures relevant to the play.

Musical references are another item that may need some research. It is often beneficial to obtain a recording of a piece of music referred to in a play and find a time to play it for the company. A recording and the sheet music are particularly handy if the piece must be performed.

A very common task is to provide definitions and pronunciations for foreign languages, slang, and a variety of words that may be uncommon or have culturally significant differences. Again, make a list of these words and their definitions for inclusion in your prompt book. Proper names are an additional source of confusion in many plays. Provide phonetic spellings for all names on the first day of rehearsal so everyone, including you, begins pronouncing them correctly.

PRODUCTION ENVIRONMENT

Once you have completed your research on the script, it is time to look around at the environment in which you will be producing this play. You will want to learn as much as you can about the theater organization and its facilities; the contracts under which various personnel will be working; the members of the production, artistic, and administrative staff; the design of the show; and even the town in which you are working. Much of this knowledge will directly affect your ability to stage manage; the rest will add to the quality of your work and help create a positive experience for the company.

Theater Organization

It would be great if someone would just hand you an organizational chart that told you exactly how a particular organization functioned. Unfortunately, it is rare that a theater company has an organizational chart and unheard of that, within the context of a production, the organization actually functions in a manner consistent with the chart. What is more likely is that there is an informal organizational structure in place, which is much more efficient and productive. This is the first thing you will want to learn about. Keep an eye out for signs of this informal structure and ask these questions:

- Who does what?
- Who makes the decisions?

- Who is the most likely person to provide the information and answers you need to be successful?
- Who can you turn to, to cut through the "red tape"?
- What is expected of you by each of the people associated with the production?

Two additional items I find extremely useful to know are (1) who is a local person and who is from out of town and (2) who has worked with whom in the past. You will be amazed at how this simple information will help in understanding who's who.

The following is a brief explanation of some of the functional areas of a theater company you will encounter and therefore must have knowledge of. Organizational structure varies wildly among theater companies, but the basic functions are consistent. In Part IV, I will discuss in detail the organization of commercial and not-for-profit theater companies. Learn who each of the people are in the organization and start a contact sheet. The Appendix provides a format for this purpose. The contact sheet should include any phone number that might put you in contact with any relevant person. Home, office, fax, girlfriend/boyfriend, parents, etc., and do not forget the address.

ARTISTIC STAFF
The artistic staff is directly concerned with the creative process of theater. Your relationship to the artistic staff is generally straightforward and well-defined. The director of the production is the leader of this team, which includes writers, composers, designers, choreographers, musical directors, their assistants, and various support functions such as dramaturgy, literary management, voice and movement coaches, etc. Producers in commercial theaters and artistic directors in not-for-profit organizations are also primary participants in creative decisions.

DIRECTOR
Clearly, as far as the stage manager is concerned, the director is the most important person in the production of a piece of theater. The relationship between the director and the stage manager is extremely important. It is vital that you know exactly what the director expects from his or her stage manager. You should meet with the director as early in the process as the situation allows. Become familiar with the director's concept for the production. Learn how she will approach the production so you become an asset to her. Discuss with the director exactly what you expect of her and what she expects of you. Do not consider anything to be a given. Consider the most obvious tasks as part of your discussion.

As I have mentioned before, every production is a new experience and calls for different solutions and methods of work. If you are fortunate enough to develop a good working relationship with a director, chances are you will work together again. The foundation will have been laid through the first experience, but with a new production there are bound to be new ideas and circumstances that will require continued conversation between director and stage manager.

WRITERS AND COMPOSERS

New plays or adaptations add another item to the stage manager's long list of responsibilities. It is critical for the stage manager to recognize the importance of the writer and composer in the process of mounting an original production. That script can change dramatically during the production period. Since this work is the heart of the production, it is vital that you build a system for managing these changes that is both nurturing to the artists and efficient in its implementation. Techniques for managing these changes are presented later in this section.

CHOREOGRAPHERS AND MUSICAL DIRECTORS

You should approach these members of the artistic staff in a manner similar to that in which you approach the director. The choreographer's and musical director's approaches to the play will be based on the director's approach, but they may have very different needs in terms of the rehearsal process. It is your charge to ascertain these needs and find a way in which they can all successfully coexist, providing each with the optimum environment for creativity to flourish.

DESIGNERS

The traditional areas of design are scenery, costumes, lights, and sound. However, with today's sophisticated technology and the continuing specialization of theater artists, you may expect to encounter additional designers or assistants specializing in properties, automation, projections, special effects, makeup, hair, etc.

PRODUCTION MANAGER/ TECHNICAL DIRECTOR

You may find both these positions in your organization. The best distinction I can draw for you is that the production manager is more involved with the overall budgeting, scheduling, and other resource allocations for the production, while the technical director manages the implementation of the design components and the engineering function. You will work very closely with both of these positions for much of the work you must do. In many organizations, you will depend on the production manager for the general allocation of rehearsal space and schedule, crew assignments, and other resources of the organization.

PRODUCTION CREWS

The production crews consist of those people responsible for turning the design for a show into reality and then operating it during performance. The organization of these crews varies significantly based on the type and size of the theater in which you are working. The first thing to determine is whether the various design components of the production are prepared "in house" or jobbed out to independent contractors. The physical location and the relationship of the workshops to the theater and rehearsal space are important factors in your ability to manage the variety of interactions and the numerous changes and concerns associated with the production of the design elements and the rehearsal process. Make a point of meeting each of the department supervisors as early as possible. Let them know you are accessible and alert them to your plan for keeping them informed throughout the rehearsal process. There is absolutely no excuse for communication problems; it is your responsibility to communicate the needs of the production.

If there are separate crews for running the show, which is typically the case for theaters of any size, then you will also need to learn the structure and personnel associated with this aspect of the production. You will at some point have to participate in determining how the show is staffed for performance, so this is a good time to learn about the people and organizational options you should consider as the show develops in rehearsal. Typically, you can expect to need people in the areas of electrics (light board operator), sound, properties, wardrobe, makeup/hair, carpenters, and flies.

> LIGHT BOARD — The console that controls all the lighting instruments. Also called the Dimmer Board and Switchboard.

CAST

Is the show cast? If not, you will most likely participate in auditions (covered at the end of this section). If it is cast by the time you begin work, you will once again want to learn as much about your cast as possible. Get a cast list or make one. Start a file for each actor in the show. Include picture, résumé, and any biographical information available. Then be sure to read the files. The rehearsal process is usually short and very intense; this advance look at the cast will provide you with a head start on your working relationship with the actors and give you some insight into what to expect from them when you begin rehearsals. In general, look for a level of experience. This experience might be further defined with regards to working with this particular company in the past or working on a similar project. What is their experience at this scale of production?

With your own experience, you will learn what to look for and what it might indicate. For example, if the actors are not local residents, do not be surprised to find them a bit distracted by the new environment and the concerns of setting up a temporary place to live. Where to buy groceries, what's going on back home, where to cash a check, and how to get to the theater are a few of the questions that will be on their minds. Be prepared to help out and be prepared to understand. You cannot make the difficulties of being in an unfamiliar place go away, but you can make them bearable and keep them from affecting rehearsals.

ADMINISTRATION

At the administration end of the organization, you will typically find a number of business functions that will directly affect your job. The administration of not-for-profit organizations is usually under the direction of a managing director, executive director, or similar title. Commercial structures are directed by the general manager. In very small organizations, the entire administration may be handled by one person. Large producing organizations will have numerous people on staff or under contract to provide administrative support. In general, the following business activities are found in the administration of a theater.

Company management — Here you can expect to find the administration of all personnel issues: contracts and benefits, housing, transportation, payroll, etc.

Accounting — The accounting function interacts with all other departments, issuing payments for salaries, per diem, accounts receivable, and payables. You can also expect accounting to generate financial reports to aid in the financial management of the company and its production activities.

Marketing/publicity — In the marketing/publicity area, the basic task of selling tickets takes place. Advertising, interviews, personal appearances, etc., are also handled here. You will need to establish a communication link with this area to avoid conflicts between the rehearsal needs and the promotional requirements of the show.

Support personnel — This group of people may not be formally involved with the production but will nevertheless be invaluable to you at times. They can include custodians, parking attendants, security guards, receptionists, even the management of the apartments or hotel in which the company is housed. You will learn their importance with experience. Get to know them and inform them about what you are doing. On more than one occasion, I have depended on an apartment manager to wake an actor who slept through the alarm going off and turned off the phone.

Facilities

APRON — Stage area in front of the proscenium.

CATWALK — An immobile platform above the stage that reaches from one end of the stage to the other, used to gain access to the stage equipment.

FALSE PROSCENIUM — A constructed proscenium that fits inside the permanent proscenium.

On one level, perhaps the most important item to research concerning the rehearsal and performance facilities is the location of the rest rooms. Funny, but everybody will want to know. Of course, you will also want to know all there is to know about emergency equipment and procedures, heating/ventilation/air conditioning operations (HVAC), and tons of other physical plant items. Once again, there is an extraordinary amount of information you will need to assimilate in a very short time, which will require tremendous organization on your part. The location of emergency exits, fire alarm signals, fire extinguishers, and first aid stations should top your list. Maps are very useful and can be posted along with signs to locate these items and other necessities.

Make sure you have a key for every door that you need to open. This includes outside doors to the building as well as rehearsal rooms, office spaces, etc. Be sure that you have a key to any door that stands between you and something you may need to get to. Keep in mind that you should identify other items, besides doors, that may be lockable. This might include circuit breaker panels, photocopy machines, supply cabinets, control consoles, thermostat controls, and much, much more.

The Rehearsal Space

GHOST LIGHT — A light left on when the theater is locked up for the night.

Check this room or rooms out well in advance for basic environmental concerns. Be sure you know where the room lights are controlled, including their circuit breakers or fuses, and that there is sufficient light to read a script comfortably. Report burnouts at once to the appropriate staff member whom you identified earlier in your survey of the theater organization. Electrical outlets and their associated circuit breakers should also be identified. You will always need to provide electrical power to something during rehearsals, so do not let this need sneak up on you. Test the heating, ventilating, and air conditioning systems to be sure they are in proper working order and to familiarize yourself with these controls. It is very important that you have the ability to control these mechanical systems to ensure the health and comfort of the company.

Begin thinking about the best orientation of the rehearsal space. Keep in mind that throughout rehearsals, people will constantly be coming and going. Devise a plan that will facilitate this activity without disturbing the rehearsal itself. The design of the show and the performance space will dictate other concerns.

THE PERFORMANCE SPACE

> GREEN ROOM — A back-stage room used by actors and crew as a waiting and meeting area.
>
> HOUSE — The part of the theater where the audience sits.
>
> PIT — The area below the front of the stage. May be used to house the orchestra. Also called Orchestra Pit.

A theater is a unique space, which, if designed properly, will meet most of the needs of your production. Having said that, let me say it is difficult to find properly designed theater spaces. There are quite a few general items that you should be aware of. Get a feel for the audience/actor relationship. Stand on stage and look out into the audience. Walk into every corner and examine the sightlines. Then move into the house. Sit in a variety of seats to understand how the audience views the stage. Identify any problem that might obstruct the audience's view.

Next, familiarize yourself with the access routes between the stage and support facilities, such as dressing rooms, green room, rest rooms, etc. You should determine what problems exist that would hinder a performer from moving quickly and safely from one area of the theater to another. Another important issue to be resolved is the location from which you will call the show. Check to see if you have the flexibility to decide on which side of the stage the stage manager's desk will be located or if you can be in a booth in the front of house if you desire.

The Design of the Production

> SIGHTLINES — Imaginary lines of sight that determine what is visible to the audience on stage and what is not.

The production design should be complete before going into rehearsals. You should review every aspect of the designs to determine any problem areas in advance and to prevent inadvertent conflicts once rehearsals begin. The first point of reference is the preliminary design requirement lists you created based on your readings of the script. See that all the items on the preliminary list are addressed and reconcile any discrepancies. The second point of reference is the fit with the performance space and the usability by performers. There are innumerable potential problems and challenges in this area, which will become easier for you to spot as you gain more and more experience. The third point of reference is the compatibility between designs. Here are a few examples that will illustrate these last two items.

SCENERY

> MASK — To hide any stage equipment or offstage area through the use of curtains, flats, etc.
>
> QUICK CHANGE — A fast costume change.

Based on your examination of the performance space, look for access problems to the entrances of the set. You will also want to be sure that there is a clear and safe crossover between stage left and stage right. Next, determine what you can and cannot see of the set from the stage manager's desk. It may not ultimately be necessary for you to see the entire set, but if you know there is a blind spot, you can be prepared. Do not overlook masking and other equipment. These items are every bit as obstructive to your sight and access routes as scenery. Upon viewing the set, you can also begin to think about the position of prop tables, quick change booths, offstage storage, and where the assistant stage managers should be stationed.

SHIFT — The process of moving from one setting into another during a play. Also to move (shift) a prop or piece of furniture.

COSTUMES

TRAPS — Removable areas of the stage floor that allow access to the area underneath the stage.

WINGS — The right and left sides of the backstage area.

WORKLIGHTS — Lights used for general illumination of the stage when not in performance.

ACT CURTAIN — Curtain usually closest to the proscenium, which when opened reveals the scene of playing area to the audience. Also called Front Curtain, Main Curtain, Working Curtain, or Grand Curtain.

CURTAIN LINE — 1) The line on the stage floor where the front curtain touches when brought in. 2) The final line in the play. Also called the Tag Line.

FIRE CURTAIN — A non-flammable curtain hung directly behind the proscenium that protects the audience from fire or smoke emitting from the stage. May be the same as the Act Curtain. Also called Asbestos Curtain or Fireproof Curtain.

PROPERTIES

Multiple set shows add another dimension to your research work as a stage manager. It is imperative that you be as knowledgeable about the plan and sequence of the scene shifts as anyone. Remember, when the show is open and the designers and construction staff are no longer in the theater, it is your responsibility.

Once you have determined that the designs address the needs of the preliminary design requirement list, there are two general areas to examine. Identify any costume or accessory that might restrict the movement of a performer or require special care in its use. Your effort in this process is not to have the designer eliminate or redesign the piece, but to identify the potential problem so you can help the performer during rehearsals to work with the restriction and to remind the director of any special considerations during staging rehearsals, if necessary. On rare occasions, you may discover a problem that will require an adjustment in the design, but this should be the exception.

A restriction, as the word is used here, may be as simple as a hat. Hats are not as popular as they once were, and actors may need time to adjust to wearing them. Often, an actor who wears a brimmed hat on stage must be diligent in her efforts to keep the brim from casting a shadow across her face. Every performer who is designated for a hat as part of his or her costume should be provided with a rehearsal hat. This will provide them with an opportunity to become comfortable while wearing hats and force everyone to deal with the hats during rehearsals. (More about rehearsal costumes in the Planning and Organization section.)

As with multiple set scenic designs, you should have a clear understanding of the costume changes indicated in the designs. You should know at what point in the script each performer has a costume change and what they should be wearing for each scene. This information, along with your knowledge of the script, should help you anticipate any costume change problems well before you begin dress rehearsals. During rehearsals you will be able to determine the exact amount of time each performer has to make each costume change, and you can plan accordingly.

Another critical area of concern is design compatibility. Imagine a scenic design that includes metal grate flooring or some other perforated treatment. It is essential that the footwear be compatible with this material. In other words, no spike-heeled boots or shoes. More common than this somewhat obvious problem is the use of relatively delicate open weave fabrics with a set constructed from coarse materials such as rough-sawn lumber. Inevitably, the fabric will snag, causing havoc with the production. Still more problems can arise when period garments are in use. Large hoop skirts can cause a great deal of difficulty for the performer who must maneuver around the confined space of a set. Just getting through a door may be awkward or impossible if the set and costume designs are not compatible.

In your review of the prop designs you must also address the issues of compatibility and interaction with the cast and the performance space.

FOURTH WALL — An imaginary wall between the actors and the audience that disallows interaction between the two groups of people.

LEGS — Narrow curtains or cloth that hang vertically on the sides of the stage to mask the backstage area. Also called Tormentors.

Ensure that the quantity of props is compatible with the available offstage storage space. There must also be adequate space to move props on and off stage as needed. Specifically, this means a prop that is to be carried on stage must fit through the entrance. This is not an uncommon problem.

I worked on a production in which the director wanted an actor to make an entrance in a sedan chair. The chair was to be carried on by two actors, and I was assured by the designer that the door opening was large enough to accommodate the chair. I felt compelled to check this for myself. Indeed, the width of the sedan chair was narrow enough to fit through the designated door. However, the overall length of the sedan chair (with carrying poles in place) was such that the chair could not be maneuvered through the set to the door. You will come up against problems like this again and again.

LIGHTS AND SOUND

The designs for lights and sound are typically not final as you begin rehearsals, since many aspects of the final designs are dependent on work that takes place during rehearsals. But you can certainly identify restrictions created by the other design elements. The placement of scenery or masking can severely limit the available lighting positions.

Do not feel you are stepping on any designer's toes by investigating these issues. Of course, the resolution to any problem in this area requires the willingness to compromise. The earlier you can catch the problem, the easier it will be to resolve. In time, doing so will become second nature to you. You will be able to spot the "red flags" a mile away.

The Contract

TRAVELER — A curtain that can open to the sides of the stage.

VELOURS — Curtains hung both to mask the backstage area and to shape the onstage area. Also called Blacks.

SWATCH — A small piece of fabric or paint used to demonstrate the color and/or texture of the material being used.

BREAKAWAY — A prop that is specifically made to break at a certain point in the play.

As part of your research into the organizational structure of the theater, it is very helpful for you to know the rules and regulations governing the working conditions of the various production personnel. Working conditions are usually part of an agreement between the theater or producing organization and various labor unions. In addition to stipulating the salary and benefits to which members are entitled, these labor agreements define the conditions under which they are employed and the rules and regulations governing their work schedule, required breaks, maximum hours, etc. As a stage manager, to work in an Equity company, you must be a member of Actors' Equity Association. In this case, you and the performers will be working under the same agreement. Equity currently has seventeen agreements with various producing organizations in the United States. The rules governing employment in these organizations can vary dramatically. It is in your best personal interest, and a necessity in a stage management position, for you to understand these rules thoroughly. Many of these rules are referred to throughout the remainder of the text.

Stagehands may also be represented by a union. In most cases the International Association of Theatrical Stage Employees (IATSE) represents stagehands. The details of their labor agreements vary from organization to organization. Some of the agreements include many specific restrictions concerning the type of work each employee can do, the number of stagehands that must be employed, and a requirement that associated employees also be members of a labor union.

> HAND PROPS — Properties that are handled by actors during the performance.

Designers, directors, and musicians are often represented by unions as well. United Scenic Artists (USA) is the union that represents scenic, costume, and lighting designers. In addition, assistant designers and scenic artists may be members of USA. Directors belong to the Society of Stage Directors and Choreographers. As the title indicates, choreographers are also represented by this union. Finally, musicians are represented by the American Federation of Musicians.

COMPANY POLICY

> HAND-OFF — The action of a crew member handling a prop for an actor at a designated time and place during a performance.
> SET DRESSING — Props that are used to decorate the set and are usually not handled by actors.

There may be many other unions and labor agreements that you will need to become familiar with in the course of your career. Box office personnel, ushers, dressers, truck drivers, and custodians may all be working under labor agreements that will have some impact on you and the production and that will demand some level of understanding on your part. Under any condition, the company will have its own policies, which you must also learn and abide by. These policies may include complimentary ticket and purchased ticket procedures, parking regulations, check-cashing policies, etc. Ask for the policies in writing, so you may include these items in your files for future reference and dissemination to cast and crew. This is also the time to begin putting together your own rules and procedures for rehearsals and performances. This should be done in consultation with the director, and the final document approved by him or her before publication. These rules and procedures should include basic etiquette with regard to food and drink, smoking, noise, and guests; sign-in and contact procedures; emergency procedures; rehearsal rules, etc.

Extras

As mother, father, sister, or brother; social director, guidance counselor, lawyer, doctor, or banker; you can save much frustration and endear yourself to any out-of-town performer or crew member by preparing a fact sheet of useful information. I suggest the following list; you can add anything else that strikes your fancy.

USEFUL PHONE NUMBERS

- all pertinent theater numbers
- time & weather
- local entertainment information
- emergency numbers
- restaurants that deliver
- taxi
- public transportation information

USEFUL BUSINESS

- company doctors, dentists, ophthalmologists, and chiropractors
- masseur
- restaurants
- groceries
- cleaners and laundry

- pharmacy
- the nearest mall
- hair stylists

TRANSPORTATION
- public transportation maps and fares
- automobile rentals
- bike rentals

ENTERTAINMENT
- movie theaters
- night clubs
- bowling alleys
- sporting events
- museums
- galleries

OTHER SERVICES
- tours

SCENERY DESIGN REQUIREMENTS

PRODUCTION: THE SEAGULL

Date: 10/17/91

Page 1 of 2

Act I Scene 1

General Description:
Exterior – "The Country" – Day – Just after sunset
A park on Sorin's estate

Page #	Scenic Element	Note:
1	Improvised Stage	Being constructed
1	Stage Curtain	Must open and close/operated onstage
1	Shrubbery	
1	Garden Table	
1	Chairs	
5	Flowers	Picked from stage/petals plucked
7	Moon	Rising
7	Elm Tree	A dark color
11	Lake	Revealed with rise of stage curtain
11	Large Stone	Sitable

FIGURE 1

Illustration courtesy of Cari Norton, Stage Manager for the Mark Taper Forum production of *Julius Caesar*.

Mark Taper Forum 1991
JULIUS CAESAR

French Scene Breakdown

ACT I–1: (97–101)

   FLAVIUS – Actor's Name #1

   MARULLUS – Actor's Name #2

   SOOTHSAYER – Actor's Name #3

   COBBLER – Actor's Name #4

   CARPENTER – Actor's Name #5

   (ARTEMIDORUS – Actor's Name #6) (En 101)

   (SECRET SERVICE ONE – Actor's Name #7) (En 101)

   (CROWD – Actors' Names #8, 9, 10, 11, 12, & 13)

ACT I–2a: (102–104)

   (ARTEMIDORUS – Actor's Name #6)

   (LUCA – Actor's Name #14)

   CAESAR – Actor's Name #15

   ANTONY – Actor's Name #16

   CASSIUS – Actor's Name #17

   BRUTUS – Actor's Name #18

   CASCA – Actor's Name #19

   (DECIA BRUTUS – Actor's Name #20)

   CALPURNIA – Actor's Name #21

   (PORTIA – Actor's Name #22)

   SOOTHSAYER – Actor's Name #3

   (SECRET SERVICE ONE – Actor's Name #7)

   (CROWD/PRESS – Actors' Names #4, 5, 8, 9, 10, 12, & 13)

ACT I–2b: (104–112)

   CASSIUS – Actor's Name #17

   BRUTUS – Actor's Name #18

   (SECRET SERVICE ONE – Actor's Name #7)

   (LUCA – Actor's Name #14)

   (ARTEMIDORUS – Actor's Name #6)

ACT I–2c: (112–114)

   CASSIUS – Actor's Name #17

   BRUTUS – Actor's Name #18

   CAESAR – Actor's Name #15

   ANTONY – Actor's Name #16

     (CONTINUED)

FIGURE 2

Illustration courtesy of Cari Norton, Stage Manager for the Mark Taper Forum production of *Julius Caesar*.

Issue #3
4/28/91
Page 1 of 3

Mark Taper Forum 1991
JULIUS CAESAR

Actor/Scene Breakdown

Actor's Name #7:
- Secret Service One (I–1, 2)
- Cicero (I–3)
- Trebonius (II–1b, 2b, III–1)
- Newsman (III–2)
- Gang (III–3)
- Cop Three (IV–1, V–1, 3, 4)
- Messala (IV–3b, V–5)

Actor's Name #22:
- Portia (I–2a, 2c, II–1c, 1d, II–4, III–2)
- Lucilia (IV–2, IV–3b, V–1, 3a, 3b, 5)

Actor's Name #3:
- Soothsayer (I–1, 2a, II–4, III–1a)
- Newsman (III–2)
- Titinius (IV–2, 3b, V–1, 3a)
- Demonstrator (V–4)

Actor's Name #16:
- Antony (I–2a, 2c, 2d, II–2b, III–1, 2, IV–1, V–1, 5)

Actor's Name #12:
- Crowd (I–1)
- Press (I–2a, III–2)
- Maid Two (II–2)
- Secretary (III–1)
- Claudia: Technician one (IV–2)
- Demonstrator: Claudia (V–1, 4)

Actor's Name #10:
- Crowd (I–1)
- Press (I–2a, III–2)
- Secret Service Four: Fortuneteller (II–2)
- Popilius Lena (III–1)
- Cinna the Poet (III–3)
- Pindarus (IV–2, V–3a)
- Demonstrator: Pindarus (V–1, V–4)

Actor's Name #14:
- Luca (I–2, II–2a, III–1)
- Press (III–2)
- Gang (III–3)
- Cop Two (IV–1, V–1, 3a, 4, 5)

FIGURE 3

2

Planning and Organization

Now that you have accumulated more information than you can possibly remember, you must find a way to organize it so it is useful. Also with this information you can begin planning the production process.

THE PRODUCTION BOOK

BLOCKING — The movement and business of an actor on stage.

CUE — A signal for the stage manager that puts into action a shift in lights, sound, or scenery.

CURTAIN — In addition to its normal definition relating to draperies, a term used to indicate the start or end of a performance such as "Five minutes to curtain" (five minutes to the start of the performance).

The Production Book is the encyclopedia and eventually the official record of the production. Take great care in putting this book together. If properly assembled and organized, it will be indispensable to your work and to the production. The production book has three primary functions. First, it is a single reference for the process of the production. Second, this book should allow anyone familiar with the function of stage management to operate the show in your absence. Remember to leave the production book in the theater at all times. If you do not make it to the theater to call a show, the book *must* be there for the show to be operated. Third, at the conclusion of the production, the production book will become the official record of the show. At this point you will begin the process of assembling the book, but it will not be complete until the final curtain. It will require constant updating and the addition of material throughout the run of the production.

The production book should be assembled in a three-ring, looseleaf binder. Many items, such as the prompt script, will need to be on reinforced paper to withstand the tendency to tear at the holes due to constant page turning.

Throughout this text I refer to the production book as a single volume. However, the quantity of information that should be included in the production book may physically require two or more volumes. Feel free to organize this information into separate books if need be. I suggest that you keep it to a maximum of two books if possible. The logical separation is for one volume to be the prompt script and the second, all other information.

The Prompt Script

As the name indicates, the prompt script is the official text for the production. This script includes all changes, additions, and deletions to the text; all necessary blocking and staging information required to recreate the show; and all cues and warnings for the production. The state of today's copying technology enables you to format the prompt script in any number of ways. It is no longer necessary or even desirable to cut and paste your script together from a published version. This is very time-consuming and limiting. Instead, copy the published version of the script onto reinforced three-hole paper in the position and size of your choice. This will be the fastest and most flexible method. An advantage to copying that you should consider is the ability to enlarge the text. This will make it easier to read and follow under distracting conditions. Please note, this is not an invitation to violate copyright laws. Playwrights and publishers depend on the purchase of published scripts as a source of income. You do not have the right to deprive them of that income.

If you are involved in the production of a new script or an unpublished script, your options may be even more plentiful. Word processing and desktop publishing software will allow you to handle script changes easily and provide you with more flexibility in formatting the script for the specific requirements of the prompt script.

The format of the prompt script is, of course, entirely up to you. In making this decision, keep these things in mind. The prompt script should allow you sufficient blank space on each page to handle all blocking and cueing notation. It should be easy to follow under restricted lighting conditions and numerous distractions. Figure 4 illustrates my recommendations for formatting the prompt script. Notice in this example that the text appears on the right-hand page of the book and a reduced ground plan of the appropriate scene appears on the left-hand page. (Left-handed stage managers may choose to reverse this configuration.) This format will accommodate a technique for blocking notation discussed in Part II. If you choose not to include a ground plan, you may designate this page for some other information or simply provide a page of the script on each side of the prompt script. This will in part depend upon the complexity of your production and your preferred method of notation.

In the research phase of this process, you broke the script down into scenes. You should now index your prompt script by placing tabs in the script locating each of the scenes you identified (Figure 5). I also recommend in some cases that you format the text so each scene begins on a new page. If you have determined that an appropriate beginning for a scene starts in the middle of a page in a published script, copy that page twice: the first time with the bottom half of the page covered, thereby removing the beginning of the new scene from the page. Then copy the page again, this time with the top half of the page covered up to the point where the new scene begins (Figure 6). The extra blank space will accommodate the increased number of cues and other notations that generally accompany the beginning and ending of a scene.

PROMPT SCRIPT — The notebook kept by the stage manager that contains all paperwork necessary to the production of the play, including a script with blocking and cues. Also called Prompt Book.

RUN — The total number of performances for a production.

GROUND PLAN — A scale diagram that shows where the scenery is placed on the stage floor. Also called Floor Plan.

Plots and Schedules

In this section, or in a separate book, include all the plots and schedules developed from the information you have been gathering. You will also add information as it becomes available during the rehearsal process. This includes:

- all preliminary design requirements
- scene breakdowns
- entrances and exits

- pronunciation guides
- facts and figures
- contact sheets
- ground plans

INSTRUMENT — A term used for any lighting device.

INSTRUMENT SCHEDULE — A list of the types of lighting instruments to be used in a show. Also called a Hookup Sheet.

LIGHT PLOT — A drawn-up plan that designates the placement of lighting instruments relative to the set.

- sections
- costume sketches
- costume plots
- light plots
- instrument schedules
- sound plots
- preset sheets
- calendars
- rehearsal and performance schedules
- due dates

In short, everything that you research and learn should be represented in the production book. For fast and efficient reference, tab this information (Figure 7).

REHEARSAL SCHEDULES

There are four components that will allow you to develop the rehearsal schedule. The first is the director's preferred method of rehearsing this production. His or her input is essential in developing the rehearsal schedule, and the director's approval is mandatory. The second component is the work you have done on scene breakdowns. The third component is the agreement governing the working conditions of various employees of the company and, most important, the actors and stage managers. The fourth component is the overall schedule indicating the start date for rehearsals, technical rehearsals, and performance dates for the show. This information is generally provided by the production manager. An example of a master calendar is illustrated in Figure 8.

Where you begin the process of developing the rehearsal schedule depends on the organizational structure of the producing company. For instance, a company that employs a production manager may, as a part of the planning and scheduling process, already have blocked out the basics of the rehearsal schedule. Expect a little overlap in this case and work closely with the production manager to ensure that you understand each other's needs.

LORT — League of Resident Theaters. A group of Equity theaters around the U.S. that have joined together and created a specific LORT contract. The theaters categorize themselves into LORT A, B+, B, C, and D, according to their box-office receipts. Each LORT level has slightly different rules. For example, in a LORT B theater, there must be an AEA stage manager and an AEA assistant stage manager, but in a LORT D theater, there only needs to be an AEA stage manager.

This seems to be an appropriate time to enter into a discussion of the rules and regulations governing employment of members of Actors' Equity Association. As I mentioned before, there is a variety of producing organizations that have entered into agreements with Equity. While the rules and regulations governing employment in these organizations are conceptually similar in most cases, the actual numbers vary. As part of your research, you should have identified the specific agreement that this company is working under. If you are not familiar with the agreement, get a copy and study it thoroughly.

This discussion is limited to those rules and regulations pertaining to rehearsal and performance schedules and uses the agreement between Actors' Equity and the League of Resident Theaters (LORT) as an example. You may obtain a complete copy of this or any other AEA agreement by contacting the local or regional office of AEA. Some of the rules are self-explanatory. If required, a brief explanation follows the rule.

RULE 44

REHEARSAL, PERFORMANCE, AND OTHER WORK RELATED RULES

A. WORK WEEK & WORK DAY

(1) The week shall mean from and including Monday to and through Sunday.

It is important that you have this in mind when making any weekly calculations.

(2)(a) During non-performance weeks, the total work week for small and medium cast plays (fourteen [14] or fewer performers on stage) shall not exceed forty-eight (48) hours, of which no more than forty-five (45) hours shall be allotted to rehearsal.

(b) During non-performance weeks, the total work week for large cast plays (fifteen [15] or more performers on stage) shall not exceed fifty (50) hours, of which no more than forty-seven (47) hours shall be allotted to rehearsal.

Within each week, you may call each actor for three hours of non-rehearsal activity, such as costume fittings, photo calls, etc. There are limits to the number of hours for these activities as well. See paragraph (D) below.

(c) In the seven (7) days prior to the first paid public performance, the total work week shall not exceed fifty-two (52) hours. The fifty-two (52) hour work week shall fall either in the last full week of rehearsal or the week of the first paid public performance, but not both.

This rule provides extra hours to account for the increased work load during technical and dress rehearsals.

(d) During combined rehearsal and performance weeks, the total work week, including but not limited to performance, rehearsals, costume calls, photographs, understudy rehearsals, brush-up rehearsals, and classes (subject to the provisions of paragraph (C)(4)(d) below), shall not exceed fifty (50) hours. (For Musical Production rehearsal hours, see Rule 31 (G).)

When calculating performance hours, you must begin from the half hour call through to the final curtain. There are also limits on the number of hours allowable for understudy and brush-up rehearsals. Musical productions have the same fifty-hour limit.

(3) Except for days when there are early student performances, the span of the work day shall not exceed twelve (12) consecutive hours.

B. PERFORMANCES

(1) There shall be no more than eight (8) performances in any week without additional compensation. Notice of the regular schedule and any additional performances known by the Theatre shall be posted at the Theatre's announced auditions. A rider describing the regular performance schedule and known additional performances shall be attached to the Actor's contract at the time of contract signing.

Remember to count Monday through Sunday and don't forget to include the performance schedule on your audition fact sheet.

(2)(a) The Actor shall be notified of any changes of the performance schedule at least two (2) weeks in advance, except in an emergency when a shorter notice period agreed to by a majority of the cast shall be permitted.

This rule generally accommodates any change in performance schedule due to holidays or local events, which you should know about in plenty of time to give the required two weeks' notice.

(b) When the Theatre's performance schedule is less than eight (8) performances per week, the Actor must receive no less than one (1) week's notice of the addition of performances up to the permitted eight (8). The Theatre shall give notice at the time of scheduling such additional performance(s) but in no event less than one (1) week's notice.

You must give notice of additional performances as soon as the theater schedules the addition. This may be several weeks in advance or even months.

(3) There shall be no more than two (2) performances in any day nor more than five (5) performances in any three (3) day period. The total number of hours worked on a two (2) performance day, including half-hour, shall not exceed nine (9) hours.

You are allowed to schedule matinées on two consecutive days under this rule. For instance, you may have matinée and evening performances on Saturday and Sunday and meet the restrictions of this rule as long as you have only one performance scheduled on Friday and Monday. Note also that the running time of the show may be a maximum of four hours to meet the nine-hour restriction. This allows a total of one hour for the half-hour call for each performance.

(4) Notwithstanding the above, if the Actor is performing solely in local tours in any week, ten (10) performances may be given. Each such performance must be limited to a maximum of one and one-half ($1\frac{1}{2}$) hours.

This rule is usually used to accommodate school tours or other local tours while working under the LORT contract.

(5) A ninth performance shall be paid for at the rate of three-sixteenths ($^3/_{16}$) of weekly contractual salary. A tenth performance shall be paid for at the rate of two-eighths ($^2/_8$) of weekly contractual salary.

This is the formula for additional compensation mentioned in (B)(1) above.

(6) Any performance which begins prior to 12:00 Noon (except to pre-school or student audiences) or which continues beyond 1:00 A.M. shall be paid for at the rate of an additional two-eighths ($^2/_8$) of weekly contractual salary. If there are to be any performances prior to 12:00 Noon, the Actor shall be so advised at the time of audition or interview. In the event the Actor is engaged without audition or interview, the Actor shall be so advised at the time of contract signing. In either event, a rider must be attached to the contract. Should there be no rider, the Actor shall not be

required to perform without the express consent of Equity.

This is another item to be sure you include in the audition fact sheet.

C. REHEARSALS

(1) At the Theatre's option, on non-performance days, rehearsal shall not exceed seven (7) out of nine (9) or eight (8) out of ten (10) consecutive hours. The Company shall receive no less than twelve (12) hours' notice of the span of each rehearsal day.

The two-hour difference allows for a maximum two-hour meal break. You may reduce this meal break under certain conditions stated below.

(2) Except as provided in paragraph (3) below, on one-performance days, (a) if the performance is three and one-half ($3^{1}/_{2}$) hours or less (including half-hour), rehearsal shall not exceed five (5) consecutive hours; (b) if the performance is over three and one-half ($3^{1}/_{2}$) hours (including half-hour), rehearsal shall not exceed four and one-half ($4^{1}/_{2}$) consecutive hours; (c) if the performance is over four (4) hours (including half-hour), rehearsal shall not exceed four (4) consecutive hours.

On a single performance day, you may rehearse the company according to the above schedule. This is for a repertory company or one that is preparing its next production with the same actors who are performing in a currently running production. The schedule might be as follows: The actors are called from 12:30 P.M. to 5:30 P.M. (five consecutive hours) for rehearsal and return at 7:30 P.M. for the half-hour call. The performance in this case must be over by 11:00 P.M. so as not to exceed the three and one-half hour limit stipulated above.

(3) There shall be no rehearsal on a two (2) performance day if only one (1) such day is scheduled in the week. Where two (2) two (2) performance days are scheduled in the week, two (2) consecutive hours of rehearsal will be permitted on one (1) such day if actors elect to do so by majority vote. In Repertory theatres, the company vote will be taken prior to the commencement of rehearsals for the second production of the season. In non-Repertory theatres, the cast vote will be taken on the first day of rehearsals for each production. If the Actors elect that there will be no rehearsal on either two (2) performance day, two (2) hours may be used in one-half ($^{1}/_{2}$) hour segments to extend rehearsals on four (4) one (1) performance days to a maximum of five and one-half ($5^{1}/_{2}$) hours.

This shall also apply to non-performing members of the cast (see paragraph (E) below).

If your performance schedule consists of two days during the week on which you perform both a matinée and an evening performance, you have two scenarios from which to choose concerning rehearsal hours. You may rehearse for two hours on one of these days or add a half hour to the rehearsals on four other days. The Equity members get to choose which of these options they prefer. I find the second option more efficient. In the example above under rule (C)(2), the rehearsal call could be extended from five hours to five and one-half under this option.

(4)(a) On a non-performance day during the seven (7) day period prior to the first paid public performance of a production, the Theatre may schedule two (2) days of ten (10) out of twelve (12) consecutive hours for each production.

The above is usually scheduled for technical or dress rehearsals and corresponds to the additional hours made available in paragraph (A)(2)(c).

(b) In no instance shall there be more than two (2) days of rehearsal of ten (10) out of twelve (12) consecutive hours in any work week. In non-Repertory companies, no ten (10) out of twelve (12) day as referred to above shall be permitted unless there has been at least a twenty (20) day interval from the previous production's last ten (10) out of twelve (12) day. No ten (10) out of twelve (12) day may be followed by two (2) consecutive two (2) performance days.

Equity defines repertory as follows:

The term "Repertory," as used in this agreement, shall be defined as a performance pattern consisting of a series of productions introduced at intervals throughout the season, some or all of which are maintained and repeatedly revived as a part of the theatre's general program.

(c) The schedule permitted in paragraphs (a) and (b) above shall fall within the maximum work week of fifty-two (52) hours where permitted (see paragraph (A)(2) above). The company shall receive no less than twelve (12) hours' notice of the span of each rehearsal day.

Take special note of the minimum requirements for notification in this and other rules. You are the one who must notify the company, and it is your responsibility to see that these minimums are met.

(d) After the official opening or one (1) week following the first paid public performance of the Actor's final production of the season, whichever comes first, rehearsals shall be limited to ten (10) hours per week for understudy, brush-up, replacements, and classes only. In the case of a new play, where the playwright is in residence a substantial portion of the time, the ten (10) hour brush-up rule referred to above may be used for revisions for four (4) weeks following the first paid public performance.

The distinction being made here between new plays, which are undergoing revisions, and all others is that rehearsals that alter or add new material are limited to new plays and only for the first four weeks of public performances. Any other play (or after the first four weeks of a new play) may only be rehearsed to maintain the production as it existed on opening night (or one week after the first paid public performance) or for the purposes of replacements and understudies. The director cannot come in after this time limit and make changes to the show.

(e) Rehearsals must be consecutive except for a break of one and one-half (1½) hours after five (5) consecutive hours of work. This break shall be reduced (or eliminated on a five and one-half (5½) hour rehearsal days when permitted under paragraph (C)(3) above) in accordance with paragraph (E) below.

This is generally the meal break.

(f) (omitted)

D. COSTUME CALLS, PHOTOGRAPHS AND PUBLICITY

(1) In addition to rehearsal time, but within the maximum hours of the work week as outlined in paragraph (A)(2) above, the Theatre may schedule a combined total of no more than six (6) hours for costume and/or photo calls per production.

This six hours is available for each actor. You should also note that while paragraph (A)(2) allows for three hours each and every week of rehearsal for these kinds of calls, you are limited to a maximum of six hours for the production. A four-week rehearsal period would have twelve hours available, but you can only use six.

(2) Costume calls must be consecutive with rehearsal hours and must be calculated in segments of no less than one-half ($^1/_2$) hour. Combined costume calls and rehearsal hours may reach a maximum of six (6) consecutive hours without a break.

This rule allows you to break rule (C)(4)(e) above, but be careful that you do not infringe on the actual length of the meal break described in paragraph (E). Also note that you may schedule additional costume, photo, or publicity calls during the actual rehearsal time. If an actor is not needed while working a specific scene, he may be scheduled for a costume fitting or other such activity. There is no limit on these calls scheduled during the rehearsal time. This is the preferred way to schedule these calls whenever possible. The actors will appreciate not having to put in the extra time, and you can save the allowable hours outside of rehearsal for emergencies.

(3) The Theatre may require the Actor to pose not only for customary and usual photographs, but also for photographs to appear in magazines or newspapers for the sole purpose of publicizing and advertising the play. Said photographing may take place on a one (1) performance day, or before or after rehearsal, subject to the limitations as set forth herein, or during the authorized rehearsal hours, but in no event during auditions or on a two (2) performance day, or after the evening performance on a day immediately preceding the day off.

(4) There shall be no more than one (1) picture call in any week and of no less than one-half ($^1/_2$) hour's duration. The Actor shall receive no less than twenty-four (24) hours' notice of a picture call. However, combined photo and rehearsal hours may reach a maximum of six (6) consecutive hours without a break.

As with costume calls, you can extend to six hours without a break, but remember the requirement for twenty-four hour notice.

(5) If the picture call takes place after a performance, refreshments shall be made available to the Actor at the Theatre's expense. No photo call may extend beyond 1:00 A.M.

Remember, stage management is prohibited from ordering any food (in this case, refreshments) for the company. You might, however, make suggestions, based on your knowledge of the company, to your friends in the marketing or public relations departments who should handle this.

(6) If the photographs are taken at a time other than hereinabove specified, or if the limitation in the number of calls in (4) above is exceeded, the Actor shall be paid not less than an additional one-eighth ($^1\!/_8$) of his/her weekly salary for each day or part thereof in which the photographing takes place.

In other words, you can break some of the rules if the producer is willing to pay for it. You must be able to give the producer a clear and concise report of the costs and options available.

(7) (omitted)

(8) (omitted)

(9)(a) & (b) (omitted)

E. BREAKS, REST PERIODS, DAYS OFF

(1) There shall be a break of no less than one and one-half ($1^1\!/_2$) hours after five (5) consecutive hours of work except as provided in paragraphs (D)(2) and (D)(4) above. If the Theatre has no objection, the Deputy(ies) may reduce this break to one (1) hour. This Deputy prerogative shall be exercised solely for the convenience and at the request of the company by a two-thirds ($^2\!/_3$) majority secret ballot vote of the Equity members of the company.

This option is usually accepted when meals are quickly and readily available. It reduces the total length of the day, providing more free time for the company.

(2) Except during run-throughs and dress rehearsals, there shall be a break of five (5) minutes after no more than fifty-five (55) minutes of rehearsal or ten (10) minutes after no more than eighty (80) minutes of rehearsal for each member of the company. During non-stop run-throughs, there shall be a break of not less than ten (10) minutes at the intermission point(s).

The ten-minute break after eighty minutes of work usually works out better for two reasons. First, it is extremely difficult to get everyone back into rehearsal after only five minutes. A five-minute break usually extends to ten or more anyway. Second, a break every hour is just too disruptive to the rehearsal process. It may seem as though you have just gotten started when you need to call another break.

(3) There shall be a break between the rehearsal, photo/costume, and half-hour call. There must be a cast vote, majority controlling, indicating whether such break shall be one and one-half ($1^1\!/_2$) or two (2) hours, except no break shall be required should the only rehearsal call for the day be for one (1) hour or less provided the Theatre schedules it just prior to half-hour and provided that in each instance there is a unanimous, secret-ballot cast vote from each Actor involved in the rehearsal.

This is, in concept, the same requirement as (E)(1) above except that the company can choose to extend the length of the required break to two hours. Also, if the rehearsal is an hour or less and the company agrees by vote, you may schedule it as follows: The actors' rehearsal call is from 6:30 P.M. to 7:30 P.M. and half-hour call at 7:30 P.M.

(4) There shall be no less than one and one-half (1¹/₂) hours and no more than three (3) hours between curtain down and a rehearsal call. The rest period may be reduced or extended by a cast majority vote. (5) There shall be no less than a twelve (12) hour rest period between the end of employment on one (1) day and the beginning of employment on the next day (see Rule 57(G)(4) for Stage Manager's Breaks). At the company's request, by a two-thirds (²/₃) majority secret ballot vote, the Deputy(ies) may reduce this period to a minimum of ten (10) hours on one (1) performance days. If the company has voted to rehearse on a two (2) performance day (see paragraph (C)(3) above), the rest period may be eleven (11) hours.

If the company is rehearsing on a two-performance day, the rest period may be reduced to eleven hours without a vote. The rest period for stage managers is only ten hours.

(6)(a) There shall be a one and one-half (1¹/₂) hour rest period exclusive of half-hour, between performances. The Theatre may reduce this period to not less than one (1) hour inclusive of half-hour, provided both performances are of the same play and provided a choice of hot or cold meal is served to the cast at the Theatre's expense. The rest period shall be computed from the time the meal is delivered.

The inevitable problem is that the food is not delivered on time. You must also understand that the time available to do your pre-show check under these conditions is limited excessively. Try and avoid this if at all possible.

(b) On local tours, where the play runs one (1) hour or less, the rest period between performances may be one-half (¹/₂) hour and no meal need be served.

This again usually is meant to address the needs of school tours.

(7)(a) There shall be one (1) scheduled full day off each week free of rehearsals and/or performances. A full day shall be twenty-four (24) hours in addition to the regular rest period required at the end of each working day.

The normal rest period for actors is twelve hours, so a full day off will mean a total of thirty-six hours between the end of work on one day and the next call. If Monday is the designated day off and the evening performance on Sunday comes down at 11:00 P.M., then the actor cannot be called until Tuesday at 11:00 A.M.

(b) There shall be no call of any kind after the evening performance on a day immediately preceding the day off.

When the curtain comes down, the actors must be free to go.

(c) The day off shall be stated in the contract and may be changed no more than three (3) times during the first twenty-four weeks of the season and three (3) times during the balance of the season upon one (1) week's notice.

The day off is usually changed to accommodate holidays or technical rehearsals. Again you are required to provide a week's notice. Planned changes in the day off for holidays, etc., should be indicated in the master calendar.

(d) There will be no rehearsal or performance on Thanksgiving Day (except during tech week) and on either December 24 or December 25 (but not both). Any change of day off required by this paragraph will not be included in the changes of day off referred to above.

If the normal day off is Monday, you may wish to change the day off during Thanksgiving week to Thursday since you are not allowed to work on this day per the above rule. In this manner you do not lose the day as a work day; you simply switch the rehearsal or performance to Monday. While this change does not count toward the maximum number of changes allowed under (7)(c) above, you are still obligated to provide a one-week notice of this change.

(e) Under no circumstances may more than eight (8) consecutive days elapse between days off, except that twelve (12) days may elapse between days off to comply with the Thanksgiving and Christmas rule above (see Rule 61(F)(1)(1)(i)).

(f) Unless the Actor is both rehearsing and performing, there shall be a daylight day of rest in the same week as the holiday, in addition to the required day off on Thanksgiving and on either December 24 or 25 (but not both). The additional daylight day of rest is not required in tech week.

This rule allows the company to make preparations for the holidays, such as shopping.

(g) Notwithstanding the above, the work week is still defined as Monday through Sunday and there must be a designated day off within each such work week.

Suppose December 24th fell on a Saturday and the 25th on Sunday and your normal day off is Monday. You might be tempted to take the 24th or 25th off and work on Monday the 26th to meet the obligations of rule (7)(d) above. However, if you plan to return to the regular day off on the next Monday you will have violated rule (7)(g) above. You have not provided for a day off in the week that begins with Monday, the 26th of December. In order to make this change work, you would have to work on the Monday before the Christmas holiday.

(8) In addition to the regular day off, there shall be a daylight day of rest for each member of the company subject to the following:

(a) This shall be made available for each production but not in the seven (7) day period up to and including the official opening.

This ensures that the critical time in the development of the production is not disrupted.

(b) There shall be at least one (1) daylight day of rest within each six (6) week period of the Actor's employment.

(c) The day selected shall be by mutual agreement, but should there be no such mutual agreement, the assignment of that day shall be made by the Theatre no later than three (3) weeks prior to the day of rest.

This is one of those scheduling issues that should be planned for well in advance and included on the master calendar. Most of the time, if the actors know well enough in advance which day is the daylight day of rest, they will have no problem agreeing to it as required.

(d) The Actor shall not be called on a daylight day of rest before 7:00 P.M., unless the cast votes, by secret ballot, by a two-thirds (2/3) majority, to end the daylight day of rest at 6:00 P.M.

The daylight day of rest is usually a day free of rehearsal and with a performance in the evening. The 7:00 P.M. limit accommodates normal curtain times; however, many theaters have instituted slightly earlier curtains on some days to attract different populations to the theater.

(e) The designated day of rest may be changed upon one (1) week's notice.

(f) During the Actor's final production of the season, after the official opening or two (2) weeks following the first paid public performance, whichever comes first, the day following the day off shall be a daylight day of rest at least once in every three (3) week period or part thereof.

Since the company has only one day off per week, this rule helps extend this time to its maximum. This often provides actors with enough time to fly home for a day or get to out-of-town auditions as they begin to look toward the end of the season.

F. NOTES

(1) Note sessions may be held after no more than four (4) preview performances. Two (2) of these may be called at the sole discretion of the director and two (2) shall require the Actor's approval.

Notes may always be given during the rehearsal call if necessary.

> READ-THROUGH — Usually the first rehearsal at which the company reads through the script.
>
> RUN-THROUGH — To rehearse the show by performing from beginning to end without stopping.

(2) Note sessions shall be limited to one (1) hour from curtain down and that hour shall be deducted from the next rehearsal day.

If you are allowed a five-hour rehearsal call on a one-performance day, and you take an hour for notes the night before, you have only four hours of rehearsal the next day, and you must calculate the overnight rest period from the end of the note session.

(3) Note sessions may be held only on a one (1) performance day.

(4) Individual Actor notes may not be posted on the Callboard, except in a sealed envelope.

Weekly Schedule

Begin with the general and work toward the details. I start with a calendar that clearly indicates the days and hours of rehearsal for the entire rehearsal period. This calendar can also indicate the general plan for the rehearsal period. This means that you should identify which days are for read-throughs, which intended for blocking, which you anticipate for run-throughs, which are technical rehearsals, what day you want the actors off book, etc. If possible, you may be able to designate which act you will be working on. Of course, this is all subject to change, so keep it general. Give as much information as you feel comfortable with but include in a prominent place on the schedule the statement "Subject to change."

Experienced directors and stage managers can be confident in their ability to predict the progress they will be able to make in rehearsal, and it is important for them to have certain milestones to gauge their progress throughout the rehearsal period. Figure 9 illustrates this kind of schedule. There are a number of computer software programs available to create a wide variety of calendars, schedules, and other useful forms for the stage manager.

Daily Schedules

Daily schedules are much more detailed and typically prepared only a day or two in advance once you are in rehearsals. These schedules should be an hour-by-hour breakdown for the entire day on which scenes are being rehearsed, which actors are required, where the rehearsal is, when lunch or dinner breaks are scheduled, etc. This schedule must also include costume fittings, photo calls, and other activities required for the actors (Figure 10). During rehearsal, note any deviation from the daily schedule and file for future reference.

NEW PLAYS

When you find yourself working on a new play, you must prepare yourself to manage script changes. This process has been vastly simplified by the personal computer, advanced software for word processing and desktop publishing, and modern copiers. In this day and age, as they say, there is no reason to go through this process without a computer and the appropriate software.

Three functions must be addressed when working on a new play and expecting the play to evolve through the production process: revision, distribution, and file management. Revisions to the script may be made on a regular basis. This could be a daily occurrence or even more frequent. Stage management must, at the very least, be responsible for revisions being correctly executed in a timely manner. See that you have access to some type of word processing system. (And that you know how to use it *before* you need it.)

Whenever a change is made, the new page or pages of the script must be distributed to all members of the cast and crew affected by the change. Do not overlook designers and the variety of artists and crafts people working on the production. Even a small cut or addition in the script could change the prop, costume, lighting, or sound requirements of a production. The turnaround time for revision and distribution should be kept to an absolute minimum. This means you must have twenty-four hour access to a copying machine or copying service. Some changes may be so slight that they may be communicated to many people by way of the daily rehearsal notes you will publish. Keep a close eye on this and decide what is best for the production. Nothing is more frustrating than a lack of information.

To keep an accurate record of the evolution of the script, it is important to maintain a file that includes every version of the script that you have come in contact with and a record of all revisions. This will become extremely useful when the director and playwright decide a recent change does not work and they wish to go back to the way the script was last Tuesday. *Do not throw anything away.*

Anyone familiar with even the most rudimentary word processing program will easily recognize the value these programs have in making changes to a script. Insertions and deletions of text are handled quickly and efficiently. More sophisticated and powerful programs offer a number of useful advantages in making and managing changes in the script. A single command can change a character's name at every occurrence in the script. The entire script can be rearranged in any order. Changes may be highlighted in many ways to call attention to the alteration for easy reference. These programs can also track changes by automatically including revision numbers or dates and times when changes are made. They may also be set up to file various versions of the script as it evolves for future reference.

PRODUCTION MEETINGS

ARENA STAGE — A stage in which the audience is seated on all four sides. Also called Theater in the Round.

CENTER LINE — An imaginary or real line that divides the stage area into two equal parts, running from downstage to upstage.

PLASTER LINE — An imaginary line that runs across the proscenium along the upstage side of the proscenium wall. This line is used by designers and technicians to position various technical elements in the theater.

Production meetings are an essential part of the production process. They may also serve as a significant irritant if not organized and managed properly. The production meeting should be attended by the director, stage manager, designers, production manager, technical director, and all functional department heads, such as the prop master and wardrobe supervisor. Establish regular dates and times for production meetings as far in advance as possible and include them on your weekly schedule. It is also advisable to send out reminder notices each week to all participants. Be sure to find a time that is convenient for all parties involved. Everyone's time must be respected.

The format and agenda for the meeting should provide an opportunity for progress reports, questions, and coordinating efforts. Avoid the tendency for production meetings to turn into design meetings. Any question that cannot be resolved in a timely manner should be held over for further discussion at another time. As a rule of thumb, if it cannot be answered in three to five minutes, move on.

I suggest an agenda that allows each person in attendance to report on his or her activities and to raise any questions. As stage manager you should start the ball rolling, setting the tempo and character of the meeting. Start with a brief and concise report on the progress of the show in rehearsal. Save your questions for others until it is their turn to report. Next, start around the table asking for a report and questions. After each member of the meeting makes his or her report and voices any questions, address the issues that have accumulated on your list since the last meeting. Remember, keep it moving. If there is not an apparent answer to a particular question, it obviously needs more thought. You will arrive at a better answer and a more efficient use of everyone's time if you hold it over for further discussion at a later date. This may require you to schedule a separate meeting to deal with the specific issue at hand, but this meeting can then be more focused and require only the people directly involved with the issue.

At the conclusion of the report and question portion of the meeting, review the calendar. Note any approaching deadlines or significant events the attendees should be aware of. Be sure to bring up any rehearsal activities that may be of interest, such as a run-through. Conclude the meeting with your thanks and a reminder of the date, time, and place of the next production meeting.

In Figure 11 you will find the basic agenda for a production meeting. The space provided between each topic is for notes as they occur during the meeting. At the conclusion of the meeting, the official record, or minutes, of the meeting should be prepared from your notes (Figure 12). The minutes should then be distributed to all interested parties and posted on the company call board.

THE REHEARSAL SPACE

Earlier, you examined the rehearsal space so you could begin planning for rehearsals. Now you must actually begin to prepare the room. You should do what you can and what is reasonable to recreate the performance space in the rehearsal room.

In your initial inspection of the room, you should have arranged for any basic maintenance or repairs to be handled in advance of your need to be in the space. So let's assume the room is clean and ready to go. Equity agreements include standards by which the safety of its members and the sanitary conditions under which they work are ensured. The rehearsal room floor requires special consideration if the production will include dancing. Actors are not allowed to dance on concrete or marble floors or any other surface that is considered unsafe. See Part II for more details.

Spiking

Start by taping out the set on the floor of the rehearsal room. This task will go quickly if you have help. You will need the ground plan of the set, a scale rule, a fifty-foot tape measure, a shorter tape measure, spike tape, chalk, chalk line, and pencils. You establish the position of the various scenic elements as they relate to two reference lines. In a proscenium theater, the plaster line and the center line are the two reference lines you want to identify. The plaster line is an imaginary line that runs stage left to stage right and is located on the upstage side of the proscenium wall. The center line is an imaginary line that runs up and down stage at a point bisecting the proscenium opening into two equal parts. Figure 13 illustrates the position of these two lines in a standard proscenium theater.

In any number of alternate seating configurations including thrust and in-the-round, the two reference lines could be two center lines that divide the performance space into four equal quadrants, similar to the plaster line and center line of the proscenium theater; or they could be any two lines appropriate to the function of positioning the set in the performance space. Check with the designer or technical director if these reference lines are not obvious to you. Figures 14 and 15 illustrate two alternative seating configurations and the reference lines used.

The ground plan should indicate the distance between the reference lines and key elements of the set. If the designer has not provided this information or only minimal amounts of information, you will need to measure the distance yourself. Since the ground plan should be a scale drawing, the process is very easy. Figure 16 shows a typical scale rule. Using the appropriate scale rule (Figure 17), measure any needed distances and record them on the ground plan for future reference (Figure 18). Once the ground plan has all the measurements you need, you can begin transferring the information to the rehearsal room floor in full-scale.

PROSCENIUM — The outlining frame of the stage opening that separates the house from the stage. Also called the Proscenium Arch.

RAKED — A stage that is built on an upward slant.

SPIKE — To mark on the stage or rehearsal floor the placement of set pieces.

SPIKE MARK — A mark on the stage or rehearsal floor, usually a piece of tape, that denotes the specific placement of a piece of scenery or a prop.

THRUST STAGE — A type of theater in which the audience is seated on three sides of the stage.

BOX SET — A set that utilizes three walls to enclose the stage area.

FRONT ELEVATION — A scale drawing that gives a front view of the set.

REAR ELEVATION — The scale drawing that gives a back view of the set.

UNIT SET — A set that can serve as several different settings by changing only one or two set pieces, or by adding different set dressing.

WORKING DRAWINGS — Drawings to scale that give the specifics of both set and prop construction.

Establish the two reference lines in positions that will allow room for the entire set to be taped out on the rehearsal room floor. This, of course, assumes that the rehearsal room is large enough to accommodate the entire set, which is not always possible. If the room restricts you from laying out the full set, tape the portion that most affects the movement of the actors. Do not forget to allow sufficient space in front of the set for you and the director to do your work. When the reference lines are established, you can chalk out the position of the key scenic elements using the full-scale measurements. If this is new territory for you, it may, at this point, be helpful to think of this as connecting the dots. Figure 19 illustrates the steps in taping out a simple single set in a rehearsal room.

More complex and multiple set shows require a little resourcefulness on your part. Colored tape can be used to distinguish between different sets or different types of scenery, such as walls and platforms. Varying widths can also be used to indicate differences in scenery. The best tape to use is a cloth-backed adhesive tape. This tape is similar in appearance to surgical tape but can be purchased or cut in various widths. It comes in large rolls and in a wide variety of colors. In the entertainment industry this tape is called *spike tape* or *gaffer's tape*. This tape is extremely durable and easy to work with.

As you have been learning about the set during the pre-production period, you may have identified some elements that may be useful to have in the rehearsal room. If the action of the play heavily depends on the use of doors, it may be worth investigating the possibility of rehearsal doors. Some theaters have these items in stock. Others may build rehearsal doors for your use. There are, of course, limits to what you can do in a rehearsal room, and in some cases the added value of providing certain elements for rehearsal may not be worth the cost. As you gain experience you will learn what is practical and what is not.

Rehearsal Furniture

You should be prepared to acquire rehearsal furniture that approximates the size and function of the designed furniture. Actors are creatures of habit in the sense that they will quickly establish patterns of performance based on their rehearsals. If they become accustomed to working with a large luxurious chair during rehearsals and then find that the real chair is a straight-backed side chair, they will have to make a significant adjustment in their performance, which could have been avoided. Only in rare cases, when an item is unique, should you expect to rehearse with the actual piece in the rehearsal room. If time and money exist, a less detailed mockup could be constructed for rehearsals. In any event, use care and caution all performers as to the delicate nature of these items.

Rehearsal Props and Costumes

Rehearsal props and costumes, like rehearsal furniture, should approximate the real thing. Your list of preliminary design requirements in these areas will provide you with the basic information you need to pull rehearsal props and costumes. As rehearsals get under way, ask the performers if there is anything else that would help them in preparing for their roles.

Providing these rehearsal items not only affords the performers a chance to work with them, it helps you develop preset lists for props and costumes. You will learn from which side of the stage an actor enters with a given prop, and you will know that the prop must be preset on that side of the stage when you move into the theater. It will also help you track the movement of these items. This ability to track props and costumes will be invaluable when you get to technical rehearsals. It is very hard to know whether an actor is remembering to strike a prop at the end of a scene if he or she is using an imaginary prop.

SUPPLIES AND EQUIPMENT

There is no telling what you are going to need in the way of supplies and equipment, so be prepared. You clearly need a fair amount of basic office supplies and equipment at all times. Another area of consideration is first aid. It's a great idea to have some first aid training and instruction in CPR. Look over the following list of items, which will perhaps inspire other ideas. Over time you will accumulate a variety of items that will prove to be indispensable at some point.

MEDICAL SUPPLIES

- ❏ aspirin
- ❏ acetaminophen
- ❏ throat lozenges
- ❏ throat spray
- ❏ cough drops
- ❏ cold tablets
- ❏ antacid
- ❏ eye wash
- ❏ eye patch

- ❏ assortment of bandages
- ❏ elastic bandages
- ❏ ice packs
- ❏ antiseptic cream or spray
- ❏ needles
- ❏ tweezers
- ❏ cotton swabs
- ❏ scissors
- ❏ surgical gauze and tape

OFFICE SUPPLIES

- ❏ #2 pencils
- ❏ erasers
- ❏ pencil sharpener
- ❏ colored pens
- ❏ felt tip markers
- ❏ highlighting markers
- ❏ rubber bands
- ❏ paper clips
- ❏ glue stick
- ❏ chalk
- ❏ self-stick note pads
- ❏ stapler and staples
- ❏ calculator
- ❏ 8½ x 11 pads of paper
- ❏ company stationery
- ❏ three-hole paper punch

- ❏ file folders
- ❏ portable file box
- ❏ ruler
- ❏ scale rule
- ❏ 12-foot tape measure
- ❏ 50-foot tape measure
- ❏ stopwatch
- ❏ transparent tape
- ❏ masking tape
- ❏ spike tape
- ❏ gaffer's tape
- ❏ electrical tape
- ❏ double-sided tape
- ❏ glow tape
- ❏ thumbtacks
- ❏ push pins

CONVENIENCE ITEMS

- ❏ matches
- ❏ disposable cups
- ❏ disposable eating utensils
- ❏ a variety of self amusement toys
- ❏ paper towels
- ❏ pre-moistened towelettes
- ❏ tissues
- ❏ sugar, sugar substitute, salt, and pepper packets
- ❏ eyeglass lens tissues
- ❏ toothpaste
- ❏ mouthwash
- ❏ dental floss
- ❏ breath mints
- ❏ bobby pins
- ❏ needle and thread
- ❏ safety pins
- ❏ extension cords
- ❏ bottle opener
- ❏ can opener
- ❏ nail clippers
- ❏ nail file
- ❏ postage stamps
- ❏ room deodorizer

TOOLS

- ❏ hammer
- ❏ slotted screwdriver
- ❏ Phillips screwdriver
- ❏ pliers
- ❏ adjustable-end wrench
- ❏ Allen wrenches
- ❏ mat knife
- ❏ work gloves

You will need to carry this stuff around with you to rehearsals. The best way to do this is with lightweight tackle boxes for the first aid kit, small office supplies, and tool kit. For the larger items, a couple of sturdy file storage boxes with lids work great. These boxes are a convenient size, have hand holes to carry the box, and a very good lid, which comes on and off easily.

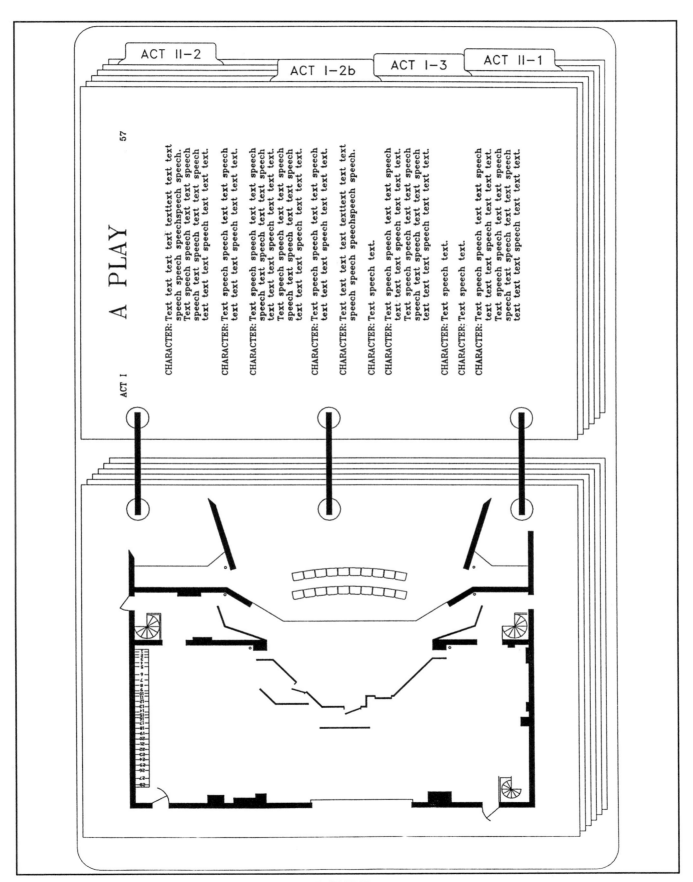

FIGURE 4

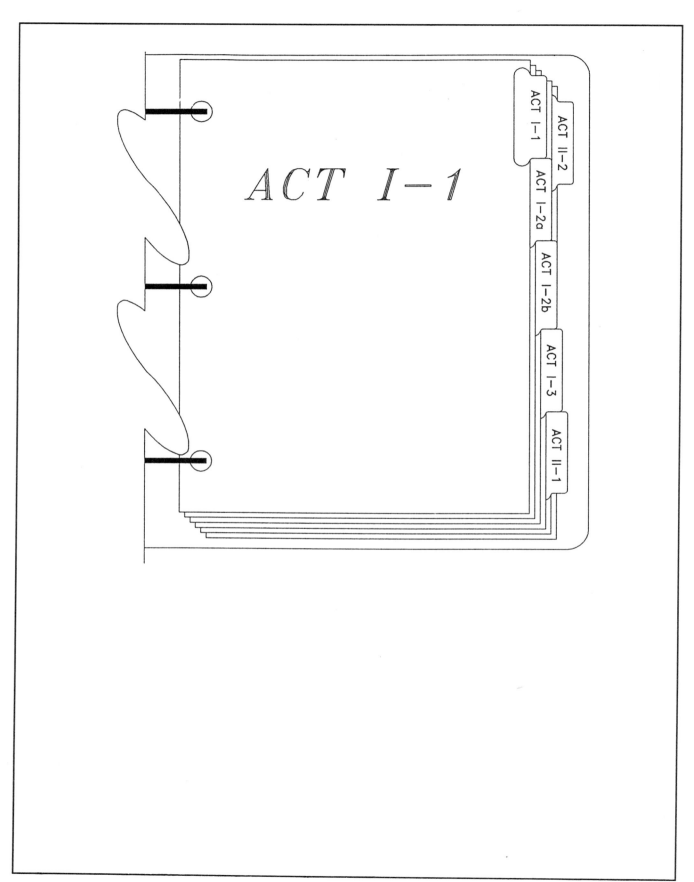

FIGURE 5

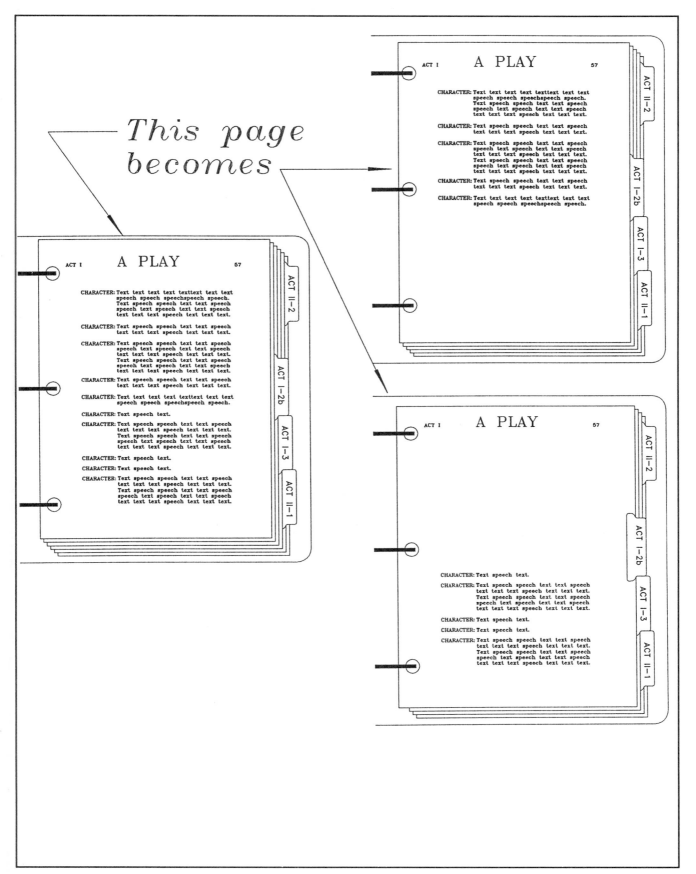

FIGURE 6

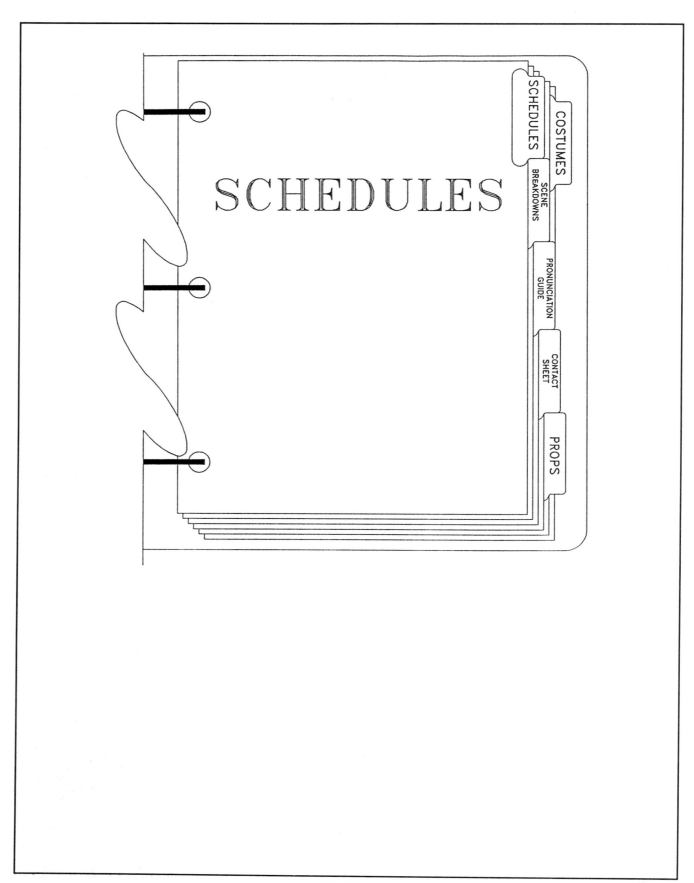

FIGURE 7

Illustration courtesy of Cari Norton, Stage Manager for the Mark Taper Forum production of *Julius Caesar.*

April 1991
CTG PRODUCTION CALENDAR

SUNDAY	MONDAY	TUESDAY	WEDNESDAY	THURSDAY	FRIDAY	SATURDAY
	1 April Fools Day	**2**	**3**	**4**	**5**	**6** Itchey Foot #5/ Tech-Cabaret Verboten ITP/Freedom Song/Barnsdall Theatre DOO/A Little Night Music - Tech
			DOO/Load-in/Night Music	DOO/A Little Night Music - Tech		
7 **⁎⁎** DOO/1st Pre/Night Music Itchey Foot #5/ Invited Dress - Cabaret Verboten Daylight Savings-- set ahead 1 hour	**8**	**9** TOO/1st Reh/The Task	**10** ITP/Freedom Song/ Tour to Cal Poly San Luis Obispo	**11**	**12** Itchey Foot#5/ Open - Cabaret Verboten	**13** ITP/Freedom Song/ begin residence at CSULA
14 TOO/Close/The Wedding	**15**	**16**	**17** DOO/Press/Night Music DOO/Press/Night Music	**18** DOO/Open/Night Music DOO/Open/Night Music	**19**	**20**
21 ITP/Freedom Song/ end residence at CSULA MTF/Close/Jelly	**22** MTF/Load-In/ Caesar TOO/Load-In/The Task	**23**	**24**	**25**	**26** ITP/Freedom Song/ UCLA 10:00 am	**27** ITP/Freedom Song/ UCLA 7:00 pm SP/Shipwreck (Getty) 1st Reh
			MTF/Julius Caesar - Tech			
28 ITP/Freedom Song/ UCLA (time TBA) MTF/1st Pre/ Caesar Itchey Foot#5/ Close - Cabaret Verboten	**29**	**30** TOO/Tech/The Task				

March						
S	M	T	W	T	F	S
					1	2
3	4	5	6	7	8	9
10	11	12	13	14	15	16
17	18	19	20	21	22	23
24	25	26	27	28	29	30
31						

May						
S	M	T	W	T	F	S
			1	2	3	4
5	6	7	8	9	10	11
12	13	14	15	16	17	18
19	20	21	22	23	24	25
26	27	28	29	30	31	

FIGURE 8

Illustration courtesy of Cari Norton, Stage Manager for the Mark Taper Forum production of *Julius Caesar*.

Mark Taper Forum 1991
JULIUS CAESAR

Rehearsal Schedule

Issue #1
3/20/91
Page 1 of 3

SUNDAY	MONDAY	TUESDAY	WEDNESDAY	THURSDAY	FRIDAY	SATURDAY
24 MARCH (diagonal)	25 (diagonal)	26 9:30 AEA Biz, 10:30 Meet & Read-thru, 2:00 Lunch, 3-6:30 REH. Reh. Rm. "C"	27 10:00-7:00 REHEARSAL, 10:00 oskar+mel mt. Reh. Rm. "C"	28 9-10 Auditions, 10:00-7:00 REHEARSAL, 2:00 oskar-KPCC Int, 2:15-3 oskar+4pel, 7:30 snd mt. Reh. Rm. "C"	29 11:00-8:30 REHEARSAL, 3-4:30 set mting. Reh. Rm. "C"	30 10:00-7:00 REHEARSAL, 7:00 Phone l'm -Ken+oskar. Reh. Rm. "C"
31 (Easter) 3:00-11:00 REHEARSAL. Reh. Rm. "C"	1 APRIL DAY OFF.	2 11:00-8:00 REHEARSAL. Reh. Rm. "C"	3 9:00am set mt., 2:45 video mt, 10:00-7:00 REHEARSAL (7:00 Prod. Mtng). Reh. Rm. "C"	4 10:00-7:00 REHEARSAL. Reh. Rm. "C"	5 11:00-8:00 REHEARSAL, 2:00 weapons mt., 8:00 Prod mt. Rm. "C" or "A"	6 10:00-8:00 REHEARSAL. Reh. Rm. "A"
7 10:00-7:00 REHEARSAL. Reh. Rm. "A"	8 2:00 T2 - Location scout DAY OFF.	9 (James starts) 9-10 Auditions, 10:00-7:00 REHEARSAL, 7:00 monitor placement, 8-9 mt Delroy. Reh. Rm. "A"	10 9:45 Audition, 2:00 Props mt., 10:00-7:00 REHEARSAL, Cable here 10-7, 7:00 make-up mt, 8:00 Call Ken. Reh. Rm. "A"	11 (Video shoots →) 10:00-7:00 REHEARSAL. Reh. Rm. "A"	12 2:30 mt w/Anthony, 11-1, 3-9 REHEARSAL, 1:00 AEA mting. Reh. Rm. "A"	13 10:00-7:00 REHEARSAL. Reh. Rm. "A"
14 10:30-7:00 REHEARSAL. Reh. Rm. "A"	15 DAY OFF.	16 (All Actors) 1-2 mt w/Anthony, 10:00-7:00 REHEARSAL, 7:00 Staff mting. Reh. Rm. "A"	17 10:00-7:00 REHEARSAL, 2:00 Watch Videos w/Karen, 7:00 Prod mt. Reh. Rm. "A"	18 10:00-7:00 REHEARSAL, 7:00 Snd mt. Reh. Rm. "A"	19 11:00-8:00 REHEARSAL, 2:30 oskar-Daily News. Reh. Rm. "A"	20 2:00 mt w/Chris re: Bald..., 10:00-7:00 REHEARSAL. Reh. Rm. "A"
21 10:00-8:00 REHEARSAL, 8:00 Lts Paper-Tech. Reh. Rm. "A"	22 (Load in) DAY OFF.	23 2:00 Ls monitors, 10:00-7:00 REHEARSAL, Focus. Reh. Rm. "A"	24 Ticket resv. deadline, 10:00-7:00 REHEARSAL, 2:00 oskar "Dramalogue". Reh. Rm. "A"	25 9:30am Prop Load-in, 12:00-5:00 TECH/DRESS, 7:00-12:00 TECH/DRESS. Taper Stage	26 5:30 video shoot, 12:00-5:00 TECH/DRESS, 7:00-12:00 TECH/DRESS, Photo Call Set-ups. Taper Stage	27 1:30-5:00 TECH/DRESS, 7:00-11:30 TECH/DRESS (Photo Call). Taper Stage

FIGURE 9

Illustration courtesy of Cari Norton, Stage Manager for the Mark Taper Forum production of *Julius Caesar*.

4/23/91

Mark Taper Forum 1991
JULIUS CAESAR
Rehearsal Schedule

Tuesday April 23, 1991 - Reh. Rm. "A"

10:00- 11:00	I - 2	William, Delroy
11:00-12:00	II-1b	Vaughn, William, Richard, Delroy, Kenny, Kimberly, Dierk
12:00-1:00	I-3	Delroy, Richard, Kenny
1:00-2:00	LUNCH BREAK	
2:00-2:30	I-2'd	William, Delroy, Richard
2:00-4:30	IV-2, V-1	William, Delroy
2:00-4:30	V-2 fight (Pav. Rm #2)	FULL COMPANY (except Casey, James, William, Delroy, Steve M.)
4:30-6:00	III-3 fight	Vaughn, Bruce, Marcus, David, Richard, Chris, Doug, James, Robert, Dierk, Steve W.
6:00-7:00	II-1	Vaughn, Lisa B., William, Richard, Doug, Delroy, Kenny, Kimberly, Dierk, Steve W.
7:00-8:30	III-2	Casey

Not Called: Stephen M.

COSTUME FITTINGS:
11:00-11:30	Marcus Chong (10:30 Annex for ride)
11:30-12:00	Bruce Beatty
12:15-12:45	William Converse-Roberts
1:00-1:30	Doug Hutchinson
5:00-5:30	Marie Chambers
5:30-6:00	Diane Robinson (5:00 Annex for ride)

FIGURE 10

Illustration courtesy of Cari Norton, Stage Manager for the Mark Taper Forum production of *Julius Caesar.*

Mark Taper Forum 1991
JULIUS CAESAR

Production Meeting Agenda

Date: Wednesday April 17, 1991 7:00pm   Reh. Rm "A"

General:
- Discuss tech scedule.
  - Begin with actors on Thursday (4/25)
  - 10/12s Thursday and Friday
  - Begin at 12:30 Thursday on stage in costume and work straight through adding all elements.
  - Schedule on stage video shoots. Friday 12:30pm?
- Anything else?

Sound/Music:
- The 5 cars starting in III-3 need to be cued separately.
- Discuss helicopter movement.
- Discuss speakers hidden with monitors.
- Discuss RF speaker in tape deck.
- Discuss location for Cicero on mike offstage.
- Is offstage mike needed for Caesar's ghost?
- Jon and Mel are meeting Thursday (tomorrow) at 9:30am.
- Recording session Monday 4/22.
- Schedule Paper Tech.
- Anything else?

Costumes:
- Dierk will be Cicero in I-2c. Discuss wig.
- New breakdown distributed with several changes.
- We are planning on shooting Caesar with his wounds for the video during Preview week.
- Discuss the garland that Titinius gives to Cassius.
- First Dress will be Thursday (4/25) 12:00 call.
- Anything else?

FIGURE 11

JULIUS CAESAR

Production Meeting Agenda Con't.

Set/Props:
- When can we get the police shields?
- When can we get a dolly for the rehearsal podium?
- What is the locking method of the DS podium?
- Discuss large US podium. How many pieces? How does it move?
- What is the locking method of the phone booth?
- Discuss using the library chairs for II-2 instead of folding chairs.
      We will therefore need 10 library chairs.
- Discuss using a 15" tv as one of the set of three and then also for
      V-5.
- Discuss small table instead of second chair for II-2.
- Discuss hanging from the front of the RC balcony. Are we going to
      be able to do it? We cannot have someone climb down from the
      balcony to the deck.
- We need a stronger metal clipboard.
- Discuss blood effects. (Michael Key)
      - When will they be completed?
      - Are we using compressed air for Cassius' death?
      - Was the blood found? Nextel?
- Any questions from new props list (Issue #5)?
- Do we need to do a "Props still needed" list?
- Schedule Prop load-in. Thursday (4/25) at 9:30am.
- Anything else?

Lights:
- Tom was able to get 3 moving lights. Discuss cost.
- When is focus?
- Schedule Paper tech if needed for Tuesday (4/23) 7:00pm
- Do we own beacon lights?
- Anything else?

Video:
- Equipment update.
- Discuss the movement of the ghost through the house.
- Discuss placement of power and video lines.
- Understudy video shoots will occur during previews.
- Anything else?

General:
-Anything else?

FIGURE 11 (cont.)

Illustration courtesy of Cari Norton, Stage Manager for the Mark Taper Forum production of *Julius Caesar*.

Page 1 of 2

Mark Taper Forum 1991
JULIUS CAESAR
Production Meeting and Daily Notes

Date: Wednesday April 17, 1991   Issue #21

DISTRIBUTION:

Oskar Eustis	Yael Pardess	Tom Ruzika	Jeff Struckman
Ken Kobland	Mel Marvin	Jon Gottlieb	Gordon Davidson
Robert Egan	Steve Albert	Karen Wood	Bob Routolo
Frank Bayer	Jonathan Lee	Toni Lovaglia	Ed Haynes
Beverly Thies	Cathy Meacham	Lisa Greenman	Annie Dippel
Hitomi Nakatani			

SET/PROPS:
- Prop load-in scheduled for Thursday (4/25) at 9:30am.
- Prop Adds: - shoe horn for Caesar in II-2.
  - Small standing ashtray for II-2. We will not need the statue ashtray.
  - We will need a total of 40 objects to throw at the cops in V-2.
  - 2 bills (orders) for Brutus in V-2.
  - 2 fake mikes for the podium in III-2.
  - Satchel (60s style) for Cinna the poet in III-3.
- Caesar's hairbrush (#45a) should be very elegant. Silver backed.
- When can we get the candels into rehearsal?
- Major Football will be using a briefcase in II-2.
- Cassius' briefcase should look very old and used.
- The letter in II-1 (#21) will be destroyed each performance.
- Casca will not be smoking in II-1.
- We should be getting the police shields by Monday at the latest.
- Both the phone booth and the DS podium will lock with cane bolts.
- The rain on the phone booth has been cut.
- We would still like to hang from the front of the RC balcony. Bob is checking on this.
- There will now be two 13" tvs and one 15" tv for Acts II and IV. The 15" will also be used for Act V.
- We still need a stronger metal clipboard. Possibly 3/16" aluminum.
- Jonathan will be talking with Michael Key about the special effects and when we will be getting them into rehearsal.
- We will be putting together a blood list ASAP.
- A "Props still needed" list will be issued Thursday (4/18).
- There will be a total of 5 Press cameras (2 strobe, and 3 flash bulb).
- Here is a list of all the guns: - 6 fake "38"s for Cops (#113)
  - 1 handgun with silencer (fires twice) (#5a)
  - 3 service 45 (fake) (#5)
  - 2 pump shotguns (each fired once) (#117)
  - 2 pump shotguns (fake) (#112)

LIGHTS:
- JBL is looking into lowering the cost of of the moving lights. If necessary we could cut the 2 search lights, or use non programable lights for the search lights.
- We are checking to see if we own beacon lights.
- Focus will probably be Tuesday night.
- We will be scheduleing a paper tech for ASAP.

VIDEO:
- Karen, JBL, and Oskar met today regarding the rights to the video clips.
- I will be scheduleing a phone paper tech with Ken ASAP.
- The movement of the ghost is now from the TV on stage and then out to the house monitors.
- There will be two locations on the deck to plug in the monitors. (RC and DC)

FIGURE 12

JULIUS CAESAR
Production Meeting and Daily Notes Con't

COSTUMES:

- Fittings scheduled Thursday (4/18):
    10:00-10:45 Lise Hilboldt
    1:30-2:15 Vaughn Armstrong
    2:30-3:15 Dierk Torsek
    3:15-4:00 David Drummond
    4:00-4:45 Robert Petkoff
    4:45-5:30 Marie Chambers
- Can we get Caesar's shoes for II-2
  into rehearsal ASAP?
- Doug's coat will be used in V-2 to
  wrap a fake tear gas canister in and
  throw it up onto the balcony.
- We discussed the ageing of Dierk as
  Cicero.
- The garland that Titinius gives
  Cassius should be a red or blue
  bandana.
- First dress will be Thursday (4/25)
  12:30 Costume Call. We should be
  in full make-up and hair on Thursday.
- We want to experiment with all the
  blood on Thursday (4/25), but we
  will do it with water packs.
- We need to get loops for the night-
  sticks on the Cops belts.
- We will be getting a costume
  breakdown in the next couple days.

MUSIC/SOUND:

- Paper tech scheduled for Thursday
  (4/18) at 7:00pm.
- Mel and Jon are meeting Thursday
  (4/18) at 9:30am.
- The cars starting will be 5 different
  cars but all on one deck.
- There will be speakers hung with each
  of the 9 house monitors.
- We need to find a space backstage
  for Cicero to speak on mike.
- Caesar's ghost will be a taped cue
  and should be put onto the video
  track. William will have to work with
  the video to learn the timing of his
  lines.
- The ghost white noise can move
  around the house.
- We do need a hand held wireless
  mike for the podium in III-2.
- There will be speakers on the top of
  each video rack on each side of the
  stage.

SCHEDULE:

- Rehearsal Thursday (4/18) will be
  from 10:00-2:00 and 3:00-7:00 in
  Reh. Rm. "A".
- First tech will be next Thursday (4/25).
    12:30 Costume Call.
    1:00-5:30 TECH/DRESS
    7:00 Costume Call
    7:30-12:00 TECH/DRESS
- There is a possibility that we can be
  in the theatre on Wednesday night
  (4/24) for a dry tech.

GENERAL:

- We rehearsed several scenes today
  including the battle and the march.

Thank you,

Cari Norton

Cari Norton, PSM

FIGURE 12 (cont.)

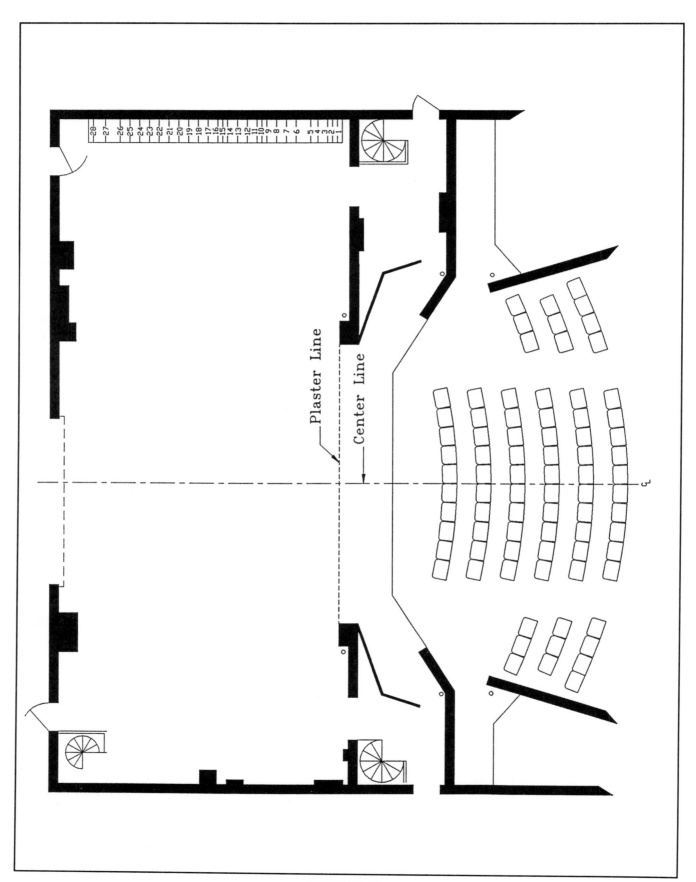

FIGURE 13

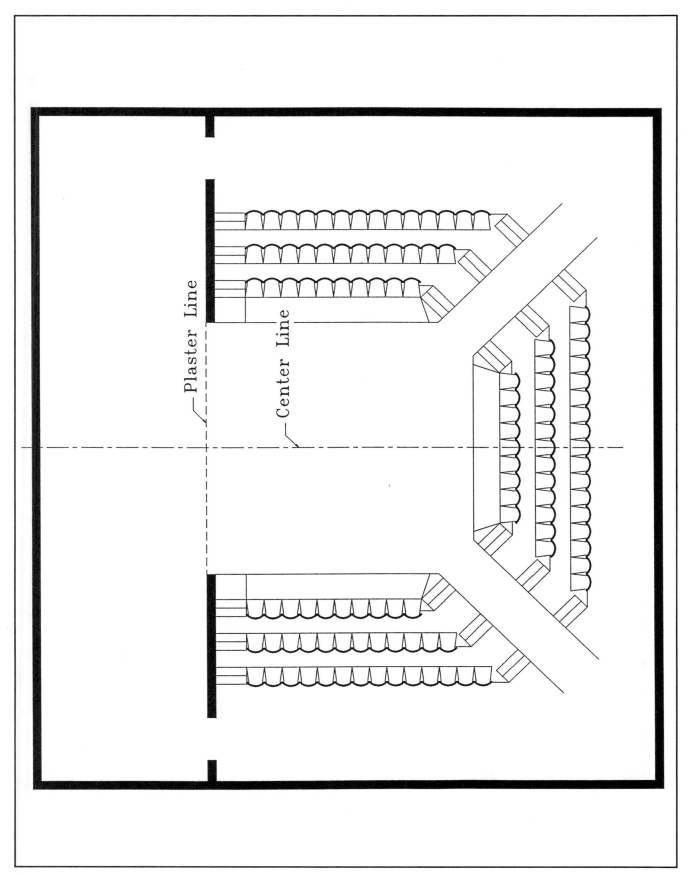

FIGURE 14

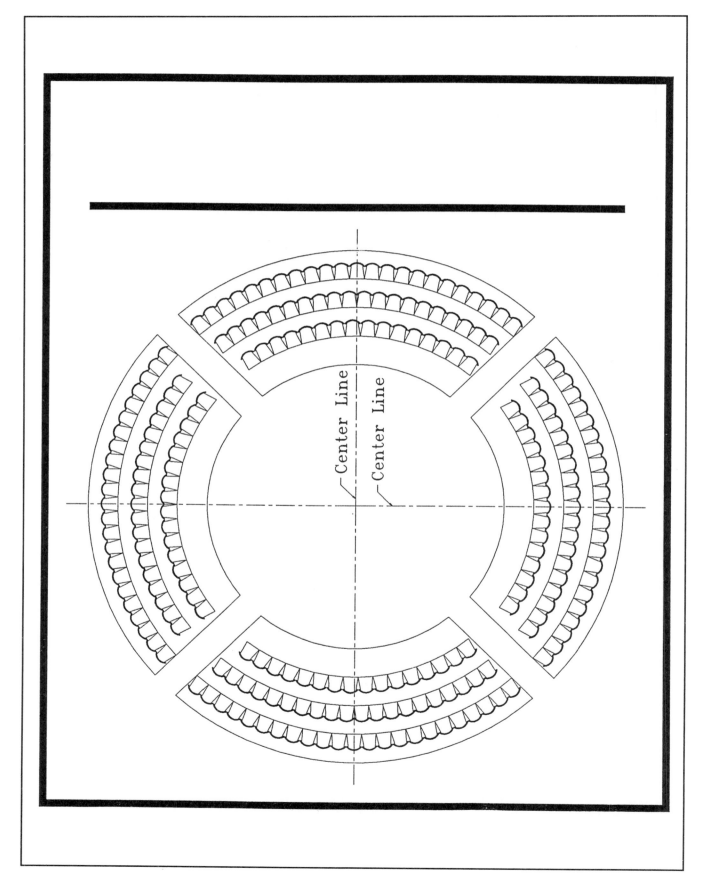

FIGURE 15

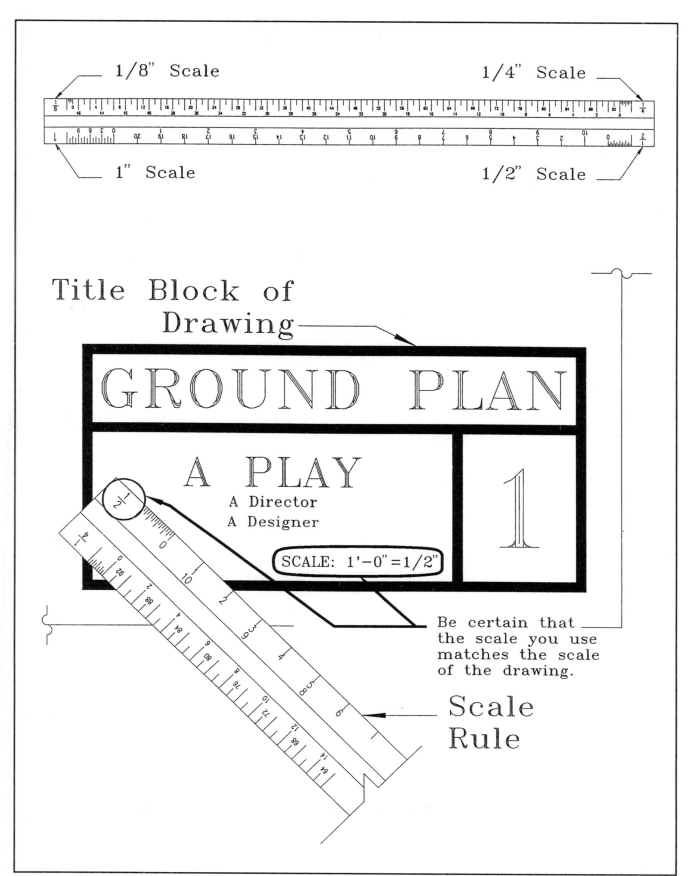

1/8" Scale

1/4" Scale

1" Scale

1/2" Scale

Title Block of
Drawing

GROUND PLAN

A PLAY
A Director
A Designer

SCALE: 1'-0"=1/2"

1

Be certain that
the scale you use
matches the scale
of the drawing.

Scale
Rule

FIGURES 16 (top) and 17 (bottom)

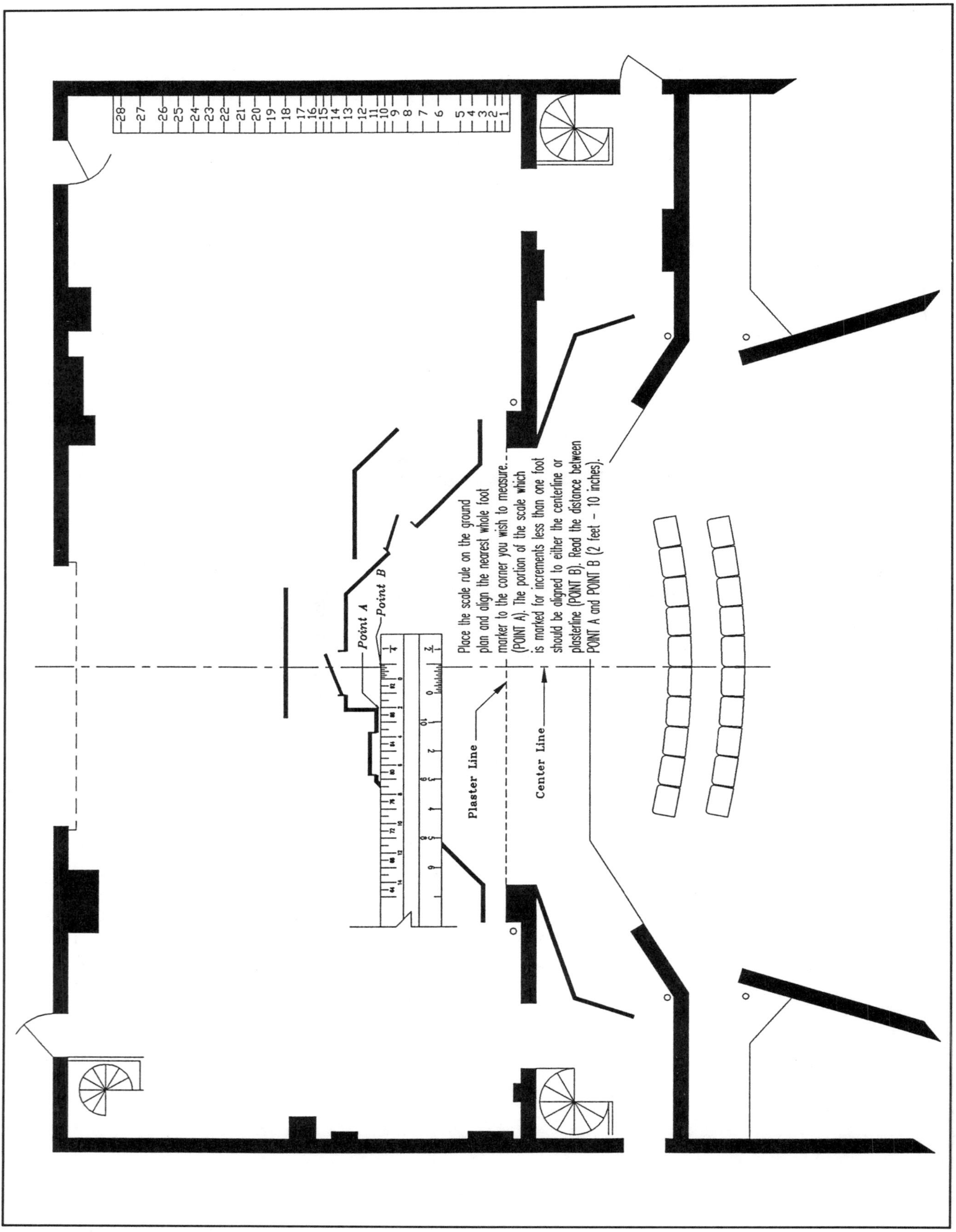
Place the scale rule on the ground plan and align the nearest whole foot marker to the corner you wish to measure. (POINT A). The portion of the scale which is marked for increments less than one foot should be aligned to either the centerline or plasterline (POINT B). Read the distance between POINT A and POINT B (2 feet - 10 inches).
Point A
Point B
Plaster Line
Center Line

FIGURE 18

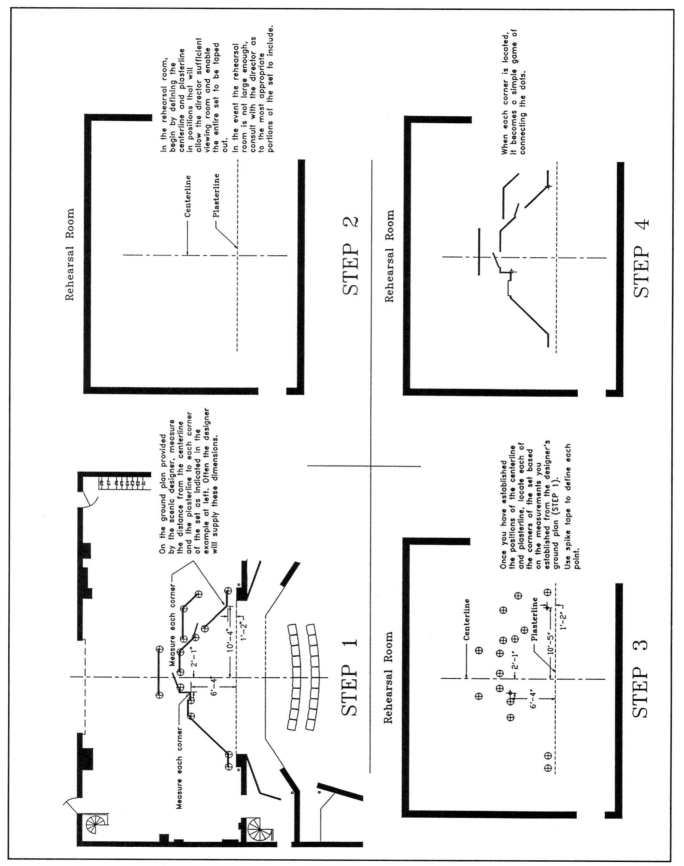

On the ground plan provided by the scenic designer, measure the distance from the centerline and the plasterline to each corner of the set as indicated in the example at left. Often the designer will supply these dimensions.

Measure each corner

In the rehearsal room, begin by defining the centerline and plasterline in positions that will allow the director sufficient viewing room and enable the entire set to be taped out.

In the event the rehearsal room is not large enough, consult with the director as to the most appropriate portions of the set to include.

Rehearsal Room

Centerline

Plasterline

STEP 1

STEP 2

Rehearsal Room

Once you have established the positions of the centerline and plasterline, locate each of the corners of the set based on the measurements you established from the designer's ground plan (STEP 1).

Use spike tape to define each point.

Centerline

Plasterline

When each corner is located, it becomes a simple game of connecting the dots.

Rehearsal Room

STEP 3

STEP 4

FIGURE 19

3

Auditions

SIDE — A bound excerpt from a play that focuses on one character's lines.

If you are fortunate enough to be involved in the audition process for your production, it will afford you a terrific advance look at the working methods of the director and at your future cast. It will also allow them to get a first look at you and the working environment they are about to enter. You must be as prepared and organized for auditions as you are for rehearsals. You must also be sensitive to the actors' needs.

Auditions can be very intimidating for actors. Every physical and psychological need they have is on the line. Getting this role will pay their bills, bolster their confidence, enhance their self-image, and raise their status amongst peers. To be sure, they will be feeling tense, insecure, nervous, frightened, and perhaps a hundred other emotions that may not be conducive to a good audition.

You can best serve the audition process by creating a comfortable and creative atmosphere for the auditions. Be friendly and helpful. Treat the actors with respect and as individuals. It may be called a "cattle call," but actors are professionals whom all theater artists rely on to present their work to an audience. Remember, you may have to do a show with them. It is not their fault that they have all asked you the same question all day long. It's yours. They simply all need to know the same things. A fact sheet posted in several prominent locations or, better yet, distributed to each actor who is auditioning, will handle the vast majority of their questions. The fact sheet should contain pertinent information about the producing organization, the title and a brief description of the play, the performance contract, rehearsal and performance dates and locations, artistic personnel, and who will be running auditions. Rule 44 of the agreement between Equity and the LORT theaters requires that the performance schedule be posted at auditions. In addition, actors must be advised of any performance that starts before 12:00 noon. You will have acquired all this information during your research. You should also include a cast breakdown describing each available role by character name, relationship to other characters in the play, and age, as well as a brief description of the character. This description should be approved by the director. Figure 20 illustrates the fact sheet for an audition.

If the audition will include reading scenes from the script, provide the scene and page numbers of the audition selections. A brief explanation of the events leading to the selected scenes will provide the actors with some background. Scripts will usually be in short supply at auditions, and this information will allow the actors to concentrate on the selected audition scenes during the limited time they have with the script (Figure 21).

The actors will need to provide you with information as well. In addition to a picture and résumé, I require all auditionees to fill out a preprinted card. This card includes his or her name, telephone numbers, union affiliations, agent's name and numbers, height, weight, hair color, and age range. The card has additional space for entries to be made by the director or casting agent. These include the character or characters the actor auditions for, comments on the audition, callback indication and role, the date, and an identification number (Figure 22). I assign each actor a number based on the order in which they audition, regardless of appointment time. This number is also indicated on their picture and résumé, which are then filed sequentially if not desired by the director during the actual audition. This avoids any confusion if the actors audition out of appointment time order, and it allows everyone viewing the audition to keep track of who they are seeing. This card follows the actors through subsequent auditions to track their progress.

The audition facility should be inspected for adequate lighting, heating, and cooling, and required safety and sanitary standards. The audition space should be set up with the necessary tables, chairs, and lighting for the director and/or casting agent, their assistants, and you. At minimum, a couple of chairs should be available for actors to use during the audition. In some cases, the director may request additional rehearsal furniture as required by the selected audition scenes. A separate room should be available for waiting auditionees. It is advisable to post signs indicating the entrance to the reception area, rest rooms, and public telephone locations, and a "Do Not Enter" sign posted on the entrance to the actual audition space. A water fountain or bottled water should be available in the facility.

I like to introduce each actor before he or she auditions to help break the ice. In the early stages of the audition process, the actor will have only a few minutes to show his or her stuff. Anything I can do to bring them quickly to a more personal and comfortable relationship with the director or casting agent is beneficial to all parties. Be sure you know how to pronounce each of the actors' names correctly and check that they are ready to perform. Encourage them to do their best, let them know what to expect during the audition, and wish them luck. The audition card, and picture and résumé if desired, is given to the director or casting agent, and the audition begins.

One of your primary responsibilities during auditions is to keep everyone on schedule. You will need an assistant working the reception room while you are in the auditions. Be sure there is enough time allotted to each audition to allow those involved in the casting decision to share any immediate responses. A minute or two is all that is required, and this time is available while you are inviting in the next auditionee.

There are a number of variations in auditions during the process of casting a show. Musicals require separate auditions for dancers, which are usually handled in large groups. This takes a tremendous organizational effort on your part. With dozens of dancers on stage, you will have to be extremely careful to identify each performer correctly. Assigning numbers to each dancer is mandatory in this case. Callbacks will be more intense explorations of the actor's abilities. The director may wish to audition performers in pairs or groups to play out an entire scene. You may also need to arrange for someone to read with an actor who is auditioning.

Once the show is cast, you will have another piece of the puzzle in place. If you have been thorough in your research during the pre-production phase and have organized this information properly, you will be extremely well prepared for the start of rehearsals.

And if you are not ready to give up at this point, Part II will take you through the rehearsal phase.

AUDITION FACT SHEET

PRODUCTION: THE SEAGULL

PERSONNEL

Director: Director's Name   Scenery: Scenic Designer's Name

Playwright: Anton Chekhov   Costumes: Costume Designer's Name

Producer: Producer's Name   Lighting: Lighting Designer's Name

Choreographer: Sound: Sound Designer's Name

Stage Manager: Your Name   Casting: Casting Agent's or Asst. Director's Name

DATES/VENUE

1st Rehearsal: 10/1/91   Opening: 11/19/91   Closing: 1/10/92

Venue: Playhouse Theater

PERFORMANCE CONTRACT
LORT B

GENERAL DESCRIPTION

Character	Age Range	Description
ARKANDINA	43	An actress
KONSTANTIN	20–25	Her son, a young man
SORIN	62	Her brother, retired from the Ministry of Justice
NINA	18–20	The young daughter of a wealthy landowner
SHAMRAYEV	52–53	A retired lieutenant, SORIN'S steward
POLINA	52–53	His wife
MASHA	22	His daughter
TRIGORIN	35–36	A novelist
DORN	55	A doctor

FIGURE 20

AUDITION SELECTIONS

PRODUCTION: THE SEAGULL

Character	Scene/Page	Description
TRIGORIN	II/25–29	With NINA
TRIGORIN	III/30–31	With MASHA
TRIGORIN	III/37–39	With ARKADINA
TREPLEV	I/2–5	With SORIN
TREPLEV	I/5–7	With NINA
TREPLEV	I/15–16	With DORN
TREPLEV	II/24–25	With NINA
TREPLEV	III/34–37	With ARKADINA
TREPLEV	IV/54	speech
TREPLEV	IV/54–58	With NINA
TREPLEV	IV/46–49	plus Ensemble
MASHA	I/1–2	With MEDVEDENKO
MASHA	I–16–17	With DORN
MASHA	III/30–31	With TRIGORIN
MASHA	IV/42–43	With MEDVEDENKO
MASHA	IV/43–44	With TREPLEV and POLINA
POLINA	I/7–8	With DORN
POLINA	II/23–24	With DORN and NINA
SORIN	I/2–5	With TREPLEV
SORIN	III/32–34	With ARKADINA
NINA	I/5–7	With TREPLEV
NINA	I/9–11	"performance"
NINA	I/12–15	plus group
NINA	II/24–25	With TREPLEV
NINA	II/25–29	With TRIGORIN
NINA	III/31–32	With TRIGORIN
NINA	IV/54–58	With TREPLEV

FIGURE 21

AUDITION INFORMATION

Name:_____ Phone #:_____

Address:_____ Service #:_____

City:_____ State:_____ Zip:_____

Agent:_____

Phone #:_____

Height:_____ Weight:_____

Hair Color:_____ Age Range:_____

(front)

No.____

Production:_____ Date:_____

Character(s):_____ Callback   YES   NO

Comments:

(back)

FIGURE 22

Part II

Rehearsals

The rehearsal phase begins with the first company reading of the play. At this point you should already know as much as you can about the play, people, design, and facilities that will be involved in the production. You should also have a very clear idea of the process you will be going through and the function you will serve in that process, as a result of your pre-production preparation.

The rehearsal phase is the most demanding phase of the production. Your time will be consumed with the management of many individuals and the extraordinary quantities of information and number of activities required to mount a show. You will perform your job better if you understand that you are managing *change*. You must learn to love chaos.

To start things off right, make sure you schedule time during the first company meeting to go over the various policies and procedures you or the producing organization have put in place in order to keep things running smoothly. You should also make available to the acting company the rehearsal and performance schedules, fact sheets, and other information you have been researching and organizing in the past few weeks. Make sure you allow sufficient time to go over each item in enough detail so the company understands its value and how to use it. In an Equity company, you will also have to hold the Deputy Elections. The Deputy is the Equity representative for the company and the liaison between the acting company, Equity, and the producing organizations.

4

Rehearsal Rules

It is important that everyone involved in rehearsals has a clear understanding of what is expected of them and what they can count on others to do. Be very specific about these issues so there are no misunderstandings. What in the beginning may seem like a trivial matter can cause great frustration when the pressure is on. You will come to each production with your own set of rehearsal rules, and through discussions with the director you will learn what everyone involved needs in order to perform best during rehearsals. The rules and procedures you set up in rehearsal will serve as the foundation for the rules and procedures for performance, so you must be consistent. If, for some reason, a change is required when moving from rehearsal to performance, inform everyone well in advance. You do not want to be faced with, "That's how we did it in rehearsal."

I have identified a few areas for special consideration below. However, before proceeding, a brief word about human behavior. Your rules and procedures will be more accepted if you provide a clear and reasonable explanation for their existence. Take the time to explain why a rehearsal rule or procedure will help you or the director do your respective jobs better. This communication will help personalize your relationship with members of the company and at the same time impress upon them the need for cooperation.

DAILY CALL PROCEDURES

If all performers were required at all rehearsals this would be a simple issue. This is not practical or desirable. You must have in place a procedure by which actors who are not in rehearsals at the end of the day (when the final schedule for the next day's rehearsal is posted) can find out what their next call is. This procedure should be simple for them to follow and should not burden the stage management staff any more than is necessary. You should not be in a position such that you have to make numerous phone calls nightly or, worse, sit by the phone waiting for actors to call in.

My recommendations are as follows. First, establish a routine that enables you and the director to discuss the rehearsal needs for the next day during your last rehearsal break of the current day. During the last rehearsal segment of the current day, an assistant can type up the rehearsal schedule, have it approved by you, and post it on the call board. This will enable performers who are participating in the final rehearsal call of the day to see the next day's schedule as they leave. You should also announce the calls personally at the end of rehearsal. This will reduce the number of performers who will need to be contacted in some other fashion.

For those people who do need to be contacted separately, publish a telephone number they can call for rehearsal information. They should know that the information will typically be available after a predetermined time. This should help eliminate unnecessary phone calls. The telephone number should belong to an employee of the producing organization who has regular office hours and is always available by phone during those hours. Make sure in advance that this employee knows how to read the schedule and take nothing for granted. You do not want that person in the position of having to interpret your rehearsal schedule.

My preferred alternative is to have a telephone recording with the day's schedule. This removes the third party communication above and is more easily and quickly adjusted. With voice mail or electronic mail becoming ever more available, you can have a very efficient and effective system at a very low cost. In any event, the procedure must become routine to ensure that proper information is available and being received.

You must also be very clear about the procedure for reporting any inability to attend rehearsal. It is mandatory that the actors call in if they are sick or will be late for rehearsal. An actor's absence can require schedule changes, which will need time to put into effect. You should impress upon the company the need for early warnings. Even if the performer is uncertain of her ability to be on time or attend rehearsal at all, with enough notice you can be preparing a response just in case.

STAGE MANAGEMENT SERVICES

This section is really about what services you will and will not provide to the actors during rehearsals and performance. Remember, consistency is very important.

Warning of upcoming entrances is one area that can cause confusion, particularly during rehearsals. If you warn the actors during rehearsals, they will expect it during performance. Then, when you confront them about their missed entrance, they will have every right to say, "You did not warn me as you did in rehearsal." I suggest that you inform all performers that they are responsible for their own entrances. You and your assistants will have enough to do during rehearsals to keep you very busy in most cases. As an alternative during rehearsals, designate an area just outside the rehearsal room where actors can wait for their entrances. The point here is that you or your assistants have other things to attend to during rehearsals and cannot be expected to know the whereabouts of each performer or have the time to search for them. As a precaution, everyone who is expected in the rehearsal should notify stage management if they are leaving the rehearsal room or waiting area and state where they will be. This is not meant to remove the performer's responsibility for making an entrance but rather to meet the need to react quickly to the constantly changing needs of the rehearsal.

Responsibility for rehearsal props and costumes also needs to be clearly defined. Once again, I believe stage management has enough to do, so my recommendation is that performers be responsible for collecting and returning their props and costumes from and to designated prop tables and wardrobe racks. As with everything else, try and be consistent and establish a routine. These routines established in the rehearsal setting will usually transfer very nicely to performance if you plan in advance. If a problem exists, it will be much more evident if a defined pattern has been broken. It will be difficult to determine in advance that a prop is missing if it is never placed in the same location twice.

THE DIRECTOR'S AND STAGE MANAGEMENT'S NEEDS

Any number of rules and procedures can be grouped into this category. The basics are perhaps policy issues of the producing organization such as those regarding smoking, eating, drinking, etc., in the rehearsal room or performance space. There may also be a number of needs based on the director's or stage management's requirements. This may include rehearsal attire, extraneous noise in the rehearsal room, guests, sign-in procedures, a phone number that will take messages, performance and rehearsal costume laundry procedures, restrictions on the use of certain entrances and exits into the rehearsal and performance space, and so on.

Managing Rehearsals

BLOCKING NOTATION

Recording the blocking as it develops is a full-time job in the early days of rehearsals. This information will be necessary to rehearse understudies and replacements, establish a variety of light and sound cues, develop presets for props and costumes, maintain the director's original intent, recreate the show, and prompt actors as they learn their blocking. You can count on the blocking changing many times during the course of rehearsals, but do not let this deter you from noting even the earliest attempts at blocking a scene. Use a hard lead pencil and carry a big eraser. If you feel that the director or an actor is uncertain about a change in blocking, it is useful to record the change, without destroying the original blocking notation until you are sure the change is permanent. This will allow you to go back quickly to the original blocking, if necessary, by simply referring to your notation and instructing the actors as to their original movements.

There are a number of methods for taking blocking notation. The system you choose or develop should, as always, be based on the needs of the production. First, make sure you are not the only person recording this information. Watch the actors carefully to be certain they are writing down their blocking. Some performers will be so caught up in the moment, they will not take the time to record their movements in the script. You and the actor should record all movement and business.

One of the simplest methods for recording blocking for a production mounted on a proscenium stage is to divide the stage into general areas of reference. Figure 23 illustrates a stage divided into six areas — three across and two deep. The notation is always referenced from the actors' perspective as they face the audience and is termed stage directions. Downstage left, noted as "DL", is the area closest to the audience and to the actors' left as they face the audience. In an effort to be more precise, you may divide the stage into as many areas as you feel are necessary. Figure 24 adds another division to the depth of the stage, resulting in nine areas. You could go further, but there are better ways to achieve precision, which will be discussed shortly.

To record blocking using the divisions in Figure 23 or 24, you simply note that the actor crosses to one of the designated areas. For example:

An actor crosses to the downstage center area. This would be noted as "XDC", where the "X" stands for cross, the "D" indicates downstage, and the "C" indicates center.

> CROSS — In blocking, to move from one area of the stage to another.
> DOWNSTAGE — The area of the stage closest to the audience.

"XML" would record the movement of an actor to the midstage left area as defined by Figure 24.

"XUR" indicates the actor has moved into the upstage right area of the stage.

As you can see, this method on its own is not very specific. On some stages each of these areas could easily measure more then ten feet wide and ten feet deep, leaving much speculation over the exact location of the actor within the area. You can develop any number of methods to increase the accuracy of your blocking notation as required by the specific production you are working on. You should examine two factors in an effort to expand the capabilities of the basic method outlined above. First, in addition to the general area designations or stage directions, look for other landmarks within the set of your production. A piece of furniture, a window, a carpet, or even another actor may provide you with a more specific location as a reference point for the actor.

For instance: An actor may cross to a table in the downstage right area of the stage, which could be noted as "XDR TABLE." Now, not only do we know the actor is in the downstage right area, we know that he or she is at the table. You can be more specific by indicating which side of the table with the notation that the actor crosses to the upstage side of the downstage right table noted as "XUS DR TABLE." Obviously, if there is only one table on stage, there is no need to use the "DR" reference; thus, "XUS of TABLE."

Another example might be "X WINDOW." This notation indicates the actor crosses to the window, which is part of the setting for the scene. If there is more than one window you will need to provide an additional reference identifying the window by stage directions, or you may choose to number the windows if the stage directions do not give you an accurate picture of the setting. In an earlier section, it was suggested that the prompt script be formatted with a page of script on the right-hand side of the book and a reduced copy of the ground plan for that scene on the left. Figures 25 and 26 illustrate how to use the ground plans you copied onto the backs of each of your script pages to identify the location and movement of the actors as referenced by numbers in the text.

The second factor you should consider is indicating in your blocking notation the distance the actor is moving. "X2DR" would indicate the actor is moving two steps toward downstage right. This technique indicates the distance and the direction the actor travels but does not specify the exact location of the actor at the end of the movement. With this technique you have to be able to track back to the actor's entrance or starting point and follow the actor's successive movements to identify his location at a given point in the script. I suggest you use this method only for small movements and that you not use this method to record a series of movements. Always insert a specific location designation to avoid tracking through a large number of blocking notes to identify the location of an actor at a given moment in the play.

For a simple production staged on a simple set, it may be sufficient to record the blocking using only stage directions, as described at the beginning of this section. In most other circumstances, you will find it necessary to implement some combination of the techniques discussed above. Figure 27 illustrates the notation for a fairly complicated series of movements. Please note the combination of methods and the references to the associated ground plan.

You may have also noted in Figure 27 the use of a set of abbreviations, which creates a "shorthand" for the stage manager. A key or legend to this shorthand should be developed and recorded at the front of the prompt script. Typically, the list of abbreviations will include character names, your stage area designations (i.e., "DR" = down right), and abbreviations for other usable landmarks such as windows, doors, furniture, etc. (Figure 28).

When working "in-the-round," you must adapt the standard stage designations or stage directions to the circular shape of the stage. First, establish a viewing reference point for yourself. I suggest you view the stage from the same direction that you will be using when you are in performance and calling the show. Looking at the stage from this viewpoint, divide the circle into the four primary compass points, with north being the farthest point from your viewing position and south the closest (Figure 29). Now add the secondary compass points and change the labels to those used for a proscenium stage as illustrated in Figure 30. These labels are usually more meaningful than the compass points and are more readily understood by actors and technicians. Some stage managers prefer to label the stage as if it were a clock face as shown in Figure 31. In any event, for additional precision add depth rings as illustrated in Figure 32. When using depth rings, your blocking notation would look like the following examples (which are based on Figure 32).

"XDR2" when the actor moves to the downstage right point in ring 2 or,

"XL1" when the actor moves to the left point in ring 1.

It is very helpful if you can provide the actors with an 8 ½" X 11" ground plan of the set that includes the stage designations you intend to use for your blocking notation. You should include on this ground plan any additional landmarks, such as your number or letter designations for doors, windows, chairs, etc. This not only gives the actors some helpful hints in taking down their own blocking but provides them with a reference that will enable them to understand you when you prompt them to "cross upstage center number two" or "move to and sit in chair number three." These plans should be available on the first day of rehearsal, and you should always keep a supply on hand for those actors who tend to lose things.

When recording the blocking for a show, you must also note the exact timing of the move. When does the actor begin the move and when does the actor complete the move? This can easily be achieved by creating for yourself a symbol that can be inserted in the text at the appropriate line or word. The first occurrence of the symbol signifies the start of the actor's move, which is noted adjacent to the line in which the symbol appears. The second occurrence signifies the completion of the move. For example:

XDC

```
GLOUCESTER: Now is the/winter of our discontent
Made glorious summer/by this sun of York;
```

In this example the / indicates the start and finish to the "XDC". Gloucester begins his cross downstage center with the word "winter" and completes the movement with the word "summer."

Determine what the *default format* should be. The default format should reflect the most common movement pattern. For instance: The majority of the time, actors may begin their movement at the beginning of a line and complete the move at the end of the line. If you determine that this pattern is your default format, there would be no need to insert a symbol.

```
GLOUCESTER: Now is the winter of our discontent
Made glorious summer by this sun of York;
```

Now Gloucester begins his cross downstage center at the beginning of his line and completes the move at the end of the line. This is the default format, so there is no need to include the arrow.

REHEARSAL CUES

At some point during the rehearsal process you will begin to provide the actors with rehearsal cues. You should, of course, consult with the director, but it is probably best to call cues from the very first day of rehearsal. I usually start with a description of the cue during the first read-through of the play. As rehearsals progress, timing becomes important, and I gain a good sense of the director's and the designers' intentions, so I provide a verbal indication of all light and sound cues, scenery and soft goods movement, and other effects necessary to the action of the play. This process will begin to familiarize the performers with the sequence of technical events that will take place during performance. Whatever sound, lighting, or special effect cues you identified in your examination of the script during the pre-production phase should be called during rehearsals.

These cues may take the form of a simple statement such as calling the "lights out" at the end of a scene or a "phone rings." An even better approach when possible is to provide a more realistic representation of the cue. This is most feasible for sound effects. It is easy to rig a bell or buzzer that can be operated by you during rehearsals. Consider this a necessary piece of stage management equipment. Some theaters may have these devices on hand. If yours does not, ask someone to make you one. It is also very useful to have a small portable cassette tape player in rehearsals. You can then request that the sound department provide a series of cassette tapes with approximations of the necessary sound cues recorded on them. Keep in mind that these tapes are not the finished products of the sound designer's work, but simulations for the purpose of rehearsals.

If this is not possible or convenient, you can make many of the sounds yourself. You will be surprised at how much this will help in setting the timing and helping the actor understand the rhythm of the cue. Test your talent for bird calls, thunder claps, and sirens. Use what's available to you to create the sounds of the show. Practice your telephone "rrrrrrrrrriiiiing" and door "buzzzzzzzzzzzz." This is no joke. If you simply say, "phone rings" at the appropriate place in the script, there is no sense of the timing. If you make the sound of a telephone ringing and try to represent accurately the length of each ring and the quiet time in between rings, you and the actors will begin to establish a pattern that will carry over into the technical rehearsals and be one less thing to work out during that time. This practice will also enable the director to identify the exact point in the script for the placement of the cue. When you go into technical rehearsals you will know exactly where to execute many of the show's cues.

Light cues are more difficult to recreate in a rehearsal setting, but you can often find some creative ways to deal with important cues. Once again, you can do a lot by speaking through the action of a cue as it is to happen on stage. You might call a slow fadeout at the end of a scene as follows: "Lights begin to fade ... fading ... fading ... and out."

The scene may conclude with the curtain coming down at the end of the light fadeout, so call it as well.

This description gives the actors a feel for the timing of the cue and again helps you establish the rhythm and mood of the cue. Do not disturb the rehearsal process by calling lighting cues that do not affect the action or rhythm of the actors. These cues are for you, the lighting designer, and the director to work out. You can, however, begin to take timing and placement notes for the cues, which will be discussed in more detail shortly.

Finally, once you start calling cues you become an active part of the rehearsal. You must be as consistent and decisive in your execution of rehearsal cues as you will be when you call the actual performances. Do not be afraid to speak out. The actors will quickly adapt to this seeming intrusion if you "perform" within the rhythm of the scene. The actors will also become very dependent on you for calling cues. If you are not on time with a cue or miss the cue altogether, you will disrupt the patterns and rhythms the actors are developing. I have seen many actors come completely out of character and stop during the middle of a scene because the stage manager missed a rehearsal cue that the actor depended on for motivation or to trigger some thought process. They will become so in tune with the cues you are calling in rehearsal that without them they will be lost.

> ON BOOK — When either the stage manager or an assistant is following the script in order to help actors when they stumble over lines.
>
> PROMPT — To help an actor with his lines when he either asks or is stumbling.
>
> PROMPT CORNER — The area from which the stage manager runs the show. Usually found just to the right or left of the proscenium backstage. The stage manager often sits in the lighting or sound booth to call the show.

PROMPTING

Prompting requires great sensitivity and an ability to respond to the pace of the rehearsal and each actors' performance patterns. Prompting should be discussed with the director prior to the beginning of rehearsals, and a set of guidelines should be established for you and your assistants to follow. The guidelines should be made known to all performers as part of the orientation during the first rehearsal. The usual procedure requires the actor to ask for a line when necessary, by simply saying "Line." This procedure removes the possibility of stage management mistaking a long dramatic pause for an actor's inability to remember a line. During early rehearsals this mistake can be quite common as actors experiment with interpretation and line delivery by constantly changing the patterns and rhythms until they and the director establish the reading of choice. This technique also discourages the actor from developing a dependence on the stage manager. As I have mentioned before, actors develop habits very quickly and if you are always right there with a line for them, forgetting their lines may become habit.

When a "line" is called for, you or an assistant should be able to respond immediately with the appropriate line. Often, the actor will require only a word or two to trigger his or her memory. When you prompt, it is important to maintain the mood and pace of the show. Speak clearly and with enough volume to be heard. Speak only the line. If your prompt is delivered in a disruptive manner or, even worse, if you prompt the wrong line, you will destroy the work going on in rehearsal. For this reason it is always desirable for you to have an assistant "on book" during rehearsals when the actors are "off book." You, as the stage manager, cannot keep track of all the goings on in rehearsal and provide effective prompting as well.

The same procedure should be established for prompting the actors on their movement. Make sure they know to ask in order to get a prompt from stage management.

One issue to resolve with the director is how to respond to the occasion when an actor makes a mistake in a line or movement. My preference is simply to take a note for the actor if the mistake is not serious or disruptive. If an actor "jumps" several lines, particularly if they are other actors' lines, you will want to stop and correct the actor. However, if the actor has simply paraphrased the line or substituted one word for another, it is best to let the rehearsal continue without interruption. You or your assistant should take a note that references the page number and line in the script and present it to the actor after rehearsal. You should keep a copy of the note as a reminder for the next time you work that scene, to make sure the problem is corrected. It may be useful to remind the actor of the problem prior to working the scene, but this is usually only necessary with an extremely forgetful actor. In the event an actor is having trouble with a particular section of the play, offer him or her an opportunity to run through the lines with you or an assistant before the next time you rehearse that section. In a one-on-one session focusing on the particular issue of lines, you will have the actor's full attention and can correct the problem without the pressure of a full rehearsal.

You should also simply note blocking errors as long as the actor gets close enough to the intended movement so as not to disrupt the rehearsal. The most common blocking mistake is simply moving at the wrong time. In early rehearsals, the actors are usually late with their movement because they tend to concentrate on the lines first. There is usually no reason to stop rehearsals for this kind of problem. A note after rehearsal is generally the most efficient way to handle this situation. Once again, your knowledge of the director's preference, the habits of individual actors, and your sensitivity to the rehearsal process and working environment will allow you to make these decisions on a case-by-case basis and from production to production.

You should also discuss with the director her preference for giving line and blocking notes. Some directors prefer to give these notes themselves. This is particularly appropriate during an actual rehearsal. When you notice a problem during rehearsal and it seems significant enough to correct right then and there, tell the director and let her make the correction. Chances are, she is aware of the problem also and is waiting for an opportune time to interrupt. You should not wade in and stop rehearsal without the director's consent.

TIMING THE SHOW

Throughout rehearsals, you will be timing run-throughs, scenes, and smaller sections of the play. One reason for timing rehearsals, and eventually performances, is to keep track of the pace of the show. Skilled directors will determine early in the rehearsal process the approximate final running time of the show, based in part on your reports on the running time of rehearsals. This target time will be something they pursue throughout rehearsals. Once they achieve this time or a time they feel is best for the show, you will use this target as one way of maintaining the quality of the show and the director's original intent. If a performance runs significantly over the target time, it may be an indication that the actors are not picking up their cues fast enough or are stretching business to the detriment of the show. You will have to make some judgment about the audience response and what role it plays in the timing of the show, but as you gain experience and become familiar with a production you will be able to gauge this impact quite well. On the other hand, if the performance is running faster than usual, look to see if the actors are rushing through the script without thinking about the words.

The running time of the show will also be required by the box office and house management staffs, so they can inform patrons and plan for intermissions and the final curtain.

> BLACKOUT — A rapid extinguishing of all light on stage.
>
> PACE — The tempo of the performance.

Another major reason to time various aspects of the show relates primarily to the process of lighting and sound design. Both designs use time as one of the variable design components. One of the controllable qualities of light is movement. The rate at which a light changes in intensity can have a significant impact on the audience's emotional response to the play.

As an example, imagine the ending of a bright, flashy musical number. The blackout at the end of the number will require an instant change from the lights' existing intensity to zero. This "blackout" will maintain the lively pace of the show and, most important, prompt the audience into wild and enthusiastic applause. In contrast, now imagine the final fadeout of the lights for a very dramatic scene. Ideally, these lights will reinforce the emotional intensity of the scene in the same manner as the "blackout" in the musical. The difference is that, in all likelihood, the emotions the lighting designer wishes to reinforce for the dramatic scene are much more somber than the high spirits of a musical comedy. This fadeout will be slow and deliberate, forcing the audience into an introspective mood, if all is working correctly. The length of time it takes an actor to complete the final movements or business of the scene will be required by the lighting designer in order to coordinate the timing of the final light cue with the final action of the scene.

There are also practical considerations that might require cues to be completed by specified moments of the play. The sound designer may need to create enough music to cover scene changes or a series of actions on stage. Through the timing of rehearsals you will be able to provide the designer with an accurate time for this sequence. Likewise, the lighting designer needs to be informed of the running times to anticipate the length of the various lighting cues for the show. The script may call for the sun to set during the course of a scene. By providing the lighting designer with the running time of this scene, the designer will be able to build the appropriate cues and assign the necessary times.

Needs will, of course, vary from production to production and designer to designer. Be helpful. Ask the designers what they would like you to do beyond the basics. You should always plan to time defined scenes and acts as a basic service. Trust me, you will need this information. On the other end of the spectrum, you may have a show that, from a design standpoint, is very time dependent. One approach to providing useful information on the timing of the show is to place interval marks in the margin of your prompt script. You will need to decide what would be the most useful interval. When I feel that a show needs this kind of detailed timing, I usually select an interval of ten to fifteen seconds. Once the show is running cleanly in rehearsal with few interruptions for missed lines and blocking, you should have an assistant sit through a run-through with a script and stopwatch. The assistant should follow the script carefully as the actors make their way through it, placing a mark in the script at every ten- or fifteen-second interval. Once this is complete, you can provide reasonable timing information on virtually any passage or section of the script by adding up the intervals from one point to the other.

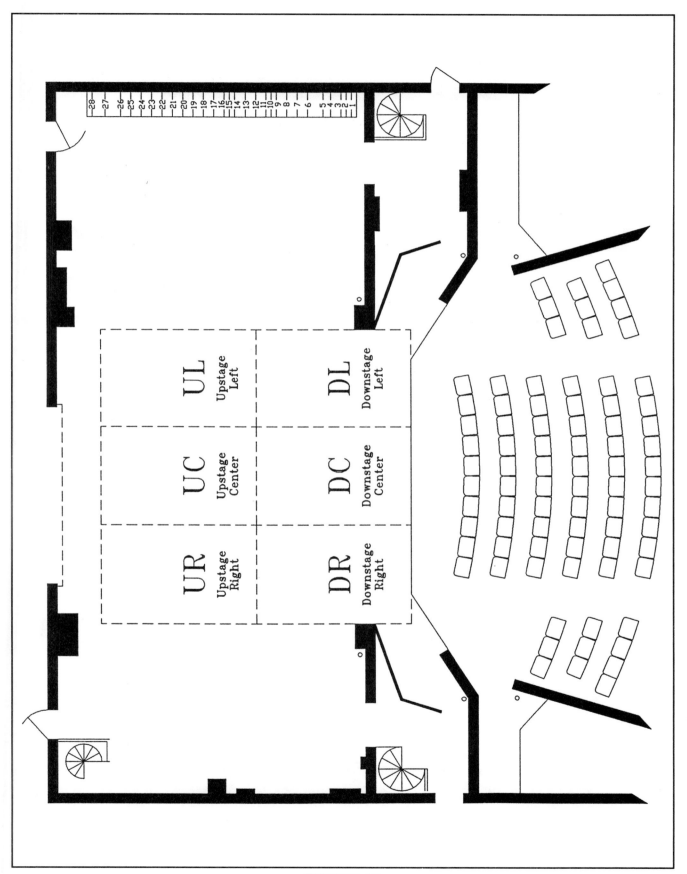

FIGURE 23

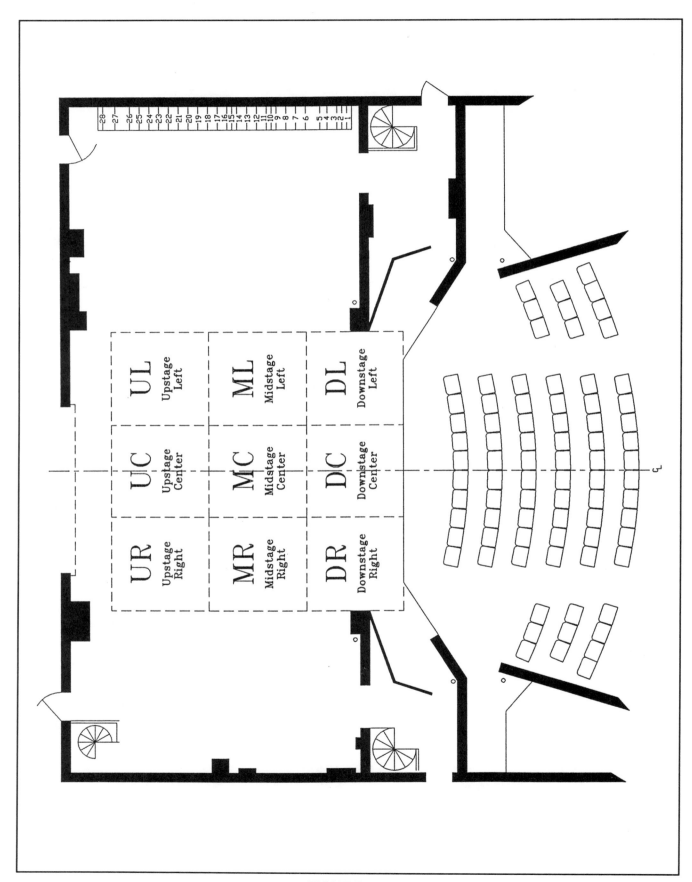

FIGURE 24

Illustration courtesy of Cari Norton, Stage Manager for the Mark Taper Forum production of *Julius Caesar.*

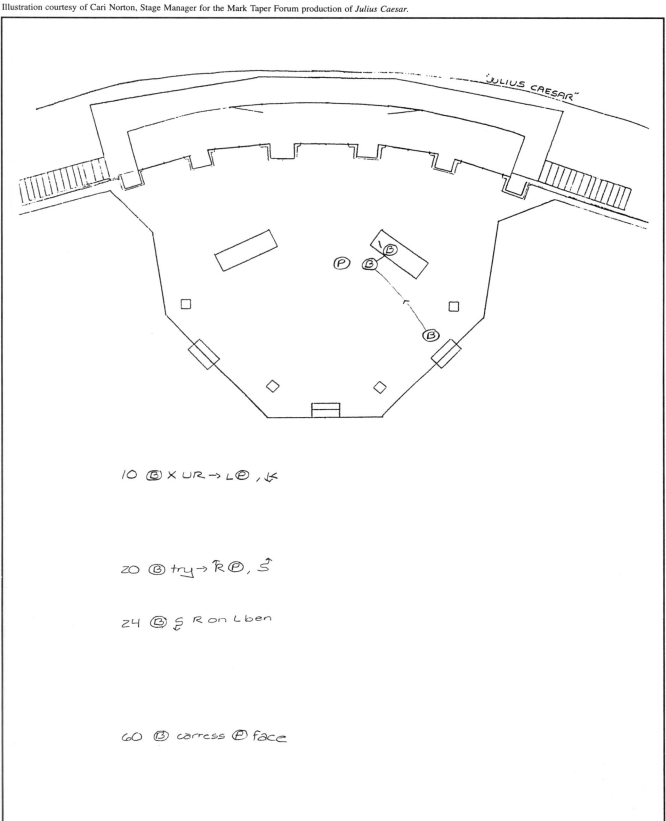

FIGURE 25

Illustration courtesy of Cari Norton, Stage Manager for the Mark Taper Forum production of *Julius Caesar.*

2.1   *Julius Caesar*

By all your vows of love, and that great vow
Which did incorporate and make us one,
That you unfold to me, your self, your half, *10*
Why you are heavy, and what men tonight
Have had resort to you; for here have been
Some six or seven, who did hide their faces
Even from darkness.

BRUTUS   *20* Kneel not, gentle Portia.

       He raises her

PORTIA

I should not need, if you were gentle Brutus. *24*   280
Within the bond of marriage, tell me, Brutus,
Is it excepted I should know no secrets
That appertain to you? Am I your self
But as it were in sort or limitation,
To keep with you at meals, comfort your bed,
And talk to you sometimes? Dwell I but in the suburbs
Of your good pleasure? If it be no more,
Portia is Brutus' harlot, not his wife. *60*

BRUTUS

You are my true and honourable wife,

279.1 *He raises her*] *not in* F   281 the] F2; tho F1

273-4 that great vow . . . one Wilson comments that *that great vow* and *incorporate*
suggest the Christian marriage service
(as in Matthew 19: 5, 'they twain shall be
one flesh').
275 your self, your half That one's marriage
partner is one's (other) self or (better) half
is, of course, proverbial (Tilley F696,
H49).
276 heavy sad, heavy-hearted
281-4 bond . . . excepted . . . limitation Legal
terms of land tenure, for a binding agreement with exceptions and time limits
(Wilson).
284 in sort after a fashion
285 keep stay, lodge (a frequent Elizabethan
sense)
comfort gladden (*OED, v.* 5, marks it ob-
solete in this sense, its latest examples
being this and one in Drayton's *Poly-
olbion*, 1612.)

286-8 suburbs . . . harlot The idea of living
in the outskirts, not the city centre, leads
to that of the brothels which Tudor
ordinances restricted to Southwark, outside London city. '"I being, O Brutus,"
said she, "the daughter of Cato, was mar-
ried unto thee, not to be thy bedfellow
and companion in bed and at board only,
like a harlot, but to be partaker also with
thee of thy good and evil fortune' (*Brutus*,
p. 118; see Appendix A).
289 You are . . . wife 'This absolute com-
munion of souls is in designed contrast to
the shallow relation of Caesar and Calpurnia. The dictator treats his wife as a
child to be humoured . . . Portia assumes
that . . . she is entitled to share her hus-
band's inmost thoughts' (F. S. Boas,
Shakespeare and his Predecessors, 1896;
repr. 1940, p. 467).

(47:22)

144

FIGURE 26

Illustration courtesy of Cari Norton, Stage Manager for the Mark Taper Forum production of *Julius Caesar.*

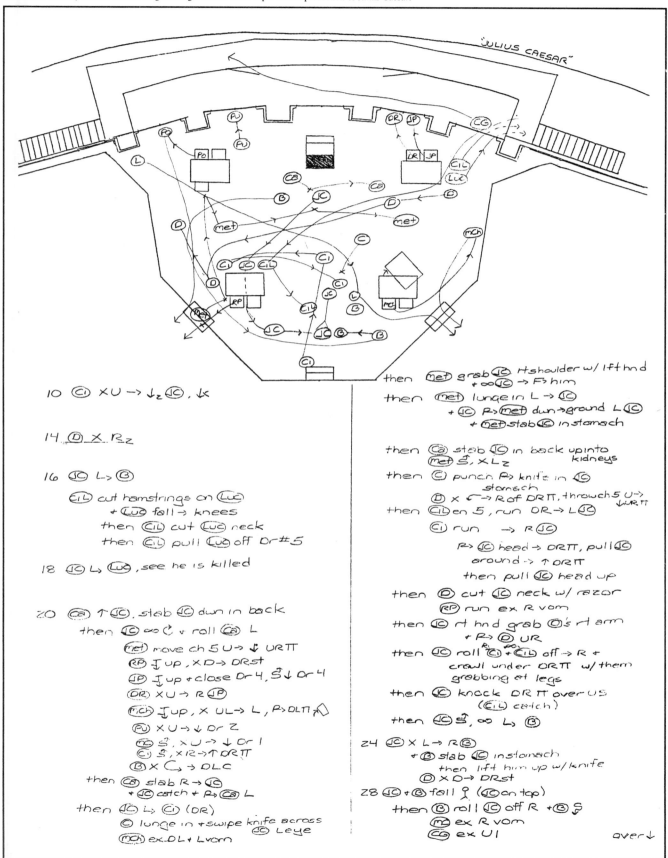

10 Ⓒⓘ XU → ↓₂ ⒿⒸ , ↓x

14 Ⓓ X R₂

16 ⒿⒸ L→ Ⓑ
    ⒸⒾⓁ cut hamstrings on ⓁⓤⒸ
      + ⓁⓤⒸ fall → knees
      then ⒸⒾⓁ cut ⓁⓤⒸ neck
      then ⒸⒾⓁ pull ⓁⓤⒸ off Dr#5

18 ⒿⒸ L→ ⓁⓤⒸ , see he is killed

20 Ⓒⓐ ↑ ⒿⒸ , stab ⒿⒸ dwn in back
    then ⒿⒸ ∞ Ↄ ↓ roll Ⓒⓐ L
      ⓜⓔⓣ move ch 5 U→ ↓ URTT
      ⓇⓅ ⌐ up , XD→ DRst
      ⒿⓅ ⌐ up + close Dr 4 , S↓ Dr 4
      ⒹⓇ XU → R ⒿⓅ
      ⓜⒸⓗ ⌐ up , X UL → L , R→ DLTT
      ⓅⓊ XU→ ↓ Dr 2
      ⒿⒸ S , X U → ↓ Dr 1
      Ⓒⓘ S , X R2 → ↑ DRTT
      Ⓑ X Ↄ → DLC
    then Ⓒⓐ stab R → ⒿⒸ
      + ⒿⒸ catch + R→ Ⓒⓐ L
    then ⒿⒸ L→ Ⓒⓘ (DR)
      Ⓒ lunge in + swipe knife across
        ⒿⒸ L eye
      ⓜⒸⓗ ex DL + L vom

then ⓜⓔⓣ grab ⒿⒸ rt shoulder w/ lft hnd
    + ∞ ⒿⒸ → F→ him
then ⓜⓔⓣ lunge in L → ⒿⒸ
    + ⒿⒸ R→ ⓜⓔⓣ dwn → ground L ⒿⒸ
    + ⓜⓔⓣ stab ⒿⒸ in stomach

then Ⓒⓐ stab ⒿⒸ in back up into
   ⓜⓔⓣ S , X L₂   kidneys
then Ⓒ punch R→ knife in ⒿⒸ
      stomach
    Ⓓ X Ↄ → R of DRTT , through 5 U→
then ⒸⒾⓁ en 5 , run DR→ L ⒿⒸ ↓URTT
    Ⓒⓘ run   → R ⒿⒸ
      R→ ⒿⒸ head → DRTT , pull ⒿⒸ
       around → ↑ DRTT
       then pull ⒿⒸ head up
then Ⓓ cut ⒿⒸ neck w/ razor
    ⓇⓅ run ex R vom
then ⒿⒸ rt hnd grab Ⓒ's rt arm
    + R→ Ⓓ UR
then ⒿⒸ roll Ⓒ + ⒸⒾⓁ off → R +
    crawl under DRTT w/ them
    grabbing at legs
then ⒿⒸ knock DRTT over US
    (ⒸⒾⓁ catch)
then ⒿⒸ S , ∞ L→ Ⓑ

24 ⒿⒸ X L → R Ⓑ
    + Ⓑ stab ⒿⒸ in stomach
      then lift him up w/ knife
    Ⓓ X D→ DRst
28 ⒿⒸ + Ⓑ fall ↓ (ⒿⒸ on top)
    then Ⓑ roll ⒿⒸ off R + Ⓑ S
    ⓜⓔ ex R vom
    ⒸⒼ ex UI   over ↓

FIGURE 27

3.1 *c*   *Julius Caesar*

Unshaked of motion; and that I am he,   70
Let me a little show it, even in this –
That I was constant Cimber should be banished,
And constant do remain to keep him so. *10*

CINNA (*kneeling*)

    (TO COVER)   O Caesar –

CAESAR   Hence! Wilt thou lift up Olympus? *14*

DECIUS (*kneeling*)

    Great Caesar – *16*

CAESAR   Doth not Brutus bootless kneel? *18*

CASCA   Speak, hands, for me! *20*

      They stab Caesar, Casca first, Brutus last

CAESAR   Et tu, Brute? *24* — Then fall, Caesar! *28*   *He dies*

CINNA

    Liberty! Freedom! Tyranny is dead!
    Run hence, proclaim, cry it about the streets! ⌐

CASSIUS   SB:

    Some to the common pulpits, and cry out   80   L-54
    'Liberty, freedom, and enfranchisement!' *60*   S-FF
      ⌈*The onlookers show signs of panic*⌉   V-75

74, 75 *kneeling*] *not in* F   76.1 *Casca . . . last*] *not in* F   77 *He*] *not in* F   81.1 *The onlookers . . . panic*] *not in* F

74 *Olympus* In Greek mythology the mountain (in Thessaly) of the gods, with whom Caesar ranges himself.

76 *Speak, hands* The staging of this crucial moment depends on how these words are interpreted – as a prayer (hands raised, instead of knees bent), or as a call (to himself and others) to act instead of speaking. The raised hands could reveal the drawn dagger.

76.1 *Casca first, Brutus last* 'Casca behind him strake him in the neck with his sword. . . . Caesar, turning straight unto him, caught hold of his sword and held it hard; and they both cried out, Caesar in Latin: "O vile traitor Casca, what doest thou?" And Casca in Greek to his brother: "Brother, help me." . . . They . . . compassed him in on every side with their swords drawn in their hands, that Caesar turned him nowhere but he was stricken at by some . . . And then Brutus himself gave him one wound about his privities' (*Caesar*, pp. 93–4; similarly *Brutus*, p. 124).

77 *Et tu, Brute* Even thou, Brutus. On the origin of the phrase see the Introduction, pp. 24–5. *Brute* (printed *Brutè* in the Folio) has two syllables.

78–81 *Liberty . . . enfranchisement* 'Brutus and his confederates . . . came all in a troop together out of the Senate, and went into the market-place, . . . boldly holding up their heads like men of courage, and called to the people to defend their liberty' (*Caesar*, p. 96; similarly *Brutus*, p. 125).

80 *pulpits* platforms (for orations); though it would be difficult for an Elizabethan to suppress the standard English sense. At 3.2.63 is a reference (echoing Plutarch) to 'the public chair', and even if Shakespeare did not expect Brutus or Antony to be seated while delivering their orations, he seems to have expected a chair to be provided.

81 *enfranchisement* Synonymous with 'Liberty, freedom'; it does not imply voting rights.

162   (1:07:54)

FIGURE 27 (cont.)

Illustration courtesy of Cari Norton, Stage Manager for the Mark Taper Forum production of Julius Caesar.

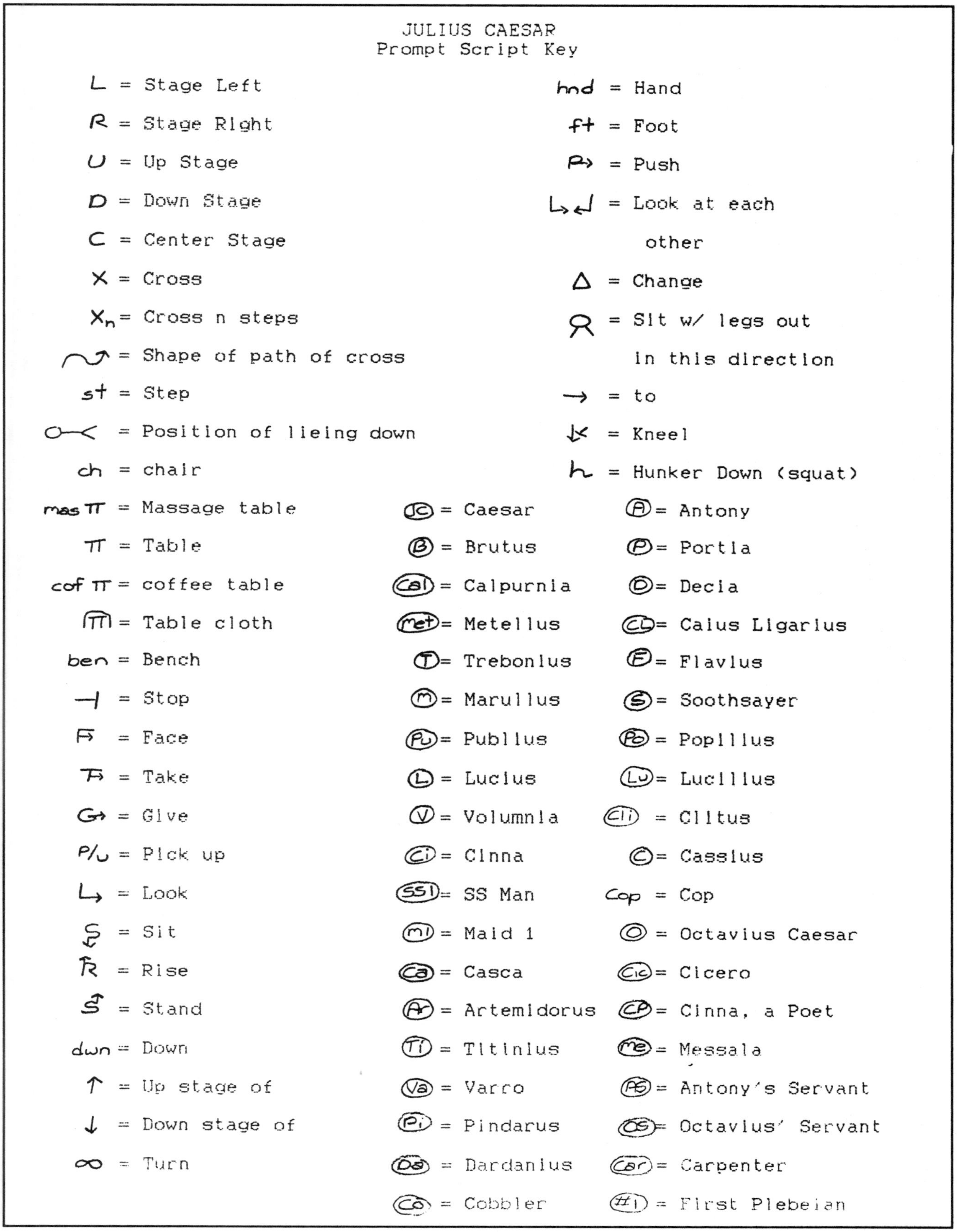

JULIUS CAESAR
Prompt Script Key

L = Stage Left

R = Stage Right

U = Up Stage

D = Down Stage

C = Center Stage

X = Cross

X_n = Cross n steps

~↗ = Shape of path of cross

st = Step

○< = Position of lieing down

ch = chair

mas π = Massage table

π = Table

cof π = coffee table

π̂ = Table cloth

ben = Bench

⊣ = Stop

F⃗ = Face

T⃗ = Take

G→ = Give

P/∪ = Pick up

⌐→ = Look

S = Sit

R̂ = Rise

Ŝ = Stand

dwn = Down

↑ = Up stage of

↓ = Down stage of

∞ = Turn

hnd = Hand

ft = Foot

P→ = Push

↳↲ = Look at each
    other

Δ = Change

Ꝑ = Sit w/ legs out
    in this direction

→ = to

↓ᴋ = Kneel

h = Hunker Down (squat)

ⓒ = Caesar

Ⓑ = Brutus

Ⓒⁱ = Calpurnia

Ⓜᵉᵗ = Metellus

Ⓣ = Trebonius

Ⓜ = Marullus

Ⓟᵘ = Publius

Ⓛ = Lucius

Ⓥ = Volumnia

Ⓒⁱ = Cinna

Ⓢˢ = SS Man

Ⓜⁱ = Maid 1

Ⓒᵃ = Casca

Ⓐʳ = Artemidorus

Ⓣⁱ = Titinius

Ⓥᵃ = Varro

Ⓟⁱ = Pindarus

Ⓓˢ = Dardanius

Ⓒᵒ = Cobbler

Ⓐ = Antony

Ⓟ = Portia

Ⓓ = Decia

Ⓒᴸ = Caius Ligarius

Ⓕ = Flavius

Ⓢ = Soothsayer

Ⓟᵒ = Popillus

Ⓛᵘ = Lucillus

Ⓒˡⁱ = Clitus

Ⓒ = Cassius

Cop = Cop

Ⓞ = Octavius Caesar

Ⓒⁱᶜ = Cicero

Ⓒᴾ = Cinna, a Poet

Ⓜᵉ = Messala

Ⓐˢ = Antony's Servant

Ⓞˢ = Octavius' Servant

Ⓒᵃʳ = Carpenter

Ⓗ₁ = First Plebeian

FIGURE 28

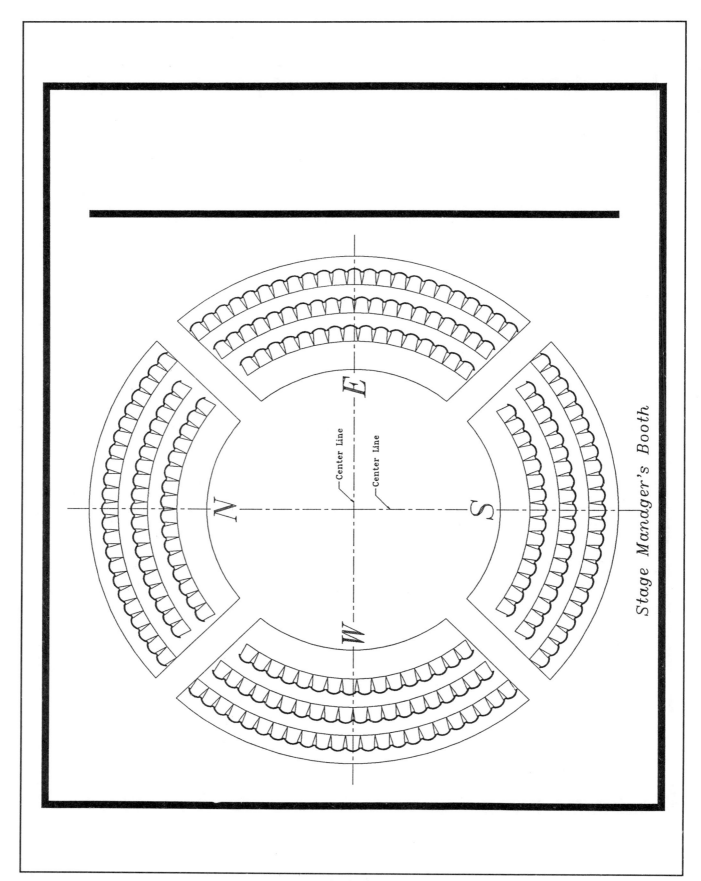

FIGURE 29

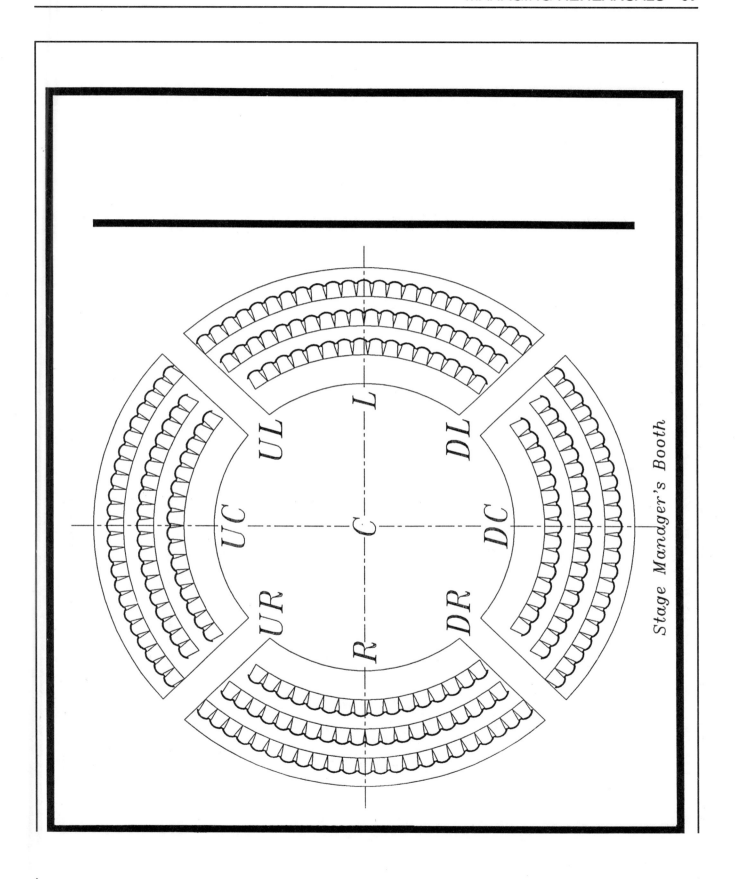

FIGURE 30

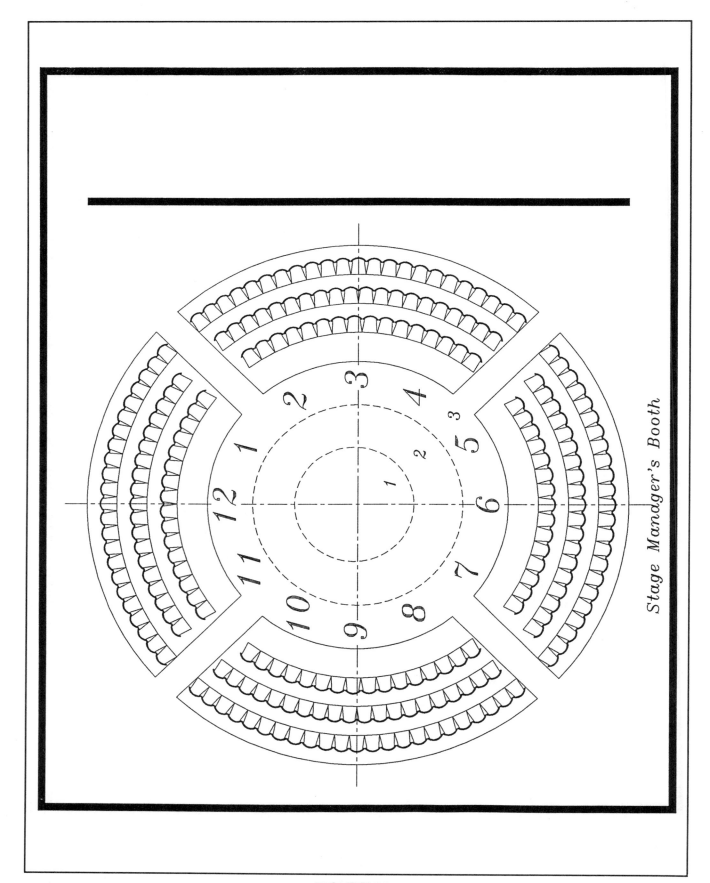

FIGURE 31

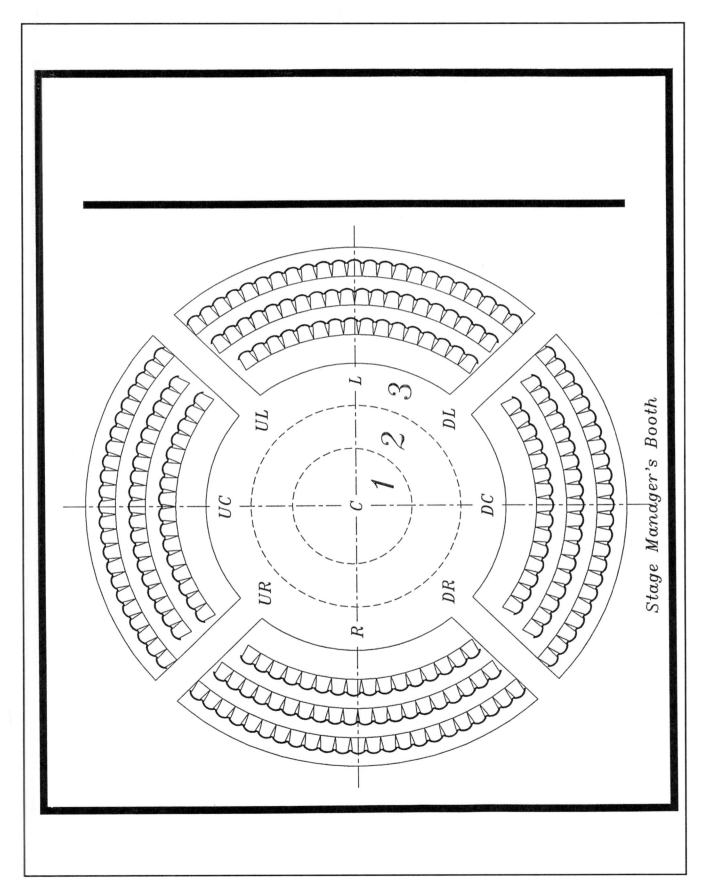

FIGURE 32

6

Information Distribution

One of the primary functions of a stage manager is to distribute information and, more than that, to keep the lines of communication open in both directions. There are three formal methods that should be considered mandatory in establishing efficient and effective communications. The first takes the form of a production meeting, which was discussed earlier in this text. These meetings provide for very effective two-way communication but can be inefficient with respect to time. It is very difficult to gather a large number of busy people together for any length of time on a regular basis. The best you can hope for is once a week for one hour. More than this and you are probably wasting valuable time needed to prepare the production.

The second involves an information distribution system, which identifies appropriate personnel and provides them with a daily report on rehearsal activities and performances. You will need to create a comprehensive distribution list if one does not exist. This list should go well beyond the production staff who attend the production meetings. Think about who might benefit from the information included in the rehearsal report and with whom you might have a need to communicate. You will certainly want to include the management of the theater company or producing organization. The following is a list of suggestions for individuals who should be included on the distribution list, in addition to the personnel who would normally attend production meetings. You may come up with others who need to be included on the list as well.

- Producer
- Artistic Director
- Managing Director
- Company Management
- Public Relations
- House Management
- Box Office
- Building or Facility Maintenance
- Security
- Other Stage Managers
- Any Appropriate Assistants
- Receptionists

Once the distribution list is established, you can use it for the dissemination of other information, such as the production meeting minutes, program copy, schedules, etc.

While this distribution system is formally a one-way communication system, the amount of two-way communication it generates is enormous.

CALL-BOARD — The bulletin board used by stage managers to post any information pertinent to actors and crew, such as rehearsal schedules and costume fittings.

As you will see in the next section, the rehearsal report can be a very flexible tool, which can be customized for the environment in which you find yourself working.

The third method involves the use of a call-board. This bulletin board should be familiar to everyone working in the theater and should be established as the official source for production information, daily calls, and rehearsal schedules. Take care that the call-board does not become too cluttered. New notices will be hard to detect if the call-board is covered with paper, so be selective about what is placed on the call-board. It will be easier to maintain if you can provide another bulletin board for the variety of other notices that will appear. You should approve any notice that appears on the official call-board.

REHEARSAL REPORTS

Daily rehearsal reports are a must for all shows. These reports provide the production staff with critical information about the development of the show and identify changing needs and potential problems. These reports will also be the official record of the rehearsal process for the production and should be filed for future reference.

The goal is to make the report form as readable and efficient as possible while still transmitting the required information. Information should be logged in as brief a form as possible. Short, concise notes reporting facts and figures are preferable to long explanations.

Ideally, these reports should take the form of a single sheet of 8½" x 11" paper divided into sections labeled for specific components of the production or specific types of information. These areas should be determined based on the organizational structure of the theater and the specific needs of the production. The basics should include:

- Show title
- Date
- Name of the person preparing the report
- Starting time of rehearsal
- Break times
- Finish time of rehearsal

The report should also provide information on the accomplishments of the day's rehearsals, the upcoming schedule, announcements, absences from rehearsal, rehearsal location, etc. Figure 33 illustrates a typical rehearsal report. Notice the divisions for scenery, costumes, lights, sound, and props. These divisions give the production staff the feeling that the report has been customized for them. They can go right to the section of the report that concerns them and get current information on the production without sifting through any other data.

For instance, the lighting designer should be able to check the report quickly to see if there is any news that will affect the design of the show. The lighting designer should not be forced to search through a variety of other details that do not concern the lighting of the show in order to find those notes that do. This organization of information will help ensure that the designer actually reads the report. If the report is too much to get through, the designer and all others involved in the production will not spend the time to read the report. This will instantly close the communication channels.

While this technique should make reading the rehearsal reports more palatable, it requires the stage manager to have a strong knowledge of the interrelationships between the numerous components of a production. What may seem like a simple prop addition as a result of the rehearsal process may require the attention of someone other than the prop department. Let's say that, during rehearsals, one of the performers develops a piece of business involving the use of a pocket watch, and the director decides it would be appropriate for the character to have a pocket watch. Your rehearsal report would show an entry under the prop heading requesting the pocket watch be added to the show. What you must also recognize is that this pocket watch must have a pocket to hold it. You have witnessed the birth of a costume note. Under the costume heading, you would include an entry notifying the costume designer and the costume department that this character in a particular scene needs a pocket for the pocket watch. If placement of the pocket is critical, include this information as well. You should also take this opportunity to request that the prop department and the costume department work out the details together. This will reinforce two-way communication between the two departments at your direction.

The "Misc." section in Figure 33 can be used for miscellaneous notes directed at a specific person or department, which are not part of the regular production functions. The illustration depicts two entries in this section. One is directed to the maintenance department and the other to house management. With these irregular notes, use a highlighting marker to call attention to the entry. You can adapt the form in the Appendix to suit the specific needs of your production or use it as is.

REHEARSAL REPORT

PRODUCTION: CANDIDE

Rehearsal # 37   Day: WED.
Location: PLAYHOUSE STAGE   Date: 5/15/91
Stage Manager: V.K. for C.K.

		Costumes:
Rehearsal Start	7:30	Cunegonde needs scarf for
Rehearsal Break	11:00	"Glitter & Be Gay".
Rehearsal Start	:	Old Woman's fruit hat needs adjustment.
Rehearsal Break	:	
Total Rehearsal Time	3:30	

Rehearsal Notes:
1st Tech – Act I
Will continue Act I tomorrow

Lights:
Dress electrical cables S.L.

Properties:
Body bag needs repair.
Need new hand mirror for Max.

Scenery:
Fix axle on large cart.
Cut projection screen.
Raise casters on cash register.

Fittings, etc:

Sound:
Speaker hanging from D.L. platform needs
to be removed.

Schedule:
Dress Parade tomorrow 5/16
@ 4:00 pm
Continue tech Act I – 5/16

Misc.
Need flashlights for backstage
Need light bulb for SM desk S.R.

FIGURE 33

7

Preparing for Technical and Dress Rehearsals

PAPER TECH — A meeting
between director, designers, and stage management to define and record
the series of technical
events required to operate the production.

TECHNICAL REHEARSAL
— The rehearsal or
series of rehearsals in
which the technical
elements of the show are
integrated with the work
of the actors. Also called
Tech.

You have several options available to prepare for technical and dress rehearsals, and you should take advantage of as many as possible. This is a critical time for planning and anticipating the technical/dress rehearsal process. If you have been using the techniques offered in earlier sections of this text, you should have a very strong foundation from which to draw up your final plans. This next section of the text should help you avoid the worst aspects of the most difficult and exciting portion of the production process. Remember, there is no substitute for planning, but make sure everyone knows the plan and that everything you plan is possible. Avoid surprises.

Technical rehearsals are notoriously inefficient and frustrating. This comes as no surprise when you recognize that the technical/dress rehearsal is the first time you bring all the elements of the production together. Scenery, which has only been two-dimensional outlines on the rehearsal room floor or crude mock-ups, abruptly becomes solid, three-dimensional scenic units, which are inevitably in the way. Lights become more than just an abstract description of the mood or atmosphere desired for each scene; they become a distraction. Sound and special effects, which you may have been brilliant at improvising in the rehearsal room, suddenly become technological nightmares understood only by rocket scientists. And costumes will become the scapegoat for every failure of an actor to make an entrance, follow blocking, or remember a line.

Technical rehearsals can be an extremely disruptive time for the actors of your company. The actors are at a point in their development where they are very comfortable with the rehearsal process and environment. They are also on the verge of completing their preparation and anxious to take the final step toward the complete realization of their character in performance. They have been the center of attention in rehearsals, and it is unfortunate that with the start of technical rehearsals they must be thrown into new surroundings and placed on the back burner just when they are ready to soar. Your effort in preparing for technical rehearsals is twofold. First, you must make the integration of the various elements as efficient and pleasant as possible. Second, you should ease the frustration of the acting company as they make the transition from the rehearsal room to the stage.

The most common and by no means mutually exclusive methods for preparing for technical/dress rehearsals are "paper techs" and "dry techs."

PAPER TECH

CUE SHEET — The page(s) used to note the cues given by the stage manager to the different technicians.

ARBOR — The metal frame that holds the counterweights. Also called the Carriage, Counterweight Carriage, or Cradle.

COUNTERWEIGHT SYSTEM — A type of rigging that uses weights to counterbalance horizontal battens containing scenery, curtains, or lighting instruments.

FLIES — The area above the stage that contains lines to be raised or lowered.

FLY — To lower or raise lines hung from the grid that are affixed with scenery or stage equipment.

FLY GALLERY — A platform that runs above the stage on one side, used in the operation of fly lines.

FLYMAN — Crew person in charge of raising and lowering the flies.

GRID — A steel framework above the stage from which the fly system is rigged. Also called the Gridiron.

A paper tech enables the director, stage management, designers, and other appropriate technical personnel to coordinate and finalize the technical and design functions of the performance. Each cue or technical activity should be defined and recorded. The definition should describe the action of the cue, its location in the script, the timing of the cue if appropriate, and the cue number or designation. This information should be recorded in the prompt script and on the master cue sheet. The completed master cue sheet should include all light, sound, and special effect cues as well as scenery shifts and costume changes.

Figure 34 illustrates an entry on the master cue sheet for a simple light cue. The cue number in this case is L25. In this method of numbering cues, the "L" stands for lights and would be called by the stage manager as "Lights 25." A sound cue would have an "S" (sound) prefix to the number, while other areas would be assigned prefixes as required by the technical complexity of the production. If a production has a significant number of scenery or curtain moves, which are handled by the theater's counterweight fly system, these cues would be designated with "F" (flies) as the prefix. Some prefer to use the designation "R", which stands for "rail" in the term "pin rail." Before counterweight systems, and still in use today in many theaters, flying scenery was operated from and secured to the "pin rail." I tend to use the "R" designation to avoid confusion with special effects cues, which are labeled "Fx".

The cues for each component of the production are numbered separately and sequentially. Figure 35 expands the master cue sheet to include an entry for Sound 18 (S18). Notice that L25 and S18 are bracketed together on the master cue sheet. This symbol indicates that the cues are to be called together as one action.

There are numerous other methods for numbering cues. One technique would have you number all cues from start to finish with no distinction between lights, sound, or any other technical component. This method depends on each crew member responsible for executing a cue in the show to keep track of which cue numbers affect them. For a production with 100 cues, the sound operator may only have cues associated with numbers 1, 4, 31, 73, and 97. This system is prone to numerous errors without some warning or reminder to the performance crew of an upcoming cue. The warning is already built into the first numbering system indicated above. This system also disregards the sequential numbering programs in most computerized lighting control systems. The lighting designer would have to specifically avoid cue numbers that did not initiate a lighting change.

Some stage managers prefer to assign numbers to light and letters to sound cues or vice versa. With the growing number of computerized lighting control systems designed to use numbers, sound cues are generally assigned letter designations. This is probably a fine technique if you have no more then twenty-six sound cues. Once you exceed this number, you will be required to use double letters such as "AA". More than fifty-two cues

LINES — Cords hung from the grid, used to fly scenery and stage equipment.

PIN RAIL — A rail connected to the fly gallery used in the securing of fly lines.

TRIM — The height to which a piece of scenery or stage equipment will be flown.

and you go into triple letters, which is ridiculous. This letter method is awkward and potentially confusing for complicated shows. The expressed advantage of this system is the clear distinction between light cues and sound cues, reducing the potential for operators to initiate a cue by mistake when hearing the stage manager call a series of cues. This advantage quickly weakens when letters and numbers are mixed as a result of adding new cues between existing cues. Suppose the sound designer wishes to add a cue between existing sound cues "L" and "M". To avoid re-lettering the entire show, the added cue would become "L1" or "L.1". Now that numbers are introduced into the designation for sound cues, the distinction is blurred.

In the first numbering system described above, cues inserted between existing cues can be designated with a decimal point and a number (L25.1, S18.1) or a letter (L25A, S18A). I prefer using the decimal point and number method because it corresponds to the scheme used by computerized lighting control systems. You should try to get through the paper tech giving each cue a whole number. Even if you find you have forgotten a cue, it's better to renumber the show and go into technical rehearsal with as much flexibility as possible. When it becomes necessary to insert a cue, remember to leave room on both sides of the new cue to insert additional cues if necessary. The first cue inserted between L25 and L26 should be L25.5. This technique allows you maximum versatility if you must insert cues between L25 and the recently added L25.5 or L25.5 and L26.

In the master cue sheet illustrated in Figure 35, the cue location for L25 and S18 is recorded by the page number of the script and the movement, action, or line that initiates the cue. L25 and S18 are called at "Door closed" "end of scene" on page 35. The prompt script will, of course, show an entry for these two cue numbers on the specified page and adjacent to the appropriate line or action. You will need to pinpoint the exact location in the text of all your cues with a symbol in a manner similar to your blocking notation as described earlier (Figure 36).

Accurately calling the cues during performance is of paramount importance. Be sure your cue notation visually dominates your blocking notation and that any symbols or abbreviations are distinctive, so as not to cause confusion. The designer has two variables with which to adjust the timing of a cue. One is the *rate* at which the cue is executed and the second is the *point in the script* at which it is initiated. The stage manager is solely responsible for the precision and consistency of the second. If a cue needs to be completed sooner, but the designer likes the rate at which the cue is moving, you will be asked to call the cue some number of seconds earlier. Be certain that you have an exact location for each cue as a result of the work you do during paper tech. This is the baseline reference for the designers. Then call each cue at its specified point until you are asked to change it.

The timing for these cues is indicated in the column labeled "Count" on the master cue sheet. Not all cues will require an entry in this category, but it is very useful to have this data whenever appropriate. This information is recorded in seconds and is admittedly speculative in some cases, but should provide a good starting point from which adjustments can be made later.

You should strive to establish a fundamental relationship among the cues, which at least indicates fast, medium, and slow. If you have done a good job of timing various aspects of the show in rehearsals and have a good feeling for the ideal pace of the show, you will be able to specify time with surprising accuracy. In most cases, the timing of the cue will require little more than fine-tuning during the technical rehearsal. Do not spend much time during the paper tech agonizing over the count of a cue. Pick a time that is close and then move on.

The final entry on the master cue sheet is a description of the cue. Returning to the example in Figure 35 (page 111), L25 is a "fade to black" and S18 is the sound of a "police siren." Many cues will be described by some action already indicated in the script. However, it is necessary to include a brief description on occasions when a cue is motivated solely by artistic interpretation. Figure 37 shows L37 as a ten-second cue, which is initiated on Macbeth's cross downstage center (Mac XDC). The description of this cue is "Lights focus DC." This cue exists to help focus the attention of the audience on the character of Macbeth during the next portion of the play. Nothing other than the blocking notation provides a clue as to the action of this particular cue. You may feel that you will remember what is going to happen during this cue, and you probably will. However, it is helpful to have a description of the cue in the prompt script to aid others who may not be as familiar with the production, in the event you are unable to call the show.

You should already have a preliminary list of cues from your pre-production evaluation of the script and updates to this list based on rehearsal activities to this point. The director and each designer will probably have additions to your list, which should be incorporated during the paper tech process. Ideally, the paper tech should be scheduled at a point far enough along in the rehearsal process so as to make maximum use of the information and decisions that are coming out of rehearsals, yet early enough to permit designers to address any issues that arise as a result of the paper tech in time for the first technical rehearsal. I recommend that you schedule a paper tech at least one week before the first technical rehearsal.

DRY TECH — A technical rehearsal without actors.

With the entire show recorded on the master cue sheet, the sheet is ready to be distributed to all participants in the paper tech and to all personnel responsible for executing the design and technical activities of performance. The master cue sheet is a step-by-step guide to the technical functions of the show, which designers and production staff can use to prepare for the technical rehearsal. The stage crew will use it to choreograph scene shifts, the lighting and sound designers will use it to build their cues, and stage management will use it to ensure that all elements of the production work together.

DRY TECH

The *dry tech* form of technical rehearsal is conducted without actors. You may choose to handle each technical component individually, in groups, or together in a single dry tech. The purpose of the dry tech is to coordinate, integrate, and practice the actual technical and design functions of the production without consuming the actors' valuable rehearsal time. It also ensures that when the actors do arrive, they will enter into an environment that will cause the least possible disruption to their development.

Based on the master cue sheet, you should be able to start with the first cue of the show and work through every cue and technical activity defined during the paper tech. All designers and production personnel responsible for the technical and design execution of the show should be present and prepared to perform every cue on request. This is the time to stop and correct any problems that cannot be handled with a note. It is extremely helpful to have available a person or two to act as stand-ins for the actors. These assistants should have scripts in hand complete with blocking notation, so they can simulate the actors' stage positions and movements and read cue lines. This technique will help refine the placement and timing of the cues.

Dry techs may also be the first time the director has an opportunity to see and hear the work of the designers. Any misunderstandings about the nature of a cue should be resolved and a plan developed to implement the change by the first technical rehearsal.

DRESS PARADE

DRESS PARADE — Designated time when the costumes are worn by the actors under stage lights in order for the director and costume designer to make any necessary changes or improvements to the costumes.

DRESSER — Crew person assigned to help with quick changes and general maintenance of costumes throughout the run of the show.

Without the actors, there is little opportunity to test the costumes prior to the first dress rehearsal. The costume department will, of course, request time for a number of costume fitting sessions to ensure the actors are properly fitted into each of their costumes, but this does not provide an opportunity to see the costumes in their performance surroundings. A dress parade satisfies this need in most cases and provides an advance look at the costumes, which should eliminate any ugly surprises during dress rehearsal.

Dress parade should be held on the set under performance lighting conditions. This approach provides reliable color rendition of the costumes and the opportunity to see the costumes against the actual background of the set. Actors should initially be viewed individually. The director and designer should discuss any design problems and required alterations to the garment. The costumer should take note of any missing components of the costume and any fitting problems. When each character in a scene has been viewed individually, they should all be brought back on stage to be viewed as a group. This review will help determine whether the color palette and silhouettes are working together for the scene.

If the production calls for quick or difficult costume changes during the course of the play, a separate rehearsal should be scheduled to practice the changes. This costume quick change rehearsal requires the actor and wardrobe crew or dressers. Each change should be rehearsed under the appropriate performance conditions, and it should be timed, to provide a realistic sense of the costume change. Any alterations to the costume that will facilitate the change being made in the available time should be communicated to the costume department to ensure a successful dress rehearsal.

MASTER CUE SHEET

PRODUCTION: A PLAY ABOUT CUES

Date: 10/15/91

CUE #	COUNT	PAGE/LINE	ACTION
L25	7	35 / Door closed – end of scene	Fade to black

MASTER CUE SHEET

PRODUCTION: A PLAY ABOUT CUES

Date: 10/15/91

CUE #	COUNT	PAGE/LINE	ACTION
L25	7	35 / Door closed – end of scene	Fade to black
S18	Bump	35 / Door closed – end of scene	Police siren

FIGURES 34 (top) and 35 (bottom)

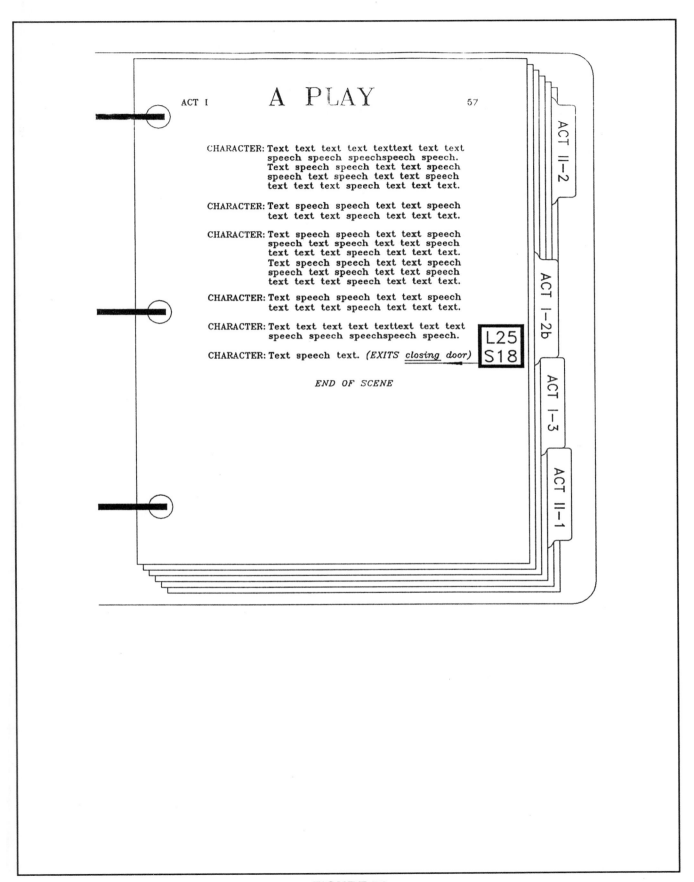

FIGURE 36

MASTER CUE SHEET

PRODUCTION: MACBETH

Date: 1606

Page 2 of 7

CUE #	COUNT	PAGE/LINE	ACTION
L37	10	13 / Mac XDC	Lights focus DC

FIGURE 37

Technical and Dress Rehearsals

There are a few more items that you must address before you actually begin the technical rehearsals. Once you have familiarized yourself and the rest of the stage management staff with the theater and its equipment, organized it to meet the needs of your production, and put into place the procedures for running the show, you are ready for the actors and running the first technical rehearsal.

MOVING INTO THE THEATER

If you have scheduled dry techs, you will have already begun the transition from the rehearsal room to the stage. This transition should be easy if you have organized rehearsals and planned the physical aspects of the production with the theater clearly in mind as suggested earlier. Prior to any technical rehearsal, you should consult with the appropriate production staff to establish the organization of the backstage space. The onstage and offstage placement of properties, furniture, and set pieces should be determined based on the placement of these items in rehearsals. Backstage equipment must be specified and put in place to ensure the efficient operation of the show during technical rehearsals and performance.

> BACKSTAGE — The area away from the acting area, including dressing rooms and the green room. Also called Off-stage.
>
> FOCUS — To direct and lock down a lighting instrument in its specified stage area.

The furniture placement as defined on the scenic designer's ground plan is often altered to some extent during rehearsals. You must recognize these adjustments as they occur and take note of the new positions in order to place the furniture on stage accurately. Spiking the furniture in the rehearsal room is the best way to keep a handle on these changes. Whenever the placement of a piece of furniture or prop is adjusted, change the spike marks. When it is time to move into the theater, you can transfer the new locations of the rehearsal spikes to a clean ground plan and, using this new ground plan, locate the furniture on the set. The position of furniture and other set pieces is not only important to the work of the actors but to the lighting designer and others. The lighting designer may key the focus of certain lighting instruments on the location of furniture or other set pieces. It is not uncommon that adjustments will continue throughout technical rehearsals. Keep the spike tape handy to keep up with the necessary changes. The furniture must be in the same place for every performance or something will go wrong. *Never be without spike tape.*

Storage of Furniture and Set Pieces

The offstage storage positions of furniture and set pieces are also important. Be sure nothing is stored in such a manner as to obstruct entrances and exits to the set or the stage itself. Also, establish crossovers around the set and know that they are clear of any impediments. In the low light conditions of the backstage area during performance, and with the actors and crews focused on the performance, it is easy to run into an item that projects into a crossover you assume is clear. In tight quarters or productions that require large amounts of offstage storage, it is necessary to spike the storage positions of these items to prevent any problems. This can be accomplished by outlining the allotted storage space on the floor with two-inch wide tape.

Property Tables

Property tables should be located offstage as needed and ideally in locations that simulate their positions in the rehearsal room. Of course, these positions were actually based on your research of the theater and the set prior to the start of rehearsal, so it should be a simple matter. This may seem like an unnecessary effort, but as stated earlier, anything you can do to keep the established patterns of behavior the same will enhance your success as a stage manager.

The property tables should be covered with kraft or butcher paper and labeled for each item to be stored there. A thick marker should be used to outline a section of the table large enough to accommodate each individual prop. This space should be clearly labeled with the name of the prop in letters large enough to read in poor light. Figure 38 illustrates the layout for a prop table. This technique enables the prop crew and stage management to know at a glance if a prop is missing, and it is an easy way to encourage the actors to pick up and return their props to the same place. This visual method of identification and storage also has benefits when a crew member or an actor is replaced. Items that are too big to place on a prop table should be subject to this same technique by graphically identifying the storage place for these items, whether placed on the floor, hung on a wall, or stored in a hallway.

In your organization of the backstage area, you should allow space for costume changes or quick change booths as necessary. This space should be equipped with sufficient light to manage any makeup changes, as well as a mirror, a costume rack or hooks, and a chair. As with everything else backstage, this space should be clearly defined for the purpose of costume changes and not for storage of anything else.

With the backstage space laid out, this is an appropriate time to make sure that there will be adequate light under performance conditions for the actors and crew to carry out their responsibilities safely. Competent electricians will usually provide for all your needs without much prompting. A few keys to focus on include sufficient lights for all crossovers and escape stairs or ramps. In addition, running lights are needed for all prop tables or prop storage areas. Clearly marked exits from the stage are required by law, so make sure these signs are visible in case of an emergency.

> ELECTRICIAN — A theater technician who installs and/or operates the lighting for a production.
>
> PROP TABLE — The table backstage on which props are laid out, usually in a mapped out order.
>
> GLOW TAPE — Tape that glows in the dark, placed in small pieces around the set so the actors and crew will not bump into anything during a blackout.

Glow Tape

In addition to running lights, it is often necessary to mark the stage and its settings with glow tape to ensure safe passage on and off stage during

ANCHOR — To secure a set piece to the stage floor.

BOOK — Two flats hinged together in order to be self-supporting when folded on the hinge. Also called Book Flat and Two-fold.

blackouts. Glow tape is treated with a fluorescent material, which, once charged with light, glows in the dark much like the luminescent hands of a clock. The tape is used to mark a path on and off the set and is placed on any object that might be an obstruction in the dark. Glow tape has an adhesive back, but under heavy traffic it does not have sufficient staying power. If the glow tape is attached to an appropriate surface, use a stable gun to secure the tape. As an alternative, a larger piece of good quality transparent tape can be placed over the glow tape for longer life. Glow tape can also be used to spike items that must be positioned in the dark. *Never be without glow tape.*

Flashlights

This discussion of running lights and glow tape would not be complete without mentioning the requirement for all stage management staff to have a flashlight. A flashlight can be used as a signaling device as well as a work light. There are many to choose from these days. I have two that I find the most useful. One is a compact, high output, focusable flashlight. It can be easily carried in a pocket, so you never have to put it down and consequently walk off without it. The other is a heavy-duty flashlight with a magnetic strip that allows you to attach the flashlight to any metal surface or equipment, freeing both hands. You may also wish to have a lighted clipboard or flexible head penlight that can attach to a clipboard. Be careful where you use your flashlight backstage during a show. It is very distracting to the audience and the performers to see little circles of light roving over the set during the course of a performance. It is often a good idea to insert a piece of blue or red color media into the lens of the flashlight to reduce the contrast between the stark white light normally emitted and the darkness of the stage. The compact flashlights mentioned above can be purchased with color filters for this purpose. *Never be without a flashlight.*

CASTER — A small wheel used on scenery and scenic equipment for ease of shifting.

CORNERBLOCK — A piece of 1/4" plywood cut in the shape of a triangle, used to connect the stile to the rail on a flat. Also called a Triangle or Corner.

DUTCHMAN — Thin strips of cloth used to mask cracks between flats.

Communication

Communication needs vary from production to production. The equipment, however, is generally the same and should be installed and checked out prior to technical rehearsals. The basics of the audio communication system are the stage monitor, intercom, page system, and house address system. The stage monitor system allows the activities on stage to be heard in other rooms. This program should be fed to all dressing rooms; the green room; actor/crew lounge or other gathering place for the performers and crew; lighting, sound, and stage management booths; the lobby; and any other room as needed. The intercom system allows two-way communication between stage management and crew. It is also used by designers during technical rehearsals to communicate with crew members responsible for execution of their designs. This system should be fairly flexible, allowing stations to be set up wherever needed. You should communicate your requirements as to location and type of equipment to the sound department. Wireless intercom systems have become much more reliable in recent years and provide the maximum flexibility.

FLAT — A cloth-covered wooden frame, usually rectangular.

GRIP — Crew member who moves scenery.

JACK — A triangular-shaped brace used to support scenery.

JOG — A narrow flat, usually between one and four feet wide.

KEYSTONE — A 1/4-inch piece of plywood used to connect the stile to the toggle bar on a flat.

The dressing room page is not essential, but it will save you miles of walking in search of actors and crew members who are not on stage when you want them. This system should not be able to be switched off or the volume lowered at the receiving end. If the actors can turn the system off, they will, and it will be useless to you. The last component is also not essential, but the house address system can be very useful in making announcements to the company. I generally find it too impersonal to address the company over a loudspeaker, but sometimes it is necessary, especially if you are calling the show from a booth in the back of the house. The house address is critical if you need to give instructions to the audience in an emergency.

To augment the audio monitoring systems, a video monitoring system is becoming increasingly more common. Not only does it provide another dimension to the monitoring capabilities of the theater, it can be used for cueing purposes. With the use of an infrared camera, you will be able to see the stage in the dark. The video signal can also be fed to the lobby for latecomers to view as they wait for an opportunity to be seated.

> CUE LIGHTS — Specific lights used by the stage manager to cue backstage technicians and actors.

Another form of communication that is very useful is the cue light. The cue light system, like the intercom system, must be flexible to allow for cue lights to be placed wherever needed. Cue lights are controlled by the stage manager and provide signals to actors and crew when the intercom is inappropriate. For instance, imagine an actor must make an entrance through a door when a specified action takes place on stage. If the cue for the actor's entrance is a visual cue (based on some physical act being performed instead of spoken dialogue), and the actor does not have a view of the scene from behind the door, a cue light is one way to solve the problem. The stage manager would turn the light on as a warning to the actor to stand by for the entrance and at the appropriate time switch the light off to cue the actor to go. The cue light itself should actually be two small lights wired together on the same circuit. Two lights are used in the event a lamp burns out. It is extremely rare that both lights would burn out at the same time, so if one burns out the other continues to work and the cue is not missed. Figure 39 illustrates a six-circuit cue light control panel labeled for a specific production.

PERFORMANCE CHECKLIST

> MUSLIN — Material used in the construction of flats.
> RIGGING — 1) The process of loading in scenery and stage equipment. 2) The way in which mobile scenery is controlled.

Moving into the theater will significantly increase your work load as stage manager. You and the rest of the stage management staff suddenly become responsible for the work of many more people and all the design and technical elements that go into the production. Organization is the key to managing this potentially chaotic and overwhelming situation. This is the time to begin formalizing the performance checklist. Many items for the checklist will have accumulated from rehearsals; others will become evident as you begin the technical rehearsal process.

It is helpful to break the lists into components of the production, and then within each area focus on the individual items that must be inspected, tested, or merely put into place. Some elements of a production, such as props and lights, are so extensive they will require specialized checklists and support documents. You will depend on your assistants and the rest of the performance crew to carry out various aspects of this task. The following list of items and descriptions generally applies to all productions. Using this list as an outline, fill in the details of your production as needed.

The Set

STAGE BRACE — An adjustable piece of stage equipment that fits into a brace cleat to support scenery.

STAGE SCREW — A screw used to fasten the bottom portion of a stage brace to the floor. Also called a Stage Peg.

BACK DROP — A large piece of canvas hung from a batten and painted to represent a particular scenic element. Also called Drop.

BORDERS — In scenery, material hung at the top of the set to hide fly system from the audience. Also called the Teaser. In lights, lighting instruments hung in battens over the stage area.

DRESSING A SET — The decoration of the set with items that are principally for aesthetic purposes only.

The set should be inspected thoroughly to ensure that it is in the proper position and secure. I like to walk the entire set, including all stairs and platforms, to be certain they are stable and free from any hazards. Look for potential problem spots as required by the production. For instance, if any actor is barefoot, you and the staff will have to be very methodical about keeping the floor free of any objects that could cause injury. As you walk the set, see that the walls and railings are solid. Do not forget the offstage scenery and escape units. In cases where the scenery is not set in place until a scene change later in the play, you or an assistant will have to examine these items once they are in place.

Take a look overhead as well. Flying scenery can be very troublesome if not handled properly. Make sure that flying units are free to travel without fouling on adjoining scenery, electrics, or equipment. I have been known to ask for each flying piece to be flown in to verify the accuracy of its spike mark and to ensure a clear run. Most stagehands will be extremely meticulous about these matters, but remember, you have the right to see for yourself. You are responsible.

In the routine of your inspection of the stage, try every door, window, curtain, window shade, or other scenic element that must be operated by the actors. Doors never open when they need to, refuse to stay open when you want them to, and always pop open when they should be closed. These units are built for a limited life span and with economy in mind. Do not be surprised when they fail to work correctly.

You must also be confident that scenic units operated by the crew are in good working order. Slip stages, revolves, jackknife wagons, elevators, and other stage machinery used to accomplish scene changes should be tested thoroughly. Computer-controlled stage machinery is becoming more prominent as the technology becomes more available. These devices are very fragile and require great care.

The final component of the set to be inspected is its appearance. Floors should be swept and mopped daily, but check further. The paint may need to be touched up from time to time. Have the scenic artist provide a touch-up kit for this purpose. See that any cosmetic repairs are handled promptly.

Masking

Masking is often considered part of the set, but it affects many other elements of the production as well. Masking must be positioned correctly so as not to interfere with the actors, scene shifts, lights, sound, etc. Be sure the masking is "dressed" neatly, is positioned at the proper trim height, covers sightlines, and is in safe operational condition.

Props and Furniture

Your inspection of the production's props and furniture should cover the same concerns as your examination of the set. First, is everything where it is supposed to be? Next, is it in good repair and operational? And finally, does it look as it is supposed to? Positioning of furniture and larger props on the set is based on the spike marks. Smaller items require another

> GROUND CLOTH — A heavy piece of muslin used to cover the stage floor. Also called Floor Cloth.
>
> GROUND ROW — A short piece of scenery, usually self-supporting, placed in front of the backdrop or cyc to mask stage equipment. Also called Cutout.
>
> PERIAKTOI — Three-sided flats that can be rotated to depict three different scenes.

technique. A sketch of a bookshelf or desk with all the props clearly indicated is one way to ensure the proper placement of these items. An instant film camera can also be used to record the placement of heavily propped productions. I generally make individual property checklists for those props that are preset on stage and one checklist each for stage left and stage right prop tables or storage locations. If you map out the prop tables for each prop stored on the table as suggested earlier, the list of props is built into the system. It is important to keep a separate list and a picture of the layout of each prop table in case the paper map is destroyed or disappears.

You will acquire prop safety habits over time. I have found it beneficial to take fail-safe measures whenever certain items are called for on stage. Most everyone has learned to put a little water in an ash tray to ensure the cigarette is snuffed out. I also place extra cigarette lighters and matches on stage in strategic locations whenever actors are required to light up in front of an audience. In addition, place sand-filled buckets backstage to catch the butts as they come off stage. Guns that are to fire blanks are also trouble. I always request a second gun offstage operated by an assistant in case the onstage gun does not fire.

Costumes and Makeup

A complete list of costumes, accessories, and makeup items for each actor should be posted in the dressing rooms. This list should be broken down by character, scene, etc. (Figure 40). It is extremely important that a full accounting of all costumes be made before and after each performance or dress rehearsal. Costumes require regular cleaning and maintenance, which makes them susceptible to that mystic garment-napper that frequently leaves us with half a pair of socks after a visit to the laundry.

Some costumes will be preset on stage or in costume quick change areas. For organizational purposes, it is easier to include these items on the prop checklists.

Lights

> SCRIM — Loosely-woven material that is used as a drop. When lit from the front scrim is opaque, and when lit from behind it is transparent. Also called Gauze and Bobbinet.

The lighting design of any production requires the intimate participation of the stage manager for much of its execution. This relationship extends to the performance checklist. Your ability to ascertain the readiness of the production's lighting component requires a specialized set of documents, a significant knowledge of lighting, and an understanding of the objectives of the lighting design. In addition to ensuring that each lighting instrument, dimmer, and system control is functioning properly, you will need to determine whether each instrument has maintained its focus and color.

Large scale productions and facilities will number instruments in the hundreds, and the design will remain fluid throughout the technical process, making it difficult to accomplish a thorough inspection on a regular basis during technical rehearsals. In Part III, I outline the process and provide examples of the paperwork you will need to complete a pre-show check of the lighting system. You should take every opportunity during technical rehearsals to gain a solid understanding of the concepts behind the design, in order to respond appropriately to any problem you encounter during your inspection.

As part of your lighting system checklist, be sure to include running lights, work lights, cue lights, orchestra lights, flashlights, house lights, audience aisle lights, and emergency exit lights. Also be sure that any electrical cable positioned on the floor or hanging overhead is secure and in no way creates a hazard. Cables on the floor should be covered with carpet or commercial cable protectors.

Sound

Sound in the theater is becoming increasingly sophisticated and complex. You may find yourself working with a system on the verge of rivaling the sound installations for concert performances. This is particularly true if your production is a musical. Do not leave anything to chance. A missing sound cue or dead microphone can do more to destroy a performance than you can imagine. The checklist should include a test of every speaker, microphone, and playback device used for the production.

Have the sound technician feed a test sound or cue through each speaker, one speaker at a time, to be sure it is receiving a signal from the mixing console. You should also ensure that the speaker selection device is functioning properly by identifying the speaker location or function as each speaker is tested. The sound technician can have a difficult time identifying a particular speaker from the sound booth. Speaker positions should be spiked for location as well as focus or direction. Once these positions are set, it should be a regular part of your checklist to see that all speakers are in their appropriate position and that associated cable is dressed properly.

Microphones must also be tested prior to each performance or rehearsal. As with speakers, you should not only test the microphone to see that the signal is reaching the mixing console, but that the controlling faders are correctly identified and matched to the corresponding microphone. Microphone cables must be positioned properly and inspected for wear if they are regularly dragged around the stage. Wireless microphones must have their batteries tested or replaced daily to ensure adequate power. Any microphone used to reinforce a musical instrument should be tested with the applicable instrument. Electronic instruments must also be tested.

All playback devices such as CD players and tape decks must be on your checklist. With a qualified sound technician, it may not be necessary for you to hear the output of every playback device, but you should have confidence in the operator, and he or she should know you expect this equipment to be tested and its status reported to you when you reach these items on your checklist. The sound technician is also responsible for the setup of the mixing console and processing equipment.

All communications systems can be checked as part of the sound check. Head to the dressing rooms and listen for the stage monitor. The page system can be tested while you are there. On stage, check the audience address system. Every crew member who is assigned an intercom station should be responsible for testing the equipment and reporting to the sound technician. The stage manager then asks the sound technician for a status report of the intercom system as part of the sound check. Do not forget to test your intercom station and equipment.

SLIP STAGE — A platform on wheels or casters that moves on and off stage during the course of a play to facilitate rapid scene changes. Also called Wagon and Jack-knife Stage.

TURNTABLE — Portion of the stage that revolves. Also called Revolving Stage.

BEAM PROJECTOR — A type of lighting instrument that has no lens, used to emit a powerful beam of light with diffused light.

CABLE — Electrical cord used in circuiting lighting instruments or other stage devices requiring electricity.

CYC LIGHTS — Type of powerful lighting instruments used to light the cyc with a smooth wash.

DIM — To decrease the intensity of a stage light.

DIMMER — An electrical apparatus used to control the intensity of the lighting instrument to which it is circuited. Found on the lighting board.

Special Effects

Special effects can take many forms and will often be the responsibility of the prop department, electricians, or stage carpenters. Your checklist should include special effects entries with the appropriate department.

Emergency Equipment

First aid kits, fire extinguishers, and other emergency equipment should be inspected on a regular basis. These items should be in their designated location, well stocked, and clearly labeled for proper use.

Dressing Rooms and Support Facilities

Your primary effort is to make sure that dressing rooms and lavatories have been cleaned and stocked with adequate supplies. During your inspection, take note of any burned-out lights and any mechanical or plumbing problems that need to be reported. Check the temperature in the dressing rooms and make any adjustments necessary.

Front of House and Facilities

In most cases, the front of house is the responsibility of the house management staff. However, I like to take a quick look around to see that everything is in order. This usually only takes a few minutes and is worth the effort. A few items to take a look at include:

- audience seating area
- auditorium lighting
- aisles and aisle lights
- emergency exits
- heating, ventilation, and air conditioning

THE ACTORS' ARRIVAL

ELLIPSOIDAL REFLECTOR SPOTLIGHT (ERS) — A type of lighting instrument that emits a hard-edged circle of light. Commonly called Leko.

FILL LIGHT — Light used to illuminate shadowy areas.

FIRST ELECTRIC — The first row of lights hung on a batten behind the proscenium. Also called X-ray Border, First Border, Teaser Border, or Concert Border.

Prior to the first technical rehearsal or the first rehearsal on the stage of the theater, the actors should be given a tour of the space and a rundown on how the place works. It is important for the acting company to make a home of the theater as soon as possible. Dressing room assignments should be posted on the company call-board in advance of the actors' arrival. If the dressing room facilities permit, post individual names on or next to the applicable dressing room doors as well. No matter what shape the rest of the production is in, make sure the dressing rooms are in good working order, clean, stocked, and ready to be occupied. This includes rest rooms and showers. In the frantic and frustrating time that is about to begin, the actors will greatly appreciate a place of their own. Believe me, you do not want to deal with the added consternation of an actor who hates his or her dressing room. Actors' Equity Association Rules and Regulations have very explicit guidelines concerning the Safe and Sanitary conditions of theaters and dressing rooms and the like (Figure 41).

Once the actors are settled into their dressing rooms, walk them through the set and its changes, if any. Show them crossovers, the most direct routes to dressing rooms and other support facilities, the backstage layout including costume quick change facilities, the location of the stage management staff during performance, and prop table locations. Point out the similarities between the rehearsal room configuration and the stage layout to instill in the actors a sense of familiarity.

RUNNING THE REHEARSAL

FLOODLIGHT — A lighting instrument that projects a diffused, unfocused beam of light. Used for general illumination.

It is time to start. Everything should be in order, so you can attempt to run the show with all the technical elements in place. A natural function of the technical rehearsal is change. The whole process can often seem to function by trial and error. In running technical rehearsals, you must be focused and able to respond quickly to required changes. The worst things that can happen during a technical rehearsal are wasting time and creating an environment in which creativity is stifled. The schedule is also very volatile during this time. If you are knowledgeable about the rules and regulations governing the scheduling of various union members and have a creative mind with regard to organization, you can save a good deal of time and energy for the company and yourself.

The Calls

HALF-HOUR — The 30-minute warning to curtain.

FLOOR POCKET — A small iron box containing an electrical outlet, sunk into the stage floor.

FOLLOWSPOT — A hand-operated lighting instrument mounted on a swivel stand that emits a high intensity beam of light, used to follow an actor on stage.

FOOTLIGHTS — Striplights used for general lighting. May be permanent or mobile.

FRESNEL — A type of lighting instrument that emits a soft-edged, diffused light.

GEL or GELATIN — Transparent material used to color the lights.

The first mistake that is usually made during technical rehearsal is an unrealistic expectation of the start time. For much of the cast and crew, technical rehearsals entail hours of waiting. Do not make them start the day by waiting. Be certain that you have allowed yourself and the crew enough time to prepare for the rehearsal adequately. During the rehearsal it is inappropriate to solve equipment problems, so make sure you have performed your inspection carefully. The actors should be given a half-hour call. A half-hour call requires the actors to arrive at the theater one-half hour before the start time of the rehearsal or performance. This thirty minutes will give the actors time to settle into the theater and focus their attention on the production. They can also inspect their props, do their warmups, and receive any last minute instructions.

You should institute a sign-in procedure with the start of technical rehearsals. A sign-in sheet, such as the one illustrated in Figure 42, should be posted on the call-board. The sign-in sheet should be for one performance only to avoid any possibility that the sheet is incorrectly marked, indicating the presence of a performer by mistake. On two-performance days, you must provide a sign-in sheet for each performance. Leave room on the sign-in sheet to indicate which understudies will be performing and any general information on the performance.

Try to anticipate the pace of the technical rehearsal to allow performers who do not appear in the early portions of the play to arrive later. The best technique for making these plans is to set goals with the director and designers. Try to reach a consensus on the time that will be required to tech each scene or act. The actors can then be given half-hour calls in anticipation of a start time for each scene or act. The key to making this scheduling plan work is an agreement among the director, designers, and you that in the event you are able to complete a scene or act ahead of schedule, you will run it or sections again and not feel the need to move on. As an example, it may be appropriate to plan an entire day on one act. If you manage to stumble through the act before the allotted time, do a run-through or work those sequences that are particularly difficult.

The Run-Through

PRE-SET — The setting on stage that the audience sees before the play begins. Refers to lights, set, and props.

RUNNING CREW — The backstage group of people who perform all the technical tasks during the show.

GOBO — A metal cutout used in an Ellipsoidal Reflector Spotlight that projects an image on stage. Also called Template.

HOUSE LIGHTS — Lights used to illuminate the area where the audience sits.

LAMP — The part of a lighting instrument that emits the light; the "light bulb" of the instrument. Also called Bottle (usually in New York).

Once the rehearsal starts, you will need to work very hard at keeping everyone's attention focused and the rehearsal on track. When the rehearsal is stopped for some technical or design adjustment, the cast and crew are likely to wander both mentally and physically. One organizational method of keeping everyone together is to post a running order for the show in strategic locations throughout the theater. The running order should list the scenes of the play in playing order and a very brief description of the scene.

Any communication to the cast and crew should go through you. They must understand that you are directing the operation of the rehearsal, and this single source of instruction will help avoid any confusion. The exception to this is the adjustments that need to be communicated to the light and sound equipment operators by the respective designers. Until the show is running smoothly, you should be stationed at the tech table in the house. The tech table should include intercom stations and lighted work space for you and the lighting and sound designers.

Often, the need to make an adjustment to some component of the production can be made while the scene is in progress. Minor changes in light levels can be made without disturbing the action on stage, and, in fact, it is desirable to adjust sound levels in relation to the action on stage. At other times it may be simply a matter of taking a note to alter the cue in some fashion the next time it is run. This is particularly true of fine adjustments in cue placement. The designer will request that you call the cue "a beat earlier" or "two beats later." You should make the change in your prompt script immediately if possible, or ask the lighting designer to give you a note if you are in standby for the next cue. Do not hesitate to interrupt the designers while they are making changes to notify them and crew members of an imminent cue. If all the necessary adjustments cannot be made before the next cue is called, you may have to stop the scene.

When it becomes necessary to stop for some technical adjustments, you should request the cast and crew to "hold" their positions. In consultation with the director and designers, you should quickly ascertain the nature of the adjustment. In some instances, the adjustment can be made or noted and the action can pick up right where it left off. To continue, request confirmation from the crew that the adjustment has been made or noted and that they are ready to continue. Inform the crew that you expect them all to be in the appropriate cue and standing by for the next cue. Warn everyone that you are ready to move on and instruct the cast to "continue please." At other times it will be necessary to modify or correct the execution of a cue. This will require that the initiation of the cue be attempted again.

As before, the cast and crew have been asked to hold their positions. While the necessary modifications are being communicated, tell the cast that you are going back and running the cue again. Identify a specific line from which you would like to start. The cast should be told that on your signal you will start from a specific character's line. Quote the specified line and ask the company to please stand by. The crew should be told to stand by for the cue in question so it may be run once again. Once the adjustments have been communicated to you or the appropriate equipment operators, you should request confirmation that the adjustments have been made or noted and that they are ready and standing by for the designated cue. Request the crew to stand by for the next cue and give the actors a "Go."

It can take a significant amount of time for some cues to be reversed in order to run them again. It is up to you to get this process moving as soon as possible. When you stop the rehearsal for any adjustment, the first issue to address, if you do not know, is the need to go back. You will quickly begin to associate the nature of a cue failure with the type of adjustment required and consequently the need to go back or not. These instructions should be communicated by you as soon as possible to avoid any delays or confusion.

I want to stress the need for you to make sure all adjustments have been recorded and understood by the operators before you continue. Nothing is more frustrating than making the same mistake twice. It is equally important to be certain the cast and crew know at what point in the script you are starting. The cue you wish to be standing in as well as the cue you are standing by for should be communicated clearly, and you should expect a response from everyone that they are indeed ready for the requested cue.

Technical rehearsals are often equated with very long days. Actors' Equity Association recognizes this phenomenon by allowing the work day for actors and stage managers to be extended for technical rehearsals. Techs also generate very intense, pressure-filled working conditions. Whether required by union regulations or not, it is a good idea to give yourself and everyone else a short break every couple of hours to relieve the stress.

If time is short or you are stage managing a particularly complex technical show, you should consider running your technical rehearsal as a cue-to-cue until you have gone through the entire play. In a cue-to-cue, you jump from one technical effect to the next, skipping any sections of the text that are without cues. This approach focuses the maximum amount of time and energy on the technical elements of the production. In deciding to skip ahead, you must consider the following: the section of script you wish to skip must take more time to perform than it takes to stop the rehearsal, inform the cast and crew of your desire to jump to the next cue, identify the pickup line, prepare for the next cue, confirm the cast's and crew's readiness to continue, and start the rehearsal again. This process can take several minutes if you are not in complete control of the rehearsal, able to communicate your instructions clearly and succinctly, and working with a cast and crew who are focused on their jobs. It may be quicker to allow the rehearsal to continue at its natural pace.

Under the right conditions, cue-to-cue technical rehearsals can be very beneficial. However, this technique does make the technical rehearsal more difficult for the actors. You will regularly need to encourage the actors to maintain performance pace and volume. These factors are particularly important for establishing the correct timing for any cue and the audio levels for sound cues. The repeated interruption of their performance will cause them to lose concentration and energy, which will result in a slower pace and poor vocal projection.

LIGHTING TREE — A vertical pipe that is placed on the side of a stage to hold lighting instruments. Also called Boom or Boomerang.

SPILL — Extraneous light that can be cut off with a shutter.

STRIPLIGHTS — A long, narrow lighting instrument used for a general wash of light. This trough-like instrument may be sunk in the floor permanently or may be mobile.

WASH LIGHT — Light used to give a general illumination of the stage; quite often a specific color is used in a wash.

Technical Notes

Once techs begin, plan a technical note session after every rehearsal. Holding the note session at the end of rehearsal ensures that the events of the day's rehearsal are clear in everyone's mind, and you preserve the maximum time available to correct any problems before the next day's rehearsal. These sessions take the place of the regular production meetings and follow a similar organizational format. If you have managed to keep the technical rehearsal from turning into an acting rehearsal, there should be little need for the director to give notes to the actors. Send the actors home with a kind word for their patience and the next day's calls. There should be sufficient time prior to the next rehearsal to give those few actor notes that are taken (usually of a technical nature).

The director should start with her list of notes. Have your prompt script handy. Directors will be unaware of cue numbers in most cases and will reference their notes based on scenes, actions, lines, etc. You will need to locate and identify the appropriate cue number for the production staff. When the director is finished, move through the rest of the staff as quickly as possible, discussing any problems and solutions. At the end of the meeting, confirm the next day's schedule including work sessions and the start time for rehearsal.

When technical rehearsals are past the initial disruptions to the actors' performance, the director will once again turn her attention to the actors. This potentially can trigger a competition for the director's time. It may not be possible to schedule the actors' note session at a time other than after the rehearsal. If this is the case, you can start the technical note session while the director gives notes to the actors. This situation should resolve itself quickly with the start of dress rehearsals. Take advantage of the time it takes the actors to get out of costume and into their street clothes to hold your production meeting.

The rules and regulations for Equity concerning notes allows four one-hour notes sessions to be scheduled: two at the sole discretion of the director and two scheduled at a time to be approved by the company.

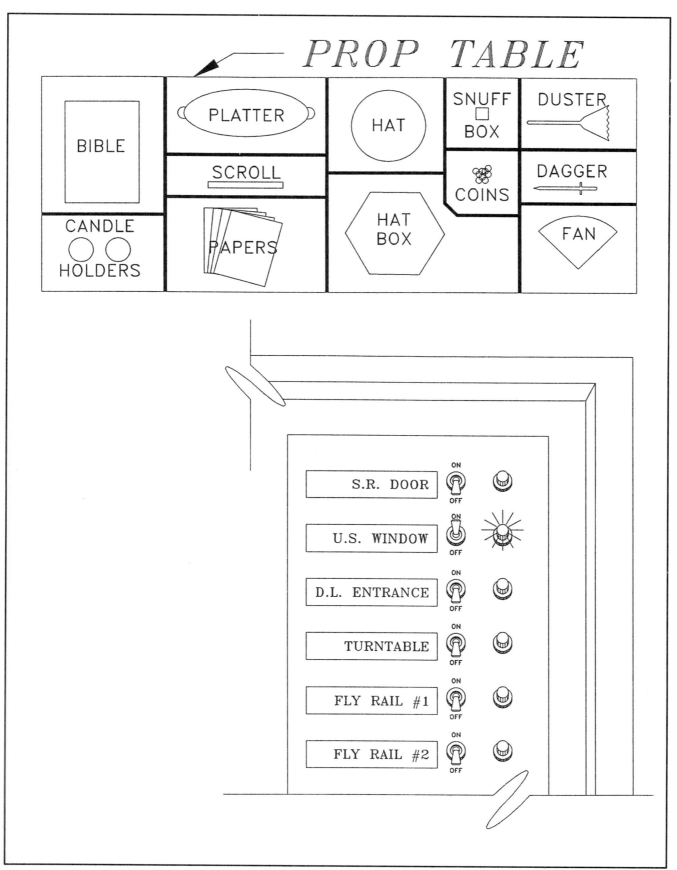

FIGURES 38 (top) and 39 (bottom)

Illustration courtesy of Cari Norton, Stage Manager for the Mark Taper Forum production of *Julius Caesar*.

ACTOR'S NAME #12

Act/Scene #	Character		Items
DRESSING ROOM:			
I–1	Crowd		Yellow print dress
			Yellow sweater
			White pumps
			Hose
			Wig – black shoulder length
			Purse
SR VOM:			
I–2a	Press	Add:	Green coat
			Grey Beads
			Green feather hat
			Wig into pony tail
STAGE RIGHT:			
II–2	Maid Two	Lose:	All but hose
		Add:	White dress
			White shoes
			White head band
STAGE RIGHT:			
III–1	Secretary	Lose:	All but hose
		Add:	Red/blue polkadot suit
			Red/cream pumps
STAGE RIGHT:			
III–2	Press	Lose:	All but hose
		Add:	Green skirt suit
			Shoes – White pumps
			Wig – black bob
			White short blouse

FIGURE 40

48. SAFE AND SANITARY PLACES OF EMPLOYMENT

The Theatre agrees to provide the Actor with safe and sanitary places of employment.

(A) (1) <u>Dressing Rooms</u>. Separate dressing rooms for male and female Actors will be provided.

(2) Dressing rooms (except quick-change booths) shall be of a permanent type, and shall not be only under canvas.

(3) Each Actor shall be provided sufficient and suitable dressing table space. All dressing rooms shall be properly heated and shall have adequate lights, mirrors, shelves and wardrobe hooks for Actors' make-up and dressing equipment. Mirrors and dressing table shall be thoroughly cleaned prior to the Actor's occupancy of the dressing room.

(4) Use of fluorescent lighting for make-up purposes is prohibited unless the fluorescent lighting is specifically warranted by the manufacturer to be for make-up purposes.

(5) All dressing rooms shall be equipped with air-conditioning systems, air-cooling systems or some similar type of mechanical device to insure proper ventilation and the circulation of fresh, cool air.

(6) The Theatre agrees to provide heat in the dressing rooms if the outside temperature falls below 60 degrees F.

(7) A telephone for the Actors shall be accessible to the dressing room areas.

(8) Alleys and roads leading to stage doors of theatres shall be accessible and properly lighted. Runways between dressing rooms and the theatre shall be covered and paved or boarded.

(9) Dressing room entrances and windows shall be properly masked from the view of the audience to insure the Actor's privacy.

(10) There shall be a fire extinguisher accessible to each dressing room.

(B) <u>Lavatory and Toilet Facilities</u>.

(1) Separate sanitary facilities will be provided for male and female Actors. Toilets and lavatories will be clean and sanitary, and will be separate facilities from those provided for the audience.

(2) The Theatre will provide soap, toilet tissue and paper towels.

(3) Sinks with hot and cold running water will be available in or reasonably convenient to the dressing rooms. "Reasonably convenient to" shall mean within the same building and in the dressing room area.

(4) In all theatres where the Actor is required to use body make-up, there shall be showers with hot and cold running water (see Rule 12 (D)).

(5) Any walkway between the dressing rooms and toilet facilities shall be masked from the view of the audience.

FIGURE 41

(C) <u>Rehearsal Space</u>. In all open-air and tent theatres, the Theatre shall make available adequate covered rehearsal space, which shall be safe, comfortable and healthful at all times. All other rehearsal areas shall provide heating and cooling devices, etc., as referred to in (A) above.

(D) <u>Aisles Ramped</u>. In all arena theatres, there shall be no riser between the runway and the stage. A ramp or other leveling device must be provided.

(E) <u>Guide Lights</u>. All ramps, stairways, levels or platforms higher than three (3) feet, entrances and exits, cross-over areas, or off-stage passageways, which may be affected by blackouts, shall be illuminated with guide lights or luminous tape. In arena theatres there shall be two (2) guide lights on the edge of the stage and one (1) on each side of every ramp leading to the stage. In addition, there shall be a guide light on each side of the aisle adjacent to the first row of seats of every aisle, and there shall be guide lights on each side of every aisle at eight (8) foot intervals. There shall be a warning light at eye-level on both sides of every pole located in an aisle, or any other obstruction in an aisle which Equity shall deem to be injurious or unsafe, and there shall be side rails on any ramp adjacent to any pit, and level guide lights on stage along the edge of any pit.

(F) <u>Aisles</u>. Aisles shall be maintained in a firm and even condition and if not constructed of a hard surface such as concrete, asphalt, or macadam, must be covered, and the coverings be secure.

(G) <u>Dancing Surface</u>.

(1) Actors shall not be required to rehearse dances or dance on concrete or marble floors or on any other surfaces which Equity shall deem to be injurious or unsafe, or on wood or on any other substance laid directly over such similar surfaces which do not provide air space of at least one and five-eighths (1 5/8) inches between the concrete or marble or similar supporting surface and the dancing surface.

(2) Where a portable stage is used, platforms must be fastened securely and the stage completely covered by a level deck or decks of such material as wood or masonite. The edge of all decks must be clearly visible or protected by securely fastened guard rails.

(3) Pits not in use shall be covered completely by a firm material.

(H) <u>Cots</u>. The Theatre shall provide two (2) cots backstage for any performer who may become ill during a rehearsal or performance. This cot shall not be in a dressing room but shall be easily available to the entire company. The Theatre may, in lieu of the above, provide a cot in each dressing room.

(I) <u>First Aid Kits</u>. Portable First Aid Kits, stocked with adequate supplies, and first aid information shall be available and easily accessible at all times wherever the Actor is required to rehearse, dress or perform.

(J) <u>Intercom System</u>. An intercom system between the stage area and the dressing rooms shall be installed in all theatres in which Equity

FIGURE 41 (cont.)

deems that the dialogue from the stage is not clearly audible in the dressing room.

(K) Drinking Water. Ample, pure, cool drinking water shall be provided wherever the Actor is required to rehearse or perform.

(L) All areas of the theatre must be equipped for air circulation, heating, safety, safe access, and proper lighting.

(M) Medical Services. An up-to-date list of medical services including doctors, dentists and hospitals, must be posted on the call board at all times and qualified medical personnel shall be available in case of emergency.

(N) Fire Safety Procedures. The Theatre must post a diagram of the locations of all fire exits and fire fighting equipment and proper procedures in case of fire. The Theatre shall consult with the local fire department and formulate safety procedures which shall be given to the Actors prior to dress rehearsal at least once for each production.

(O) Smoking Areas. In theatres and rehearsal areas where smoking is permitted, areas shall be designated by the Theatre as smoking areas, and smoking shall not permitted outside said areas.

(P) Toxic Materials.

(1) Equity and LORT shall meet jointly in committee and work together (with such experts as are necessary) to identify and eliminate hazardous, toxic, or unsafe materials and procedures from the working environment.

(2) A mutually approved smoke machine and chemical substance shall be used when chemical smoke is required. Ventilation for the removal of the chemical smoke shall be provided during its use.

(3) The Theatre shall post such notices as are required by the regulations of the Occupational Safety and Health Administration.

(Q) Inspection and Compliance. The Theatre agrees that Equity's representative shall have the right to inspect the theatre to determine whether the Safe and Sanitary requirements set forth in the foregoing Rules have been complied with. Any deficiencies shall be reported in writing to Equity and the representative shall furnish the Theatre with a copy of such report. Upon receipt of such report, Equity may notify the Theatre, in writing, to correct the deficiencies. Unless the Theatre then either corrects the deficiencies noted or gives Equity assurances satisfactory to it that such deficiencies will be promptly corrected, Equity's Council or its Executives may certify the theatre as unauthorized for rehearsal, for performances, or both, as the Council or its Executives may determine. Upon such certification and until correction of the deficiencies or the giving of assurances satisfactory to Equity that they will be corrected within a reasonable time, Equity may require its members to refrain from rehearsing and/or performing in the theatre.

(R) A joint committee shall meet, as necessary, to discuss the Actors' safety in the working environment.

FIGURE 41 (cont.)

SIGN-IN SHEET

PRODUCTION: THE SIGN PLAY

Date: 10/16/91   Call: 7:30 PM
Time: 8 PM   Performance # 14

NAME	NAME
Actor #1	Actor #16
Actor #2	Actor #17
Actor #3	Actor #18
Actor #4	Actor #19
Actor #5	Actor #20
Actor #6	Actor #21
Actor #7	
Actor #8	
Actor #9	
Actor #10	
Actor #11	
Actor #12	
Actor #13	
Actor #14	
Actor #15	

AT THIS PERFORMANCE:

NOTES:

FIGURE 42

PART III

Performance

Presenting your show to its first audience is one of those great dichotomies. For some members of the company nothing will be more frightening yet vitally necessary than the audience to breathe life into the production. The intimate group of talented artists you have been nurturing for several weeks in private will be exposed to a great unpredictable public. All the hard work you have just been through to perfect the timing and placement of every cue in the show will be undone. You will suddenly have a house full of people you must satisfy and care for. All your past work is meaningless without them. The rewards that an audience can bring are right around the corner.

Whether it is your first preview performance or opening night, your production is entering into a new phase and your job is to make the transition as easy as possible. You must maintain momentum in spite of new challenges. The working environment you created must survive the feelings of apprehension that will exist. Your best bet for success is being prepared, and all your pre-production work and rehearsals are meant to condition you for this and future audiences. The audience becomes an important factor in the final shape of a production. The basic routines that have been established will continue, with the necessary adjustments and additions required by the presence of an audience. You must diligently continue to anticipate every possible scenario.

Pre-Performance

Prior to any performance, there is a wide variety of duties that must be carried out by the cast and crew in preparation for the show. The stage manager must set the tone and create the structure by which these preparations are completed in a timely and meticulous fashion before each performance.

CHECKLIST

In Part II we discussed in detail the procedure and components of the stage manager's pre-show checklist. This routine inspection continues throughout the run of the show. The lighting instrument check requires special consideration and a significant amount of time. You should by now have a clear understanding of the concept for the lighting design and how it is implemented. As part of the inspection, you must ensure that each lighting instrument and its associated dimmer and controller are working properly. You must also ascertain that each instrument is focused as intended by the lighting designer.

The lighting designer should provide you with current copies of the light plot, instrument schedule, and magic sheet, and discuss this paperwork with you in detail. The light plot and instrument schedule, illustrated in Figures 44 and 45, are the documents that translate the designer's vision into the practical application of the equipment and technology available for stage lighting. These documents provide detailed information on the type of instrument and its location, focus, color, and control. You will notice on the light plot in Figure 44 that the instruments are selected and placed in a position chosen by the designer to achieve some aspect of the design. Each instrument is numbered and coded for its focus, color, and control channel. The key in the lower right-hand corner of the light plot deciphers this code and illustrates the symbols that define each type of lighting instrument used in the design. The instrument schedule in Figure 45 organizes this information in a purely textual format and provides additional details on the equipment and its purposes.

The instrument schedule can be formatted in any number of ways. Figure 45 is organized by instrument position and number. You can also have the same information organized by control channel. This format is typically called a *hook-up*. Since computerized lighting control systems make provisions for sequencing through control channels or dimmers automatically, it is easier to conduct your instrument check using a hook-up. With

AREAS — In lighting design, the divided portions of the stage used to apportion the light.

BATTEN — A bar made of wood or steel from which scenery, lights, or curtains may be hung and flown in and out. Also called Pipe.

BEAMS — The hidden area above the audience where lighting instruments are hung.

BRIDGE — A mobile platform suspended over the stage or audience that provides access to lighting instruments.

CROSSFADE — A lighting action in which a particular light cue fades down as the next light cue fades up.

HANGING — The process of putting a lighting instrument in its designated spot according to the light plot.

HOT SPOT — The area of the greatest illumination projected by a lighting instrument.

PATCH — To connect a circuit to a dimmer.

PATCH PANEL — The board on which one connects circuits to dimmers.

this information in hand, you should instruct the electrician to bring up the first control channel or dimmer. One by one you will continue through every control channel or dimmer used in the production to ensure each instrument is working and maintaining its focus.

You must also examine the color media in each instrument to determine whether it has faded to an unacceptable level. After a time, you will be able to establish regular color changes based on the number of hours the lighting instruments are in operation. The electrician should then be scheduled to conduct this maintenance procedure as a matter of routine.

The paperwork described above is the ultimate reference for any problems discovered in your inspection. However, if you are very familiar with the lighting for the production, you will find it easier to use the designer's magic sheet to conduct the instrument check. A magic sheet is a visual representation or quick reference guide to the lighting design. It usually centers on the control channel and functions or focus for each instrument or group of instruments in the design.

Every designer has a different way of developing a magic sheet. Figure 46 uses a fairly common approach. In this method, the designer's basic areas of focus are represented on a picture of the stage by the numbers of their control channels. In modern lighting control systems, the control channel regulates the power flow from the dimmer to the lighting instrument, which in turn controls the intensity of the instrument. The handy thing about using the magic sheet is that the focus location of the instrument is graphically illustrated in relation to the set. In Figure 47, one focus area from the magic sheet has been isolated. Each number is now defined as to its purpose or location. Once you know the key to the magic sheet, it is a simple matter to request the activation of each control channel by number and to make your inspection. Notice that the lighting designer has organized the control channels sequentially by function. For instance: The back light for each of the twenty-three focus areas is all 200 level channels (i.e., 201 = back light for area 1, 202 = back light for area 2, 203 = back light for area 3, etc.). If you look at another group such as the front lights, you will see they follow a similar pattern.

Additional instruments are indicated either by control channel numbers positioned where the lighting instrument is located, by direction, or by a simple description of use. Returning to Figure 46, you will notice in the upper left-hand corner a short list of control channels and very simple definitions, which completes the magic sheet.

A word of caution. It is possible and probable that a portion of the dimmers and/or control channels will operate more than one instrument. Be sure that whatever paperwork you use to conduct your instrument check clearly identifies the number of lighting instruments that should be operating with each channel or dimmer.

You should plan to complete your instrument check and the pre-show inspection of all the items outlined in Part II before the actors' half-hour call to the theater. Once the actors arrive, you will have one crisis after another, which you must solve with imperturbable confidence and undivided attention. The actors will also need your encouragement and support.

CAST AND CREW CALLS

The first call for any performance should be yours. Always allow a few moments to collect yourself and get your head into the game. Post the sign-in sheet for the performance, including any other announcements pertinent to the current performance, such as understudies who will be performing, VIPs who will be in attendance, rehearsal calls for the next day, etc. Once the crew arrives, you will be on a strict time schedule with little time for these responsibilities.

> PLACES — The request for cast and crew to take their positions for the start of the performance. Also Beginners.
>
> PAPER THE HOUSE — To give away free tickets to a performance in order to fill the house.

The crew should be called at least one hour before curtain in order to carry out the pre-show check and make any necessary corrections before the curtain goes up. If the production literally does not use a curtain or is particularly complex, this call will have to be 1½ hours before curtain. The actors' call is one-half hour before curtain (half-hour call). From the half-hour call you will give the actors and crew regular calls until curtain. The usual calls take place at "15 minutes" before curtain, "5 minutes" to places, and, of course, the "Places" call. These announcements become a significant part of the pattern of the actor's preparation. You must be consistent. Even if the actors are face to face with a clock, they are on "your" time and that is the only time that matters. I think it is best to give these calls in person. This puts you in touch with the performers and can give you a sense of their mood and energy, which may have an impact on the performance. It is also one of the few times during the routine of performance that you can easily personalize the working environment backstage with a friendly conversation. This is one of the many reasons you want to have your pre-show duties completed before half-hour.

Sometime after the half-hour call and before "Places," stage management should collect "valuables" from the actors. These personal items should be stored in a secure location such as a safe or a locked drawer of the stage manager's desk. Valuables should then be returned personally to each actor after the performance. If possible, this service should be provided anytime the actors are called.

FRONT-OF-HOUSE

The term *front-of-house* generally refers to everything on the audience side of the curtain. This includes the audience seating area, lobby, and other public spaces. The house manager is responsible for these facilities and for the audience. There are a few ground rules you must establish with the house manager concerning your production. As discussed above, your pre-show check should be complete one-half hour before curtain. This is the traditional time the "house is opened" or the audience is allowed into the auditorium. While it will always be your intention to meet this deadline, from time to time you will discover a problem that must be corrected before opening the house. Establish a procedure by which you inform the house manager you are ready to open the house. Some house managers assume that because the curtain is down or the pre-show lights are up, you are ready. This is a common occurrence, because in most cases it is true. To avoid any confusion over this matter, I always insist that the house be opened only after I have given the house manager a verbal "OK." This way, there are no surprises.

If you discover a problem that could potentially delay the opening of the house, you should alert the house manager immediately. He or she deserves as much warning as possible in order to appease the waiting crowd. Some people, especially house managers, believe if the problem is upstage of the curtain you should be able to correct the problem with the curtain down and the audience being seated. This is sometimes true. However, before you are persuaded to open the house, be certain that there is absolutely no reason in the world that you will have to open the curtain or perform any work in the auditorium in order to correct the problem. In addition, understand that the noise created by any required repairs must not be audible to the audience. This includes stagehands yelling instructions across stage. If you harbor any doubt, hold the house.

You and the house manager should also predetermine the starting time for the show under normal circumstances. If everything is running smoothly, there will be no need for actual communication at curtain time. The house manager will have seated the audience by the agreed-upon time and you will begin. This targeted starting time is normally a few minutes after the advertised performance time to compensate for the normal tardiness of a modern audience. If it looks as though there will be some trouble in getting the audience seated by the specified time, it is incumbent upon the house manager to notify you as soon as possible. With experience, you should be able to anticipate delays due to poor weather conditions, known traffic problems, and even those caused by a capacity crowd.

Once you have ascertained the nature and severity of the problem, you may wish to adjust your calls to the cast and crew to account for any anticipated delays. I always establish a revised starting time with the house manager in order to maintain the production's routine. You must avoid having the actors in place for the start of the show and waiting for the house manager to tell you it is time to begin. From the "Places" call to the rise of the curtain is somewhat like the final countdown for the launch of a spacecraft. Once the sequence has begun, you should either start or go back and begin the process again.

Let's say your normal start time for an eight o'clock show is five minutes after eight. There is a moderate rain falling on this particular night. You know from past experience that this rain will hinder traffic and congest public transportation, delaying the arrival of the audience. You and the house manager should consider the impact this will have on the curtain time and, if other conditions warrant, revise the target start time. Given the anticipated size of the house based on advance ticket sales, you agree to revise the starting time to ten minutes after eight. You can then make the necessary adjustments to your calls required by the delay and continue as usual. Remember to try and make any adjustments to the actors' calls before the five minute call and without doubt before the "Places" call. This will cause the least disruption to their routine.

There is still one more procedure you must establish with the house manager. This deals with the sensitive issue of latecomer seating. Once the show begins, it is vital to the audience's understanding of the play and the actors' performance that the tone and pace of the show be established without distraction and that the audience be quickly transported into the world of the play. This process is virtually impossible with ushers and tardy audience members stumbling through the dark aisles of the theater in search of their seats. I believe that anyone who misses a curtain should go home, but this is not feasible. What you must do is find a point during the early part of the act that can survive this intrusion. Look for a scene change, the end of a musical number, or some other naturally occurring pause in the action. This moment should be clearly communicated to the house manager and identified as the opportunity to seat latecomers. Prior to this time, they should be kept in the lobby or quietly brought in to stand at the back of the house. If the equipment exists, have a video and audio feed sent into the lobby to accommodate the latecomers' suddenly urgent need to see the play. This may seem like harsh treatment to someone who might have a legitimate excuse for being late (if such a thing exists), but you owe the highest quality experience possible to the performers and to those audience members who arrived on time.

You may also encounter the problem of audience members returning late to their seats after intermission. This, however, is a much more controllable problem. You must be firm on this issue with the front-of-house staff. Announcements must be made, lights flashed, bells rung, concession areas closed, rest rooms emptied, and people prodded to return to their seats in a timely manner. An extended intermission can have devastating effects on the ability of an audience to maintain its emotional attachment to the play. The actors will suffer too. Make it clear to the house manager that you intend to start at an exact time, and put the responsibility for retrieving the audience by this time squarely on his or her shoulders.

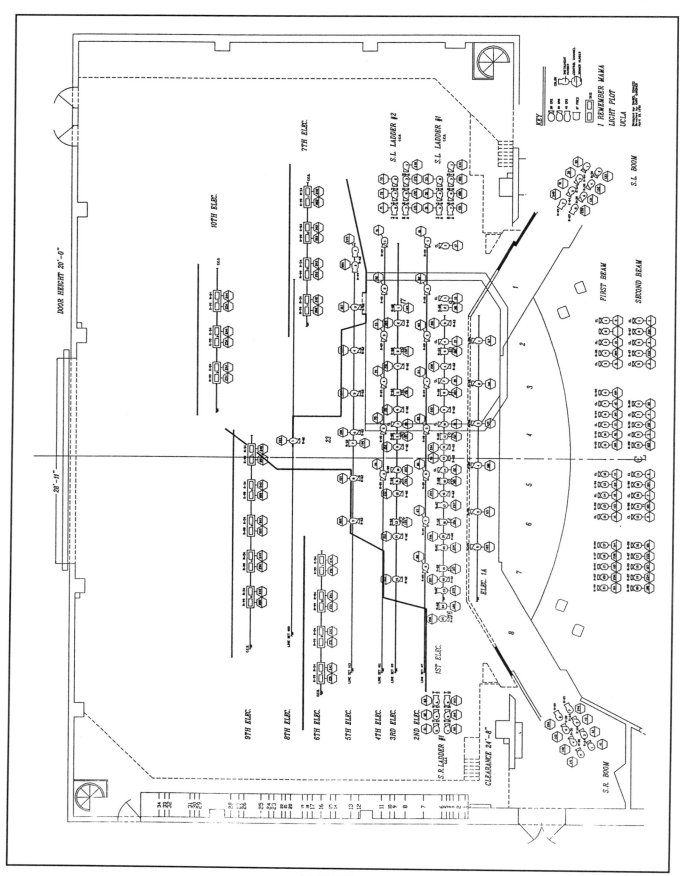

FIGURE 44

I REMEMBER MAMA
Instrument Schedule

NO	POSITION	CHANNEL	DIMMER	CIRCUIT	TYPE	COLOR	FOCUS
1	2ND BEAM	1	17		20ERS	CL	AREA 1 COOL
2	2ND BEAM	231	18		20ERS	R-07	LEAF GOBO 1 & 2
3	2ND BEAM	2	19		20ERS	CL	AREA 2 COOL
4	2ND BEAM	232	20		20ERS	R-07	LEAF GOBO 3 & 4
5	2ND BEAM	3	22		20ERS	CL	AREA 3 COOL
6	2ND BEAM	101	23		20ERS	R-99	AREA 1 WARM
7	2ND BEAM	4	24		20ERS	CL	AREA 4 COOL
8	2ND BEAM	102	25		20ERS	R-99	AREA 2 WARM
9	2ND BEAM	5	27		20ERS	CL	AREA 5 COOL
10	2ND BEAM	103	28		20ERS	R-99	AREA 3 WARM
11	2ND BEAM	6	29		20ERS	CL	AREA 6 COOL
12	2ND BEAM	104	30		20ERS	R-99	AREA 4 WARM
13	2ND BEAM	7	31		20ERS	CL	AREA 7 COOL
14	2ND BEAM	105	32		20ERS	R-99	AREA 5 WARM
15	2ND BEAM	8	34		20ERS	CL	AREA 8 COOL
16	2ND BEAM	106	35		20ERS	R-99	AREA 6 WARM
17	2ND BEAM	233	36		20ERS	R-07	LEAF GOBO 5 & 6
18	2ND BEAM	107	37		20ERS	R-99	AREA 7 WARM
19	2ND BEAM	234	39		20ERS	R-07	LEAF GOBO 7 & 8
20	2ND BEAM	108	40		20ERS	R-99	AREA 8 WARM
1	1ST BEAM	9	41		20ERS	CL	AREA 9 COOL
2	1ST BEAM		43		20ERS		
3	1ST BEAM	10	44		20ERS	CL	AREA 10 COOL
4	1ST BEAM	200	46		20ERS	R-05	CHAIR SP
5	1ST BEAM	11	48		20ERS	CL	AREA 11 COOL
6	1ST BEAM	109	50		20ERS	R-99	AREA 9 WARM
7	1ST BEAM	12	51		20ERS	CL	AREA 12 COOL
8	1ST BEAM	110	52		20ERS	R-99	AREA 10 WARM
9	1ST BEAM	13	54		20ERS	CL	AREA 13 COOL
10	1ST BEAM	111	55		20ERS	R-99	AREA 11 WARM
11	1ST BEAM	100	57		20ERS	R-05	KATRINE SP
12	1ST BEAM	14	59		20ERS	CL	AREA 14 COOL
13	1ST BEAM	112	60		20ERS	R-99	AREA 12 WARM
14	1ST BEAM	15	62		20ERS	CL	AREA 15 COOL
15	1ST BEAM	113	64		20ERS	R-99	AREA 13 WARM
16	1ST BEAM	16	67		20ERS	CL	AREA 16 COOL
17	1ST BEAM	114	68		20ERS	R-99	AREA 14 WARM
18	1ST BEAM	235	69		20ERS	R-07	LEAF GOBO 13 & 14
19	1ST BEAM	115	70		20ERS	R-99	AREA 15 WARM
20	1ST BEAM	236	71		20ERS	R-07	LEAF GOBO 15 & 16
21	1ST BEAM	116	74		20ERS	R-99	AREA 16 WARM
1	S.L. BOOM	33	1		20ERS	R-64	D.S.R. COOL SIDE
2	S.L. BOOM	133	2		20ERS	R-30	D.S.R. WARM SIDE
3	S.L. BOOM	32	185		30ERS	R-64	D.S.C. COOL SIDE
4	S.L. BOOM	132	186		30ERS	R-30	D.S.C. WARM SIDE
5	S.L. BOOM	31	188		30ERS	R-64	D.S.L. COOL SIDE
6	S.L. BOOM	131	187		30ERS	R-30	D.S.L. WARM SIDE

FIGURE 45

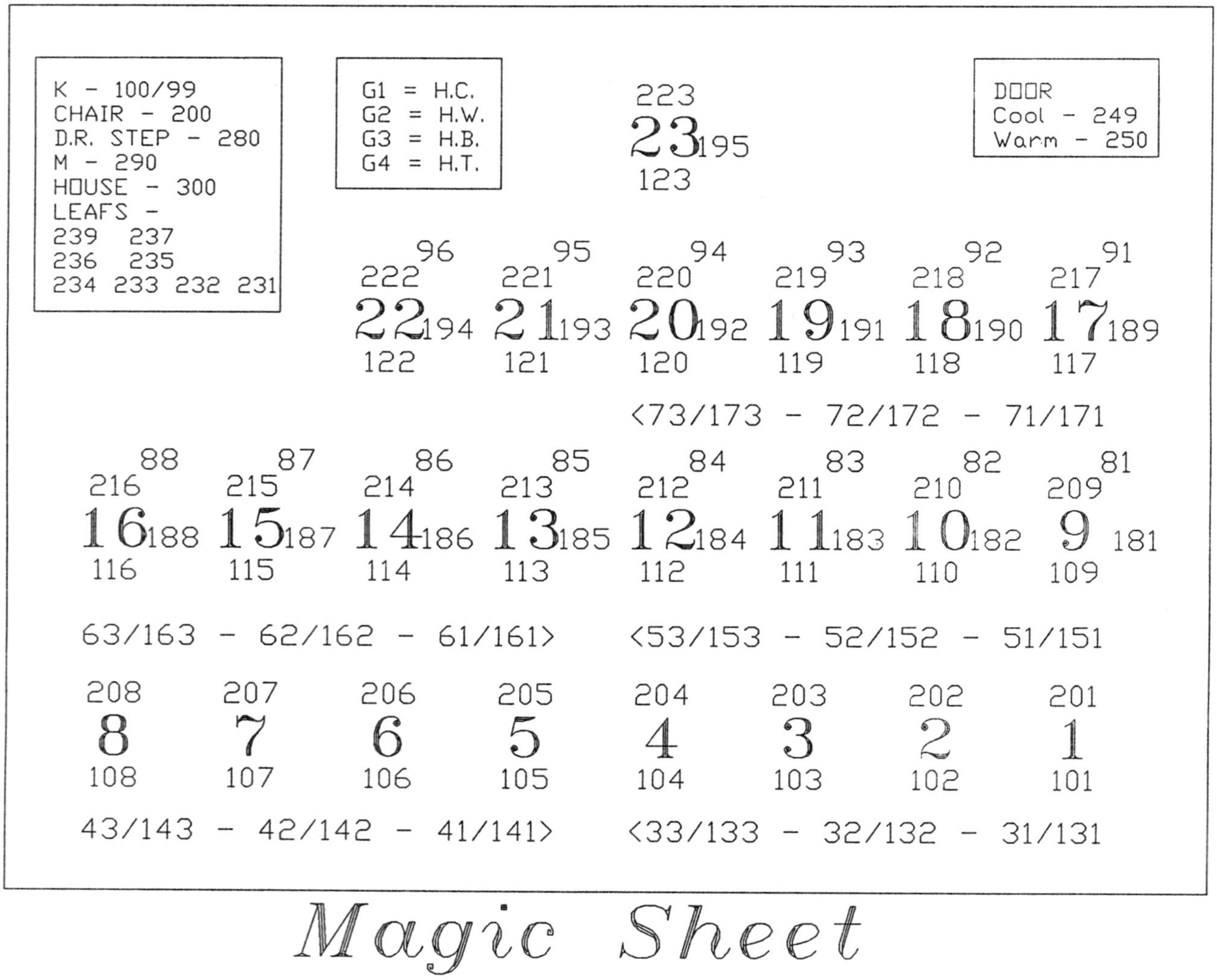

```
┌─────────────────────┐   ┌─────────────────┐                              ┌─────────────────┐
│ K - 100/99          │   │ G1 = H.C.       │         223                  │ DOOR            │
│ CHAIR - 200         │   │ G2 = H.W.       │         23 195               │ Cool - 249      │
│ D.R. STEP - 280     │   │ G3 = H.B.       │                              │ Warm - 250      │
│ M - 290             │   │ G4 = H.T.       │         123                  └─────────────────┘
│ HOUSE - 300         │   └─────────────────┘
│ LEAFS -             │
│ 239  237            │
│ 236  235            │
│ 234 233 232 231     │
└─────────────────────┘
```

```
            96         95         94         93         92         91
       222        221        220        219        218        217
       22 194     21 193     20 192     19 191     18 190     17 189
       122        121        120        119        118        117

                                    <73/173 - 72/172 - 71/171

        88         87         86         85         84         83         82         81
    216        215        214        213        212        211        210        209
    16 188     15 187     14 186     13 185     12 184     11 183     10 182     9  181
    116        115        114        113        112        111        110        109

    63/163 - 62/162 - 61/161>          <53/153 - 52/152 - 51/151

    208        207        206        205        204        203        202        201
    8          7          6          5          4          3          2          1
    108        107        106        105        104        103        102        101

    43/143 - 42/142 - 41/141>          <33/133 - 32/132 - 31/131
```

Magic Sheet

FIGURE 46

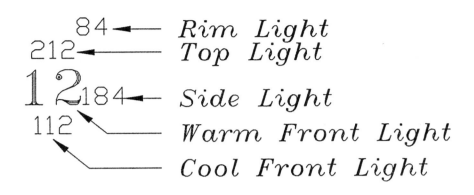

FIGURE 47

10

The Performance

With the cast, crew, and audience in place, you are ready to raise the curtain. Your responsibility now is to be an active participant in the performance. You are one more artist whose performance can dramatically affect the presentation. Take a deep breath, kill the work lights (always write this in your prompt script before the first cue), and call the first cue.

CALLING THE SHOW
All through the rehearsal process you have been fine-tuning the placement of cues and synchronizing your calls to the actions of the cast and crew. You should have a good idea of how quickly each crew member responds to a called cue. You know exactly when an actor flicks a switch to turn on a table lamp. Your calls are perfect. Well, don't be too disappointed if they are not so perfect with an audience in attendance. The people sitting in those seats in front of the curtain have not had a chance to rehearse their laughter or applause. They have no idea what's coming next and unfortunately, with regard to the audience's response, neither do you. Your first few audiences will teach you and the cast a small portion of the many and varied responses of an audience to your play. It is very important to recognize and accept that the audience is now an active player in the performance as well. They can slow the show down or speed it up. They can make it difficult or impossible to hear or concentrate. You must respond and adjust to them. You will be able to feel and react to most of the required adjustments if you "perform" your part just as an actor does. Your prompt script indicates the ideal placement and timing of each cue, and it is up to you to make the necessary adjustments for each audience to achieve the desired effect. You cannot blindly call the show with no regard for the audience's input.

Keep a pencil and note pad handy to jot down any major problems during the early performances. You may discover that the crew cannot hear the "go" for a specific cue because of the thunderous applause. You may have to change to a cue light. The volume of some sound cues may be too low or the length of the cue too short because of the audience's response. These major adjustments are often required with musicals and comedies in which the audience does frequently respond with applause or laughter after a musical number or punch line.

If you wish the crew to be extremely responsive and predictable to the cues you call, you must be very consistent. I announce a warning for each cue or series of cues between fifteen and thirty seconds before the cue, depending on the speed at which the cues are coming. The sequence goes like this for cue "L25":

"Warning lights 25"

(15-30 seconds elapsed time)

"Lights 25 ... GO"

The interval between "Lights 25" and "GO", whether it is one second, two, or three, must be very reliable. In this way the crew member responsible for executing the cue will be able to anticipate the "GO" and provide you with the timing you desire. If he or she cannot anticipate the "GO", the cue will often be late. This is not to say that the crew should have a hair-trigger response. They must never execute a cue without actually hearing the "GO". It is very much like conducting an orchestra. In order for everyone to play together, you must establish and adhere to a tempo. Whenever the rhythm must change, notify the players.

I often request confirmation from the crew that they heard the cue warning. The crew usually responds to the "Warning" with "Standing by." However, there are times when it may just be impossible to have all that chatter going on over the intercom.

The prompt script page illustrated in Figure 48 provides an example of a much more complicated series of cues. In this sequence, notice that the warning is given for L25-29, S16 and 17, F5 and 6, and T2 at the same time. These cues would be called as follows:

"Warning Lights 25 through 29 (L25-29), Sound 16 and 17 (S16 & 17), Flies 5 and 6 (F5 & 6), and Turntable 2 (T2)."

(15-30 seconds elapsed time)

"Lights 25 ... GO"	Blackout
"Lights 26 and Sound 16 ... GO"	Scene shift lights and music up
"Flies 5 ... GO"	Cyc flies out
"Turntable 2 ... GO"	Turntable revolves to scene two
"Flies 6 ... GO"	Cyc flies in
"Lights 27 ... GO"	Scene shift lights out
"Lights 28 and Sound 17 ... GO"	Scene lights up and music out
"Lights 29 ... GO"	Table lamp on

You may prefer to initiate the fly and turntable cues with cue lights to reduce the amount of communication required over the intercom system. It may also be necessary from time to time to request a confirmation from the crew that a specific cue is complete. Such may be the case with cues F5, T2, and F6 in the sequence above, if you cannot see that each of these moves is complete before calling the next cue. I prefer to eliminate this communication unless it is necessary for the initiation of another cue.

CYCLORAMA or CYC — A curved drop or wall used as a background to partially enclose the set. Quite often used to depict the sky. May be painted or lit.

PERFORMANCE REPORTS

Performance reports will take the place of rehearsal reports with the occurrence of your first audience. These reports are similar to rehearsal reports in that they are the official record of each and every performance of the play. The format of these reports shifts from the technically-oriented organization of the rehearsal reports to an audience, business, and artistic focus. (See Appendix.) Figure 49 shows a completed performance report. Notice that the basic information is the same as that of the rehearsal reports. The name of the show, day, date, number of the performance, and name of the person preparing the report are included. Next you will see an area designed for a detailed accounting of the running time of the show. In the example, the show is performed in two acts. Other productions may be played without an intermission or be presented in three acts. This area should be customized for the specific needs of your production.

The form allocates space for front-of-house (FOH) information such as weather conditions, number of people in attendance, general audience response, and reports of any problems, delays, accidents, etc. There is also an area designated to report the absence of any cast or crew member and their replacements or understudies. Any rehearsal or work calls should be noted in the space designated "Additional Calls." This may be a brush-up or understudy rehearsal, a crew call to maintain the technical elements of the show, a public relations activity such as an interview, a fitting for a replacement costume, or anything outside the normal business of performance.

The form concludes with performance and technical notes. The performance notes will call for your opinion on the quality of the performance and any specific successes or failures. Generally, this is not a place for individual actor notes but an overall evaluation of the entire production. Technical notes should be given for any desired repairs, execution problems during the show, equipment failures, etc.

The performance report must be filed with the other records of the show and distributed to the producer and his or her representatives, appropriate artistic staff, and production supervisors. This report is an important communication device between those involved in the day-to-day operation of the show and the producing organization.

MAINTAINING THE SHOW

During the run of a show, you will need to provide maintenance services not only for the technical elements but for the performances. You are the director's representative and are charged with adhering to the director's vision and maintaining the show in the state in which it was left to you. The morale of the company will have a great deal to do with the quality of their performances. Part IV will discuss some of these issues in detail.

On the practical side, there are a few common areas of concern that you should be aware of. Actors must maintain their volume and projection. This is crucial to the audience's ability to understand the play. You and the rest of the cast and crew will be so familiar with the script that you will subconsciously fill in any words you do not actually hear or understand. The audience is hearing it for the very first time and is not capable of this filling-in process.

Follow the blocking to ensure it is correct. Be particularly watchful for actors who upstage their scene partners and for those who seem not to be in the scene at all. All the actors in a scene must maintain a common focus in order for the audience to stay focused. If some performers in the background are daydreaming or causing some distraction, it will make it harder for the rest of the performers to hold the audience.

I have already referred to the need to keep a close eye on the pace of the show. Varying performance times that cannot be explained by audience reaction are a clear signal that something is wrong. Perhaps the actors are so comfortable with their parts that they no longer think about what they are saying and rush through the show at breakneck speed. Or maybe they have become lazy or self-indulgent to the point of extending the playing time by several minutes.

AD-LIB — To improvise lines or speeches that are not part of the script.

BREAK CHARACTER — When an actor says or does anything that is not in keeping with the character.

DISCOVERED — A person or an object on stage when the curtain goes up.

DARK THEATER — A day or night when there is no performance.

Expanding (usually the case) or contracting "stage business" should also be a cause for concern. During the course of a few weeks, I watched one actor go from throwing a small piece of paper into a wastebasket to re-enacting the final minutes of a championship basketball game. The wastebasket was now a basketball hoop and the "small" piece of paper became a large sheet crumpled into a "basketball." A sure sign that this piece of business had gotten out of hand was when the cast and crew began referring to the scene as the "basketball" scene. The stage manager was obviously not paying attention or for some reason thought this was clever. Nothing should be added to the show without the director's consent. If an actor has a problem with this basic rule, he or she should take it to the director.

As stage business expands so do an actor's lines. Ad libbing or rewriting the script is another common problem you will face during a long-running show. Some actors have a very bad habit of placing "handles" on their lines or developing speech habits for their characters that add words to the script and disrupt the rhythm and meaning of the author's play. I discussed this issue with one actor who was defiant in her need to change the text. She felt that changing the dialogue was a legitimate way of making the character her own. This is a very selfish and destructive approach to a collaborative art. If an actor wants to write, give her paper and pencil. If she wants to perform, give her the script to study — tactfully.

You will need to correct these problems with determination and diplomacy. In some cases, a note or personal conversation with an actor may handle it. In other cases, it will be necessary to request a brush-up rehearsal so everyone involved in the scene can participate in the correction of the problem. If there is a general problem such as pacing or audibility, you may need to address the entire cast.

Some actors do not take very kindly to receiving notes from a stage manager. Gather your confidence and approach the problem with care and all the finesse you can muster. Try to avoid any confrontation or quality assessments of their ability. Discuss with them what you feel is wrong and request their help in finding a way to return to the director's version of the play.

Understudies   Over a run of any length, you can expect to send on an understudy for an ailing actor or to replace a performer who leaves the show. The difference between an understudy and a replacement is significant. Understudies must perform the part as if they were the actors they are replacing. In essence, they are giving a performance of a specific actor playing the role. A replacement will have the freedom within the context of the existing production to bring some new interpretation to the role.

Actors should be assigned or hired to understudy as early in the rehearsal process as possible. Throughout the rehearsal process, they should attend every rehearsal, technical rehearsal, dress rehearsal, and preview with script and pencil in hand to note all blocking, stage business, and interpretation of the character they are understudying and of those with whom they will be performing. During the run of the show, understudies should see an actual performance every week. The art of understudying is duplicating the performance of the original actor. The understudy must fit into the very narrow limits of another actor's performance. This is due in large part to the fact that understudies are allotted very little time, if any, to rehearse with the cast. In most cases, their preparation consists of watching rehearsals and performance, working through the show with the stage management staff and other understudies, and if they are lucky, having a "speed-through" of some of the more complex scenes immediately prior to going on in front of an audience.

You must make sure understudies are always up on their parts because you never know when you will need them. In some rare cases, you may have as much as twenty-four hours' notice. At the other extreme, I have sent on an understudy for the second act of a show. There must be a regular routine established to alert them as early as possible that they will be performing. The rule must be that you can communicate with them at a designated number or they must provide you with an itinerary of their whereabouts. The actor shares responsibility for determining each and every performance if he or she is needed.

When understudy assignments are made from the cast, you will often find that the absence of one actor will require changes in many roles. Be sure every role is covered. Small roles may be covered by doubling (one actor playing two roles) or eliminating the character and splitting up the role's lines and responsibilities among two or more performers.

Replacements   When one actor or several leave the show and are replaced by other performers, you will go through a substantial rehearsal process. These rehearsals are usually conducted by the original director or her representatives, and the performers are allowed to create the role anew within the context of the existing production. Once the replacement is brought up to speed on staging and knowing lines, you can schedule a full cast rehearsal. A new performer can change the way the show is run, and you will need to schedule a series of technical and dress rehearsals to acquaint the replacement with the technical elements and make any alterations required by the new performance.

BACKSTAGE ETIQUETTE

A few thoughts on backstage etiquette. You may feel a need to formalize some of these items and include them in the company rules or policies, but I think you will get a better response if you can develop an atmosphere in which courtesy and a fundamental awareness of the needs of each company member thrive.

- No visitors after half-hour. Some people require privacy and a calm environment in order to prepare for their performance.

- No unnecessary noise or activity for the reason mentioned above. Try to provide an isolated for vocal and physical warmups or suggest these activities be completed before half-hour.

- All visitors must be announced and should wait to be greeted at the stage door. This prevents guests from stumbling around and disrupting others in their search for friends in the cast or crew.

- Respect the dressing room and property of others. Dressing rooms become the home away from home for many performers. Do not barge in unannounced or rifle through the contents of the room without notifying the occupant of your needs. Privacy is very hard to maintain in the close quarters of a theater, and the dressing room is one area where it may be possible to sustain some sense of it.

- No unnecessary talk backstage. This is a somewhat sweeping remark, but everyone should be aware of the need for stage management, crew members, and actors to concentrate on the show during performance. It would be very easy for you to miss a cue if an actor or a crew member felt the need to tell you the latest gossip at an inopportune time. Be sure everyone knows that you are dying to hear all the dirt when you have a moment. Take advantage of the half hour before curtain when your immediate responsibilities are minimal to catch up on all the news of the company.

CLOSING THE SHOW

I have found the biggest problem in closing a show is the overwhelming need of some company members to turn the last performance into a showcase for pranks, practical jokes, and their comedic talents. Without turning into a humorless, stick-in-the-mud ogre, you should discourage any such attempts and remind the company that the final audience is just as deserving of a quality performance as any other. The company's emotions are high, filled with a mixture of relief at finally being done with the show, apprehension for what is to come next, and sorrow over the disbanding of their working family. It is your job to keep everything on an even keel. Don't let the party or the wake start until the show is over.

As for the more practical responsibilities of closing a show, this will depend on the organization and the future of the show. Well before the final performance, you and the producer should clearly define the disposition of all the physical elements of the show and what your duties are in regard to these arrangements. If the show is going out on tour or moving to another theater, you will need to participate in the organization and inventory of the technical components whether *you* are taking the show out or not. Your knowledge of the show and how it is run will have some impact on how the

> STRIKE — The removal of all stage equipment, scenery, props, lights, and costumes from the stage area.

elements are packed and transported. Keep an eye out for souvenir hunters. Whether the show is continuing or not, the props, costumes, sets, and all other physical assets of the production belong to the producer.

At minimum, you must see to it that the records and documents for the development and performance of the play are in good order, complete, and properly filed for future use by the producing organization. Stage management equipment and supplies must be packed up and returned to the producer or other appropriate location.

Everyone should be instructed to have his or her personal belongings removed after the final show. It is wise to encourage people to begin this process in the week prior to closing. This not only makes it easier to handle all the items that have accumulated over the run of the show, it mentally prepares people for the end. These things have a way of sneaking up on you. Actors' Equity Association requires the posting of a closing notice two weeks in advance. Take this opportunity to begin the process of closing the show.

Now, if you have really developed the characteristics of a good stage manager and embraced the notion of being prepared and anticipating every need, you will not have waited until the final curtain to begin looking for your next job.

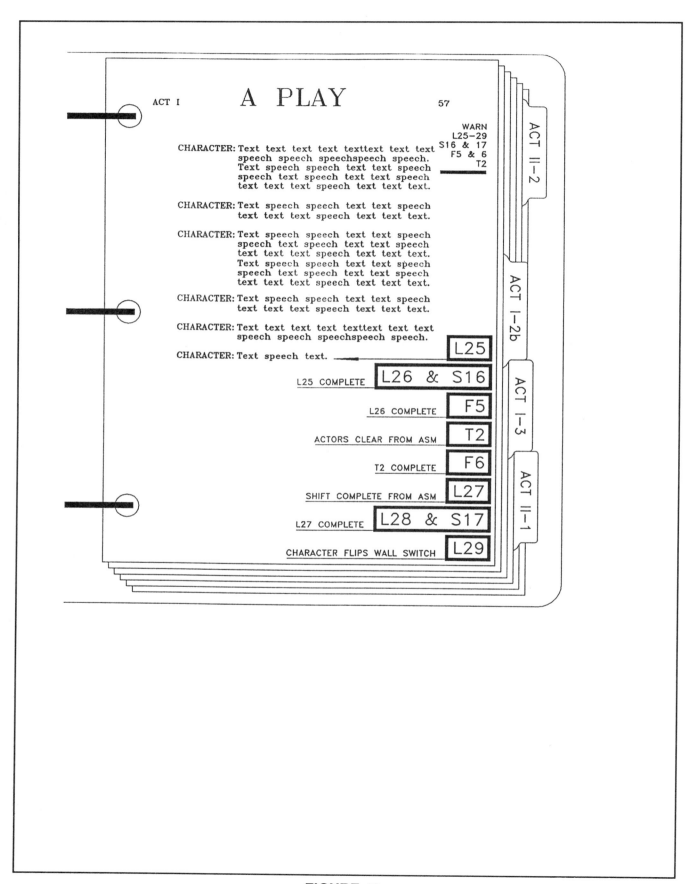

FIGURE 48

PERFORMANCE REPORT

PRODUCTION: CANDIDE

Performance # 7   Day: Saturday
Stage Manager: C.K.   Date: 6/1/91

ACT I Up	8:13	**F.O.H.**
ACT I Down	9:21	Held house for 15 min. due to error in CSS.
ACT I Running Time	1:08	Very full house.
Intermission Up	9:21	
Intermission Down	9:39	
Intermission Time	:18	
ACT II Up	9:39	
ACT II Down	10:33	
ACT II Running Time	:54	
TOTAL RUNNING TIME	2:02	
TOTAL ELAPSED TIME	2:20	

Additional Calls: **IN/OUT**

Brush–up rehearsal for Act II
6/4 @ 6:30 pm.
Photo Call following perfomance
6/6.

Performance Notes:

Good performance – pace much better.
J.S. ill tonight – not able to appear in finale or curtain call.

Technical Notes:

Shutter hit electric #5 while flying out – no apparent damage.
Problem with ASM headset – corrected
CSS failed prior to opening of house – corrected.

FIGURE 49

PART IV

Human Behavior in Organizations

In this final section of the book, I will introduce two topics vital to a long-term, successful career as a stage manager. Over the course of a long-running show or after years of work as a stage manager, you will be able to perform most of the tasks outlined in the previous sections of this book as a matter of routine. What will remain is the very difficult task of motivating people to perform at their peak and maintaining a quality standard that ensures everyone's satisfaction.

To accomplish this feat, it is important to know about the organizational structure of the theater you are working in and how human beings behave within that organization. The information contained in this section is in no way meant to be a definitive or exhaustive discussion of these topics. In fact, these topics are the subjects of complete courses of study and careers. I hope, however, to provide a perspective on the duties and responsibilities of a stage manager that goes beyond the mechanical techniques put forth in the first three sections of this book.

11

Organizational Structure

The organizational structure of a theater has a great impact on your specific responsibilities as stage manager, as well as on how you and others function within the working environment. A commercial producing organization such as those mounting productions for Broadway is organized differently than a regional resident theater or a stock company. There are many types of organizational structures and many more variations on each type, but there are two primary organizational structures that most theaters seem to follow. The first organizes the theater along functional lines and is most often represented in resident (regional) theaters. The second is organized along project lines and is more often seen in commercial producing entities. The reality of most theater companies is that they are organized using some combination of the two principal forms. In order to understand clearly the difference in these two forms, the information that follows assumes a structure very close to a pure functional or project organizational structure.

FUNCTIONAL ORGANIZATION

When any theater company uses the functional form of organization, Shakespeare's famous line delivered by Prince (turned playwright) Hamlet, "the play's the thing," is not quite true. In fact, the organization is set up, at least in theory, to produce *any* play and this is exactly what you must be aware of. This type of structure in the theater usually means all production functions and services are handled as in-house operations. Establishing a company of actors, designers, technicians, managers, publicists, accountants, marketing specialists, and development personnel without a specific play in mind does not guarantee the best people or even capable people for any one play. Rather it means a generic approach to churning out what can be a wide variety of productions. This approach can have a tendency to result in mediocre theater. The chart in Figure 50 illustrates the basic organization of a theater along functional lines. Notice that almost every business and production function is fulfilled by in-house employees of the company.

In order to make the point, here is an admittedly extreme analogy. A theater company organized along strict functional lines is like a car manufacturer trying to produce a low-priced, fuel-efficient, economy family car and a 250 mile-per-hour, high performance sports car with the same personnel, equipment, and facilities. It does not appear very likely that either of these vehicles will be served by the ultimate expertise, skills, and resources available and necessary to achieve the desired product successfully. A theater company that can produce world class Shakespeare may not be able to produce an equally successful musical with the same personnel, equipment, and facilities; nor should they be expected to.

In a more real world setting, you may find that rather than providing the support to produce a specific play, the company chooses a play or group of plays they can produce successfully. In many cases this manifests itself into a showcase for the talents of the actors, director, or designers. The play becomes secondary, because the people are in place on a more or less permanent basis and plays become interchangeable. Under these conditions, there is no assurance that the company does indeed recognize their limitations and is making the right choices. A company can develop a blind spot when it comes to assessing their own capabilities. Can the acting company really perform the material? Are the design and technical services capable of producing the physical requirements of the production? Will the right audience be found and persuaded to attend the theater? Does the ticket price support the cost of the production? The questions can and should go on and on, and some of them should certainly be examined by the stage manager, so he or she can be prepared to make the necessary adjustments in the production process.

I am not attempting to make a qualitative judgment of this type of theater organization; I only point out that the goals of the organization are and must be different from those of a theater that can adapt its resources to producing any script. The inspiration for artistic expression may not be a script but the vision of the production or performance instead. There are some distinct advantages to this kind of structure. Clearly the organization can and will establish a set of ongoing procedures that will streamline the production process. Communication channels should be easy to define and maintain. In essence, the mechanism is in place to produce theater. The question remains of whether it is the right mechanism for the play.

There are some notable examples of companies that have successfully operated with this organizational structure and have produced high quality theater. Their success was the result of recognizing what they were good at producing, selecting material that would be enhanced by their production style, or producing material that exploits the unique talents of their company. The Guthrie Theater in Minneapolis, under the direction of Tyrone Guthrie, developed a very distinctive production style, which drove the company's artistic decisions. Designers, directors, performers, and even the performance space were chosen or constructed with Guthrie's artistic vision in mind and indeed helped define the Guthrie Theater itself. Likewise, the early days of the Royal Shakespeare Company focused on producing Shakespeare. Every organizational choice was based on this goal. Both these companies maintained a group of theater artists and a single production focus over a period of several years.

PROJECT ORGANIZATION

The other end of the spectrum is a company organized specifically for the project. Each participant, resource, and component is selected for its uncompromising ability to meet the needs of a specific play. Without the play and the desire to present it to an audience, the producing entity does not exist. Each artist, technician, manager, and office worker is selected with the needs of the play as the primary criteria. These people are then organized into a unique entity, which is custom-built to produce this particular play. This type of structure should provide an opportunity to engage the most appropriate people, facilities, and equipment to produce the play. Figure 51 illustrates the project organizational structure.

Broadway, in many cases, provides the example of this organizational structure. At the top of the producing organization, a group of investors is put together by a general partner for the purpose of producing a specific play for the Broadway stage. Individuals are then hired for the design and production team based on their unique talents and abilities to meet the needs of the play and the production environment. An appropriate Broadway theater is reserved, and the construction of the show is contracted out to the desired scenic studio and costume workshop. A public relations and marketing firm is contracted to create a marketing plan specifically for the play and the Broadway market.

The advantages present in the functional form of organization are not shared by the project structure. In fact, the most troubling aspect of this kind of organization is the need to reinvent the producing mechanism for every production. Areas of responsibility and communication channels must be clearly defined for all participants. Many separate companies and individuals, who may be unfamiliar with each other, must be coordinated to ensure an efficient and productive collaboration. The production timetable is short and allows little time to work out the "bugs" and make adjustments to the "chemistry" of the group.

These disadvantages are acceptable if you consider the opportunities this structure allows. Finding the most appropriate director for the production, or getting the chance to assemble the perfect design team, can enhance the quality of the production immeasurably. Once the production is conceived and designed, you can provide the technical support to guarantee the successful realization of the physical aspects of the production. Clearly, the performers can benefit from a rehearsal process that does not simply conform to some existing schedule but is designed to provide the coaching, training, rehearsal time, facilities, and other resources that will enable the actors to reach their full potential.

THE MATRIX

Most theater organizations, whether commercial or not-for-profit, are structured in such a way as to combine aspects of each of the two fundamental organizational structures discussed above. This combination in which the functional structure and the project structure overlap is often referred to as a *matrix*. Typically, the closer the component is to the actual artistic expression, the more closely the structure resembles that of a company organized along project lines. For instance: In most theaters, performers are generally cast on a per-project basis. Even in repertory companies, an individual may be cast based on suitable roles available for the performer during the current season. In regional theaters, some directors and designers are jobbed in for specific shows, while resident directors and designers of the company handle the rest. Most often these theaters maintain workshops to construct the sets, props, and costumes, but certain craftspeople and artisans are brought in whenever a production requires their special skills and talents.

Commercial producers will often maintain long-term relationships with business management and public relations firms as well as the theater owners and operators. These less creative aspects of production tend to move toward the functional format. Producers also become very familiar with the scenic studios, costume workshops, and equipment rental houses providing services to Broadway or other commercial and touring productions.

Figure 52 illustrates one version of the matrix system for a regional theater. It is important for you to recognize the organizational structure of the theater in which you find yourself working, so you can identify the strengths and weaknesses of the structure. This knowledge will also help you understand the relationship between the production personnel and the producing organization. These relationships can have a considerable impact on the performance of the artists and technicians working on the production.

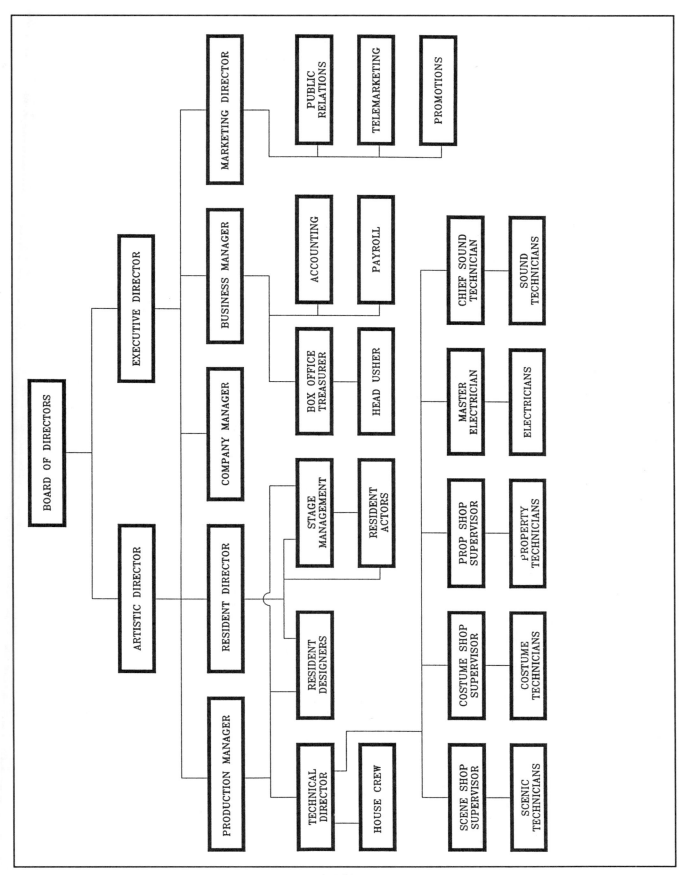

FIGURE 50

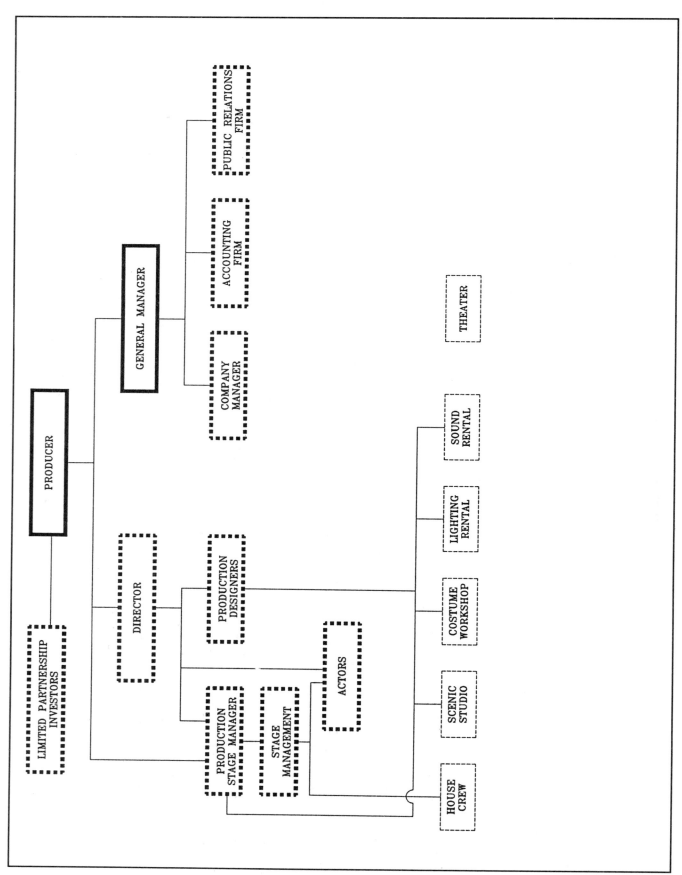

FIGURE 51

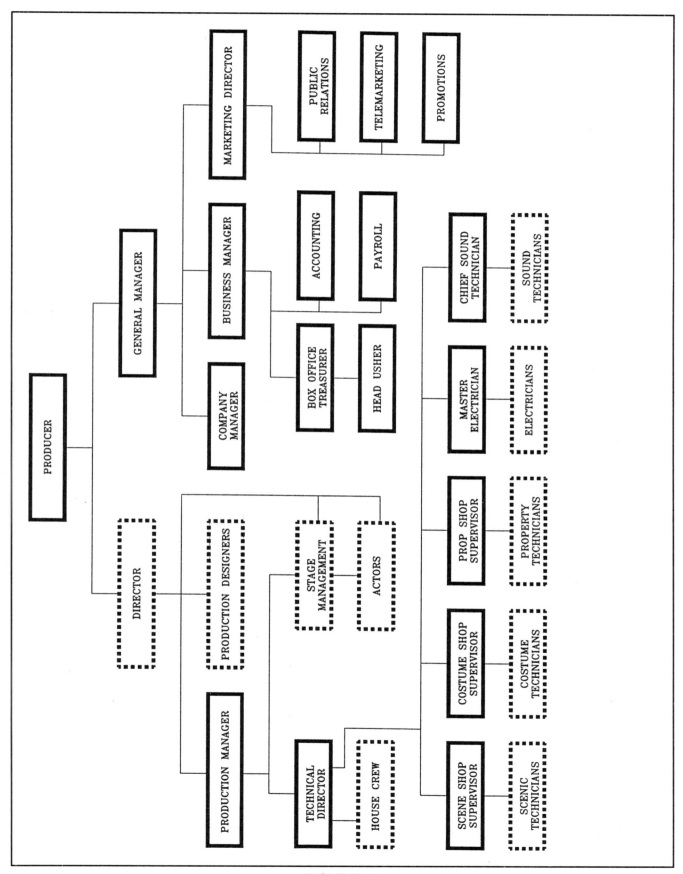

FIGURE 52

12

Human Behavior in Organizations

Early in this text I discussed the need to create a working environment in which the creative process could flourish. As a stage manager, there are two aspects of human behavior that you should be aware of and prepared to embrace in your work process. Motivation and job satisfaction of employees have been studied for decades, and many theories have been put forth over the years, with varying degrees of acceptance. These factors are related but not identical and have a tremendous impact on the success or failure of a project. Motivation pertains to the effort expended in order to attain a specified goal. Satisfaction is the feeling of contentment associated with the work.

Two prominent theories on work motivation and job satisfaction are Maslow's Hierarchy of Needs and Herzberg's Two-Factor Theory. There has been much debate through the years over the validity of both these theories, which I will not attempt to resolve here. However, because of their longevity and intuitive appeal, they provide a suitable introduction into the study of human behavior in organizations, and they are relatively accessible to the novice.

HIERARCHY OF NEEDS

Abraham H. Maslow's theory of motivation defines a set of needs that he believed we all share. These needs provide a personal motive that drives us toward fulfillment. The set of needs is arranged in a hierarchy implying that basic needs are met before higher order needs are addressed. Subsequent studies refute this theory and hypothesize that we may in fact be striving to fulfill several needs concurrently and that we may have individual hierarchies that differ from person to person. These individual differences may be the result of personal values (cultural, political, moral, etc.), the various stages of our careers, maturity, or psychological state. It is important to recognize the dynamic nature of this process. Our needs may be constantly changing, and each member of the company may be driven by different internal needs.

Maslow's Hierarchy of Needs is as follows.

Physiological Needs

This classification includes basic life-sustaining items such as food, water, shelter, sleep, etc. Most jobs provide us with money that can be exchanged for these physiological needs. As a stage manager, you have very little control over the amount of money performers or technicians are to receive for their work and even less control over the amount of money they need to sustain themselves. However, if someone is seeking to fulfill physiological needs, you must acknowledge that a pat on the back and words of praise will not go very far in motivating this individual. He or she is working from a deficit and is concerned with survival.

Money may not be the only problem here. An adverse working environment may deprive an individual of certain physiological needs. A person who cannot sleep at night due to stressful conditions at work is being deprived of a basic bodily need.

Safety Needs

These needs not only refer to physical safety, which in most cases is regulated by some external agency such as Actors' Equity, but the sense that employees are safe from emotional injury. The physical safety of performers and technicians is relatively easy to ensure unless you are dealing with some form of neurosis. Emotional safety is much more complex and is a good example of why it is difficult to think of Maslow's Hierarchy of Needs as isolated goals to be achieved in order. The emotional safety of an individual may have a great deal to do with higher order needs such as group acceptance, and it should be thought of in conjunction with these needs.

Love and Belongingness Needs

These needs relate to the "chemistry" of a group of individuals and the ability of each individual to feel he or she is an integral part of the group. The need to interact with others in an exchange of love and good will is an important aspect of working in a collaborative art. Performers are very exposed and vulnerable and must feel supported by the group to ensure their emotional safety and success.

Esteem Needs

People who are seeking esteem will consider both their personal standards and the standards of others within their work group, social group, and the theater community at large. We all tend to measure our self-respect in part by the respect we receive from others. One of the basic questions we must all ask ourselves is: "Is my occupation worthwhile?" If we believe it is, then are we good at it? There has always been a controversy concerning critics and their evaluation of art. Actors must struggle with this issue throughout their careers and most likely will be motivated by esteem needs on a permanent basis.

Self-Actualization

Self-actualization concerns becoming what constitutes your ideal, and it is influenced by factors that go well beyond work. In fact, most jobs cannot supply a means to achieve this goal. However, high level management, professional, and artistic positions such as designers, writers, directors, and performers do provide an opportunity for individuals to fulfill their self-actualization needs because they involve so much of what a person is. As an artist in the theater, part of the job is an expression of yourself, and there is little inherent in the job itself to inhibit you from reaching your ideal. The difficulty lies in the audience's willingness (or lack thereof) to support your expression.

Rewards are commonly used to motivate individuals. In the context of Maslow's theory, a good reward will appeal to an active need. A good salary should help meet physiological needs and may also function as a reward if a person is seeking esteem and believes money is some measure of success and acceptance. Clearly this is a common belief in many cultures. For the actor who has no deficiency in physiological needs and has attained consistent success, money may no longer be a motivator. The need for esteem may only be fulfilled by praise, good reviews, and recognition.

Helping each person fulfill his or her needs is, in theory, the best means toward motivation. As a stage manager, you must determine what people's needs are and, within the context of their jobs, what you can do to help them achieve their goals.

TWO-FACTOR THEORY

The Two-Factor Theory is an effort to explain job satisfaction. Frederick Herzberg's principal hypothesis is that satisfaction and dissatisfaction are not end points on a single continuum. The Two-Factor Theory presumes that satisfaction and dissatisfaction are provoked by different components of a job. Elements within the content of a job lead to satisfaction, while those aligned with job context lead to dissatisfaction.

Those items that lead to job satisfaction are considered motivators, and those leading to dissatisfaction are called hygiene factors. To make the distinction, the lack of a health plan may cause an employee dissatisfaction; however, the inclusion of a health plan in a benefits package will not provide motivation. The health plan does not lead to job satisfaction. Figure 53 lists a number of satisfiers and dissatisfiers according to Herzberg. Note the relationship many scholars have established between Maslow's higher order needs and Herzberg's satisfiers and the lower order needs with dissatisfiers.

The Two-Factor Theory has been carefully scrutinized over the years since its introduction and has been faulted by many. Two principal reasons have been put forth for its failures. As with Maslow's Hierarchy of Needs, individuals are unique and appear to have different sets of motivators and hygiene factors. Second, when research is conducted and employees are interviewed concerning job satisfaction, they often take credit for their satisfaction and will blame other factors for their dissatisfaction. In other words, it is never their fault that they are unhappy, and their own hard work is the sole reason for their success. This bias has caused a good deal of skepticism over the usefulness of Herzberg's theory.

As I stated earlier, the two theories offered here are only the smallest taste of the material available for study on human behavior in organizations. However, I believe Maslow and Herzberg are fairly accessible to the uninitiated and come with a certain amount of logic, which in my experience makes them generally useful concepts and helpful in beginning to understand the complex nature of motivation and satisfaction.

IN CONCLUSION

If you choose to pursue a career as a stage manager, you have my respect. If you are successful, you have my admiration. My own career has been closely tied to my good fortune in working with some uniquely talented stage managers, and they have my eternal gratitude.

Buona Fortuna!

HERZBERG'S TWO-FACTOR THEORY	MASLOW'S HIERARCHY OF NEEDS
SATISFIERS Achievement Recognition The Work Itself Responsibility Advancement The Possibility of Growth	**HIGHER ORDER NEEDS** Self-Actualization Esteem
DISSATISFIERS Company Policy Administration Technical Supervision Working Conditions Interpersonal Relationships Salary Status Job Security Personal Life	**LOWER ORDER NEEDS** Love & Belongingness Safety Physiological

FIGURE 53

Bibliography

ACTING

Adler, Stella. *The Technique of Acting*. New York: Bantam, 1990.

Benedetti, Robert. *The Actor at Work*, 5th ed. Englewood Cliffs, NJ: Prentice-Hall, Inc., 1990.

Brebner, Ann. *Setting Free the Actor: Overcoming Creative Blocks*. San Francisco: Mercury House, 1990.

Brook, Peter. *The Empty Space*. London: MacGibbon & Kee Ltd., 1968.

——. *The Shifting Point*. New York: Harper & Row, 1987.

Chekov, Michael. *Lessons for the Professional Actor*. New York: Performing Arts Journal Publications, 1985.

——. *On the Technique of Acting*. New York: Harper Perennial, 1991.

Hagen, Uta. *A Challenge for the Actor*. New York: Charles Scribner's Sons, 1991.

——. *Respect for Acting*. New York: Macmillan Publishing Company, Inc., 1973.

Richardson, Don. *Acting Without Agony: An Alternative to the Method*. Boston: Allyn & Bacon, Inc., 1988.

Stanislavski, Constantin. *An Actor Prepares*. New York: Theatre Arts Books/Routledge, 1964.

——. *Building a Character*. New York: Methuen Theatre Arts Books, 1977.

——. *Creating a Role*. New York: Theatre Arts Books/Routledge, 1961.

COSTUMES

Anderson, Barbara and Cletus. *Costume Design*. New York: Holt, Rinehart, and Winston, 1984.

Corey, Liz, and Rosemary Ingham. *The Costume Designer's Handbook*. Englewood Cliffs, NJ: Prentice-Hall, Inc., 1983.

Emery, Joy Spanabel. *Stage Costume Techniques*. Englewood Cliffs, NJ: Prentice-Hall, Inc., 1981.

Holkeboer, Katherine Strand. *Costume Construction*. Englewood Cliffs, NJ: Prentice-Hall, Inc., 1989.

Kohler, Carl. *A History of Costume*. New York: Dover Publishers, Inc., 1963.

Prisk, Berneice. *Stage Costume Handbook*. New York: Harper & Row, 1966.

Russell, Douglas A. *Stage Costume Design: Theory, Technique, And Style*. New York: Appleton-Century-Crofts, 1973.

DIRECTING

Bartow, Arthur. *The Director's Voice: Twenty-one Interviews*. New York: Theatre Communications Group, 1988.

Carra, Lawrence, and Alexander Dean. *Fundamentals of Play Directing*, 4th ed. New York: Holt, Rinehart & Winston, 1980.

Catron, Louis E. *The Director's Vision: Play Direction from Analysis to Production*. Mountain View, CA: Mayfield Publishing Company, 1989.

Clurman, Harold. *On Directing*. New York: Collier, 1972.

Cohen, Robert, and John Harrop. *Creative Play Directing*. Englewood Cliffs, NJ: Prentice-Hall, Inc., 1984.

Hodge, Francis. *Play Directing: Analysis, Communication, and Style*, 3rd ed. Englewood Cliffs, NJ: Prentice-Hall, Inc., 1988.

LIGHTING

Bellman, Willard F. *Lighting the Stage: Art and Practice*, 2nd ed. New York: Chandler Publishing Company, 1974.

Gillette, J. Michael. *Designing with Light*, 2nd ed. Mountain View, CA: Mayfield Publishing Company, 1989.

Hood, W. Edmund. *Practical Handbook of Stage Lighting and Sound*. Blue Ridge Summit, PA: Tab Books, Inc., 1981.

McGrath, Ian. *A Process for Lighting the Stage*. Boston: Allyn and Bacon, 1990.

Palmer, Richard H. *The Lighting Art: The Aesthetics of Stage Lighting Design*. Englewood Cliffs, NJ: Prentice-Hall, Inc., 1985.

Pilbrow, Richard. *Stage Lighting*. New York: Drama Book Publishers, 1991.

Rosenthal, Jean, and Lael Wertenbaker. *The Magic of Light*. Boston: Little, Brown and Company, 1972.

MAKEUP

Arnink, Donna J. *Creative Theatrical Makeup*. Englewood Cliffs, NJ: Prentice-Hall, Inc., 1984.

Buchman, Herman. *Stage Makeup*. New York: Watson-Guptill Publications, 1989.

Corson, Richard. *Stage Makeup*, 8th ed. Englewood Cliffs, NJ: Prentice-Hall, Inc., 1989.

Westmore, Michael. *The Art of Theatrical Makeup for Stage and Screen.* New York: McGraw-Hill, Inc., 1973.

PROPS

James, Thurston. *The Theater Props Handbook.* White Hall, VA: Betterway Publications, Inc., 1987.

Motley. *Theatre Props*. London: Studio Vista, 1976.

SCENERY

Bay, Howard. *Stage Design*. New York: Drama Books, 1978.

Burris-Meyer, Harold, and Edward C. Cole. *Scenery for the Theatre.* Boston: Little, Brown and Company, 1971.

Burroughs, Robert C., and Dennis J. Sporre. *Scene Design in the Theatre.* Englewood Cliffs, NJ: Prentice-Hall, Inc., 1990.

Gillette, A.S. *Stage Scenery*, 3rd ed. New York: Harper and Row, 1980.

Gillette, J. Michael. *Theatrical Design and Production*, 2nd ed. Mountain View, CA: Mayfield Publishing, 1991.

Nelms, Henning. *Scene Design: A Guide to the Stage.* New York: Dover Publishers, Inc., 1975.

Parker, W. Oren, and R. Craig Wolf. *Scene Design and Stage Lighting*, 6th ed. New York: Holt, Rinehart, and Winston, 1990.

SOUND

Burris-Meyer, Harold, Vincent Mallory, and Lewis S. Goodfriend. *Sound in the Theater*, rev. ed. New York: Theater Arts Books, 1979.

Collison, David. *Stage Sound*, 2nd ed. London: Cassell, 1982.

Walne, Graham. *Sound for the Theatre.* New York: Theatre Art Books/ Routledge, 1990.

TECHNICAL THEATER

Beck, Roy A. *Stagecraft*, 3rd ed. Lincolnwood, IL: National Textbook Company, 1990.

Carter, Paul. *Backstage Handbook*, 2nd ed. New York: Broadway Press, 1988.

Glerum, Jay O. *Stage Rigging Handbook.* Carbondale & Edwardsville: Southern Illinois University Press, 1987.

Sweet, Harvey. *Handbook of Scenery, Properties, and Lighting.* Boston: Allyn & Bacon, Inc., 1989.

Welker, David. *Stagecraft: A Handbook for Organization, Construction, and Management*, 2nd ed. Boston: Allyn & Bacon, Inc., 1987.

Wolfe, Welby B. *Materials of the Scene: An Introduction to Technical Theater.* New York: Harper & Row, 1977.

JOURNALS AND DIRECTORIES

Art Search
c/o TCG
355 Lexington Avenue
New York, NY 10017
212-697-5230

Drama-Logue
P.O. Box 38771
Hollywood, CA 90038
213-464-5079

Call Board
2940 16th Street, Suite 102
San Francisco, CA 94103
415-621-0427

Chicago Reader
11 E. Illinois
Chicago, IL 60611
312-828-0350

Theatre Crafts
P.O. Box 470
Mount Morris, IL 61054

Lighting Dimensions
P.O. Box 425
Mount Morris, IL 61054

Theatre Communications Group
Theatre Directory
TCG, Inc.
355 Lexington Avenue
New York, NY 10017
212-697-5230

Stage Managers Directory
Broadway Press
120 Duane Street, #407
New York, NY 10007
212-693-0570

Charles, Jill, ed. *Regional Theatre Directory:* Vermont: Theatre Directories, annual.

———. *Summer Theatre Directory:* Vermont: Theatre Directories, annual.

UNIONS

Actors' Equity Association (AEA)
National Office
165 W. 46th Street
New York, NY 10036
212-869-8530

Branch Offices

6430 Sunset Blvd.
Hollywood, CA 90028
213-462-2334

203 N. Wabash Avenue
Chicago, IL 60601
312-621-0393

465 California Street, Suite 210
San Francisco, CA 94104
415-781-8660

International Alliance of Theatrical Stage Employees (IATSE or IA)
14724 Ventura Blvd.
Sherman Oaks, CA 91403

1515 Broadway
New York, NY 10036
212-730-1770

Society of Stage Directors and Choreographers (SSDC)
1501 Broadway
New York, NY 10018
212-391-1071

United Scenic Artists (USA)
Local 829
575 8th Avenue, 3rd Floor
New York, NY 10018
212-736-4498

Appendix

AUDITION FACT SHEET

PRODUCTION:

PERSONNEL

Director_____   Scenery_____

Playwright_____   Costumes_____

Producer_____   Lighting_____

Choreographer_____   Sound_____

Stage Manager_____   Casting_____

DATES/VENUE

1st Rehearsal_____   Opening_____   Closing_____

Venue_____

PERFORMANCE CONTRACT

GENERAL DESCRIPTION

Character	Age Range	Description

AUDITION SELECTIONS

PRODUCTION:

Character	Scene/Page	Description

CONTACT SHEET

PRODUCTION:_____

Date:_____   Page____ of____

NAME/TITLE	PHONE #s	ADDRESS	NOTES

SCENERY DESIGN REQUIREMENTS

PRODUCTION:_____

Date:_____   Page___ of___
Act_____ Scene_____

General Description:		
Page #	Scenic Element	Note:

LIGHTING DESIGN REQUIREMENTS

PRODUCTION:_____

Date:_____   Page___ of___

Act____ Scene____

General Description:

Page #	Effect	Note:

SOUND DESIGN REQUIREMENTS

PRODUCTION:_____

Date:_____   Page____ of____
Act____ Scene____

General Description:		
Page #	Effect	Note:

COSTUME DESIGN REQUIREMENTS

PRODUCTION:_____

Date:_____   Page___ of___
Act____ Scene____

General Description:

Page #	Character	Costume	Note:

PROPERTY DESIGN REQUIREMENTS

PRODUCTION:_____

Date:_____   Page___ of___
Act____ Scene____

General Description:

Page #	Prop	Use	Note:

REHEARSAL REPORT

PRODUCTION:_____

Rehearsal #_____   Day:_____

Location_____   Date:_____

Stage Manager_____

Rehearsal Start	:	Costumes:
Rehearsal Break	:	
Rehearsal Start	:	
Rehearsal Break	:	
Total Rehearsal Time	:	

Rehearsal Notes:

Lights:

Properties:

Scenery:

Fittings, etc:

Sound:

Schedule:

Misc.

PERFORMANCE REPORT

PRODUCTION:_____

Performance #_____   Day:_____
Stage Manager_____   Date:_____

ACT I Up	:	F.O.H.
ACT I Down	:	
ACT I Running Time	:	
Intermission Up	:	
Intermission Down	:	
Intermission Time	:	
ACT II Up	:	
ACT II Down	:	
ACT II Running Time	:	
TOTAL RUNNING TIME	:	
TOTAL ELAPSED TIME	:	

Additional Calls: IN/OUT

Performance Notes:

Technical Notes:

SIGN-IN SHEET

PRODUCTION:_____

Date:_____   Call:_____

Time:_____   Performance #_____

NAME _____   NAME _____
_____   _____
_____   _____
_____   _____
_____   _____
_____   _____
_____   _____
_____   _____
_____   _____
_____   _____
_____   _____
_____   _____
_____   _____
_____   _____
_____   _____
_____   _____
_____   _____
_____   _____

AT THIS PERFORMANCE:

NOTES:

MASTER CUE SHEET

PRODUCTION:_____

Date:_____   Page___ of___

CUE #	COUNT	PAGE/LINE	ACTION

Index

Improve Your Theater Craft With Betterway Books!

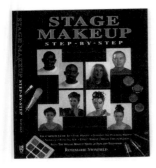
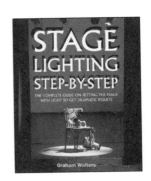

SECOND EDITION

Field Experience Guide

Resources for Teachers of Elementary and Middle School Mathematics

for

SIXTH EDITION

Elementary and Middle School Mathematics

Teaching Developmentally

John A. Van de Walle
Virginia Commonwealth University

Prepared by

Jennifer M. Bay-Williams
University of Louisville

Boston   New York   San Francisco
Mexico City   Montreal   Toronto   London   Madrid   Munich   Paris
Hong Kong   Singapore   Tokyo   Cape Town   Sydney

ISBN: 0-205-49314-9

Printed in the United States of America
10 9 8 7 6 5 4 3   11 10 09 08 07

Contents

NCATE Standards

The National Council for Accreditation of Teacher Education (NCATE) provides guidance on the knowledge, skills, and dispositions that teacher candidates should develop in their teacher preparation, including coursework and field experiences. The target for the design, implementation, and evaluation of field experiences and clinical practice is stated as follows:

- Field experiences allow candidates to apply and reflect on their content, professional, and pedagogical knowledge, skills, and dispositions in a variety of settings with students and adults.
- Both field experiences and clinical practice extend the unit's conceptual framework(s) into practice through modeling by clinical faculty and well-designed opportunities to learn through doing.
- During clinical practice, candidate learning is integrated into the school program and into teaching practice.
- Candidates observe and are observed by others.
- They interact with teachers, college or university supervisors, and other interns about their practice regularly and continually.
- They reflect on and can justify their own practice.
- Candidates are members of instructional teams in the school and are active participants in professional decisions.
- They are involved in a variety of school-based activities directed at the improvement of teaching and learning, including the use of information technology.
- Candidates collect data on student learning, analyze them, reflect on their work, and develop strategies for improving learning. (NCATE, 2002, p. 26)

NCATE also provides targets for developing candidates' knowledge, skills, and dispositions. These statements are shared in the appropriate chapters of this field guide.

This field guide provides a rich collection of diverse experiences. Field experiences vary greatly from institution to institution. For some students, their initial visits to schools may be when they are in mathematics methods courses; for other students, it may be their final field experience prior to student teaching. The field experiences offered in this book were designed to respond to both the variety of teacher preparation programs and the NCATE recommendation that students have the opportunity to engage in diverse activities. In addition, NCATE states that teacher candidates reflect a thorough knowledge of teaching based on professional standards. For mathematics teachers, those standards include the *Principles and Standards for School Mathematics* (NCTM, 2000) and the *Professional Standards for Teaching Mathematics* (NCTM, 1991).

Part I is organized by specific knowledge, skills, or dispositions for teacher candidates outlined in NCATE, such as pedagogical knowledge and assessment. Within each is a menu of possible tasks for teacher candidates to use. In one setting, it may be appropriate to focus on one or two of the NCATE categories, such as assessment and content knowledge, using numerous activities from those sections. In another setting, it may be more useful to use one or two activities from each category. An instructor might select the tasks that are most appropriate for use in their setting, or allow students to pick from a selection of tasks that have the same goal. It is also important to note that although many of the activities in the field guide are placed in one chapter, they are also applicable to other areas.

Part II has a collection of lessons and tasks for each of the content standards of the National Council of Teachers of Mathematics (NCTM) (Number, Algebra, Geometry, Measurement, Data Analysis, and Statistics). Each content area has at least one lesson for each grade band (K–2, 3–5, 6–8). See p. 84 for a detailed list of lessons and grade bands. These lessons can be linked to the experiences described in Part I. For example, if students are designing appropriate accommodations for a student with special needs (Activities 8.4 and 8.5 in Part I), they might select a task or lesson from this collection, use a lesson that is provided by the methods instructor or the classroom teacher, or find a lesson on their own.

Part III of this guide contains a full set of reproducible Blackline Masters referenced in the 6th edition of *Elementary and Middle School Mathematics* as well as additional Blackline Masters for use with the Expanded Lessons in Part II.

The goals of *Field Experience Guide* are as follows:

- To meet the needs of various teacher preparation programs and background and experience of teacher candidates
- To provide useful templates and graphic organizers that are user friendly for both teacher candidates and instructors
- To provide a collection of diverse tasks (e.g., interviews, observations, teaching experiences) within a focus area, such as assessment
- To facilitate the process of linking field experiences to NCATE *Standards*
- To elaborate and provide activities that can further a candidates' understanding and application of the content offered in *Elementary and Middle School Mathematics* (6th edition)

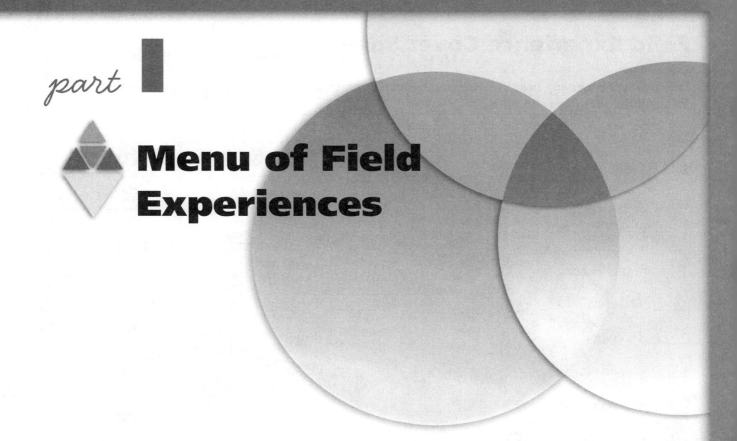

part **I**

Menu of Field Experiences

Getting Started

This section provides recording sheets that can be used for all of your field experiences:

- Field Experience Cover Sheet
- Field Experience Activity Log

Field Experience Cover Sheet

When you conduct any field experience assignment, attach this as a cover sheet (or provide this information on a cover page).

Your name: _____ Date: _____

School visited: _____

Cooperating teacher: _____ Grade(s) of students: _____

Activity completed (if it is a Field Guide task, give the number): _____

Type of experience

_____ Observation   _____ Teaching

_____ Interview   _____ Project

_____ Reflection   _____ Other: _____

Other pertinent information:

Field Experience Cover Sheet

When you conduct any field experience assignment, attach this as a cover sheet (or provide this information on a cover page).

Your name: _____ Date: _____

School visited: _____

Cooperating teacher: _____ Grade(s) of students: _____

Activity completed (if it is a Field Guide task, give the number): _____

Type of experience

_____ Observation   _____ Teaching

_____ Interview   _____ Project

_____ Reflection   _____ Other: _____

Other pertinent information:

Field Experience Activity Log

Use this log to record the date, time, purpose, and descriptions of each visit to the school. The first table gives an example. You may use this page, or create one of your own.

Activity Log

Name: _____

Date	Times	Purpose of Visit	Brief Description of Visit
3/6/07	8:30–9:00	Observe questioning strategies	I observed Ms. Bergen's 2nd-grade lesson on adding two digit numbers. After the lesson I asked her a few follow-up questions.
3/7/07	1:00–2:00	Teach an inquiry math lesson	I cotaught a 2nd-grade lesson on growing patterns (with my teaching partner). After the lesson, we met with our supervisor and received feedback.
	2:00–2:30	Assist students as they worked on end-of-quarter portfolios	Ms. Bergen invited me to stay and help students select their "best" work to illustrate what they had learned on specific objectives.

Field Experience Activity Log

Date	Times	Purpose of Visit	Description of Visit

1 Professional and Pedagogical Knowledge: Classroom Environment

Field Experiences in this Section

Alignment

NCATE

Standard 1: Knowledge, Skills, and Dispositions
Professional and Pedagogical Knowledge and Skills

Teacher candidates reflect a thorough understanding of professional and pedagogical knowledge and skills delineated in professional, state, and institutional standards. They develop meaningful learning experiences to facilitate learning for all students. They reflect on their practice and make necessary adjustments to enhance student learning. They know how students learn and how to make ideas accessible to them. They consider school, family, and community contexts in connecting concepts to students' prior experience and applying the ideas to real-world problems. (NCATE, 2002, p. 15)

NCTM

The teacher is responsible for creating an intellectual environment where serious mathematical thinking is the norm. More than just a physical setting with desks, bulletin boards, and posters, the classroom environment communicates subtle messages about what is valued in learning and doing mathematics. Are students' discussion and collaboration encouraged? Are students expected to justify their thinking? If students are to learn to make conjectures, experiment with various approaches to solving problems, construct mathematical arguments and respond to others' arguments, then creating an environment that fosters these kinds of activities is essential. (NCTM, 2000, p. 18)

The Professional Standards for Teaching Mathematics: Learning Environment

The teacher of mathematics should create a learning environment that fosters the development of each student's mathematical power by

- Providing and structuring the time necessary to explore sound mathematics
- Using the physical space and materials in ways that facilitate students' learning of mathematics
- Providing a context that encourages the development of mathematical skill and proficiency
- Respecting and valuing students' ideas, ways of thinking, and mathematical dispositions

And by consistently expecting and encouraging students to

- Work independently or collaboratively to make sense of mathematics
- Take intellectual risks by raising questions and formulating conjectures
- Display a sense of mathematical competence by validating and supporting ideas with mathematical argument (NCTM, 1991, p. 57)

Elementary and Middle School Mathematics by John Van de Walle

Chapters 1, 2, and 3 address mathematical learning environment.

1.1 Observation: Physical Environment

As you enter a classroom, imagine you are a prospective parent visiting for the first time and trying to decide if it's the right environment for your child. As you walk around, jot down your responses to these questions:

1. Describe the mathematics pictures, posters, or other displays. What do they depict?

2. Describe any bulletin boards that have math information or interactive math activities.

3. What manipulatives and tools are evident? Are they accessible to the students (can students get tools at any time, or does the teacher determine when they are available)?

4. Are there any computers or calculators in the class? Describe.

5. Draw a sketch of the location of the desks, calculators, computers, overhead projector, whiteboard (or chalkboard), and other math-related resources.

6. What physical aspects of the classroom do you feel "create a spirit of inquiry, trust, and expectation"? See "An Environment for Doing Mathematics" on page 14 of *Elementary and Middle School Mathematics* to assist in answering this question.

1.2 Observation: NCTM *Professional Teaching Standards*

The following template can be used with a live or videotaped math lesson. As described in *Elementary and Middle School Mathematics*, the NCTM *Professional Teaching Standards* describes five "Shifts in Classroom Environment." During your observation, note the evidence that the teacher is modeling each shift in his or her practice and note ideas for incorporating the five shifts in your own practice.

Five Shifts in Classroom Environment	Evidence in Classroom	Observer's Additional Ideas or Future Actions
1. Toward classrooms as mathematical communities and away from a collection of individuals.		
2. Toward logic and mathematical evidence as verification and away from the teacher as the sole authority for right answers.		
3. Toward mathematical reasoning and away from mere memorizing procedures.		
4. Toward conjecturing, inventing, and problem solving and away from an emphasis on the mechanistic finding of answers.		
5. Toward connecting mathematics, its ideas, and its applications and away from treating mathematics as a body of isolated concepts and procedures.		

1.3 Teacher Interview:
An Environment for Learning

Ask a practicing teacher if you may interview him or her about how he or she organizes the mathematics classroom, or the environment for mathematical learning (questions adapted from *Professional Standards for Teaching Mathematics*, NCTM, 1991, p. 57).

1. Describe how a typical lesson is organized. What is your role? What is the students' role?

2. How do you decide how much time to provide learners to explore a math task?

3. How does the way you've arranged the room (e.g., the seating, location of materials) affect the students' learning of mathematics?

4. How important do you think it is to use real contexts or problem situations in teaching a math concept or skill? How do you use contexts or situations to develop mathematical skills and proficiency.

5. What do you do about the learner who says that he or she doesn't like math or is anxious about doing math?

6. Do learners ask questions or make conjectures during your math instruction? Do you encourage this? How?

7. What do your learners do that helps you understand that they are making sense of math? How do you foster and encourage those actions?

1.4 Student Interview: Attitudes and Environment

In this interview you will prepare interview questions in three areas: (1) students' attitudes toward mathematics, (2) the typical math environment, and (3) what learning environment preferences students have. In advance, write 2 or 3 questions in each area. You may want to pull some of your questions from the ones below. Each question can be followed with a "Why?" or "Why not?"

4th-Grade Attitudinal Questions, Adapted from National Assessment of Educational Progress (NAEP)	
1. Do you think everybody can do well in math if they try? 2. Are you good at mathematics? 3. Do you like solving mathematics problems? 4. Is math easier for boys? 5. Is math mostly memorization? 6. Is math useful for solving everyday problems?	7. Is there only one correct way to solve a math problem? 8. Do people use math in their jobs? 9. If you had a choice, would you continue to go to math class? 10. Do you understand what goes on during math?

Interview Questions	Responses from Student
Student's attitude	
Typical math class	
Learning preferences	

Complete these questions after completing the interview.

1. How do you think the classroom environment affects students' attitudes?

2. How do you think students' attitudes toward mathematics impact their success in learning mathematics?

1.5 Teaching: Establishing Your Environment

For this experience, the goal is to teach a lesson that communicates expectations that all students are to contribute to every lesson. When teachers begin their school year, they often plan lessons that have some math embedded in them, but the goal of the lesson is as much about learning to participate appropriately as it is about the mathematics.

The activity should have these characteristics:

1. Allow students to interact in cooperative groups.
2. Each student must contribute to his or her group in order for the task to be successfully completed.
3. Interdependence is important to achieving success in the task.
4. The task lends itself to having a follow-up discussion that focuses on how the task was solved and the cooperation required in the task.
5. The task should be interesting and accessible to every student in the class.
6. Assessment includes individual student performance on the task and participation in the group.

What you need to do:

1. Find an appropriate task for the age and experiences and needs of your students.
2. Create a three-phase lesson (before, during, and after).
3. In the *after* phase of the lesson, include discussion prompts related to the task and to the role of participation.
4. Teach the lesson to the class of students.
5. Write a brief reflection on (1) how successful the lesson was in meeting its objectives and (2) how the activity served to communicate expectations that all students are to be engaged in math learning.
6. Turn in the lesson plan, activity, and reflection (see next page).

Possible alternative or addition: Try out the lesson with one small group of students.

Title of Lesson:	Source/Citation:
Mathematics Learning Objectives:	Participation/Social Objectives:

Lesson Plan

Before

During

After

Reflection

1. Did each student learn what you intended for the math objectives? How do you know? Describe evidence and include samples of student work.

2. Did each student learn what you intended for the participation/social objectives? How do you know?

1.6 Project: Assessing School Environment

The focus of this project is to find out the ways the school advocates for the learning of mathematics. Use the prompts below to help you prepare a report on the way your school promotes the importance of learning mathematics. You may interview teachers and/or the principal. Some of the questions you will be able to answer simply by walking around the school and observing. Once you have completed your inquiries in the school, prepare a brief report highlighting the ways the school supports the learning of mathematics and your suggestions for additional support.

Areas of Inquiry	Descriptions and Notes
Parent/community involvement • How are families involved in math instruction? (e.g., Back to School Nights, Family Math, tutoring, problems of the week)	
Displays of math • How are hallway and classroom bulletin boards used to showcase math? • Based on the displays, what seems to be important about math?	
Views of faculty/staff • What do the principal and/or teachers feel are the priorities for math in the school?	
Resources • Does the library have resources for teaching math? Children's books for teaching math? Support for students? • Does the school have classroom sets of calculators? Manipulatives? Computers? • What is the school's math curriculum based on (e.g., problem-based, aligned with standards, skill practice)?	
School goals • What are the school objectives for math for the year? • How do they plan on meeting these goals? • How are students assessed and their progress monitored?	

2 Professional and Pedagogical Knowledge: Planning

Field Experiences in this Section

Alignment

NCATE

Standard 1: Knowledge, Skills, and Dispositions
Professional and Pedagogical Knowledge and Skills

Teacher candidates reflect a thorough understanding of professional and pedagogical knowledge and skills delineated in professional, state, and institutional standards. **They develop meaningful learning experiences to facilitate learning for all students.** They reflect on their practice and make necessary adjustments to enhance student learning. They know how students learn and how to make ideas accessible to them. They consider school, family, and community contexts in connecting concepts to students' prior experience and applying the ideas to real-world problems. (NCATE, 2002, p. 15)

NCTM

Learning Principle

Students must learn mathematics with understanding, actively building new knowledge from experience and prior knowledge. (NCTM, 2000, p. 20)

Curriculum Principle

A curriculum is more than a collection of activities: it must be coherent, focused on important mathematics, and well articulated across the grades. (NCTM, 2000, p. 14)

Elementary and Middle School Mathematics by John Van de Walle

Chapters 4 and 5 provide lots of suggestions and strategies for effective planning.

2.1 Teacher Interview: Selecting Goals and Objectives

The following is the beginning of an interview protocol to learn how a teacher determines goals and objectives of lessons. You may want to add your own questions, based on your state's specific standards and testing.

1. In your long-term planning, what resources do you use in deciding the topics that you will cover in a year?

2. Are you familiar with the NCTM *Principles and Standards*? Are they used in your planning? How?

3. Are you familiar with [our state standards]? Are they used in your planning? How?

4. Does [this school district] have grade-level expectations or other guidelines about what to teach?

5. Can you describe goals and objectives you would have for a single lesson (like one you are teaching this week)?

6. How is student learning used to determine your lesson objectives?

7. How do you make the objectives accessible and challenging for the wide range of skills and interests of students in your classroom?

2.2 Observation: Evidence of Higher-Level Thinking

Incorporating higher-level thinking into teaching requires careful planning. Higher-level thinking can be defined a variety of ways. Most commonly, it is used to distinguish between knowledge questions and those that involve analysis, application, and so on. You can usually distinguish between higher-level and lower-level thinking by the level of discussion and effort that is required to solve the task. In this observation, focus on the opportunities for students to engage in higher-level thinking.

1. Did the teacher encourage higher-level mathematical thinking? If so, what were some of the teacher's actions? Cite specific examples and strategies (questions posed, tasks presented, etc.).

2. Did the students make conjectures or engage in mathematical arguments? Were they expected to defend or support their arguments and conjectures? How do you know? Describe the students' actions in this lesson.

3. Circle any of the verbs below that you think describe the activities students were asked to do during the lesson.

explore	investigate	conjecture	solve	justify
represent	formulate	discover	construct	verify
explain	predict	develop	describe	use

4. To what extent were *all* students expected to use higher-level thinking? In other words, when a question or task was posed, what did the teacher do to ensure all students were thinking about and answering the question? How was the classroom structured so that all students were engaged?

5. What tools (technology, manipulatives, visuals, etc.) were used to support higher-level thinking?

2.3 Teaching: Mathematics Task Analysis

Using the Activity Evaluation and Selection Guide on page 52 of *Elementary and Middle School Mathematics*, find a task in one of the following sources and evaluate it. Possible sources include a textbook used in the classroom or school where you are placed, a K–8 math textbook series available at your college or university, a mathematics teacher resource book (e.g., Navigations series), and Web sites that post K–8 mathematics activities.

Steps for Evaluation and Selection	Your Evaluation
1. How is the activity done? Actually do the activity. Try to get inside the task of activity to see how it is done and what kinds of thinking might go on. How would children do the activity or solve the problem? • What materials are needed? • What is written or recorded by the student?	
2. What is the purpose of the activity? What mathematical ideas will the activity develop? • Are the ideas concepts or procedural skills? • Will there be connections to other related ideas?	
3. Will the activity accomplish its purpose? What is problematic about the activity? Is the problem aspect related to the mathematics you identified in the purpose? What must children reflect on or think about to complete the activity? Is it possible to complete the activity without much reflective thought? If so, can it be modified so that students will be required to think about the mathematics? What difficulties might students encounter in solving the task?	
4. What must you do? What will you need to do in the *before* phase of your lesson? • How will you prepare students for this task? • What will be the students' responsibilities? What difficulties might you anticipate seeing in the *during* phase of the lesson? What will you want to focus on in the *after* phase of your lesson?	

2.4 Teaching: Worthwhile Task Evaluation

Using the prompts below, adapted from the *Professional Standards for Teaching Mathematics*, Standard 1 (NCTM, 1991), rate an activity from an elementary or middle school mathematics textbook series. Add comments, as appropriate. You can also use this template to contrast a parallel activity in another textbook series as a way to compare textbook programs.

1 = No evidence of this element in the lesson/activity and/or the activity does not lend itself to having this element built in.
2 = This element is included in minor ways, or it appears that incorporating this element is possible.
3 = This element is evident in this lesson and is important to the success of the lesson.
4 = This element is central to this lesson or explicit in the design of the lesson.

Standard 1: Worthwhile Mathematical Tasks	Score				Comments
Task is based on . . .					
1. Sound and significant mathematics	1	2	3	4	
2. Knowledge of students' understandings, interests, and experiences	1	2	3	4	
3. Knowledge of the range of ways that diverse students learn mathematics	1	2	3	4	
And . . .					
4. Engages students' intellect	1	2	3	4	
5. Develops students' mathematical understanding and skills	1	2	3	4	
6. Stimulates students to make connections and develop a coherent framework for mathematical ideas	1	2	3	4	
7. Calls for problem formulation, problem solving, and mathematical reasoning	1	2	3	4	
8. Promotes communication about mathematics	1	2	3	4	
9. Represents mathematics as an ongoing human activity	1	2	3	4	
10. Displays sensitivity to and draws on students' diverse background experiences and dispositions	1	2	3	4	
11. Promotes the development of all students' dispositions to do mathematics	1	2	3	4	

2.5 Teaching: Planning a Problem-Based Lesson

Use the nine-step procedure to help you plan a problem-based lesson. Refer to *Elementary and Middle School Mathematics*, pages 61–63 for explanations of each step.

Step 1: Begin with the math!
Step 2: Think about your students.
Step 3: Decide on a task.
Step 4: Predict what will happen.
Step 5: Articulate students' responsibilities.
Step 6: Plan the *before* portion of your lesson.
Step 7: Think about the *during* portion of the lesson.
Step 8: Think about the *after* portion of the lesson.
Step 9: Write your lesson plan.

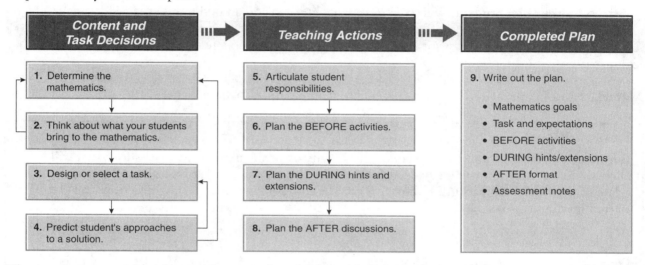

The next page provides a lesson plan template for a problem-based lesson. Keep in mind that it may not be developed sequentially. Typically, as stated above, you start with a math goal. A teacher to whom you've been assigned may say, "Please do a lesson on area of rectangles." Or you may not have any restrictions on what to teach, in which case, you will likely start with the state standards (or national standards) for that grade level.

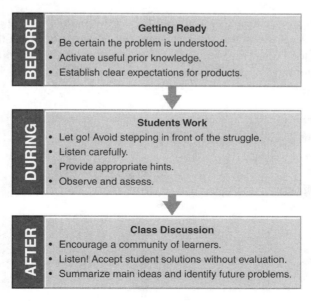

Lesson Planning Template

Lesson Title: _____   **Grade:** _____

Alignment with State Standards: List the grade level expectations from your state that align with this lesson.

Mathematics Goals: Describe the exact learning expectations for students. You must phrase the expectations in a way that you will be able to say a student did or did not learn it (the verb must be something you can observe).

> **Example:** Students will be able to *explain* a strategy for determining if a number between 10 and 50 is even or odd.
>
> **Nonexample:** Students will *understand* what an even and an odd number is.

Thinking of Students: What prior knowledge and experiences do students have related to the lesson goals?

Materials and Preparation: List transparencies, manipulatives, handouts, etc.

Lesson Plan

Before: Describe how you will introduce the activity or problem. Consider questions that will elicit students' prior knowledge needed for this activity, get students curious about the task, and/or relate to their personal background or interests. In addition, consider giving directions for getting started on the focus task.

During: Describe the expected actions of the students during this phase. What are they to be doing? How you are making sure each child is accountable? What will you ask students as you observe (ask good questions related to your objectives; don't just say "good job!"). Describe possible extensions or challenges you will have ready for early finishers.

After: This is the most important part of a problem-based lesson! What questions will you ask students that will help them understand the mathematics they explored in their task or activity? How will you structure those questions (e.g., think-pair-share, share with an "elbow partner") so that all students will participate in answering each question? Will students be presenting findings? How will this be structured?

Assessment Notes: How will you determine who knows which objectives? Describe the tools, handouts, and techniques you will use.

Accommodations: What strategies will you use to support the diverse needs of students in the class?

2.6 Teaching: Using Children's Literature in Math Teaching

For this teaching experience, you will share a piece of children's literature as an entry point into a problem-based lesson. There are hundreds of excellent books at every grade level. Preferably, you will start by identifying a math topic. The teacher may suggest a topic. Then you will find a book that is a good match. The book will serve as the first part of the *before* part of your lesson, followed by a problem that you will pose from the book. A shortened lesson plan template is provided on the next page to help you.

Resources

Where do you find the right book? There are many places to find lists of children's books for teaching mathematics. Here are a few:

1. See "Literature Connections" at the end of most chapters in *Elementary and Middle School Mathematics: Teaching Developmentally*.
2. The NCTM journals *Teaching Children Mathematics* and *Mathematics Teaching in the Middle School* often have articles offering good children's books to use in math instruction. NCTM also has a book titled, *Wonderful World of Mathematics*, which is an annotated bibliography of hundreds of children's books.
3. Use the Math Forum web site and search for sites that have children's literature
4. Use the Math & Literature books written by various authors, but originated by Marilyn Burns (Math Solutions Publications). Also, the Math Solutions web site has many ideas.
5. The librarian in your school's media center can be a great resource. Describe the lesson you want to teach and they can often point you to several books that are in the library.

Recommendations

Remember, that children's literature is not just picture books or fictional stories. Students enjoy poetry, news articles, and nonfiction books (like World Records books).

In selecting the book, poem, or article that you are going to read, it is important to consider the experience and interests of your students. If, for example, you have many Latino/a students, you might pick a book that has a Latino heroine. Be sensitive to the cultural, economic, and family backgrounds of your students.

A book (or poem) is to be enjoyed. Try not to stop repeatedly during the story. If you want students to pick up a detail, go back after you have read and re-read particular passages.

If the literature is too long, which is more likely a problem in grades 4–8, you can read the start of the book, and skip to the aspect you want to read, but provide opportunities for students to read the entire book. Another option is to tell the story as a storyteller, reading only the passage related to the math problem you have selected.

Literature and Math Lesson Template

Lesson Title: _____ Grade: _____

Children's Book: _____

Author(s): _____

Brief Description of Story:

Goal of the Lesson (math concept):

Objectives:

Materials:

Lesson Plan

Before: What will you ask students prior to reading the book? What will you ask them following the story?

Write the problem-solving task as you will pose it to the students (it must relate to the book you read):

During:

After: How will students be presenting findings? How will this be related to the story that was read to them?

3 Content Knowledge

Field Experiences in this Section

3.1 Observation: Conceptual and Procedural Knowledge
3.2 Observation: Prior Knowledge
3.3 Teacher Interview: Selecting a Worthwhile Task
3.4 Student Interview: Prior Knowledge

3.5 Student Interview: Conceptual and Procedural Knowledge
3.6 Teaching: Create a Web of Ideas
3.7 Teaching: Design (and Teach) a Lesson
3.8 Reflection: Student Understanding

Alignment

NCATE

Standard 1: Knowledge, Skills, and Dispositions
Content Knowledge

Teacher candidates have indepth knowledge of the subject matter that they plan to teach as described in professional, state, and institutional standards. They demonstrate their knowledge through inquiry, critical analysis, and synthesis of the subject. (NCATE, 2003)

NCTM

NCTM Content Standards: Number, Algebra, Geometry, Measurement, Data Analysis and Probability

See Appendix A in *Elementary and Middle School Mathematics* for NCTM Specific Content Expectations for Students in K–12.

Elementary and Middle School Mathematics by John Van de Walle

Chapter 3 provides lots of suggestions for developing content knowledge.

Key Points

- Teaching should reflect constructivist learning theory, allowing students opportunities to construct or build meaning.
- Understanding can be defined as a measure of the quality and quantity of connections that an idea has with existing ideas.
- Mathematical knowledge includes both conceptual knowledge and procedural knowledge.
- Manipulatives and physical materials can support students' development of new knowledge.

Part II of the Field Guide includes lessons for each content standard that may be used for the experiences provided in this section.

3.1 Observation: Conceptual and Procedural Knowledge

This observation is for a whole class math lesson. Record notes throughout the lesson, recording the questions and tasks the teacher poses and the actions and responses of the students.

Conceptual knowledge of mathematics consists of logical relationships constructed internally and existing in the mind as a part of a network of ideas.

Procedural knowledge of mathematics is knowledge of the rules and the procedures that one uses in carrying out routine mathematical tasks and also the symbolism that is used to represent mathematics.

Learning Objectives

1. After watching the lesson, list what you determined to be the learning objectives of the lesson.

2. Which of the objectives are conceptual? Procedural? Both? Explain.

Questioning

3. In what ways do the teacher's questions promote conceptual knowledge? Give examples of questions the teacher used.

4. In what ways do the teacher's questions promote development of procedural knowledge? Give examples of questions the teacher used.

Student Engagement

5. What were the students doing during the lesson that would help them develop conceptual knowledge? Give examples of activities, actions, or explanations you observed students doing.

6. What were the students doing during the lesson that would help them develop procedural knowledge? Give examples of activities, actions, or explanations you observed students doing.

Analysis

Read your notes on this lesson and your responses to the questions above. Respond to the following:

1. Do you feel there was an appropriate balance on concepts and procedures? Explain.

2. What would you do to enhance students' conceptual knowledge in this lesson?

3. What would you do to enhance students' procedural knowledge in this lesson?

3.2 Observation: Prior Knowledge

Record notes throughout the lesson in the appropriate box in the table. After completing the observation, add to your notes, as appropriate. After the observation, write a summary paragraph on the use of prior knowledge in this lesson, including strengths and what you may have added to incorporate prior knowledge.

Observation Questions	Field Notes
1. What is the purpose (learning objectives) of the lesson? What mathematical concepts and/or procedures does the activity develop? What other goals do you think the teacher has for this lesson?	
2. What prior knowledge is needed to learn the concepts and procedures of this lesson? Create a list.	
3. What does the teacher do to build on prior knowledge? How does the teacher set up the activity (demonstrations, instructions, examples, etc.)? What questions does the teacher ask? What task does the teacher use to introduce the lesson? What adaptations does the teacher make to build background for the diversity represented in the classroom?	
4. In what ways does students' prior knowledge impact their success in this lesson? How are students applying prior knowledge? How does a context or situation help students to make sense of the task? How do tools support their development of understanding? Does a lack of prior knowledge prevent a student from being successful in this lesson? Explain.	

3.3 Teacher Interview: Selecting a Worthwhile Task

The following is an interview that should take no more than 30 minutes. When asking if and when you might conduct an interview, tell the teacher that the interview will focus on a task, activity, or lesson they have recently selected to use with their students. You may use any or all of the questions below, or you can add your own questions.

1. Describe the mathematics task that you recently selected to use with your students.

2. Why did you select this particular task?

3. What do you expect students to learn once they have participated in this lesson?

4. Do you feel that it represents the concepts and procedures appropriately? Explain.

5. Is this task appropriately challenging for all the students? Explain.

6. In what ways were/are the students engaged in the task? In what ways are they "doing" mathematics?

7. What student characteristics did you consider when you chose this task? In other words, how does this task fit your students' background, including their prior knowledge, culture, and learning needs.

8. Does the task appeal to your students' interests, disposition, and experiences? Will you/did you alter it in any way to make it more appealing?

9. In general, what do you feel are the most important considerations when selecting a math activity, lesson, or task? What makes a task worthwhile?

Add your own questions:

10.

11.

12.

3.4 Student Interview: Prior Knowledge

The goal of this interview is to find out what prior knowledge a student has related to a particular topic. The goal is not to teach, but to get information to determine a student's readiness for the topic. Ask your cooperating teacher if you can interview a student. You may also ask for suggestions on a topic that has not yet been taught, but will be taught later that year.

Preparation for the Interview

1. Select the topic you are going to use.
2. Select a task from Part II of this book, from *Elementary and Middle School Mathematics*, from the math textbook the student is using, or from any other math resource book.
3. Create a list of skills and concepts that a student would need in order to be ready to learn this topic.
4. Consider contexts (situations) and manipulatives that can be used with the skills you listed.
5. Prepare 1 to 3 tasks to have student do and explain. For each task, prepare questions to ask the student (see next page for a Template).

Interview Suggestions

- Prior to arriving, be sure you have chosen a quiet place to complete the interview.
- Depending on the age of the student, the interview should be 15–30 minutes.
- Begin by introducing yourself to the child and telling him or her why you are conducting the interview (you want to know how students think about math, you have "homework" for your class, you are trying to learn what kinds of math a third grader can do, etc.).
- Do not jump in and help as the student is working. You can rephrase a question, but if a student is stuck, move to another task.

Example Interview

Focus Concept:

Finding perimeter of a rectangle (see "Garden Fence" in Part II for a possible activity on finding perimeter of rectangles)

Readiness Skill/Concept 1: Properties of a rectangle (e.g., opposite sides are the same length)

Interview Task 1a:

I am going shopping to buy fencing for a cage I am making for my rabbit (draw a picture of a rectangle). The pet storeowner suggested that the long side be 7 feet long and the short side be 4 feet wide.

Related Questions to Probe Student:

Can you label the picture for me?

Can you tell me what the measures of the other sides are, or do we not have enough information?

Interview Task 1b:

Show a collection of rectangles of different shapes (including some squares). Ask student to describe the characteristics of a rectangle.

Related Questions to Probe Student:

What can you tell me that is true for all rectangles?

What is never true for rectangles?

What is sometimes true for a rectangle, but not always?

Readiness Skill/Concept 2: Addition and being able to double

Interview Task 2a:

What is 26 + 26?

Related Questions to Probe Student:

How did you solve it?

If student solved it with the standard algorithm:

Can you do it another way?

Can you do it in your head?

Interview Form

> **Focus Concept:**

> **Readiness Skill/Concept 1:**
>
> **Interview Task 1a:**
>
> **Related Questions to Probe Student:**
>
> **Interview Task 1b:**
>
> **Related Questions to Probe Student:**

> **Readiness Skill/Concept 2:**
>
> **Interview Task 2a:**
>
> **Related Questions to Probe Student:**
>
> **Interview Task 2b:**
>
> **Related Questions to Probe Student:**

Copy this page, as needed, for additional readiness skills/concepts.

3.5 Student Interview: Conceptual and Procedural Knowledge

Knowing how to calculate 23 × 4 and understanding multiplication are not synonymous. In fact, the first is a subset of the latter. This interview involves finding out what a student knows about one of the operations for whole numbers or for rational numbers.

1. Select a type of number and an operation from the lists below.

Type of Number:	**Operation:**
Whole Number	Addition
Fractions	Subtraction
Decimals	Multiplication
Integers	Division

2. Complete the Link Sheet yourself.

3. Ask a student to complete the Link Sheet. Have questions and materials ready for each of the four boxes. Young students will need more room to write, so you will need to adapt the template accordingly.

4. Write a summary of the knowledge the student has related to the topic you selected, including the following points:

   - Student's understanding
   - Gaps in student understanding
   - What experiences you believe the student needs, based on these results.

For more about Link Sheets, see Shield, M., & Swinson, K. (1996). The link sheet: A communication aid for clarifying and developing mathematical ideas and processes. In P. C. Elliott & M. J. Kenney (Eds.) *Communication in Mathematics, K–12 and Beyond: NCTM Yearbook.* Reston, VA: NCTM.

LINK SHEET

TOPIC: _____

Mathematics Example	Situation/Context

Illustration/Model/Picture	My Explanation of the Operation

Source: Adapted from Shield & Swinson, 1996

3.6 Teaching: Create a Web of Ideas

In order to assist students in using prior knowledge and developing a relational understanding, it is essential that the teacher first analyzes and understands the relationship among mathematics concepts. See *Elementary and Middle School Mathematics*, pages 26–28 for more details on relational understanding.

For this field experience, you will be creating a Web of Ideas, sometimes called a Concept Map. Your topic may be one that fits any of the following criteria:

1. A topic you plan to teach in your field experience this semester
2. A topic provided in Part II of this book
3. A topic in the chapter you are reading in *Elementary and Middle School Mathematics Methods*
4. A topic assigned by your supervisor or instructor

Web of Ideas for _____
(Mathematics Concept)

3.7 Teaching: Design (and Teach) a Lesson

The purpose of this lesson is to engage students in a conceptually based activity and to assess what they know about the topic prior to and after the activity. You may select an activity from Part II of this book, or from any other resource. For guidance on what to write for each lesson part, see *Elementary and Middle School Mathematics*, Ch. 5, Planning in the Problem-Based Classroom, pages 61–63.

Title of Activity:
Mathematics Concept(s)
Conceptual knowledge:
Procedural knowledge:
Before
Questions/input to determine student understanding (prior knowledge) of selected concept:
How I will engage the students in the lesson:
How I will introduce the focus task (communicate clear expectations):
During
Questions I will ask as students are working on their task to help them focus on the objectives (e.g., probe their understanding, help them get through a "struggle point"):
How I will observe and assess:
After
Questions I will ask to see if they know the concepts and procedures listed above (include how students will respond to questions so that every child is accountable):
How I will have students summarize the main ideas of the lesson:

3.8 Reflection: Student Understanding

This reflection is a natural follow-up to the lesson plan provided in this section, but can also be used to follow any teaching experience.

Upon completion of teaching your lesson, respond to the following questions. Attach your lesson plan to this reflection.

1. What math concepts did you, the teacher, have to understand in order to teach this lesson well?

2. To what extent did students understand the procedures and concepts prior to the start of the lesson? (What did they already know?)

3. What was challenging for the students to understand?

4. What did you notice best supported their development of concepts and/or procedures? (e.g., teacher actions, use of tools, aspects of the task itself)

5. If you were to teach a follow-up to this lesson, what would be the focus of the next lesson? How would you build on what you did in this lesson?

6. Based on your own knowledge and your experience from this lesson, what do you feel is the relationship between conceptual and procedural knowledge?

4 Pedagogical Content Knowledge: Instruction

Field Experiences in this Section

Alignment

NCATE

Standard 1: Knowledge, Skills, and Dispositions
Pedagogical Content Knowledge and Skills

Teacher candidates reflect a thorough understanding of pedagogical content knowledge delineated in professional, state, and institutional standards. They have in-depth understanding of the subject matter that they plan to teach, allowing them to provide multiple explanations and instructional strategies so that all students learn. They present the content to students in challenging, clear, and compelling ways and integrate technology appropriately. (NCATE 2003, p. 15)

NCTM

Teaching Principle

Effective mathematics teaching requires understanding what students know and need to learn and then challenging and supporting them to learn it well. (NCTM, 2000, p. 16).

Process Standards: Problem Solving, Reasoning and Proof, Communication, Connections, and Representation

See pages 4–5 of *Elementary and Middle School Mathematics* for a brief description of each process standard.

Elementary and Middle School Mathematics by John Van de Walle

Chapter 4 specifically discusses the problem-based approach to teaching mathematics. In addition, all the chapters in Section II (Chs. 9–24) address the specific pedagogical content knowledge (PCK) areas for teaching mathematics.

4.1 Observation: The Process Standards

You may observe a video or live classroom for this experience. As you observe, note evidence of each of NCTM's process standards. Following the observation, consider adaptations or additional ideas for incorporating each process standard. The table below can help you to identify each of the processes.

The Five Process Standards from *Principles and Standards for School Mathematics*	
Problem Solving Standard Instructional programs from prekindergarten through grade 12 should enable all students to—	• Build new mathematical knowledge through problem solving • Solve problems that arise in mathematics and in other contexts • Apply and adapt a variety of appropriate strategies to solve problems • Monitor and reflect on the process of mathematical problem solving
Reasoning and Proof Standard Instructional programs from prekindergarten through grade 12 should enable all students to—	• Recognize reasoning and proof as fundamental aspects of mathematics • Make and investigate mathematical conjectures • Develop and evaluate mathematical arguments and proofs • Select and use various types of reasoning and methods of proof
Communication Standard Instructional programs from prekindergarten through grade 12 should enable all students to—	• Organize and consolidate their mathematical thinking through communication • Communicate their mathematical thinking coherently and clearly to peers, teachers, and others • Analyze and evaluate the mathematical thinking and strategies of others • Use the language of mathematics to express mathematical ideas precisely
Connections Standard Instructional programs from prekindergarten through grade 12 should enable all students to—	• Recognize and use connections among mathematical ideas • Understand how mathematical ideas interconnect and build on one another to produce a coherent whole • Recognize and apply mathematics in contexts outside of mathematics
Representation Standard Instructional programs from prekindergarten through grade 12 should enable all students to—	• Create and use representations to organize, record, and communicate mathematical ideas • Select, apply, and translate among mathematical representations to solve problems • Use representations to model and interpret physical, social, and mathematical phenomena

Source: Reprinted with permission from *Principles and Standards for School Mathematics.* Copyright © 2000 by the National Council of Teachers of Mathematics. All rights reserved.

Process Standard	Evidence	Additional Ideas
Problem solving		
Reasoning and proof		
Communication		
Connections		
Representation		

Summary Reflection

1. What is the relationship between these processes and student engagement?

2. How do students of diverse backgrounds respond to an environment that incorporates the process standards?

4.2 Observation: Classroom Discourse

Classroom discourse includes the ways of representing, thinking, talking, agreeing and disagreeing in the classroom. Observe the interactions in a classroom (video or live) and used the statements from the *Professional Standards for Teaching Mathematics* Standards on Discourse to note evidence of discourse (NCTM, 1991).

Strategies for Orchestrating Discourse	Evidence
Teacher's Role	(Record teacher statements or actions in the appropriate box.)
Pose questions and tasks that elicit, engage, and challenge each student's thinking.	
Listen carefully to students' ideas.	
Ask students to clarify and justify their ideas orally and in writing.	
Decide when and how to attach mathematical notation and language to students' ideas.	
Monitor students' participation in discussions and decide when and how to encourage each student to participate.	
Students' Role	(Record student statements or actions in the appropriate box.)
Listen to, respond to, and question the teacher and each other.	
Use a variety of tools to reason, make connections, solve problems and communicate.	
Initiate problems and questions.	
Make conjectures and present solutions.	
Explore examples and counterexamples to explore a conjecture.	
Try to convince themselves or others of the validity of particular representations, solutions, conjectures, and answers.	

What do you feel are key teacher actions to develop a classroom with a high level of student involvement in the discourse?

4.3 Observation: Cooperative Groups

Ask your teacher if you can observe the class on a day that he or she is using cooperative groups. The purpose of this observation is twofold: first, for you to identify management strategies for ensuring that each child participates and learns, and second, to analyze the ways cooperative groups can support student learning.

Introducing the Cooperative Learning Activity

1. **Organization.** Describe how the teacher organizes groups (e.g., how many students are in a group? Is there an ability mix? Gender mix? Do students pick their groups?).

2. **Accountability.** Describe what the teacher does to have individual accountability within group work (e.g., are group roles assigned to individuals in each group? Are other strategies used to make sure each individual contributes to the group?).

3. **Management.** Discuss how the teacher organizes the classroom to facilitate cooperative groups (e.g., how does the teacher transition between the whole class and small groups? What does the teacher do while students are working in groups? Are materials accessible to students?).

Choose one group to observe during the cooperative group task. The following questions refer to just the group you selected.

1. **Interaction.** Describe how the members of the group interact (e.g., do students listen to, respond to, and question one another? Does everyone contribute equitably? Do students pose and explore conjectures?).

2. **Support for Learning.** Describe how members of the group interact with someone who doesn't understand or is struggling with an idea (e.g., are they left out? Helped? Does the teacher assist, or expect the team members to help?). Does the teacher coach the students on how to help each other?

3. **Accountability.** Describe the actions of the individuals within the group (e.g., do they interact to make sure each person learns, or do some students rely on others to do the work for them? How do the groups record and report their answers?).

4. **Assessment.** Explain strategies that are used to identify what each individual child has learned (e.g., does the teacher informally interview students while they work? Does she use a checklist? Individual recording sheets? How does the teacher know who learned the objectives of the lesson?).

Postobservation Analysis

Based on this observation, readings in *Elementary and Middle School Mathematics*, and your own experiences, respond to the following two questions.

1. Take a position on whether students should or should not learn a new concept in cooperative groups and defend your answer.

2. Describe what you believe to be the critical features for cooperative groups to serve as effective learning communities.

4.4 Teacher Interview: Teaching for Understanding

Van de Walle defines understanding as "a measure of the quantity and quality of connections that an idea has with existing ideas." The purpose of this interview is to learn, from the teacher, how a topic he or she is about to teach ties into other mathematics concepts. In addition, you are to explore the way in which he or she is going to develop the topic so that students make those connections. These two objectives are worded in general questions below, but prior to your interview, you will need to plan three to five more specific questions for each. Chapter 3 in *Elementary and Middle School Mathematics* is a good resource to help you plan and implement this interview.

1. How does _____ relate to the other mathematics that students have learned and will be learning?

    a.

    b.

    c.

    d.

    e.

2. What experiences are you planning/have you planned for the students so that they connect this concept with prior learning and/or real life contexts?

    a.

    b.

    c.

    d.

    e.

Following your interview, you will need to write up the responses the teacher gave to each question and conclude with a brief paragraph explaining what you learned about (1) the topic you discussed, (2) instructional strategies for that topic that were new, and (3) ideas of your own that would enhance a student's understanding of the topic.

4.5 Student Interview: Learning Mathematics Developmentally

The purpose of this interview is to find out how a student who is learning through a developmental approach (see p. 34 of *Elementary and Middle School Mathematics*) views mathematics. You can use this interview with any student. Comparison of the responses from a student using a different approach could be very interesting. Some questions are provided below, but you will need to adapt them for phrasing appropriate for the age level of the student.

Introduce yourself and your purpose: "I am learning how to teach math. You can help me by telling me what you know and think about math. Can I ask you some questions?"

Interview Prompts	Additional/Adapted Questions
Mathematics as a Subject	
If I had no idea what math meant, what would you tell me? What is math?	
What are the important math topics?	
Why do you think you are learning math? How will you use it? Can you give some examples?	
Is there usually one way to solve a problem or more than one way?	
Your teacher says, "It's time for math." What is going to happen (what will you be doing, what will the teacher be doing)?	
Attitudes/Beliefs About Mathematics	
When you visualize someone who is good at math, what kinds of things can this person do?	
Do you think everybody can do well in math if they try?	
Who is good at math?	
Is math something that is useful to know? Why or why not?	
Are you good at math? Why do you think so?	
How is math best learned?	
How do you best learn math?	
Is math your favorite subject?	

4.6 Teaching: Teaching a Small Group

The purpose of this field experience is to give you an opportunity to practice posing a quality task, using good questioning, and observing student thinking. Use this page as a guide in completing this experience. You will turn in (1) your lesson plan, (2) the task you used, and (3) a one to two paragraph reflection describing your students' reactions to the task and your own reflections on the task.

1. **Selecting a worthwhile task.** Select one problem that will engage students and lends to working together (you might consult the teacher for ideas). You can select from:

    a. Lesson outlines in Part II of this guide.
    b. Activities that are provided in Activity Boxes in the Van de Walle text.
    c. A problem-based resource, such as *Navigations* (NCTM, 2000).

2. **Identify the learning objective for the activity.** Describe what it is students will be able to do after they complete the activity you have selected.

3. **Determine exactly how you will implement the activity for the small group.** Complete a shorter version of the lesson plan format (see p. 18).

Lesson Plan

Before: Describe how you will introduce the activity or problem. Record questions that you will pose. Plan directions for getting started on the focus task.

During: Describe the expected actions of the students during this phase. What are they to be doing? How will you redirect them if they are stuck, without giving away the challenge of the task? What questions will you ask to extend their thinking?

After: How will students show what they learned from the task? Will each student be presenting what he or she learned?

---

4. **Ask students questions regarding their reactions to the task.** For example, "How difficult did you think the problem was? Did you like to be challenged?"

4.7 Teaching: Teaching a Standards-Based Lesson

The focus on this experience is on teaching. Most of the time, teachers do not create a lesson from scratch but rather take an activity from a textbook or other resource and determine how they will use it with a whole class of students. That is what you will be doing in this field experience.

1. Select one of the Expanded Lessons in Part II of this guide (also downloadable on the Companion Web site at www.ablongman.com/vandewalle6e). As an alternative, you can use a full lesson plan from another source that uses a developmental approach to teaching.

2. Consider each component of the lesson, and think of what **teaching strategies** you can use to make the component effective with students. For example, will you have students discuss a key question with a partner? Will you have students write down an idea before asking them to share? Will they use manipulatives?

3. Consider **management** of the lesson. In particular, how long do you plan to spend on each part? How will you plan for transitions from whole class to small groups and back to whole group again? What exact instructions will students need?

4. What **resources** will the students need? Are they easily accessible?

5. After teaching the lesson, reflect on the instructional strategies, management, and resources you planned. What worked? What would you do differently if you were to teach it again? (See p. 44 in this guide for lesson reflection template.)

4.8 Teaching: Putting It All Together

For this instructional field experience, you will select a mathematics topic, find an appropriate task, develop it into a lesson, teach it, and reflect on the instruction. This is the complete cycle of a lesson. Consult with your teacher to determine the mathematics topic and to determine the knowledge and interest of your students.

You will submit the completed lesson plan and the reflection together. Use these steps to guide your work.

1. With the teacher, determine the mathematics topic and/or the state standard that will be the focus of your lesson.

2. Complete the lesson plan (p. 17–18).

3. Submit lesson to teacher and/or supervisor for feedback.

4. Teach the lesson to the students.

5. If possible, get feedback from the teacher (see p. 45).

6. Complete reflection (p. 59).

4.9 Reflection: Reflecting on Teaching and Learning

1. To what extent did the lesson tasks, activities, and/or discussion support the lesson objectives?

2. To what extent was each child engaged throughout the lesson?

3. What instructional strategies seemed effective? Ineffective?

4. What management strategies seemed effective? Ineffective?

5. To what extent were you able to determine if each child learned the objectives? Be specific.

6. What do you feel were the most successful aspects of this lesson?

7. What would you do differently if you were to teach this lesson again?

4.10 Feedback on Teaching

This form is to be used by the classroom teacher and/or your supervisor to observe your teaching (see Chapter 3 of *Elementary and Middle School Mathematics* for more background on each of these categories).

Category	Evidence	Suggestions
Creating a mathematical environment • Students try out ideas • No passive observers • Students take risks		
Posing worthwhile tasks • Task is problematic to students • Students actively look for relationships, • Task leads to students learning important math concepts		
Using variety of grouping structures • Pairs, small groups allowed to work together • Individuals in groups are participating • Teacher observing and questioning		
Using models • Manipulatives, calculators, and/or visuals support objectives • Management of tools is effective		
Using discourse and writing • Opportunities to explain thinking verbally • Opportunities to write and/or illustrate ideas • Effective questioning		
Justification of student responses • Students explain how they arrived at the solution • Students justify why it works		
Listening actively • Lesson child centered, not teacher centered. • Adequate wait time • Prompts that extends students' explanations		
Other		

Observer's Final Comments
Strengths:

Goal(s) for next teaching experience:

5 Pedagogical Content Knowledge: Technology

Field Experiences in this Section

Alignment

NCATE

Standard 1: Knowledge, Skills, and Dispositions
Pedagogical Content Knowledge and Skills

Teacher candidates reflect a thorough understanding of pedagogical content knowledge delineated in professional, state, and institutional standards. They have in-depth understanding of the subject matter that they plan to teach, allowing them to provide multiple explanations and instructional strategies so that all students learn. They present the content to students in challenging, clear, and compelling ways and **integrate technology appropriately.** (NCATE, 2002, p. 15)

NCTM

Technology Principle

Technology is essential in teaching and learning mathematics; it influences the mathematics that is taught and enhances students' learning. (NCTM, 2000, p. 24)

Elementary and Middle School Mathematics by John Van de Walle

Chapter 8 offers suggestions for using technology.

5.1 Project: Learning Online

For this experience, you may complete Part I, Part II, or both. The Illuminations Web site (http://illuminations.nctm.org) has various interactive applets that enable you to explore mathematics concepts. For this field experience, you will select one of these tasks and explore it.

Part I: Personal Reflections on Online Applets

1. Describe the applet that you explored.
2. What was the learning goal of the applet?
3. Compare and contrast a parallel task that could be done without the use of technology. What would be gained or lost?
4. How do you believe students at the appropriate grade level would respond to doing this applet as their activity for learning about the intended objective(s)?

Part II: Observe a Student Exploring Online Applet

Find a student (grade 3–8) who is willing to be interviewed. The student might be from the class you have been assigned or another student you know.

1. Explain to the student how to use the applet (not how to solve the problems in the applet).
2. Ask the student to take some time to explore and see if he or she can figure out the task.
3. Upon completion, ask the student (1) what he or she learned from using the applet and (2) what he or she thinks of learning using the computer.
4. Write up your observations of what the student did while exploring the applet, what the student told you, and what you learned about students using technology.

5.2 Project: Evaluating Mathematics Software or Web Sites

In order to complete this field experience, you will need to ask what math software is used in your assigned school and/or consult your university library to see if there is K–8 math software available to review. The purpose of this experience is to think critically about the learning opportunities that a particular software offers. There is a wide range of quality and as a teacher, you will need to be discerning in making choices for your students. The criteria below are adapted from *Elementary and Middle School Mathematics*, pages 115–116.

Name of software or Web site: _____

URL for Web site or publisher of software: _____

Scale: 1 = False   2 = Probably false   3 = Neutral   4 = Probably true   5 = True

Criteria	Rating	Comments
The software or Web site provides better opportunities to learn than alternative approaches.	1 2 3 4 5	
Students will be engaged with the math content (not the frills).	1 2 3 4 5	
The software or Web site provides opportunities for problem solving.	1 2 3 4 5	
The program develops conceptual knowledge and supports student understanding of concepts.	1 2 3 4 5	
The program develops procedural knowledge and supports student understanding of skills.	1 2 3 4 5	
The software or Web site allows the teacher to assess student learning through records and reports.	1 2 3 4 5	
The program is challenging for a wide range of skill levels.	1 2 3 4 5	
The program is equitable in its consideration of gender and culture.	1 2 3 4 5	
Software or Web site promotes good student interaction and discussion.	1 2 3 4 5	
The software or Web site has quality supplemental materials, such as blackline masters.	1 2 3 4 5	

5.3 Teaching: Using the Calculator to Support Learning

The calculator is so much more than a tool to improve the speed and accuracy of computation, it is a tool for challenging students and helping students learn. In this field experience, you will teach a lesson that uses the calculator as a tool for learning. Use the Lesson Plan Template from the Planning Section (p. 18).

Resources for finding calculator lessons:

1. *Elementary and Middle School Mathematics.* See activities throughout the text (see calculator icons to find the activities employing calculators).

2. **Math Forum Web Site.** If you go to the Math Tools site (http://mathforum.org/mathtools), you can search by grade level and by the type of technology you wish to use (e.g., calculator).

3. Texas Instruments has a collection of calculator activities to review (http://education.ti.com/us/activity/main.html). Select "General Math" and then you will be able to pick the grade band you need.

4. Casio has several calculator activities to review for elementary and middle school (www.casioeducation.com/contents/lesson.php).

5.4 Teaching: Develop a Calculator Learning Center

In this field experience, you will create a calculator-dependent activity that is appropriate for a learning center. A learning center is usually set up in a classroom so that it is always accessible to students who have extra time and are looking for an interesting challenge, or it may be part of a series of learning activities. An effective teacher will provide tasks that extend what is being learned in the classroom.

In order for a learning center to be effective, the tasks should have the following characteristics.

1. **Kid-friendly instructions.** The students should be able to read and follow all instructions without needing clarification from the teacher.

2. **Multidimensional and/or repeatable tasks.** If the task has one solution, a student will complete that task and not want to spend more time in the learning center. See, for example, the Range Game (p. 255 of *Elementary and Middle School Mathematics*), in which the student can try to get in the range but the activity can be easily extended by having the student create his or her own Start and Range (or do this with a partner).

3. **Promotion of conceptual development, not merely skill practice.** Notice that the Range Game focuses on estimation and promoting students' understanding of multiplication.

4. **Final product.** Completion of the task should result in a tangible product that is turned in to the teacher.

The template on the next page is intended to be a guide. You can also create your own template. The final product should look intriguing to the age group you are targeting. Without much time invested, you can download artwork from the Web or place other illustrations on the page to increase the visual appeal and perhaps help to clarify the task.

Calculator Learning Center Planning Template

Title:

Topic: Grade:

Instructions (written to student):

Tasks/Problem/Examples:

Extension(s)/Alternatives:

Attach a page entitled "Student Recording Sheet," designed to match the task above.

5.5 Reflection: Reactions to Learning with Technology

After teaching or observing a lesson that uses computers or calculators as a means for learning mathematics, respond to the following prompts.

1. What were the learning objectives of the lesson?

2. In what ways did the technology support or inhibit the learning of those objectives?

3. If technology were not available, what impact would that have had on the lesson?

4. How did students respond to using the technology? Did students respond differently? Explain.

5. Based on this lesson, readings, and your personal beliefs, describe what you think the appropriate use of calculators should be for the grade that you taught or observed.

6 Dispositions

Field Experiences in this Section

6.1 Observation: Parent Conference
6.2 Teacher Interview: Communicating with Parents
6.3 Parent Interview: What Is Important to You?

6.4 Teaching: Prepare a Family Math Take-Home Activity
6.5 Reflection: Growing in the Profession

Alignment

NCATE

Standard 1: Knowledge, Skills, and Dispositions
Professional and Pedagogical Knowledge and Skills

Candidates work with students, families, and communities in ways that reflect the dispositions expected of professional educators as delineated in professional, state, and institutional standards. Candidates recognize when their own dispositions may need to be adjusted and are able to develop plans to do so. (NCATE, 2002, p. 16)

NCTM

The Teacher's Role in Professional Development

Teachers of mathematics should take an active role in their own professional development by accepting responsibility for

- Experimenting thoughtfully with alternative approaches and strategies in the classroom;
- Reflecting on learning and teaching individually and with colleagues;
- Participating in workshops, courses, and other educational opportunities specific to mathematics;
- Participating actively in the professional community of mathematics educators;
- Reading and discussing ideas presented in professional publications;
- Discussing with colleagues issues in mathematics and mathematics teaching and learning;
- Participating in proposing, designing, and evaluating programs for professional development specific to mathematics; and
- Participating in school, community, and political efforts to effect positive change in mathematics education. (NCTM, 1991, p. 168)

Elementary and Middle School Mathematics by John Van de Walle

Chapter 2 describes a new vision of mathematics learning, which has implications for the way that you perceive and teach mathematics:

> your challenge [is] to reconceptualize your own understanding of what it means to know and do mathematics so that the children with whom you work will have an exciting and accurate vision of mathematics. (p. 12)

6.1 Observation: Parent Conference

This conference may be one that is scheduled because of a concern for the child, or the regularly planned, end-of-quarter conferences. Ask in advance if the teacher will be discussing math specifically and if you could quietly observe the conference. Use the table below to record the interactions over one math-related issue and after the interview respond to the prompts at the bottom of the page.

	Topic/issue addressed: Who initiates issue:	Actions to be taken as a result of discussion
Student's role in discussion		
Parent's role in discussion		
Teacher's role in discussion		

1. What strategies has the teacher used to create a welcoming environment for the family (if you aren't sure, ask the teacher)?

2. In what ways does the teacher incorporate the student's strengths as part of the conversation?

3. How would you characterize the conversation (i.e., is there a balance of who is listening and who is talking?)?

4. What does the teacher share as evidence of the student's math learning (e.g., grades, work samples, student portfolio)?

6.2 Teacher Interview: Communicating with Parents

For this field experience, prepare an interview in which you can learn about what the teacher does to communicate with parents, how they do the things that they do (e.g., if they do a newsletter, find out what it looks like, how often it goes out, who contributes to the writing).

Ask a practicing teacher if you may interview him or her about how he or she involves parents in their child's math learning. Your interview should address four areas:

1. What communication they use and how they use those approaches (see possible communication strategies below)
2. What they consider most important in terms of communication with parents (specific to math teaching and learning)
3. What strategies they use to involve parents who are not likely to show up on their own (due to their own bad experiences in school, cultural background, etc.)
4. How they build support for using reform practices in mathematics (see Ch. 1 in *Elementary and Middle School Mathematics* for details on this). If the teacher is not using reform practices, you may replace this item with asking what they want parents to know as the priorities in their math class.

Parent Communication Strategies

1. Teacher → parent communication
   Includes:
   - homework
   - newsletters
   - notes to individual parents
   - back-to-school nights

2. Parent → teacher communication
   Includes:
   - Emails
   - Phone calls
   - Visits to the school

3. Teacher ↔ parent communication
   Includes:
   - Family math nights
   - Student/parent conferences (these can be one-way, but should be two- or three-way)
   - Parent volunteers in classroom

After completing your interview, respond to the questions on the following page.

Summary of Communication with Parents

1. Summarize the ways the teacher communicates with parents.

2. Analyze the ways the teacher communicates with parents in term of one-way and two-way communication.

3. What strategies does the teacher use (or suggest) for communicating with hard-to-reach parents?

4. What strategies does the teacher use to gain the confidence and support from parents in terms of his or her instructional approach to teaching math?

5. What have you learned from this interview that you would prioritize in your own classroom in terms of communicating with parents?

6.3 Parent Interview: What Is Important to You?

Find a parent who has at least one child in grades K–8. The purpose of this interview is for you to gain a perspective on the perspectives of parents in terms of their children's achievement in math and their own beliefs about math. This background is of critical importance when you consider your own relationship with parents and how you will sell your math program to the families of your students. A few questions are provided for you. Add your own questions that are relevant to the local community.

Interview Questions	Parent Response
1. What do you think are the important things your child will learn this year?	
2. How do you think people learn math? How does your child learn best?	
3. What is your opinion of the use of calculators? Explain.	
4. What is your opinion of students working together on a math problem or assignment?	
5. What math do you think your child needs in order to have access to the careers he or she may desire?	
Other questions:	

Summary

After completing your interview, discuss the following:

1. How are the parents' views aligned with or in contrast to how you would teach math?
2. Take one issue for which the parent had a different view. Describe two to three strategies you would use to avoid or address a possible conflict.

6.4 Teaching: Prepare a Family Math Take-Home Activity

For this experience you will put together a family math activity (a Take-Home Kit).

Family Math Nights are common in schools and are excellent for developing parent support for math and getting to know your students' families. A Family Math Night can be done for your classroom, collaboratively for all students at a particular grade, or for the entire school.

The key to the success of a Family Math Night is to have engaging tasks that parents and their children can enjoy and that illustrate important mathematics concepts. Good tasks for Family Math Night are ones that can be used over and over again. Where can you find these?

1. Visit the Family Math Program, which includes a series of books that are full of good ideas, at www.lhs.berkeley.edu/equals. The university or school library may have one of these books. If not, there are a few on the Web site that can be downloaded. These books are available in English and Spanish.
2. Look at the activities throughout *Elementary and Middle School Mathematics*. Examples that could be adapted include Activities 14.6, 15.11, and 20.14.
3. National Council of Teachers of Mathematics (NCTM) has high-quality activities and resources available at www.nctm.org/families/index.htm.
4. Games or activities in the class's math textbook. If you have engaging activities built into your units, this is a great way to have families support their children's math learning and for you to show off the quality of your math program.
5. There are so many teacher resource and activity books. If you select carefully, you can find excellent activities for Family Math Nights.

Family Math Take Home Activity Example (Adaptation of Activity 15.11)

> **Down the Line!**
> In this activity, students and parents will build and predict what happens down the line.
>
> **Take-Home Kit (in a zip-lock bag) including the following**
>
> 1. **Detailed, kid-friendly instruction card.** In the instructions, students and families will first predict how many tiles for the 5th or 7th figure for the cards you have in the kit. Then, they will be instructed to create their own. The parent can create the first three steps and ask their child to predict "down the line" (such as step 8); then they can trade roles.
> 2. Several patterns on cards, such as the ones in Activity 22.4 that use tiles.
> 3. 50–60 1" square tiles (cut colored cardstock).
> 4. Optional: laminated card with a table (for recording how many tiles are needed for step 1, 2, 3, . . .) and an overhead nonpermanent marker.

6.5 Reflection: Growing in the Profession

As noted in Chapter 3 of *Elementary and Middle School Mathematics*, "constructing knowledge requires reflective thought, actively thinking about or mentally working on an idea." The idea you are working on is the goal of becoming an effective mathematics teacher. This reflection can be used after a single lesson but can also be used to comprehensibly review a series of teaching opportunities. The purpose is for you to consider your strengths and target areas for growth.

This form can be completed by preservice teacher for self-reflection, a cooperating teacher collaboration with the preservice teacher, or by a university supervisor.

	Strengths	Target Areas for Continued Growth
Classroom environment		
Planning		
Content knowledge		
Instruction		
Use of technology		
Assessment		
Diversity		

7 Student Learning

Field Experiences in this Section

Alignment

NCATE

Standard 1: Knowledge, Skills, and Dispositions

Teacher candidates accurately assess and analyze student learning, make appropriate adjustments to instruction, monitor student learning, and have a positive effect on learning for all students. (NCATE, 2003, p. 16)

NCTM

Assessment Principle

Assessment should support the learning of important mathematics and furnish useful information to both teachers and students. (NCTM, 2000, p. 22)

The Professional Standards for Teaching Mathematics: Analysis of Teaching and Learning

The teacher of mathematics should engage in ongoing analysis of teaching and learning by

- Observing, listening to, and gathering other information about students to assess what they are learning
- Examining effects of the tasks, discourse, and learning environment on students' mathematical knowledge, skills, and dispositions

In order to

- Ensure that every student is learning sound and significant mathematics and is developing a positive disposition toward mathematics
- Challenge and extend students' ideas
- Adapt or change activities while teaching
- Make plans, both short- and long-range
- Describe and comment on each student's learning to parents and administrators, as well as to the students themselves

Elementary and Middle School Mathematics by John Van de Walle

Chapter 6 provides suggestions and tools for assessment.

7.1 Observation: Assessing to Inform Instruction

The goal of this observation is to assess how the students in the classroom are performing on the topic they are learning and later to determine what you feel are the appropriate next steps for this group of students. When you schedule this observation, make sure that they will be learning a new concept.

Begin the observation by asking the teacher what he or she hopes the students will learn in the lesson (these objectives may be posted on the board). These will be the focus of your observation, not behavior, teaching strategies, or anything else.

1. Does each child have the prior knowledge to learn the new topic?

2. Does each student demonstrate evidence of understanding the task or activity they are supposed to be doing? If they do not understand, can you determine the cause of their confusion (e.g., don't understand instructions, don't know the math, are not familiar with the mathematics language)?

3. How successful is each student at demonstrating understanding of the lesson objectives? What is your evidence for this assessment? Be sure to respond to this in terms of individuals (e.g., three of the students . . .) and to use the evidence you used to reach this conclusion (e.g., their work on a handout, their oral explanation).

4. For the students who did not complete the task, what did you see as their gaps in understanding or other reasons for not completing the task?

Postobservation:

5. Given what you recorded in your observation, describe what next steps you would take with this class of students (i.e., what you would have as the focus of the lesson the next day).

7.2 Student Interview: Assessing for Understanding

The goal of a diagnostic interview is to find out where a child is at a particular time in terms of concepts and procedures. Ask your supervising teacher if you can interview a student and then follow the steps below.

Preinterview

1. Select a topic that will be in their curriculum this year but has not yet been taught.
2. Select or design one to three tasks for the student to demonstrate and/or explain this concept. You must select items so that the student can complete them in 10–20 minutes (depending on student's age).
3. Schedule a time to visit with the student.

Interview

4. Introduce yourself to the student and explain the purpose of your discussion. Tell the student that you are interested in learning about his or her thinking, so you will be asking the student to explain what he or she is thinking and doing.
5. Explain each task clearly (preparing a script is recommended). Watch the student solve the task; do not assist the student. Give the student enough time. If the student is stuck, ask the question a different way, simplify the task, or remind the student of something that might help to jog his or her memory.
6. If appropriate, when a student solves a problem, ask if he or she could solve it another way.
7. Thank the student for helping you to learn more about teaching math. Tell the student he or she did a good job.

Postinterview

8. Write a summary of how the student performed on each question you asked. Include any work samples you have from the interview.
9. Describe what future instruction you feel is appropriate for this student (related to your specific topic).

Sample Interview for Primary Grades

MATH: Counting strategies (Grades K–1)

Task 1:

Provide student with 17 counters. Ask the learner, "How many counters are here?"

Observe what strategy the student originally uses (counting by 1s, 2s, 5s, 10s).

Possible interview questions:

1. If the student counted by ones, ask "Can you count them another way?" or "Is there a quicker way you could count them?"
2. If student counts by 1s and 2s, ask what other ways they know how to count.
3. If the counters were placed into piles, say, "Tell me why you chose to do that."
4. Ask the student, "What do you do to remember which counters you already counted?"
5. If counters were counted more than once, present the same counting task with fewer than ten counters. Ask yourself whether the child conserves number (i.e., the child can avoid double-counting despite the arrangement of the counters and knows when to stop counting to have counted them all). The task may be developmentally beyond the learner right now.

Task 2:

Provide student with 42 counters. Ask the learner, "How many counters are here?"

Observe what counting strategy the student uses and how he or she organizes the counters (e.g., were the counters moved into pile(s) as they were counted? How?).

Possible interview questions:

1. If the student begins to count by ones, ask "Can you count them a quicker way?" or "Can you organize the counters so they will be easier to count?"
2. Can you count by 2s (or 5s) to find out how many?
3. Ask the student, "What do you do to remember which counters you already counted?"
4. If student has been successful on these tasks, ask "What if you had a whole box of counters, how would you figure out how many were in the box?"

Math Concept: _____

Task 1:
Key Questions
1.
2.
3.

Task 2:
Key Questions
1.
2.
3.

Task 3:
Key Questions
1.
2.
3.

7.3 Student Interview: Learning Through Problems

The focus of this interview is to observe a student solving a problem and ask questions to see what the student knew in order to solve the task and what was learned as a result of doing the task. You may use any task, but there is a collection of good tasks on pages 81–82 of *Elementary and Middle School Mathematics*. You need to do only one task, but you may want to have an extension ready in case the one you selected is too easy for the student. Prepare two to four questions that extend the problem and ask the child to explain his or her strategy.

After having a student solve the task, respond to the following prompts:

1. What prior knowledge did the student have to have in order to solve this problem?

2. What strategies did the student use to solve the problem? Did the student try different approaches?

3. In what ways did the questions you asked extend the student's thinking?

4. What did the student learn from the task itself and/or the questions you posed?

7.4 Teaching: Assessing Student Understanding with Rubrics

In Part II of this guide are three balanced assessment items. Balanced Assessment–Mathematics Assessment Resource Service Project (www.educ.msu.edu/mars) was designed to create high-quality performance tasks across the curriculum that could be assessed to more comprehensively assess what a student knows in mathematics. The tasks and rubrics illustrate how problem-based tasks can be used to assess student understanding.

Select one of the Balanced Assessment Performance Tasks and ask a student or small group of students to complete the task. Be sure they are clear about what they are to do before getting them started on the performance task.

Once they have completed the task, use the rubrics provided and the example assessed work to help you apply the rubric to the students who have completed the task.

Complete the following questions and submit this along with the student completed tasks and your scoring of each one.

Reflection on Using Balanced Assessment Items

1. As the student worked on the task, what problems were particularly challenging?

2. What strategies did the student use to solve the more challenging tasks?

3. Do you think that the student learned something as a result of doing the performance task? Explain.

4. What did you learn about the student as a result of his or her completion of this task?

7.5 Teaching: Creating and Using Rubrics

For this experience you can use a task from a lesson you plan to teach, a task that your cooperating teacher has used, or one that has not been used.

Assessment is to involve the learner. Rubrics should be shared with students prior to completion of the task, so that they can clearly see what the expectations are. The expectations must be heavily weighted on what the objectives of the lesson are. It is not appropriate to have behavior included in a rubric that is designed to assess students understanding of area, for example. Neatness and clarity are legitimate items to include, but should not overshadow the learning objectives.

PART I. Develop the Rubric

Using a four-point rubric as a guide, create a rubric that is specific to the task that you have selected.

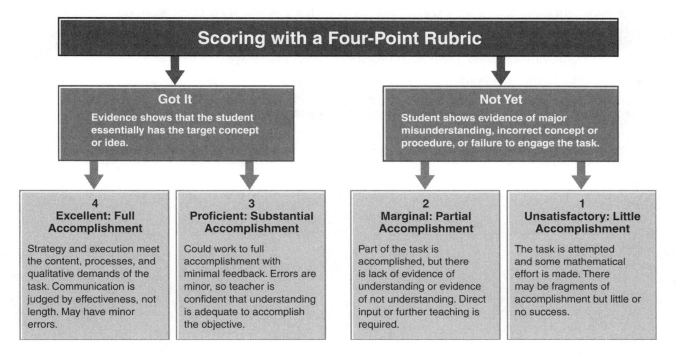

Scoring with a Four-Point Rubric

Got It
Evidence shows that the student essentially has the target concept or idea.

Not Yet
Student shows evidence of major misunderstanding, incorrect concept or procedure, or failure to engage the task.

4
Excellent: Full Accomplishment

Strategy and execution meet the content, processes, and qualitative demands of the task. Communication is judged by effectiveness, not length. May have minor errors.

3
Proficient: Substantial Accomplishment

Could work to full accomplishment with minimal feedback. Errors are minor, so teacher is confident that understanding is adequate to accomplish the objective.

2
Marginal: Partial Accomplishment

Part of the task is accomplished, but there is lack of evidence of understanding or evidence of not understanding. Direct input or further teaching is required.

1
Unsatisfactory: Little Accomplishment

The task is attempted and some mathematical effort is made. There may be fragments of accomplishment but little or no success.

PART II. Use the Rubric

After using this rubric in the lesson you teach (or the cooperating teacher taught), use it to assess the student work you collected. For all students, you should be able to underline the descriptions of their work in each section of the rubric. This communicates to children what they accomplished and what areas need improvement.

PART III. Reflection and Revision of Rubric

Typically, a first-draft rubric doesn't quite capture what you had hoped and you realize this after struggling over whether a piece of student work is a 3 or a 4. For Part III, revise your rubric. In addition, comment on the impact the rubric had on the quality of the student work.

7.6 Teaching: Using Anecdotal Notes to Assess Students

One strategy teachers use to assess student learning is to keep anecdotal evidence, using note cards or sticky notes. These notes are used throughout a unit. See Figure 6.3 in *Elementary and Middle School Mathematics* for a visual of what this can look like. As students work on the *during* part of a lesson, the teacher observes and keeps notes on who is and is not achieving the objectives.

The goal of this experience is for you to use anecdotal notes to assess student learning. You can attempt to do an entire class of students, or a fraction of the class. You can observe one lesson or a series of lessons.

1. Select a style you are going to use to record your notes (note cards on a clipboard, the template provided and sticky notes, or a format the teacher recommends).
2. Prepare cards/notes. Organize your materials in such a way that it will be easy to take notes during the lesson.
3. Record notes on each student. You will want to try to observe them at several points during the lessons/series of lessons. You will need to visit and revisit students.
4. At the end of your observation (or series of observations):
    a. Summarize to what extent each child learned the objectives of the lesson or unit.
    b. Describe what you see as the benefits and limitations of using anecdotal notes (e.g., note cards or sticky notes) to assess student learning.

Rubric Format for Anecdotal Notes

See Figure 6.4 in *Elementary and Middle School Mathematics* to see an example of this format. You may want to use sticky notes in the right column, which allows you to write students' names and brief notes. Using sticky notes means you can move them to new categories or revise their notes without having to erase the form.

Math Concept: _____

Level of Understanding	Names of Students (post students names)
SUPER Clear understanding. Communicates concept in multiple representations. Shows evidence of using idea without prompting. Specific descriptors: 1. 2.	
ON TARGET Understands or is developing well. Uses designated models. Specific descriptors: 1. 2.	
NOT YET **Some confusion or misunderstands. Only models idea with help.** Specific descriptors: 1. 2.	

7.7 Teaching: Using a Checklist to Assess Students

For this field experience, you will use a checklist format to assess student learning. Although it is called a checklist, you can also add anecdotal notes to the form as a way of tracking students. This is intended for a lesson that you have planned but can also be used with a lesson that you are observing.

For this task you will

1. Observe a lesson using one of the forms provided here or one you have created.
2. Record how each student in the class has achieved the objectives of the class.
3. Respond to the following reflection prompts.

Postobservation Reflection

1. Briefly describe the lesson, in particular describing the goals of the lesson.

2. To what extent did students learn the objectives? In other words, who learned which objectives?

3. Based on your response to item 2, what needs to be planned for these students for their upcoming math lesson?

4. What are the benefits and limitations of using checklists in classroom assessment?

Full-Class Observation Checklist

List student names in the left column. See *Elementary and Middle School Mathematics*, page 87 for a model.

Topic:_____	Objective 1	Objective 2	Objective 3	Notes
1.				
2.				
3.				
4.				
5.				
6.				
7.				
8.				
9.				
10.				
11.				
12.				
13.				
14.				
15.				
16.				
17.				
18.				
19.				
20.				
21.				
22.				
23.				
24.				
25.				
26.				
27.				

8 Diversity

Field Experiences in this Section

Alignment

NCATE

Standard 4: Diversity
Design, Implementation, and Evaluation of Curriculum and Experiences

Curriculum, field experiences, and clinical practice help candidates to demonstrate knowledge, skills, and dispositions related to diversity. They are based on well-developed knowledge bases for, and conceptualizations of, diversity and inclusion so that candidates can apply them effectively in schools. Candidates learn to contextualize teaching and to draw upon representations from the students' own experiences and knowledge. They learn how to challenge students toward cognitive complexity and engage all students, including students with exceptionalities, through instructional conversation. Candidates and faculty review assessment data that provide information about candidates' ability to work with all students and develop a plan for improving their practice in this area. (NCATE, 2002, p. 29)

NCTM

Equity Principle

Equity in mathematics education requires equity—high expectations and strong support for all students. (NCTM, 2000, p. 12)

Elementary and Middle School Mathematics by John Van de Walle

Chapter 7 provides information on the types of diversity one is likely to encounter and strategies for supporting those learners.

8.1 Observation: One Child's Experience

The purpose of this observation is to focus on one child who has a special need (e.g., gifted, LD, ELL) and observe his or her learning in a lesson. You will have to communicate with the teacher about the purpose of the observation and have him or her assist in selecting the student. Also, you will need to be careful that in observing the student, you do not make him or her feel uncomfortable. Use the template below to record notes.

Focus Area	Evidence of Accommodations or Modifications	My Additional Ideas
Physical Environment • Desk arrangement • Placement of student • Bulletin boards, displays • Posters • Accessibility of tools		
Instructional Strategies • Explanation of the task • Building on prior knowledge • Use of manipulatives, models, visuals • Use of overheads and whiteboard to write/illustrate		
Classroom Discourse • Asking students to clarify thinking • Student–student and student–teacher communication • Different student approaches to problem • Involving all students in the task and discussion		
High Expectations • Goals of the lesson for each child • Task completion expectations • Support (hints, tools, etc.) offered to students		

Postobservation Reflection

For each of these questions, you are responding in relation to the one student you observed.

1. Describe the specific learning needs of this student.

2. What struggles did this student encounter in the lesson (language was difficult, lesson wasn't challenging, etc.)?

3. What structures or strategies were in place that seemed to best support this child's learning?

4. What additional strategies or ideas do you feel would have enhanced the learning for this child?

8.2 Teacher Interview: Student Diversity

The purpose of this interview is to learn about the individuals in a classroom. It is recommended that you always find out this information prior to planning and teaching so that you can create a lesson that meets the specific needs of the learners in the classroom.

Who is in your class?	Ask the teacher to share 1–3 strategies and/or activities that she or he uses to make mathematics accessible and meaningful to students for each category in this table.

Gender
   Number of Females: _____
   Number of Males: _____	

Special Needs In this box, list any special needs that are represented in your class and how many of each there are (e.g., learning disabled, gifted, sight impaired)	
Culture/Ethnic Group In this box, list the different culture/ethnic groups that are represented in your class and how many of each there are.	
Language How many of your students are English Language Learners (ELL):	
Performance How many of your students are performing Below grade level? _____ Above grade level? _____	

Additional Interview Questions

1. What community and family characteristics impact your planning and teaching of mathematics?

2. What district/school/classroom issues impact your students' math learning (e.g., time allotted to study math, ability grouping)?

3. In general, what strategies do you use to meet the needs of the diverse learners in your classroom? (How do you plan a lesson to meet the needs of every child?)

8.3 Teacher Interview: Environment and Students

Ask a classroom teacher if you may interview him or her about how they use knowledge of students, family, and community to make decisions for their math teaching.

A classroom environment that nurtures all learners reflects both the best practices in teaching mathematics *and* the needs of the specific learners. As the NCTM Equity Principle states, we must have "High expectations and strong support for all students." Here you will design five questions to ask a classroom teacher, so that you will learn about how he or she develops an environment with high expectations that supports all learners. This might include, but is not limited to, cultural and/or linguistic background, involving families learning styles, learning differences, personalities, skills/ backgrounds, local community interests/events, interests of individual students, and seasonal considerations.

Interview Questions	Teacher Response
1.	
2.	
3.	
4.	
5.	
Other:	

Summary

After completing your interview, describe how you believe the teacher keeps expectations high and supports all learners. How does the teacher use the backgrounds and interests of her or his students? Offer suggestions of your own that you would try to incorporate if you were the teacher of this particular classroom.

8.4 Teaching: Lesson Adaptations

The purpose of this experience is for you to apply what you know about students, what you know about adaptations for various special needs, and your knowledge of mathematics teaching. Adaptations include both accommodations and modifications. Accommodations are strategies you use to help a student learn (e.g., showcasing key vocabulary, putting a child in a particular seat, pairing a child with a certain student). Modifications are changes to the lesson itself (e.g., altering the objectives, changing the activity).

In this task, you will develop accommodations and/or modifications that directly relate to the learners in the classroom that you would be teaching and then teach the lesson. The following steps are offered as a suggested approach:

1. Complete the Student Diversity sheet (see p. 75) or use your own form for finding out what the special needs are within your classroom.
2. Select a task and plan a lesson for the class, or use one of the extended lessons available in this guide.
3. Review you student diversity sheet and for each child, list the strategies you will use to make the lesson accessible to him or her.
4. Teach the lesson.
5. Complete the reflection on Meeting Individual's Needs (p. 81).

Title of Lesson: _____

Mathematics Topic in the Lesson: _____

Name of Student	Description of Special Need	Accommodations or Modifications

8.5 Teaching: Sheltering a Lesson for English Language Learners

The purpose of this field experience is for you to identify and incorporate those instructional strategies that can support an English language learner (ELL). In Chapter 7 of *Elementary and Middle School Mathematics*, you will find a description of the following ways to support the ELL:

1. Write and state the content and language objectives
2. Build background
3. Encourage use of native language
4. Comprehensible input
5. Explicitly teach vocabulary
6. Use cooperative groups

In addition, Chapter 5 of *Elementary and Middle School Mathematics* has lesson planning suggestions for ELLs.

For this experience you are going to take an existing lesson from a textbook or teacher resource (you can also use one of the Expanded Lessons in this guide) and "shelter" it. That means that you will take each component of the lesson (the objectives, the before, during, and after, and the assessment) and determine the accommodations or modifications you would make (see Table 5.1 of *Elementary and Middle School Mathematics* for specific guiding questions. If you have access to a classroom with English language learners, discuss with the teacher their level of language proficiency so that the adaptations you are making fit the needs of those specific students.

Use this page to record any accommodations or modifications to the lesson you selected. Attach this cover page to that lesson.

Lesson	Accommodations/Modifications for English Language Learners
Mathematics goals	
Thinking about the students	
Materials and preparation	
Lesson Plan	
Before	
During	
After	
Assessment	

What instructional strategies are already embedded in the lesson that will support the English language learner?

1.

2.

3.

4.

5.

8.6 Reflection: Meeting the Needs of Individuals

Complete this reflection after teaching a lesson. This could be a lesson you developed for 8.3 or 8.4, or any other lesson.

1. Did all students learn the mathematics you identified in your objectives? How do you know?

2. What instructional strategies enabled your diverse students to be successful? Respond with specific strategies for each type of diversity.

3. In what ways did student interaction support the learning of all students (grouping, discussions, etc.)?

4. The NCTM Equity Principle states that we need high expectations and strong support for all students.
   a. In what ways did your lesson goals and instructional strategies communicate high expectations?

   b. In what ways did your lesson goals and instructional strategies provide strong support (without lowering expectations)?

Bibliography

National Council for Accreditation of Teacher Education. (2002). *Professional Standards for the Accreditation of Schools, Colleges, and Departments of Education.* Washington, DC: NCATE.

National Center for Educational Statistics. (2003). *National Assessment of Educational Progress,* http://nces.ed.gov/nationsreportcard.

National Council of Teachers of Mathematics. (1991). *Professional Standards for Teaching Mathematics.* Reston, VA: NCTM.

National Council of Teachers of Mathematics. (2002). *Professional Standards for School Mathematics.* Reston, VA: NCTM.

part **II**

Resources for Teaching

In this section, we offer various lessons and tasks that can be used with the field experience activities in Part I or on their own. They are organized into three categories: Expanded Lessons, Mathematics Tasks, and Balanced Assessment Items. Consult *Elementary and Middle School Mathematics*, Chapter 9, "Planning in the Problem-Based Classroom," for additional support.

Expanded Lessons (prepared by John A. Van de Walle)

In this section, you will find detailed lesson plans that span each grade band and each content area. These provide substantial support in planning, though the preservice teacher will need to adapt the lesson to the particular classroom based on students' backgrounds and interests. These expanded lessons can be used with various experiences outlined in Part I of this Field Experience Guide.

Mathematics Tasks

These tasks have been selected because they have the potential for teaching important mathematical concepts, but planning the details is left to the preservice teacher. A brief overview of the lesson is provided as a starting point for planning. This is what often happens in teaching—you are handed an activity and then you determine how to use it with students. If you just hand it out and collect it, you aren't going to see the learning that you will if you carefully plan how you will organize the *before*, *during*, and *after* components of the lesson. Part I, Experience 2.5, provides a lesson plan format that can guide the planning process.

Tasks from Balanced Assessment

These are detailed mathematics tasks that include scoring rubrics and sample solutions that have been scored. These items are intended to assist preservice teachers in learning to assess student learning. Like the Mathematics Tasks, the preservice teacher will also need to plan the lesson in which these tasks are used.

All Three Types of Lessons: Accommodations and Modifications

Classrooms are diverse. Learners can differ in skills, rates of learning, language proficiency, abilities to abstract, physical abilities, sociability, motivation, as well as prior knowledge. For each lesson or mathematics task, think about ways to differentiate the task to meet the needs of each of the diverse learners in the classroom.

PART II RESOURCES ORGANIZED BY CONTENT

ACTIVITY	STRAND/CONCEPT	K–2	3–5	6–8
Whole Number				
9.1 Exploring Subtraction Strategies	Subtraction strategies	E		
9.2 Close, Far, and in Between	Number sense, relative magnitude of numbers		E	
9.3 Two-More-Than/Two-Less-Than	Two more and two less	E		
9.4 Learning About Division	Repeated subtraction/division	E		
9.5 Estimating Groups of Tens and Ones	Place value and estimation to 100	E		
10.1 The Find!	Counting strategies/skip-counting	T		
10.2 Odd or Even?	Patterns in numbers	T		
10.3 Factor Quest	Factors		T	
10.4 Interference	Least common multiples			T
10.5 Target Number	Exponents, order of operation, operation sense			T
11.1 Magic Age Rings	Order of operations		BA	
Rational Number				
9.6 Dot Paper Equivalencies	Equivalent fractions	E		
9.7 Multiplication of Fractions	Multiplying fractions		E	
9.8 Friendly Fractions to Decimals	Converting fractions and decimals		E	E
9.9 Division of Fractions Using the Partition Concept	Division of fractions			E
9.10 How Close Is Close?	Density of rational numbers; multiple representations			E
9.11 Comparing Ratios	Proportional reasoning			E
10.6 Fraction Find	Finding fractions between two fractions		T	
10.7 Illustrating Ratios	Ratios in tables and graphs		T	
Algebraic Thinking				
9.12 One Up and One Down: Addition	Number patterns in addition	E		
9.13 Predict How Many	Growing patterns		E	
9.14 Create a Journey Story	Interpreting graphs			E
10.8 Building Bridges	Building, extending and generalizing growing patterns		T	
10.9 Compensation Decision	Comparing linear and exponential growth			T
10.10 Solving the Mystery	Using symbolic manipulation to find equivalencies			T
11.2 Grocery Store	Creating mathematical model (equation) to represent a situation			BA
Measurement				
9.15 Crooked Paths	Measuring length of nonstraight lines	E		
9.16 Fixed Areas	Contrasting area and perimeter		E	E
10.11 Cover All	Estimating and finding area using square tiles		T	
11.3 Bolts and Nuts!	Measuring length and analyzing patterns in tables		BA	
Geometry				
9.17 Shape Sorts	Sorting shapes by different characteristics	E		
9.18 Diagonal Strips	Properties of diagonals of quadrilaterals		E	
9.19 Triangle Midsegments	Exploring properties of triangles			E
Data Analysis and Probability				
9.20 Using Data to Answer Our Questions	Creating a survey and representing results in a bar graph	E		
9.21 Create a Game	Equally likely events	E		
9.22 Bar Graphs to Pie Graphs	Creating bar graphs, interpreting graphs		E	
9.23 Testing Bag Designs	Probability of simple event		E	
9.24 Toying with Measures	Impact of outliers on the measures of central tendency			E

9 Expanded Lessons

EXPANDED LESSON 9.1

Exploring Subtraction Strategies

Grade Level: Second or third grade.

Mathematics Goals

- To develop flexible strategies for subtracting two-digit numbers with an emphasis on adding-up methods.
- To promote the use of tens in computational strategies.

Thinking About the Students

The students have been working on a variety of invented strategies for adding two-digit numbers. It is not necessary that this skill be mastered before beginning subtraction. This lesson may or may not be the first subtraction lesson. The assumption is that students have not been taught the traditional algorithms for addition or subtraction.

Materials and Preparation

Prepare two story problems either on a transparency or duplicate on a sheet of paper. If duplicated, leave half of the page for each problem.

LESSON

Before
The Task

- Provide students with two story problems either on paper or on the overhead. Here are two possibilities:

    David's book has 72 pages. He has already read 35 pages. How many more pages does David have to read to finish his book?

    Tara keeps her books on two bookshelves. She has 24 books in all. On the top shelf she has 16 books. How many books does Tara have on the bottom shelf?

    Students are to solve each problem using any method that they want.

Brainstorm

- Read the first problem together with the students. Have them think how they would go about solving the problem. What would they do first?
- Give students some time to think of a way to solve the problem and then call on several students to share their ideas. Try to elicit some details. For example, if a student says, "I would start with 35 and add up to 72," ask what she would add on first. You want to give students who do not know where to begin some good ideas. Ask other students if they would begin differently. It is not sufficient to say, "I would subtract." If students use a take-away strategy or even a counting-by-ones approach, that is okay. Do not force any method.

Establish Expectations

- Students are to show how they solved each problem. They should provide enough information so that if someone picked up their paper they would be able to tell how they got the answers. Remind students that they will be sharing their ideas with the class.

During

- Monitor students' work. For students who are stuck, ask them to tell you what ideas they have thought about. Try to make a suggestion that builds on the student's ideas. For example, if the student says, "I want to take 35 from 72," you might suggest that the student try taking away 10 at a time. After making a suggestion, walk away. Do not be overly guiding.

- Watch for students who solve the problem but have not written enough to explain their solution. Ask them about their method and then require them to write some more to explain what they have just told you. You may have to help some students with ways to record their ideas.
- Do not correct students who have made errors.
- Watch for students to share their methods. If usually reluctant students have a solution, advise them that you may call on them to share their ideas.
- Challenge early finishers with a three-digit problem: 314 – 197.

After

- When all students have completed their work, ask for answers to the first problem. Record these on the board. Pick one of the answers and ask, *Who got this answer?* Select a student to share his or her method.
- As the students explain their thinking, try to record their process on the board. Avoid aligning the two numbers vertically as in the traditional algorithm. One good strategy is to use a blank number line. As students explain what they did, you can indicate each portion on the number line, recording each jump as they explain. For example, suppose that a student starts with 35 and adds 10 and 10 and 10 (to get to 65), then adds 5 (to get to 70), and then 2 more. Your record on the board may look like this:

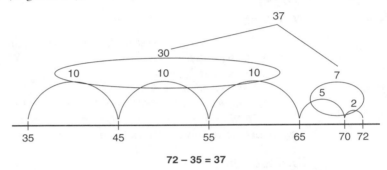

72 – 35 = 37

- For each jump on the number line, indicate the size of the jump. For adding-up strategies, the answer will usually be the sum of the jumps. For take-away strategies, the answer will be where the jumps end.
- When more than one answer has been offered, be sure to have a method shared for each answer. By asking the class if they agree with, understand, or have questions for the student who is sharing, the responsibility for deciding what is correct falls to the class, not you. In any case, try to get several solution methods for the problem.
- Have students share their solution strategies for the second problem in a similar manner.

NEXT STEPS

Assessment Notes

- Watch for students who are solving these problems by counting by ones. Some may even count both numbers by ones rather than count on. Others may make tallies or use counters for the larger number and then mark off or remove the subtrahend.
- Try to keep track of students who are using a take-away method and those who use an adding-on approach. For some problems, take-away strategies are often more difficult.

EXPANDED LESSON 9.2

Close, Far, and in Between

Grade Level: Third or fourth grade.

Mathematics Goals

- To develop number sense through thinking about relative magnitude of numbers.
- To develop strategies for mental mathematics.

Thinking About the Students

Students should have had experience pulling smaller numbers apart to do addition and subtraction (e.g.,

to add 18 and 25, they can think, "Take two away from 25 and add that to 18 to get 20. 20 + 23 is 43"). That is, students are familiar with using 5 and 10 as benchmarks. Students are also familiar with using a number line.

Materials and Preparation

- There are no materials to prepare for this lesson.
- You will need to think ahead of time about the numbers that you will use. (See "The Task.")

LESSON

Before

Begin with a simpler version of the task:

- On the chalkboard or overhead, write the numbers 27, 83, and 62.
- Draw a number line on the chalkboard or overhead and label the points for 0 and 100. Ask a student to come forward and place one of the numbers on the number line and explain why he or she placed the number in that location. Ask the class if they agree or disagree with the placement and the reasoning. Discuss as needed. Repeat this process for the other two numbers.
- Ask questions such as these: *Which number is closest to 50? Which two numbers are closest? How far apart are 27 and 100, 62 and 100, and 83 and 100?* With each question, give students time to think individually. Then ask students to share their ideas and strategies for doing these comparisons. The methods that they use will be quite varied. Therefore, do not stop with the ideas from just a single student. Look for students who are breaking numbers apart and using tens rather than simply subtracting numbers to find the difference.

The Task

You will need to decide on three numbers for students to compare. The numbers can be chosen purposefully to either assess the understanding of a particular idea or to increase the likelihood that students will grapple with a particular idea or strategy. For example, if students have not yet explicitly used the notion of using hundreds as a benchmark, the numbers chosen might be 298, 402, and 318. Because 298 is so close to 300 and 402 is so close to 400, at least some students will use this idea to compare 298 and 402 to each other and the third number. For this lesson, we will use 219, 457, and 364.

Write the numbers 219, 457, and 364 on the board along with the following:

The task is to answer these questions:
- Which two are closest? Why?
- Which is closest to 300? To 250?
- About how far apart are 219 and 500? 219 and 5000?

Establish Expectations

Students are to explain how they answered the questions using words, numbers, and/or a number line, so that they can remember what they did and be ready to discuss their ideas with the class.

During

- For students who are having difficulty getting started, suggest that they use the number line as an aid to identify benchmarks such as 200 or 450. Once the students have identified possible benchmarks, ask them how they might use a benchmark to get closer to one of the numbers. Give no more assistance than is absolutely necessary to get students started.
- Look for different strategies students are using so that you can highlight the variety of ways to think about comparing numbers.
- For students who finish quickly, ask them questions about finding particular multiples between given numbers (e.g., *Name a multiple of 25 between 219 and 364*).

After

- Ask students to share their strategies for responding to each question. Record ideas on the board in a manner that illustrates students' thinking.
- As students share, you might have to ask questions to either slow down a student's explanation so that classmates have a chance to process the ideas or to make explicit a subtle idea that you want students to think about.
- Do not evaluate the strategy but ask students if they agree and understand the strategy and if they have questions. Allow other students to offer ideas for the same question.
- As new strategies emerge, ask students to compare and contrast them to strategies already shared. The discussion might pertain to which strategies seem quicker or more efficient and why or how various strategies use the notion of place value and/or benchmarks.

NEXT STEPS

Assessment Notes

- Look for students who are simply counting up or down by ones to determine how far away numbers are from each other. They likely need more work with using 5 and 10 (which includes multiples of 5 and 10) as benchmarks to move between numbers.
- Are students using a variety of strategies depending on the numbers or do they always use the same strategy? Being able to develop and use different strategies is evidence of number sense as well as the ability to think flexibly.
- Many students will simply subtract numbers with pencil and paper. Encourage them to find methods that do not involve subtraction.

EXPANDED LESSON 9.3

Two-More-Than/Two-Less-Than

Grade Level: Late kindergarten or early first grade.

- Mathematics Goals
- To help students develop the paired relationships of two-more-than and two-less-than for numbers to 12.
- To provide continued exposure to patterned sets with the goal of instant recognition.

Thinking About the Students

Students must be able to count a set accurately and understand that counting tells how many. They may or may not be able to recognize patterned sets or be able to count on and count back from a given number. For those students still having difficulty match-

ing the correct numeral and set, the written component of the activity can be omitted.

Materials and Preparation

- This will be a station activity. (Alternatively, students can do the activity at their seats.) Each student doing the activity at the same time will need the materials described.
- Place four dot cards, showing 3 to 10 dots each, in a plastic bag.
- Each bag should also have at least 12 counters and a crayon or pencil.
- Make one two-sided recording sheet for each student. The backside of the sheet is the same as the front except that it says "2 Less Than" at the top. (See the Blackline Masters 60 and 61.)

LESSON

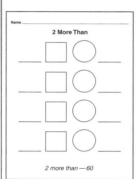

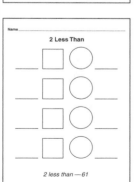

Before
The Task

- For each dot card, the task is to make a set that has two more counters than dots on the card. Similarly, students will make sets that have two fewer counters than dots on the card. The task is completed with the counters.

Establish Expectations

- Show the class (or a small group) a bag of cards and counters. Empty the counters and select one card. Have a student count the dots on the card. Have a second student use counters on the overhead (or on the carpet, if in a circle setting). Say: *Make a set that has two more counters than dots on this card.*
- Discuss with the students how they can decide if the set is actually two more. Accept students' ideas and try them. For example, they might say: *Count each set. Set a counter aside for each dot. Make the counters into a pattern that is the same as on the dot card.*
- Show students the recording sheet. Point out the words "2 More Than" and "2 Less Than" on the top. Explain that they will record their two-more-than sets on the 2 More Than side. Demonstrate how to first draw the same number of dots as are on the dot card. Next show how to draw dots in the oval to show the number of counters that they made for their two-more-than set. Beside each set they should write the corresponding number.
- If students are ready, have them tell how they think the 2 LESS THAN side should be completed. (You may choose to do only one side of the sheet at a time.)
- Explain that bags with counters and dots will be at stations. (Or pass out bags at this time to each student.) Bags will be different, so each student's paper will also be different.

During

- Observe the methods that students use to count the dots on the cards and to create their sets.

- Challenge students to explain how they know their set is correct. Focus on the actual counters and dot cards rather than on the record sheet because that is less important.
- Challenge task for capable students: Make sets and record numbers for sets that are 10-more-than the given sets. Look for understanding of the teen numbers.

After (when all students have completed the station)

- Show students a sheet of paper with 6 dots in a patterned arrangement. Ask: *How many dots? How can we tell how many are two more than this?* Students' suggestions should be tied to the methods they used in the activity. Some students may know immediately that 8 is two-more-than 6. Begin with students who are likely to be still developing this idea. Have different students explain how they did the activity.

NEXT STEPS

Assessment Notes

- How do students count or know how many dots are on the cards? Do they recognize patterned sets or do they count each dot? Which patterns do they know?
- How do students create their two-more-than sets? Is there indication of the two-more-than relationship developing or being already developed? If students are working on both sides of the paper, look for similar two-less-than concepts.
- Look for ease or difficulty in recording. Do students correctly write numerals with sets?

EXPANDED LESSON 9.4

Learning About Division

Grade Level: Late third grade, early fourth grade.

Mathematics Goals

- To develop the measurement (repeated subtraction) concept of division.
- To connect this concept of division to multiplication and addition.

Thinking About the Students

Students have explored multiplication concepts, but it is not necessary that they have mastered multiplication facts. This lesson could be used as an introduction to division. For students who have been exposed to division, the lesson can further develop early ideas and help connect the ideas to contextual situations.

Materials and Preparation

- Students will each need about 35 counters.
- If possible, provide students with small paper cups or portion cups that will hold at least 6 counters. Alternatively, students can stack counters in piles.

LESSON

Before

Begin with a simpler version of the task:

- Draw 13 dots on the board. Ask: *How many sets of 3 dots can we make if we have 13 to work with? How many will be left over?* Most students should be able to answer this question mentally. After receiving several answers, have a student come to the board and demonstrate how to verify the answer of 4 sets of 3 and 1 left.
- Ask: *What equation could we write for what we have on the board?* Accept students' ideas. Correct ideas include:
  - $3 + 3 + 3 + 3 + 1 = 13$
  - $4 \times 3 + 1 = 13$ ($3 \times 4 + 1$ technically represents 3 sets of 4 and 1 more.)
  - $13 \div 3 = 4 \text{ R } 1$

  Note: If this is the introduction to division symbolism, you may want to use 12 instead of 13 so that there are no remainders. However, it is also okay to begin this way.
- Say: *Think of a situation in which someone might have 13 things and wants to find out how many sets of 3. Make up a story problem about your situation.* Have several students share their story problem.

The Task

- Begin with a set of 31 counters. Use the counters to see how many sets of 4 you can make. Repeat with a set of 27 counters and find out how many sets of 6 you can make.

Establish Expectations

- Write the directions on the board:
  - 31 counters—how many sets of 4?
  - 27 counters—how many sets of 6?
- Explain (and record on the board) that for each of these tasks students are to:
  - Write three equations: one addition, one multiplication, and one division.
  - Write a story problem to go with their division equation.

During

- Ask students to explain why their equations go with what they did with the counters. Do not correct incorrect equations or story problems. You only want to be sure students are attempting to connect the activity with the symbolism and the stories.

- Challenge early finishers to see if they can do the same thing for a set of 125 things in piles of 20. However, they will have to figure it out without using counters.

After

- For 31 counters in sets of 4, ask how many sets and how many are left over. Most students should agree that there are 7 sets and 3 left over. Draw a picture that looks similar to those you have seen on students' papers.
- Have a number of students share their equations. After several equations are on the board, ask those who have different equations to share theirs as well.
- Have students explain how their equations match what was done with the counters. If students disagree, have them politely explain their reasoning. Students should be comfortable with their ideas about the multiplication and addition equations. For an introductory lesson on division, you should correct any misunderstandings about the division equation and what it means.
- Have several students share their story problems. Students should explain how the story situation matches the action of finding how many sets of 4 in 31. For example: "There were 31 apples in the basket. If each apple tart requires 4 apples, how many tarts can be made?"
- If time permits, repeat with the $27 \div 6$ situation.

NEXT STEPS

Assessment Notes

- The key idea in this lesson is the connection between the action of finding how many equal sets in a given quantity, and the manner in which a multiplication equation and a division equation are connected to this action. Look for evidence that this idea is clear to students. Do not be overly concerned about the use of 4×7 instead of 7×4.
- Story problems should indicate the action of measuring sets of 4 rather than creating four sets, a sharing or partition concept. If students make this error, simply have them discuss whether or not the story fits well with the action. Do not indicate that the story is incorrect. It is also possible that students will create multiplication stories (31 being the unknown amount). Here ask students which equation best represents the problem.

EXPANDED LESSON 9.5

Estimating Groups of Tens and Ones

Grade Level: Late first or second grade.

Mathematics Goals

- To connect a count-by-ones understanding to a count based on the number of groups of 10 and leftovers for quantities to 100.
- To provide opportunities to measure lengths using nonstandard measures.

Thinking About the Students

Students have not yet developed a full understanding of two-digit numbers in terms of tens and ones. They are able to count a collection of objects to 100. They have talked about numbers in terms of bunches of tens and have discussed number patterns on the hundreds chart.

Materials and Preparation

- Decide on about 8 lengths for the students to measure. All lengths must be such that students can place measuring units end-to-end along the full length. Vertical distances can be measured with Unifix cubes or other snap cubes that can easily be made into a long bar.
- For each length, make a corresponding measurement "kit." Each kit should have more than enough individual units to measure the length it is paired with. Also, for each kit prepare 10 connected units, for example, a bar of 10 Unifix cubes, a chain of 10 paper clips, or 10 toothpicks sandwiched between two pieces of transparent tape.

For Unit	Use Lengths
Unifix	2 to $5\frac{1}{2}$ feet (60 cm to 180 cm)
Small paper clips	2 to 9 feet (60 cm to 270 cm)
Large paper clips	3 to 12 feet (90 cm to 4 m)
Toothpicks	5 to 12 feet (1.8 m to 4 m)

- A transparency of the recording sheet and a copy for each student. (See the Blackline Master 62.)
- A kit of units that can be used in the BEFORE portion of the lesson.

LESSON

Before

Begin with a simpler version of the task:

- Decide on a unit of length, such as Unifix cubes. Show students a length that is somewhere between 25 and 45 units long. For example, you might use the edge of a teacher's desk, a length of ribbon or rope, or a poster set on the chalk tray.
- Explain that you want to make an estimate of how long it is in terms of Unifix cubes. Accept some estimates. Expect students' guesses to be quite varied. Then suggest that it might be helpful to estimate in terms of groups of 10 units and leftovers. Show students a bar of 10 Unifix (or 10 of whatever unit you are using).
- Hold the 10 units at one end of the length to be measured and accept students' new estimates. Write the first child's estimate in the blank on the transparency. Explain that an *estimate* is what you think it might be by looking at the 10 units. It is not just a wild guess.
- Pass out the recording sheets and have students record their own estimate in the first box. Ask several students what their estimates are.
- Have two students use individual units to measure the length. It is important that they line units along the entire length so that when they have finished they will have as many actual units as required for the measure. Have two students put the units into groups of 10. Count the groups of 10 and count any leftovers separately. Record this in blanks labeled "Actual" on the recording sheet transparency and have students do likewise on their papers.
- Finally, ask students how many units there are. Have the class count the entire group by ones as you set them aside or point to each. Write the number word and the number (e.g., *thirty-four 34*) on the transparency. Have students record on their papers.

The Task

- For each length and corresponding unit, students are to see how good an estimate of the length they can make in terms of groups of 10 and leftovers.
- They then check their estimates by actually measuring, making, and counting groups of 10 and leftovers and, finally, counting all of the units.

Establish Expectations

- Explain that there are measuring kits and a length for each kit. For each length, students are to:
  - Hold the 10 units at one end of the length and estimate the measure of the length in terms of 10 and leftovers. Each student should record his or her estimate on the recording sheet. They may want to do this step independently to see who is the better estimator.
  - They are then to measure the lengths by using units—laying them end to end.
  - When they have placed units along the full length, they should make sets of 10. They count and record the number of groups of 10 and leftovers.
  - Finally, they should count all of the units and record this as a number word and as a number. Refer to your example.
- Students are only to measure three different lengths. As long as they use the kit that goes with the length, it does not make any difference which lengths they measure.

During

- Be sure that students are making and recording estimates by comparing the length to the provided strip of 10. They are not to change their estimates.
- Pay attention to how students count the total number of units. Some may already know that 4 tens and 6 leftovers is 46. However, most should probably be counting the total by ones. Challenge students who just count groups: *Are you sure you will get 46 if you count them all by ones?*

After

When all students have completed at least three estimates and measures, discuss what it means to estimate—it is not the same as a guess. Ask: *How did using a group of ten units help you make an estimate? How does counting the groups of tens and leftovers help tell you how many units you had?* This last question is the key to this lesson. Avoid telling students how to relate the groups and leftovers to the actual number.

NEXT STEPS

Assessment Notes

- Look for students who do not make connections between the groups and leftovers, and the actual counts. These students have not yet developed base-ten concepts.
- Students who confidently state the total when they have the number of groups and leftovers have indicated at least a beginning understanding of base-ten concepts.

EXPANDED LESSON 9.6

Dot Paper Equivalencies

Grade Level: Third or fourth grade.

Mathematics Goals

• To develop a conceptual understanding of equivalent fractions; the same quantity can have different fraction names.
• To look for patterns in equivalent fractions.

Thinking About the Students

Students should have a good understanding of what the top and bottom numbers (numerator and de-

nominator) in a fraction stand for. Although this is an early activity in developing equivalent fraction concepts, it is probably not the best first activity.

Materials Preparation

• A transparency of a centimeter dot grid (Blackline Master 35).
• Copies of the "Fraction Names" worksheet for each student (Blackline Master 63) plus a transparency for use in the AFTER portion of the lesson.

LESSON

Before

Begin with a simpler version of the task:

• On the dot transparency outline a 3 by 3 rectangle and shade in $\frac{2}{3}$ of it as shown here.

• Tell this story: *Two students looked at this picture. Each saw a different fraction. Kyle saw $\frac{6}{9}$, but Terri said she saw $\frac{2}{3}$. Ask: How can they see the same drawing and yet each see different fractions? Which one is right? Why?*
• Have students come to the front of the class and offer explanations for how Kyle saw the picture and how Terri saw it. When students in the class agree on and also understand a correct explanation, draw the corresponding unit fraction to aid in understanding. For example, you can explain: *Terri saw a row of three squares as $\frac{1}{3}$.* (Draw a row of 3 squares to the side of the rectangle.) *If a row of 3 squares is $\frac{1}{3}$, then there are two rows of three squares shaded. Therefore, the shaded portion is $\frac{2}{3}$.* Similarly, be sure that students see that one square is $\frac{1}{9}$ of the whole. *Since there are 6 squares shaded, the shaded part is $\frac{6}{9}$.*

The Task

• For each outlined region on the worksheet, find as many fraction names as possible.

Establish Expectations

• For each fraction name, students draw a picture of a fractional part and use words to tell how they found that fraction name for the shaded portion.

During

• For students who are having difficulty getting started, draw a fractional part for them. For example, for 1, draw a two-square rectangle. Ask: *How many rectangles like this make up the whole?* Try not to give more assistance than is absolutely necessary to get students on track.
• Students who do not seem to understand counting the fractional parts may need more development of the meaning of top and bottom numbers.
• For students who seem to have finished quickly, make sure first that their explanations reflect their capabilities. Also, consider challenging them to find even more names. In number 2, for example, a small triangle can be used as a unit to produce $\frac{12}{24}$.

After

- Use a transparency of the worksheet to help students share their ideas. For each drawing on the worksheet, first make a list of all of the fraction names that students have found for the shaded region. Record these on the board without comment even if some are incorrect. Then have students explain how they got the fractions. Let one student explain one fraction, not all of them. Be sure students all agree and understand. For some explanations, other students may have used a differently shaped unit fraction. For example, in the first drawing, four squares make $\frac{1}{6}$ and can be used to name the shaded region as $\frac{4}{6}$. Some students may have used a column of four squares and others a 2-by-2 arrangement of four squares. Although completely the same, students should be allowed to discuss this.
- The first region can be named $\frac{2}{3}$, $\frac{4}{6}$, $\frac{8}{12}$, and $\frac{16}{24}$. Of course, a 1-by-1 square could be halved to produce $\frac{32}{48}$. Also, note that three squares is $\frac{1}{8}$ of the whole. Can the shaded region be named with eighths? Yes! The shaded region contains $5\frac{1}{3}$ eighths; $5\frac{1}{3}$ in the numerator. It is unlikely that students will think of this.
- The second region can be named $\frac{1}{2}$, $\frac{2}{4}$, $\frac{3}{6}$, and $\frac{6}{12}$. If a small triangle is used, it can be seen as $\frac{12}{24}$. If a trapezoid of three triangles is used, it is $\frac{4}{8}$. Students may divide it up in other ways as well.
- The last region also has lots of names from $\frac{1}{4}$ to $\frac{8}{32}$.
- If time permits, you may want to focus attention on all of the names for one region and discuss any patterns that students may observe.

NEXT STEPS

Assessment Notes

- The issue of greatest concern will be the students who, even after marking off an appropriate unit fraction, cannot correctly name the shaded portion. For example, in the third figure, if the full shaded region is used as the unit (fourths), some students may write $\frac{1}{3}$ (1 region to 3 regions) or in other ways still not know how to name the fraction. These students will need further foundational work with fraction concepts.
- Do not be concerned if students do not find all of the fraction names that are possible. The goal is not to exhaust the possibilities but to develop the understanding that a given quantity can have multiple names.
- For students who seem to find this activity easy, see if they can generate other fraction names for these regions by looking at the fractions they have already found and seeing if they can discover a rule for generating more.

EXPANDED LESSON 9.7

Multiplication of Fractions

Grade Level: Fourth grade.

Mathematics Goals

- To develop the meaning of multiplication of fractions through informal explorations.
- To emphasize that a fraction is connected to a particular whole and that the whole can change in a context.

Thinking About the Students

Students understand that multiplication can be thought of as repeated addition; that is, 3 × 6 means 3 sets of 6. They understand that in the context of part-whole fractions, the whole is divided into equivalent parts. They also understand the symbolic notation of fractions; that is, they know what the top number in the fraction means (the number of parts) and what the bottom number in the fraction means (the kind of parts we are counting).

Materials and Preparation

Make copies of Blackline Master 64 for each student and also a transparency of 64.

LESSON

Before

Begin with a simpler version of the task:

- Ask students what 3 × 4 means. Have them either draw a picture or give a word problem to show what 3 × 4 means. Listen to students' ideas. Capitalize on ideas that emphasize that 3 × 4 means 3 groups of 4.
- Pose the following word problem to students: *There are 15 cars in Michael's toy car collection. Two-thirds of the cars are red. How many red cars does Michael have?*
- Encourage students to draw pictures not only to help them think about how to do the problem but also as a way to explain how they did the problem. Have students share their work with the class. Many students will draw 15 rectangles (cars) and then divide the 15 into three equal parts. At this point, make sure to have the students explain why they divided the 15 into three equal parts (e.g., looking for thirds because $\frac{2}{3}$ are red). Once they have three equal parts or thirds, they count two of those sets because they need $\frac{2}{3}$.
- Help students connect this situation with multiplication with whole numbers. Just as 3 × 4 means 3 groups of 4, $\frac{2}{3}$ × 15 means $\frac{2}{3}$ of a group of 15.

The Task

Students are to solve the problems on the worksheet and be ready to explain their thinking.

> You have $\frac{3}{4}$ of a pizza left. If you give $\frac{1}{3}$ of the leftover pizza to your brother, how much of a whole pizza will your brother get?
>
> Someone ate $\frac{1}{10}$ of the cake, leaving only $\frac{9}{10}$. If you eat $\frac{2}{3}$ of the cake that is left, how much of a whole cake will you have eaten?
>
> Gloria used $2\frac{1}{2}$ tubes of blue paint to paint the sky in her picture. Each tube holds $\frac{4}{5}$ ounce of paint. How many ounces of blue paint did Gloria use?

Establish Expectations

Students should use both words and pictures to help them think through the problems and to show how they solved them. They should be prepared to explain their thinking.

During

- Look for students who use different representations to think about the problems. Highlight those different ways in the "After" portion of the lesson.

- If students have difficulty getting started, have them represent the information in the first sentence of the task. Have them explain why their picture represents this information. Then have them read the first part of the "if" statement in the second sentence and identify what part of their original picture this statement refers to. Have them color the part they just identified with a different color to make it stand out. Now have them read the question at the end of the task and think about how the part they just colored can help them answer this question.
- For students ready for a challenge, pose the following task in which the pieces must be subdivided into smaller unit parts: *Zack had $\frac{2}{3}$ of the lawn to cut. After lunch, he cut $\frac{3}{4}$ of the grass he had left. How much of the whole lawn did Zack cut after lunch?*

After

- Starting with the first problem, ask a student to come to the board to explain his or her strategy for thinking about the problem. Ask questions about why the student drew what he or she did to make sure everyone in the class follows the rationale. Encourage the class to comment or ask questions about the student's representation or thinking.
- Help students make explicit what the whole is at each stage of the problem.
- Ask if others solved the problem in a different way. If so, have the students come forward to share their solutions.
- As students share their solutions, it is important to have them compare and contrast the different solutions. Some solutions that at first appear to be different are actually equivalent in many ways. Through questioning, help students make these connections.
- Help students connect fraction multiplication with the meaning of multiplication: $\frac{1}{3} \times \frac{3}{4}$ means $\frac{1}{3}$ of a group of $\frac{3}{4}$.

NEXT STEPS

Assessment Notes

- Look for students who struggle when the whole changes in the problem. They need more experience working with parts-and-whole tasks.
- Are students correctly using the meaning of the numerator and denominator? These problems are easily solved by thinking of the fractional parts as discrete units. For example, $\frac{2}{3}$ of $\frac{3}{4}$ is $\frac{2}{3}$ of three things called fourths.
- Are students answering the question that is being asked?

EXPANDED LESSON 9.8

Friendly Fractions to Decimals

Grade Level: Fourth or fifth grade.

Mathematics Goals

- To help students connect decimals and familiar fraction equivalents in a conceptual manner.
- To reinforce the notion of the 10-to-1 relationship between adjacent digits in our numeration system.

Thinking About the Students

Students are familiar with the 10-to-1 relationship between adjacent digits in our numeration system. They have worked with decimals and can add and subtract decimals somewhat successfully, but they appear to have at best a procedural understanding of the process. Students also understand the part-whole meaning of fractional parts and the meaning of the numerator and denominator in a fraction.

Materials and Preparation

- Provide each student with at least two sheets of 10 × 10 grids (see Blackline Master 27).
- Make a transparency of the 10 × 10 grid sheet to use in the before and after portions of the lesson.

LESSON

Before

Begin with a simpler version of the task:

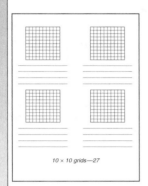

10 × 10 grids—27

- Write the number 34 on the board. Remind students that 34 is 3 tens and 4 ones. Ask students to describe 34 with tens and ones in other ways. As students suggest names such as 2 tens and 14 ones, focus on the 10-to-1 relationship between adjacent digits: A larger unit can be exchanged for 10 of the next smaller unit and vice versa.
- Ask students what it means to have $\frac{1}{10}$ of something. Highlight the idea that the whole is divided into 10 *equal* parts and $\frac{1}{10}$ means you have one of those parts. Showing students the 10 × 10 grid, ask them to shade $\frac{1}{10}$ of the grid. Ask students to share different ways to shade $\frac{1}{10}$ of the grid. It might be helpful to illustrate using base-ten materials as one way to think about this task (i.e., the flat hundreds piece is used as the whole and the long ten stick is then used as a tenth). Suggest to students how you could represent 1.3 with the base-ten materials (e.g., if the flat piece is the whole, one flat piece and three long pieces).

The Task

Using a 10 × 10 grid, for each of the following fractions determine the decimal equivalent and explain your reasoning.

$$\frac{3}{4} \qquad \frac{2}{3} \qquad \frac{3}{8}$$

Establish Expectations

Using the 10 × 10 grids, students should:
- Shade the fractional amount.
- Identify the decimal number that also represents this amount.
- Be prepared to explain their reasoning.

During

- Look for students who are shading their 10 × 10 grids differently. Highlight those different ways in the "After" portion of the lesson.
- If students have shaded their grid in a way that does not use long rows of ten, ask students how they would cover the area using strips and squares if they could use no more than nine tinies.
- The $\frac{3}{8}$ task is the most challenging. A useful hint is to ask students how they would find $\frac{1}{8}$ if they had $\frac{1}{4}$.

- You may need to remind students that as they need something smaller than the smallest square on the grid, that the next smaller pieces are tenths of the little squares. Since a small square is $\frac{1}{100}$, one-tenth of it would be $\frac{1}{1000}$ and half of it would be $\frac{5}{1000}$.

After

- Students are likely to shade their grids differently. It is important to compare and contrast between different shadings so that students see that they have shaded an equivalent amount. For example, for fourths, students might shade a 5 × 5 section (half of a half). Others may shade two and a half rows of ten. Ask students to determine how these both show one-fourth.
- For some shadings, it may be difficult for students to see the decimal equivalent. For example, when students shade a 5 × 5 section to show a fourth, it can be difficult for them to translate that representation into a decimal. You might focus students' attention to finding tenths within the 10 × 10 grid by looking at rows of 10. One way to help them think about this is to ask students how they would cover the area using strips and squares if they could use no more than nine tinies.

NEXT STEPS

Assessment Notes

- Some students will be very successful with shading equal parts but have difficulty connecting this to the decimal representation. As you suggest to them to use strips and tinies, make sure they can explain why they are using these groupings rather than, say, strips of 5.
- Students who are able to move quickly between the equal parts for fractions and the decimal equivalents in this task are ready to think about the decimal equivalent for one-third.

EXPANDED LESSON 9.9

Division of Fractions Using the Partition Concept

Grade Level: Fifth or sixth grade.

Mathematics Goals

- To develop the partitive meaning of division with fractions through informal explorations.
- To reinforce the partitive meaning of division.

Thinking About the Students

Students solved both partition and measurement problems with whole numbers. They understand the symbolic notation of fractions (i.e., they know what the top number in the fraction means—the number of parts—and what the bottom number in the fraction means—the kind of parts we are counting). The students can add fractions and find equivalent fractions.

Materials and Preparation

- Prepare a transparency with the problems in the lesson.

LESSON

Before

Begin with a simpler version of the task:

- Ask students how they would solve the following story problem if they did not know their multiplication facts:

    Marie bought 24 pieces of bubble gum to share among herself and her 3 friends. How many pieces of gum will each person get?

- Have them draw a picture or think about how they would act out the story to determine the answer. Listen to students' ideas. Capitalize on ideas that emphasize the sharing action in the problem.

The Task

- Students are to solve the following problems:

    Cassie has $5\frac{1}{4}$ yards of ribbon to make three bows for birthday packages. How much ribbon should she use for each bow if she wants to use the same length of ribbon for each?

    Mark has $1\frac{1}{4}$ hours to finish his three household chores. If he divides his time evenly, how much time can he spend on each?

Establish Expectations

- Students should draw pictures and have a written explanation for their solutions. They should also be prepared to explain their thinking. Before you come together as a class, have students explain their ideas to a partner.

During

- Be sure that students are drawing pictures to help them think about how to do the problems and explain their thinking.
- Look for students who use different representations to think about the problems. Highlight those different ways in the "after" portion of the lesson.
- For students who finish early, pose another problem to them in which the parts must be split into smaller parts (like the second problem in the task). For example, *Ryan has $6\frac{2}{3}$ yards of rope to hang 4 bird feeders. How much rope will he use for each feeder if he wants to use the same length of rope for each?*

After

- For each problem, first get answers from the class. If more than one answer is offered, simply record them and offer no evaluation.
- Have students come to the board to explain their strategies for thinking about the problem. You may need to ask questions about drawings or explanations to make sure everyone in the class follows the rationale. Encourage the class to comment or ask questions about the student's representation or thinking. Ask if others used a different representation or solved the problem in a different way. If so, have the students come forward to share their solutions. If there are different answers, the class should evaluate the solution strategies and decide which answer is correct and why.
- Discuss the different representations students use (e.g., some students use circles or rectangles, whereas others may use a number line) and how the action in the story is one of sharing.
- For problems that require the parts to be split into smaller parts, students will likely use different approaches. For example, for the second problem in the given task, some students will first divide the hour into thirds and then the quarter hour into twelfths, whereas other students will divide the $1\frac{1}{4}$ hours into twelfths and share the twelfths between the 3 hours. It is important to have students compare and contrast the different approaches. Some solutions that at first appear to be different are actually equivalent in many ways. Through questioning, help students make these connections.
- Help students notice that while they are answering these questions, they are also asking, "How much is in the whole?" or "How much for one?" This mode of thinking will help students when the divisor is a fraction because the sharing concept seems to break down at that point.

NEXT STEPS

Assessment Notes

- Are students using their understanding of the meaning of fractions to help them draw a representation or solve the problem in another way? Using the meaning of the fraction is imperative when the problem requires splitting the part into smaller parts.
- Look for students who struggle with identifying the whole. They need more experience working with part-and-whole tasks.

EXPANDED LESSON 9.10

How Close Is Close?

Grade Level: Seventh or eighth grade.

Mathematics Goals

- To develop the concept of density of the rational numbers.
- To reinforce the idea that fractions and decimal numbers are different symbolic notations for the same quantities.

Thinking About the Students

Students are skilled at finding equivalent fractions and at converting fractions to decimals.

Materials and Preparation

- Have available copies of 10×10 grids (see Blackline Master 27) for students who need them.
- Have a transparency of the 10×10 grid sheet available for the "after" portion of the lesson.

LESSON

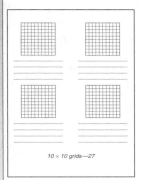

10 × 10 grids—27

Before

Begin with a simpler version of the task:

- Ask students to list four fractions between $\frac{1}{9}$ and $\frac{8}{9}$. This should be an easy task and should not require much, if any, discussion. Now ask students to find four fractions between $\frac{1}{2}$ and $\frac{9}{10}$. Have students share the fractions that they have identified and the strategies they used to find them. Resist telling students any method to use. The fractions $\frac{6}{10}$, $\frac{7}{10}$, and $\frac{8}{10}$ are easy to find; a fourth fraction may be a challenge if students are looking for fractions with common denominators. However $\frac{2}{3}$, $\frac{3}{4}$, $\frac{5}{6}$, $\frac{7}{8}$, and are among the many other possible solutions. Listen to and encourage the class to discuss students' ideas about approaches to finding the fourth fraction.

The Task

- As a class, select two fractions that students believe are "really close." The task is to find 10 fractions that are between the two that the class decides on.

Establish Expectations

- Students can use any method they wish to find their fractions, but they have to be able to explain their methods and defend their results.

During

- Look for students who are identifying fractions using various strategies. Possible strategies include:
  - Trying different fractions without a system (often leading to fractions not in the desired interval).
  - Getting a large common denominator and then using consecutive numerators.
  - Converting the given fractions to decimals and using decimal representations instead of fractions.
- Resist telling students how to find the fractions. They will have to rely on their own understanding of fractions to come up with a solution.
- Think about what information you can glean from students' strategies about their understanding of fractions.

After

- Have students share the fractions they have identified and the strategies they used to find them. Listen to, but do not judge, students' ideas. Instead, encourage the class to discuss students' ideas about approaches to finding the fractions.
- If students convert the fractions to decimals, see if they can convert one or more of the decimal numbers to fractions. Use this strategy to highlight that these are different symbolic notations for the same quantities. If you suspect that students are not convinced that the fraction and decimal number represent equivalent quantities, give them a copy of the 10×10 grids and ask them to represent the fraction quantity on one grid and the decimal quantity on another grid and compare the amounts.
- Ask students if they think they could find 10 more fractions between two of the closest fractions they found in this activity. Encourage students to discuss their conjectures. If there is any doubt, have the class work together to find 10 more fractions.
- At the conclusion of this lesson, explain that what they have been exploring is the concept of the *density of the rational numbers*. Students may be able to come up with their own definition of what it means to say that the rational numbers are *dense*.

NEXT STEPS

Assessment Notes

- Do students have a systematic way to determine fractions between the given fractions or are they haphazardly identifying possibilities?
- If students convert the fractions to decimals, do they only identify decimals in between the two given quantities? Can they also solve the problem using fractions? If they struggle with using fractions, this may indicate a weak understanding of equivalent fractions.
- How do students respond to finding more fractions between two of the closest fractions identified in the activity? Are they hesitant or do they seem to understand the concept of density?

EXPANDED LESSON 9.11

Comparing Ratios

Grade Level: Seventh or eighth grade.

Mathematics Goals

- To develop proportional reasoning (multiplicative as opposed to additive).
- To develop conceptual strategies for comparing ratios.

Thinking About the Students

Students understand equivalent fractions. They are also familiar with the term *unit fraction* (e.g., $\frac{1}{3}$, $\frac{1}{4}$, $\frac{1}{9}$).

Students have had experiences with ratios, but some may still not be able to distinguish between additive and multiplicative relationships. Some students may have also used symbolic or mechanical methods for solving proportions in a prior year, but the assumption is that these methods are not understood.

Materials and Preparation

- Prepare copies of Blackline Master 65 and also make a transparency.

LESSON

It's a matter of rates—65

Before

Brainstorm

- Show the first problem on the Blackline Master and read it together. Ask students to simply make a guess at which of the two runners they think is faster. Get a show of hands for Terry and then for Susan.
- Next, have students think for a moment about how they could decide which of the two runners is actually faster. Students should share their ideas with a partner.
- Accept student ideas without evaluating them. Do not pursue any of the proposed strategies.

The Task

- Pass out the worksheet with the four problems. Students should solve any three of the problems in any manner they wish and be prepared to explain why their answers make sense.

Establish Expectations

- Students must be able to explain their reasoning. Simply doing a series of calculations is not sufficient.

During

- For students who are having difficulty, look at one ratio in a problem and ask what the unit rate is. For example, *How fast can Terry run in one minute? How often does Jack eat one berry?* In all four of these problems, one or both of the ratios can be converted to a unit rate.
- For students who are ready for a challenge, change the numbers so that neither rate is easily reducible to a unit rate.
- Do not give students an algorithm. Instead, encourage them to make sense of the numbers in the given context.

After

- For each problem, ask students to share their strategies. Do not evaluate students' approaches but allow the class to discuss and question the different strategies. Through questioning, help the students compare and contrast the different approaches.
- If students use unit rates in their strategies, help the class relate unit rates to the concept of unit fractions.

- Change the numbers in one or more problems so that unit rates are not easy to use. For example, suppose that Terry runs 5 laps in 12 minutes and Susan runs 2 laps in 5 minutes. How students respond to this problem will give you insight into problems for the next lesson.

NEXT STEPS

Assessment Notes

- Look for students who focus on additive relationships. They are not seeing the multiplicative relationship of proportionality.
- Which students are using a unit rate approach? Which are not? Another possible approach, a "building up" approach, uses the idea that a ratio does not represent absolute values but represents instead a multiplicative relationship between the two numbers forming the ratio. Therefore, multiples of the two numbers forming the ratio can be used to solve the problems by finding a common element in each of the ratios.
- Watch for students who are using a mechanical method (such as the cross-product algorithm). These methods do not develop proportional reasoning and should not be encouraged (or introduced) until students have had many experiences with intuitive and conceptual methods. If students are using such methods, insist they also come up with another way to find a solution.

EXPANDED LESSON 9.12

One Up and One Down: Addition

Grade Level: Late kindergarten, first grade, or second grade.

Mathematics Goals

- To discover and explore number patterns within the context of addition.
- To help understand how complementary changes in two addends leave the sum unchanged.

Thinking About the Students

Students need not know their addition combinations to engage in this lesson. However, they should have been exposed to the plus and equal sign and understand how an addition equation is a representation of two parts of a whole.

Materials and Preparation

- Students should have access to simple counters, pencil, and paper.
- Optional: In late first or second grade, students should have access to calculators.

LESSON

Before

Introduction to the Task

- Explain this problem: *The other day, a friend of mine was thinking about adding* 7 + 7. (Write 7 + 7 on the board.) *She wondered what would happen if she made the first 7 one more and the second 7 one less.* With students' help, write this new sum, 8 + 6, on the board. Have students complete each equation.

Brainstorm

- Ask: *Why do you think the answers are the same?* Have students offer their ideas. Ask: *Do you think this will work if we started with 5 + 5 or 8 + 8?* Discuss this briefly.

The Task

- (For kindergarten and early first grade): The task is to use counters and try to figure out why 7 + 7 and 8 + 6 have the same answers. Then try another sum, like 5 + 5, and see if it works for that sum also.
- (For late first grade and second grade): The task is to use counters and try to figure out why 7 + 7 and 8 + 6 have the same answers. Will it work for any double (like 5 + 5, 6 + 6, 8 + 8, and so on)? What if the two numbers you begin with are not the same?

Establish Expectations

- Students should use pictures, numbers, and words to show their thinking. If someone picks up the papers, they should be able to understand what students' ideas are. (Optional: You may want to have students work in pairs. Work could be shown on large newsprint to be shared with the class.)

During

- Some students may use their counters and complete each sum independently without relating one to the other. Ask these students to show you 7 + 7 with counters. Be sure that there are two separate piles of seven and not a single pile of 14. Ask: *How could you change these piles to show 8 + 6?* Whatever your hint, avoid simply showing students how to move a counter from one part of the sum to the other. Always try first to listen to the ideas that students have.
- Encourage students to get their ideas on paper for the 7 + 7 case before they explore further.

- How much you push students to explore further depends on the abilities and maturity of the students. In the lower grades, you might remind them to try another double such as 5 + 5 and see if the same thing works there. Older students can be challenged with more open-ended explorations, such as: *Does it always work? Do you have to start with a double? What if you change the numbers by 2 or some other number? What about really big numbers like 87 + 87?* (For large numbers, students should be encouraged to use calculators, even if they cannot compute the sums by hand.)
- For those students who may find this exploration rather easy, challenge them to see how this might work for subtraction.

After

- Select students to share their ideas. Perhaps call first on students who have struggled and need to be encouraged. Although it is good for students to see the more sophisticated ideas, it is important to also focus on emerging ideas as well. For each student who shares, encourage students to ask questions or to offer additional ideas.
- Some students may have difficulty articulating their ideas. Suggest that they use counters on the overhead or magnetic counters on the board so that they can show students their thinking.
- Ask students how this idea could help them if they forgot how much 5 + 7 was. (5 + 7 will be the same as 6 + 6. Similarly, 6 + 8 is double 7, and so on.)

NEXT STEPS

Assessment Notes

- Especially for very young students, be aware of students who do not have a clear connection between a model for addition—especially a part-part-whole model—and the symbolic equation that represents this. Many students learn only to use counters to get answers but do not see the counters as a way to show what the equation means.
- Students who shove counters together and begin counting at once to solve an addition equation are the most likely to have difficulty with this activity.
- A few students will see this activity as rather simple. These students have a good understanding of what addition means.

EXPANDED LESSON 9.13

Predict How Many

Grade Level: Fifth grade.

Mathematics Goals

- To explore growing patterns using three representations: pictures or drawings, table of values, and a rule.
- To practice searching for relationships between the step number and the step in a growing pattern as a foundation for the concept of function.

Thinking About the Students

Students have had some experience with growing patterns. They have extended growing patterns with appropriate materials and explained why their extensions followed the patterns. Students have created tables to record the numeric component of patterns (the number of objects at each step). They have found and described recursive relationships (i.e., how the pattern changes from one step to the next). They have not begun to use variables in their explanations.

Materials and Preparation

- Make transparencies of the Windows and the Predict How Many worksheets (Blackline Masters 66 and 67).
- Make a copy of both worksheets for each student.

LESSON

Windows—66

Predict how many—67

Before
Brainstorm

- Distribute the Windows pattern worksheet and display it on the overhead. Explain that the table shows how many bars or sticks are needed to make all of the windows for that step. Have students draw the next two steps and fill in the next two entries of the table.
- Ask: *If we wanted to find how many sticks it would take to have 20 windows—the twentieth step—what patterns can we use to help us so that we would not have to draw all of the steps?* Suggest that students look for ways to count the sticks in groupings and try to connect the groupings to the step numbers. Have students work for a while in pairs and then solicit ideas from the class. Here are some possible ideas that students may suggest:
  1. *The tops and bottoms have the same number of sticks as the step number. There is one more vertical stick than the step number.* [Step + Step + Step + 1]
  2. *There is a square of four sticks, then each new step adds three more. That is, four plus three times one less than the step number.* [4 + 3 × (Step − 1)]
  3. *One stick (at either end), then there are as many sets of three as the step number.* [1 + 3 × Step]
  4. Looking only at the table and not the drawing: *Start with 4 then add 3, one less time than the step number.* This gives the same result as idea number 2. Help students make the connection to the drawing.
- For each suggestion that you get, write the idea in a manner similar to the expressions shown here. Notice in these expressions that "Step" is actually a variable and could be replaced by *n* or *S* or any other letter. It is not necessary that students come up with all of these ideas. Erase the ideas that have been suggested.
- Have students use an idea that they like and explain their rule on the Windows worksheet. Then have them use the rule to finish the table.
- Pass out the second worksheet, Predict How Many.

The Task

Determine the number of items in the twentieth step of the pattern on the Predict How Many worksheet without filling in the first 19 entries.

Establish Expectations

- Students should extend the pattern for two more steps, making table entries accordingly.
- Students should describe in words the pattern they see in the picture. They should use the picture and/or the table to determine the number of dots in the twentieth step.

During

- Be sure students understand what they did with the Windows worksheet before they continue with Predict How Many.
- If students are having difficulty finding a relationship, suggest that they look for ways to count the dots without having to count each one. If they use the same method of counting for each step, they should begin to see how their counting method relates to the step numbers. Have them write a numeric expression for each step that matches their counting procedure. For example, step two is 2×3, step four is 3×4, and so on.
- Once students think they have identified a relationship, make sure they test their conjecture with other parts of the table and picture.

After

- Ask what entry students found for step 20. List all results on the board without comment. The correct result is 420, but do not evaluate any responses.
- Ask students to come to the board to explain their strategies for identifying and extending the pattern. Encourage the class to comment or ask questions about methods of counting the dots or thinking about the rule for step 20.
- For students who use only the table to find a pattern, have the class see how their idea can be related to the drawings of the dots.

NEXT STEPS

Assessment Notes

- Are students able to see the connections between the pictorial representation of the pattern and the table of values?
- Look for students who are simply generating all the entries in the table to determine the twentieth entry. These students need to be encouraged to look for patterns in the manner that they count the dots.

EXPANDED LESSON 9.14

Create a Journey Story

Grade Level: Seventh or eighth grade.

Mathematics Goals

• To develop the way that graphs express relationships.

Thinking About the Students

Students have explored their rate of walking with a Calculator-Based Ranger (motion detector) to learn how walking rates are modeled in a graph. For instance, they understand that the faster they walk, the steeper the line that is generated in the display. Students have experienced graphing ordered pairs in a coordinate plane. (The motion-detector experience is not a prerequisite for this lesson.)

Materials and Preparation

• Make copies of the Create a Journey Story worksheet for each student (Blackline Master 68).
• Make a transparency of the Create a Journey Story worksheet.

LESSON

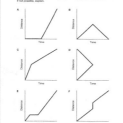

Create a journey story—68

Before

Begin with a simpler version of the task:

• Ask students to sketch a graph of the distance a car travels in the following story:

> *A car is traveling along a road at a steady speed and comes to a stop sign. It stops for the sign and then accelerates to the same speed as before.*

• Point out that the horizontal axis should represent *time* and the vertical axis should represent *distance*.
• Have students share their sketches. Resist evaluating the sketches. Encourage students to comment on and question classmates' ideas. Draw attention to different periods of time on the horizontal axis and how the distance changes within that period. A reasonable sketch might look like one of these:
• The graph on the right has a curve following the stopped (horizontal) segment, indicating speeding up from stopped to the former speed. The left graph is quite adequate.

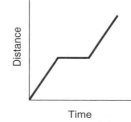 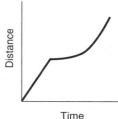

The Task

• The Create a Journey Story worksheet shows time–distance graphs created by a student. Each is supposed to represent the journey of a single vehicle or person. For each of the graphs, make up a plausible journey story or explain why it is not possible to do so.

Establish Expectations

• For those graphs that can represent a journey, students should make up a simple yet plausible journey story. The story may involve walking, running, or driving a car.
• Point out that some of the graphs cannot represent any credible journey. For those graphs, they are to explain why.

During

• As individual students write their stories, ask them to explain to you what is happening in their stories at various points in the graph.

- If a student is having trouble getting started, cover up all but the first part of the graph he or she is working on. Ask the student to think about what that part of the graph tells him or her about the distance traveled or the time elapsed. Help the student translate that information into a story context. Repeat with the next part of the graph.
- For students ready for a challenge, ask them to graph the *speed* of the car in the "before" portion of the lesson over the same interval of time.

After

- Have students share one of their stories without telling which graph the story is supposed to match. Have the class discuss which graph best fits the story.
- Ask students to explain why the impossible graphs are impossible. (Graph D is impossible because it shows different positions at the same time. Graph F is impossible because in the vertical segment the position changes but no time elapses.)
- Discuss the steepness (slope) of lines in different segments of the graph. Ask what it means if the graph is steeper in one portion than in another.
- After identifying stories for each graph, compare stories for the same graph. Have students discuss the similarities and the differences.

NEXT STEPS

Assessment Notes

- Look for students who create journey stories that mimic the shape of the graph by the movement of the journey but that do not reflect the relationship of distance versus time. For example, for graph A, such a student might describe walking on a straight path and then veering off the path to the left. This story does not interpret the graph as a relationship between distance and time but rather as a map.
- Are students able to articulate through their stories the reason for different slopes in different parts of the graph? That is, steeper lines indicate faster speeds. Downward sloping lines indicate moving backward or toward the starting point. (A person/car could turn around and move forward or go backward without turning around. The graph would be the same.)

EXPANDED LESSON 9.15

Crooked Paths

Grade Level: Late kindergarten or early first grade.

Mathematics Goals

- To help students understand that length is an attribute that need not be in a straight line. For example, a distance around an object or a nonstraight path has length just as does a straight object.
- To provide the opportunity to use an intermediary object as a basis of comparison.

Thinking About the Students

Students have made comparisons of straight objects or paths and have learned the meaning of *longer* and *shorter* in that context. Students have not used units or rulers to measure lengths.

Materials and Preparation

- This will be a station activity. Set up three identical stations around the room. Each station consists of two crooked paths made of masking tape. Try to make them about the same in each station. Path A is a zigzag of four straight line segments that total about 9 feet in all. Path B is more S-shaped and is about 7 feet long. Make path B "look" longer by spreading it out more.

- Make one recording sheet for every two students. (See Blackline Master 69.)
- Use rope, string, or yarn that is at least 10 feet long for each station.

LESSON

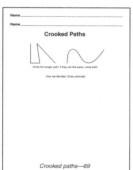

Before

Begin with a simpler version of the task:

- Show the class pairs of straight objects such as a meter stick and teacher, pencil and crayon, or two lines drawn on the board. For each pair, ask: *Which is longer? Which is shorter? How can we tell?*
- On the board draw a half circle and beneath it a line segment about as long as the diameter. Ask: *How can we tell which of these is longer?* Solicit ideas. Be sure students hear the idea that the curve is longer than the segment and that some students provide good reasons. For example, say: *If you had to walk on these, it would take longer to walk the curved path.*

The Task

- Gather students around one station. Say, *One path might be longer or they might be the same. Your task is to decide.*

Establish Expectations

- Show students the worksheets and explain how to use them. Explain that they are to circle the path that is longer or circle both paths if they think they are the same. Then they draw a picture to show how they decided. Have children work in pairs.
- Ask students which path they think is longer or whether they think they are the same. Say: *Before you begin work, put an X on the picture of the path that you think is longer. This is your guess.* Have a few students share their guesses and their reasoning.
- Show students that there is string for comparing lengths, but they can use their bodies, or blocks, or whatever materials they want to help them decide.

During

- Monitor station activity but do not interfere. Be sure students are completing worksheets to the best of their abilities.
- If a pair seems unable to make a decision, ask: *If a toy car was going to go along these paths, which path would it travel longer on?* Or: *Could you use some blocks from over in the block corner to help?*
- Challenge task for capable students: Make a long row of blocks in a straight line that is just as long as the curvy path.

After (when all students have completed the station)

- Remind students of the task of comparing the two paths. Return their worksheets so that they can use them to talk about what they did.
- Ask: *How many thought the zigzag path was longer?* (Count and record on the board next to a zigzag.) *How many thought the curvy path was longer?* (Count and record.) *How many thought they were about the same?* (Count and record.) Ask students if the guesses they made were the same as the result that they figured out. Were they surprised? Why?
- Select pairs to explain what they did. Begin with timid students who are correct. Then ask students with different results. Get as many different ideas and methods as possible.
- If students disagree about which path is longer, have them explain their reasoning in a way that might convince those who disagree. Give students the opportunity to change their minds but ask, *What made you change your minds?*

NEXT STEPS

Assessment Notes

- Look for students who understand how length can exist on a curved path (correctly compare or make appropriate attempt). This can be a checklist item based on the discussion or observations.
- If students used the string, did they exhibit correct understanding of intermediate units? (This is not a requirement of the activity.)
- For students who used units, did they use like-sized units or make appropriate use of materials?

EXPANDED LESSON 9.16

Fixed Areas

Grade Level: Fifth to eighth grades.

Mathematics Goals

- To help contrast the concepts of area and perimeter.
- To develop the relationship between area and perimeter of different shapes when the area is fixed.
- To compare and contrast the units used to measure perimeter and those used to measure area.

Thinking About the Students

Students have worked with the ideas of area and perimeter. Most students can find the area and perimeter of given figures and can state the formulas for finding the perimeter and area of a rectangle. However, they still often become confused as to which formula to use.

Materials and Preparation

- Each student will need 36 square tiles such as Color Tiles, at least two sheets of centimeter or half-centimeter grid paper (see Blackline Masters 35 and 36), and a recording sheet (see Blackline Master 70). Have extra sheets of grid paper on hand.
- This activity can be done in pairs. If students are paired, still provide each student 36 square tiles, as each student needs to explore how the rectangles can be constructed.
- Overhead tiles and a transparency of the grid paper and recording chart will be helpful to introduce the activity as well as to share students' ideas afterward. If overhead tiles are not available, the Color Tiles will suffice, although they will be opaque and more difficult for students to see the individual tiles.

LESSON

Before

Begin with a simpler version of the task:

- Have students build a rectangle using 12 tiles at their desks. Explain that the rectangle should be filled in, not just borders. After eliciting some ideas, ask a student to come to the overhead and make a rectangle that has been described.
- Model sketching the rectangle on the grid transparency. Record the dimensions of the rectangle in the recording chart, for example, "2 by 6."
- Ask: *What do we mean by perimeter? How do we measure perimeter?* After helping students define perimeter and describe how it is measured, ask them for the perimeter of this rectangle. Ask a student to come to the overhead to measure the perimeter of the rectangle. (Use either the rectangle made from tiles or the one sketched on grid paper.) Emphasize that the units used to measure perimeter are one dimensional, or linear, and that perimeter is just the distance around an object. Record the perimeter in the chart.
- Ask: *What do we mean by area? How do we measure area?* After helping students define area and describe how it is measured, ask for the area of this rectangle. Here you want to make explicit that the units used to measure area are two dimensional and, therefore, cover a region. After counting the tiles, record the area in the chart.
- Have students make a different rectangle using 12 tiles at their desks and record the perimeter and area as before. Students will need to decide what "different" means. Is a 2 by 6 rectangle different than a 6 by 2 rectangle? Although these are congruent, students may wish to consider these different. That is okay for this activity.

The Task

- See how many different rectangles can be made with 36 tiles. Determine and record the perimeter and area for each rectangle.

Name _____
Rectangles made with 36 tiles

Rectangle Dimensions	Area	Perimeter

Rectangles made with 36 tiles—70

Establish Expectations

Write the directions on the board:
1. Find a rectangle using *all* 36 tiles.
2. Sketch the rectangle on the grid paper.
3. Measure and record the perimeter and area of the rectangle on the recording chart.
4. Find other rectangles using *all* 36 tiles. Record as before.

During

- Observe how students are generating new rectangles. Are they using some systematic way (e.g., changing the length of the rectangle by one each time) to ensure they have found all rectangles? Are they haphazardly finding rectangles with no apparent strategy?
- How do they measure the perimeters? Do they count or measure all four sides or do they double the sum of length and width? Are they aware that the perimeters change?
- Do students realize that the areas must remain the same since all of them use 36 tiles?

After

- Ask students what they have found out about perimeter and area. Ask: *Did the perimeter stay the same? Is that what you expected? When is the perimeter big and when is it small?*
- Ask students how they can be sure they have all of the possible rectangles. As a class, decide on a systematic method of recording rectangles on the recording chart. For example, start with a side of 1, then 2, and so on. After everyone has had time to consider the information in the chart, have students describe what happens to the perimeter as the length and width change. (The perimeter gets shorter as the rectangle gets fatter. The square has the shortest perimeter.)

NEXT STEPS

Assessment Notes

- Are students confusing perimeter and area?
- How do students react to the idea that the perimeter changes? Do they think they made a mistake in determining the perimeter?
- Are students looking for patterns in how the perimeter changes before you guide them toward that idea?
- As they form new rectangles, are they aware that the area is not changing because they are using the same number of tiles each time? If not, these students may not know what area is, or they may be confusing it with perimeter.
- Are students looking for patterns in how the perimeter changes before you guide them toward that idea?

EXPANDED LESSON 9.17

Shape Sorts

Grade Level: Kindergarten through second grade or early third grade.

Mathematics Goals

- To develop an awareness of the wide variety of ways that two-dimensional shapes can be alike.
- To establish classifications of shapes by various properties, both traditional categorizations and informal, student-generated categories.
- To introduce the names of common shapes or important properties (when and if the opportunity arises within the activity).

Thinking About the Students

Students need no prerequisite knowledge for this lesson. The activity will naturally adjust itself to the ideas held by the students. The level of vocabulary and the types of observations that students make will depend on the geometric experiences of the students and their verbal skills.

Materials and Preparation

- Each group of three to five students will need a collection of 2-D Shapes. Blackline Masters 41 to 47 provide a collection of 49 shapes. Duplicate each set on a different color of card stock and cut out the shapes. You may want to laminate the card stock before you cut out the shapes.
- Students will need a large surface (floor or table) on which to spread out the shapes.

LESSON

Before

Begin with a simpler version of the task:

- Gather students in a circle where all can see and have access to one set of shapes.
- Have each student select a shape. Ask students to think of things that they can say about their shape. Go around the group and ask students to hold up their shape and tell one or two of their ideas.
- Return all shapes to the pile and you select one shape. Place this "target" shape for all to see. Each student is to find a shape that is like the target shape in some way. Again, have students share their ideas. You may want to repeat this with another shape.

The Task

- Each group of students is to select a shape from the collection to be the target shape just as you did. Then they are to find as many other shapes that are like the target shape as they can. However, all the shapes they find must be like the target shape *in the same way.* For example, if they use "has straight sides" as a rule, they cannot also use "has a square corner." That would be two different ways or two rules.

Establish Expectations

- Explain that when you visit each group, you want to see a collection of shapes that go together according to the same rule. You will see if you can guess their rule by looking at the shapes they have put together.
- When you have checked their first rule, you will select a new target shape for them. They should make a new collection of shapes using a different rule. When they have finished, each student should draw a new shape on paper that would fit the rule. All of the drawings should then be alike in the same way. (For kindergarten and first-grade students, you will probably explain this part as you visit their group.)

During

- Listen carefully for the types of ideas that students are using. Are they using "non-geometric" language such as "pointy," "looks like a house," "has a straight bottom," or are they beginning to talk about more geometric ideas such as "square corners," "sides that go the same way" (parallel), or "dented in" (concave)? If they are using shape names, are they using them correctly?
- Gently correct incorrect language or, when appropriate, introduce correct terms. However, do not make terminology and definitions a focus of the activity. Allow students to use their own ideas.
- You may want to challenge students by quickly creating a small group of shapes that go together according to a secret rule. See if they can figure out what the rule is and find other shapes that go with your collection.

After

- Collect students' drawings, keeping the groups intact. Gather students together so that all will be able to see the drawings. (This could be done the day after the DURING portion of the lesson.)
- Display the drawings from one group. Have students from other groups see if they can guess the rule for the drawings. If the drawings are not adequate to see the rule, have those who made the drawings find a few shapes from the collection of shapes that fit the rule.
- To expand students' ideas or interject new ideas, you may want to create a set using a secret rule as described previously. Base your rule on an attribute of the shapes that the students have not yet thought of.

NEXT STEPS

Assessment Notes

- Do not think of this activity as something that students should master. This lesson can profitably be repeated two or three times over the course of the year. As students have more and more experiences with shapes, they will be able to create different, more sophisticated sorting rules.
- Watch for students who talk about shapes in terms of relative attributes such as "bottom," "pointing up," or "has a side near the windows." These same students will not recognize a square as such if it has been turned to look like a "diamond." When this happens, pick up the shape, turn it slowly, and ask the student if it is still pointing up (or whatever). Point out that the shape doesn't change, only the way it is positioned.
- If you have introduced vocabulary that is important, you can informally assess students' knowledge of that vocabulary during this activity. Every type of shape that a primary-grade student needs to know is included in the set. There are examples of right angles, parallel lines, concave and convex shapes, shapes with line symmetry, and shapes with rotational symmetry.

Diagonal Strips

Grade Level: Fifth grade.

Mathematics Goals

- To investigate the properties of the diagonals of quadrilaterals.
- To provide opportunities to clarify the meaning of the terms *quadrilateral, diagonal, perpendicular,* and *bisect,* as well as the names of specific types of quadrilaterals.

Thinking About the Students

Students should be able to identify different types of quadrilaterals (rectangle, parallelogram, trapezoid, kite, rhombus) and talk about their properties in terms of the length of sides and angles formed by the sides. They should also understand the terms *quadrilateral, diagonal, congruent, perpendicular,* and *bisect.*

Materials and Preparation

- For each pair of students, prepare three strips of tagboard about 2 cm wide. Two strips should be about 30 cm and the third about 20 cm. Punch a hole near each end. Divide the distance between the holes by 8 and use this distance to space 7 holes between the ends. Each student also needs a brass fastener to join two diagonal strips.
- Make copies of Blackline Master 71 and the 1-cm square dot grid paper (Blackline Master 37) for each student.
- Make a transparency of Blackline Master 71 and at least two transparencies of Blackline Master 37.

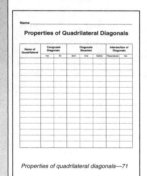

Properties of quadrilateral diagonals—71

LESSON

Before

Begin with a simpler version of the task:

- On the board write the terms *congruent, bisect,* and *perpendicular.*
- Using the two diagonal strips that are equal in length, show students how to join them with the brass fastener. Join the diagonals so that they bisect each other at a right angle. Lay the diagonals on the overhead and ask students to tell what they can about how the two are related. Refer to the terms on the board. As students share their observations, record the properties on the first line of the L-3 transparency by putting Xs under *congruent, bisect each other,* and *perpendicular.* Clarify the meaning of terminology as necessary. Now ask students to think about what quadrilateral would be formed if the ends of the diagonals were connected. On the overhead, mark the vertices through the holes at the end of each diagonal. Use a straightedge to connect the vertices and, thus, form a square.
- On the dot-grid transparency, show students how they can draw two intersecting lines with the same properties (congruent, bisecting each other, and perpendicular). Then connect the endpoints of these lines to form the quadrilateral. Have students draw a pair of intersecting lines on their own paper. Have them use lines that are either shorter or longer than the two on the transparency. When they connect the endpoints, all students should get squares regardless of the lengths of their diagonals.

Brainstorm

Together generate a list of possible types of quadrilaterals that might be formed. You may wish to put this list on the board.

The Task

Students are to use the three strips of tagboard to determine the properties of diagonals that will produce different types of quadrilaterals.

Establish Expectations

- Before giving students the task, remind them that they can use the third shorter diagonal with one of the longer diagonals to form a quadrilateral with noncongruent diagonals.
- Make clear to students that they are to work in pairs to identify the properties of the diagonals and the quadrilateral formed by the diagonals. They are to record their findings on the worksheet and also draw a corresponding pair of diagonals and the quadrilateral on their dot grid. They should put the name of the quadrilateral on each drawing.

During

- Observe how students are determining the properties of diagonals that produce different quadrilaterals. Do they start with the diagonal relationships to see what shapes can be made? Or do they start with examples of the shapes and determine the diagonal relationships? Either approach is fine.
- If students are having difficulty getting started, suggest that they try creating diagonals with one set of properties from the worksheet.
- Do they have a systematic way of generating different quadrilaterals? For example, do they use the same two diagonals, keep one property constant (e.g., diagonals are perpendicular), and then look for ways to vary the other property (e.g., diagonals bisect or do not bisect each other)?
- For students who are ready for a challenge, have them determine the properties that will produce a nonisosceles trapezoid.

After

- As students share their findings, have them draw the diagonals and quadrilateral on your transparency of Blackline Master 10.
- Referring to the descriptions (properties) of the diagonals, ask students if *all* quadrilaterals of a given type have the same diagonal properties. For example, will all rhombuses have these same diagonal properties? Use the transparency of the dot-grid paper to have students make drawings to test various hypotheses regarding the quadrilateral type and their diagonals.
- Ask students to look at the quadrilaterals that have a diagonal property in common (e.g., all quadrilaterals whose diagonals bisect each other) and to make conjectures about other properties in the quadrilaterals that happen as a result of the common diagonal property.

NEXT STEPS ───────────────────────────────────

Assessment Notes

- Are they testing their hypotheses with different sizes of quadrilaterals using the grid paper? Or are they convinced without using the grid paper? If so, how are they convinced? Are they even questioning what might happen with different examples of the same quadrilateral? The answers to these questions will provide evidence that students are or are not beginning to think at van Hiele level 2.

EXPANDED LESSON 9.19

Triangle Midsegments

Grade Level: Eighth grade.

Mathematics Goals

- To look at the relationship between a triangle's midsegment and its base.
- To develop the rationale for why particular relationships exist in a triangle.
- To develop logical reasoning in a geometric context.

Thinking About the Students

- Most students are beginning to function at the van Hiele level 2, where they are ready to grapple with "why" and "what-if" questions. Students are aware of the properties of angles formed by cutting parallel lines with a transverse line. They also have experience working with similar triangles.

- To do the lesson with a dynamic geometry program, students should be relatively competent with the program tools and be able independently to draw different geometric objects (e.g., triangles, lines, line segments), label vertices, find midpoints, and measure lengths and angles.

Materials and Preparation

- This lesson can be done either with computers or as a paper-and-pencil task. As described, the lesson only assumes a demonstration computer with display screen. Although desirable, a computer is not required.
- The computer used in the lesson requires a dynamic geometry program, such as *The Geometer's Sketchpad*.
- Students will need rulers that measure in centimeters.

LESSON

Before
Brainstorm

- Have each student draw a line segment measuring 16 cm near the long edge of a blank sheet of paper. Demonstrate using the computer. Label the segment BC.
- Have students randomly select another point somewhere on their papers but at least a few inches above BC. Illustrate on the computer that you want all students to have very different points. Some might be in the upper left, upper right, near the center, and so on. Have them label this point A and then draw segments AB and AC to create triangle ABC. Do the same on the computer.
- Next, students find the midpoints D and E of AB and AC, respectively, and draw the midsegment DE. Do the same on the computer. You can introduce the term *midsegment* if you wish as the line joining the midpoints of two sides of a triangle. Terminology is not important, however.
- Have students measure their midsegments and report what they find. Amazingly, all students should report a measure of 8 cm. On the computer, measure BC and DE. Move point A all over the screen. The two measures will stay the same, with the length of DE being half of BC. Even if B or C is moved, the ratio of BC to DE will remain 2 to 1.
- Ask students for any conjectures they may have about why this relationship exists. Discuss each idea briefly but without any evaluation.
- On the computer draw a line through A parallel to BC. Have students draw a similar line on their paper. Label points F and G on the line as shown here.

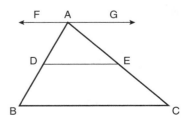

- Ask students what else they know about the figure now that line FG has been added. List all ideas on the board.

The Task
- What conjecture can be made about the midsegment of any triangle?
- What reason can be given for why the conjecture might be true?

Establish Expectations
- Students are to write out a conjecture about the midsegment of a triangle.
- In pairs, students are to continue to explore their sketch, looking for reasons why this particular relationship between the midsegment of a triangle and its base exists. They should record all of their ideas and be ready to share them with the class. If they wish to explore an idea on the computer sketch, they should be allowed to do so.

During
- Resist giving too much guidance at first. See what students can do on their own. Notice what they focus on in forming conjectures.
- For students having difficulty, suggest that they focus on angles ADE and ABC as well as angles AED and ACB. (These pairs of angles are congruent.)
- Suggest that they list all pairs of angles that they know are congruent. Why are they congruent?
- If necessary, ask students to compare triangle ABC with triangle ADE. What do they notice? They should note that the triangles are similar. Why are they similar?

After
- Have students discuss their initial arguments for why the midsegment relationship holds. They can use the demonstration computer to share their ideas.
- Using their ideas, help students build arguments so that one can see how one point flows to the next in a logical sequence.

NEXT STEPS

Assessment Notes
- Look for students who struggle seeing the connections or relationships between properties. They may not be functioning at level 2 of the van Hiele levels of geometric thought.
- Do students see the difference between simply observing a relationship and considering the reasons the relationship exists?

EXPANDED LESSON 9.20

Using Data to Answer Our Questions

Grade Level: First through third grades.

Mathematics Goals

- To learn how different graphing techniques are used to answer questions about a population.
- To learn how to use data to create graphs.

Thinking About the Students

- This lesson assumes that students have had experiences with several different types of graphs, at least cluster graphs and some form of bar graph. Bar graphs may be picture graphs, real graphs, or simple bar graphs of columns or rows of squares. Tallies or numbers may also have been used to represent data. Students may have access to and have used a computer program that will produce graphs. Most such programs include circle graphs as an option. If that is the case, the computer should be available as an option in this lesson.

Materials and Preparation

- Students should have ready access to large pieces of paper such as chart paper. Paper with a large grid, such as a 1-cm grid should also be available. (See Blackline Master 35.) Because the lesson allows students to make their own choices about graphing techniques, these materials simply need to be available to students.

LESSON

This lesson may require several days to complete. It is more of a project than a typical problem-solving lesson. Nonetheless, a problem spirit should be employed in each of three phases of the lesson: (1) What question do we want to answer, and how will we collect the data? (2) What type of graph should we use to answer our question? (3) How do our graphs answer the question? For young students, these issues will need to be addressed separately and perhaps on different days. Here they are presented as two tasks with the third phase dealt with in the AFTER portion of the second task.

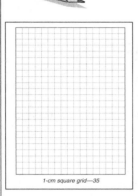

1-cm square grid—35

Before (1)
The First Task

- Decide on a question you would like to answer and how you will gather data to answer it.

  How you guide this discussion will vary with the age of your students and perhaps their recent experiences, such as a field trip or unit of study in science, or a book that has been read to the class. Regardless, the first problem is to decide: What do we want to know or learn? Consider such ideas as favorites (books, food, etc.), nature or science (weather, what lives in our yards), comparisons (something about your class as compared with another class, children compared to adults), measures (heights, arm spans), how many (pets, hours watching TV, minutes spent brushing teeth), and so on.

  After focusing attention on a general topic, brainstorm ideas about what students want to know. It would be useful to have different groups explore different aspects of the same broad topic. For kindergarten, the class will need to work jointly on a topic.

  Once a question or questions are determined, talk about how information (data) can be gathered. If a survey is required, you will probably need to help formulate one to three questions that have simple responses—not full sentences or explanations. What is important is that students are personally invested in the decisions.

During (1)

- Set students to gathering the data. If the collection involves getting data from home or from another class, you will need to help students be very organized about doing this so that real data are available when you need it.
- Monitor the data collection to be sure it is being gathered in a useful manner.

After (1)

- When the data have been collected, briefly discuss what data the class, groups, or individuals have gathered. At this point, a new problem develops as follows.

Before (2)
The Second Task

- Decide on a type of graph to make with the data that will help answer your question. Make the graph.

Brainstorm

- Engage the class in thinking about the various types of graphs that they know how to make and ask for ideas that match a type of graph with the question to be answered and the data gathered. You may need to remind students about techniques they have seen or that are available on the computer.

Establish Expectations

- Show students the types of materials available to them (including the computer if appropriate). They are to select a type of graph, use the data they have collected, and create a presentation of the data in a way that they believe answers the question. Students will work best in groups of two or three, even if multiple groups are working on the same data and question.

During (2)

- Be sure students are profitably working. Do not worry excessively with details or precision. If the bars in a graph do not represent the quantities, help students use squares or other methods. However, even if the graph is not exactly accurate, as long as it approximately represents the data and will not distort conclusions, it should be left alone.
- Encourage students to add words to their posters or presentations to tell what the graph stands for.

After (2)

- Have groups display their graphs. Take turns having students explain their graphs and how the graph answers their question. Ask the other students if they agree that the graph shows the answer to the question. There may be some discussion about which graphs best answered the question and why. (Note that this means the best *type* of graph for the data and the question.)
- Ask students if they can answer other questions using the graphs or what else the graphs show.

EXPANDED LESSON 9.21

Create a Game

Grade Level: Second or third grade.

Mathematics Goals

- To develop the ability to analyze a one-stage experiment and identify all possible outcomes—the sample space.
- To explore informally the probability of an event in a one-stage experiment when all of the outcomes are equally likely.
- To contrast the concept of chance or luck with that of probability.

Thinking About the Students

- Although students need not have a firm understanding of probability, they should have been exposed to the basic idea that the outcome of an experiment can lie at different points along the probability continuum from impossible to certain.

Materials and Preparation

- Each pair of students will need a paper lunch bag or the equivalent and a collection of colored chips or cubes of four colors. Color tiles or Unifix cubes are suggested. Another option is to cut up squares of colored poster board.

LESSON

Before

Begin with a simpler version of the task:

- Discuss children's favorite games. Ask: *Have you ever wondered how games are created? Today we are going to make up our own games.* Explain that the game will consist of putting tiles (or whatever is to be used) in a bag and taking turns drawing out a tile. Each player will be given a color. The person whose color is drawn gets a point. After ten draws, the game is over.
- Say: *Suppose we wanted to put in two colors of tiles, red and blue. We want four tiles in the bag. How many of each tile should we put in?* Accept whatever ideas the class agrees on. Play the game quickly between two halves of the class. Be sure to return the tile to the bag after each draw. Make a big point of this so that students will not forget to return the tiles to the bag when they play. Ask if they think this is a good game or not. Is it fair? Why?
- Now suggest putting in five tiles and three different colors. How would they design the game for two players? One player has to get a point with each draw. Give students a moment to design a game with five tiles and three colors. Have students share their ideas. For different ideas, ask which side they think will win or is it even—a fair game. Of course, there is no way to create a fair game with five tiles. Do not explain this to the students! It is not necessary to play this game.

The Task

- Design a game with 6 red, 1 yellow, 2 green, and 3 blue tiles. Make a list of colors for each player. The tiles are drawn one at a time and returned to the bag. By playing the game to ten points, decide if your game is fair or not.
- Repeat the same task for a bag with 2 red, 3 blue, and 7 yellow tiles.

Establish Expectations

- Students are to make a list of the colors for each player and then play the game. Ten total points is a full game. Have them play the game two times without changing the color list.
- Next they decide if the game is fair or not fair to both players. They should explain their reasoning on their papers and be prepared to discuss this with the class.

- Students then design a new game with the second set of colors (write these on the board). For this new game, they again play the game, decide if it is fair, and explain why.

During

- Be sure that students are playing the game correctly and following the rules they have established.
- After a team has played two times, be sure that they first write down their ideas about the game before designing a second game.
- Listen to the ideas that students use in deciding if the game is fair or not. With only 10 points in a game, it is possible that the score will produce a winner even if the game is designed fairly. For the second set of tiles, a truly fair game is impossible. Listen to see if students realize that before they play. Do they still believe in what they thought after the game has been played? Listening to these discussions will give you insights into students' understanding of luck versus probability.

After

- Have groups share their designs, explain their thinking about the fairness of the game, and how the game turned out. When there are discrepancies between their thinking about the design and the results, confront this. *You thought the game was fair but Sandra won both times. Why do you think that happened? If you play a lot of times, who do you think will win the most times?* Engage the class in this discussion of game designs, luck, probability, and short- and long-term results. Rather than describe probabilities with fractions, use language like this: *Player A can win with 6 of the 12 tiles and Player B can win with 6 of the tiles.*
- In the first set of tiles, a fair game design will result in one player with only one color and the other player with three colors, 6 red versus 1 yellow, 2 green, and 3 blue. Some students may focus on the number of colors rather than the number of tiles for each color.
- Repeat the discussion for the second set of tiles in which a truly fair game is impossible. Even with a 5 to 7 ratio, however, the player with fewer chances to win may still win.

NEXT STEPS

Assessment Notes

- Pay attention to students who seem to believe more in chance or luck than in observable probabilities. This is a main idea that you want to develop at this point in their understanding of probability.
- If students are leaving colors out of the game, they do not have a good understanding of sample space.
- Try to decide how well your students are able to determine the probabilities of the outcomes in these games. Students who correctly analyze these games—who can tell if a game is fair or not and who can design fair and unfair games—are ready to progress further.

EXPANDED LESSON 9.22

Bar Graphs to Pie Graphs

Grade Level: Fourth or fifth grade.

Mathematics Goals

- To introduce the use of a circle or pie graph to represent data.
- To informally explore the concept of percent.

Thinking About the Students

Students have previously made a variety of graphs such as bar graphs, line plots, and tally charts but have limited or no experience with circle graphs. They have not been introduced formally to the idea of percentage. If students have explored the connections between decimals and fractions, the lesson can be used to both expand that connection and also introduce the concept of percent.

Materials and Preparation

- Make copies of the hundredths disk (Blackline Master 28) and 2-centimeter grid paper (Blackline Master 34) for each student. Also make transparencies of the grid paper and the hundredths disk. Cut out one of the hundredths disks for use with the class.
- Students will need access to scissors, tape, and crayons.
- Five pieces of yarn or string, each about 10 to 12 feet long. You will also need a heavy weight such as a brick or large book. The ends of the string will be anchored to this weight as the center of a class-sized circle graph.
- You may want to do the "before" portion of the lesson somewhere other than the classroom so that there is room to form a circle of all your students.

LESSON

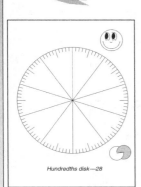

Hundredths disk—28

This lesson may take two days. Prior to this lesson, students must have gathered data to answer a question of their own. This can be a common data set for the class or individual students, or groups can have data sets from different questions and gather their own data. Use questions that lend themselves to being grouped in three to five categories. The following are only offered as examples:

- What are the favorite _____ (e.g., TV shows) _____ of students in the fourth grade? (Gather data by listing four shows and "other.")
- What are the populations of the top 50 cities in our state? (Get data from the Internet. Group the data into three categories.)
- How many students buy lunch at our school on each day of the week? (Get data from the cafeteria staff.)

Before

Begin with a simpler version of the task:

- Ask a question in which each student will have one of three to five choices. For example: What are the colors of our eyes? Write the choices on the board (brown, blue, green, other).
- Quickly make a bar graph on the transparency, coloring in one square for each student as he or she tells you the color of his or her eyes.
- Have the students form a human bar graph by aligning themselves in rows for each color. Next help the students rearrange their rows into a circle formed of all the students in the class. In the center of the circle place the weight with the strings attached. Extend a string to be held by students between each different color of eyes (between the brown and green, the green and blue, and so on). To explore the idea of percents, place a hundredths disk at the center where the strings come together. With the strings fairly straight you can estimate the percentage of students in each category.

The Task

Decide on an appropriate way to graph the data gathered earlier to answer the students' question(s).

Establish Expectations

Students are to make one or more graphs to illustrate the data they collected to answer their question. Allow students to use whatever graphing technique(s) they choose.

During

Discuss with individual students or groups how their graphs will help others answer their question. Keep their focus on good ways to answer the question.

After

- Have several students or groups display their graphs and have the class decide if the graphs help answer the question the data were collected to answer.
- If students have not made a bar graph of their data, have them do so. Each bar should be colored differently or marked with pencil to distinguish the bars. Have students cut the bars from the graph and tape them end to end to form a long strip. The two ends of the strip are then taped together to form a loop. This loop is similar to the circle of students made at the start of the lesson.
- Have students place the loop on the paper with the hundredths disk and form the loop into a circle. The center of the circle should be the center of the disk. Next they draw straight lines from the center of the disk to the divisions between the different bars, as they did earlier with the strings in their human graph. If the loop is smaller than the disk, extend the lines to the edge of the disk. Demonstrate all of this on the overhead projector using the transparent disk and one of the students' bar graph loops. Show how the first line drawn should align with one of the major subdivisions on the disk.
- Examine the transparent disk and note that it has ten large subdivisions each with ten smaller divisions for a total of 100 sections. Each is *1 percent of the whole*. Explain that 1 percent is the same as $\frac{1}{100}$.
- With this information, students can now label their own circle graphs as another representation of the data they collected. Have a discussion about which graph, the bar or circle graph, is best for answering their question.

NEXT STEPS

Assessment Notes

This is an example of a lesson in which students are introduced to a new convention. The circle graph does not arise out of a problem or task. Rather, you are showing students how such a graph is made.

- Since you are introducing a convention—how to make a circle graph—you are mainly looking for students who are having difficulty understanding how the graph is made. Students who need help making their graphs should be given help freely.
- Once the circle graphs have been made, see how well students seem to understand how the circle graph represents the data.

EXPANDED LESSON 9.23

Testing Bag Designs

Grade Level: Third to fifth grade.

Mathematics Goals

- To refine the idea that some events may be more or less likely than others.
- To explore the notion that for repeated trials of a simple experiment, the outcomes of prior trials have no impact on the next.
- To determine that the results for a small number of trials may be quite different than those experienced in the long run.

Materials and Preparation

- Collect and display the designs made by the students in "Design a Bag."
- Provide a lunch bag and color tiles or cubes for each pair of students.

LESSON

Before

Estimate

- Have students share their reasoning for the number of each color they put in their designed bag for "Design a Bag." Some students may think that the colors used for the other tiles make a difference, and this point should be discussed. Do not provide your opinion or comment on these ideas. Select a bag design that most students seem to agree on for the 20 percent mark and instruct them to fill the bag as suggested.
- Ask what they think will happen if they draw a tile from their bag and replace it ten times. How many of the designated color do they think they will get? Encourage a discussion of their thinking.

The Task

Students are to test a bag designed to create the chance of drawing a designated color about 20 percent of the time. (The mark on the probability line is an indicator of the targeted percent.)

Establish Expectations

Once students fill the bag according to the design, they shake the bag and draw out one tile. If a tile of the designated color is drawn, a tally mark is recorded for Yes. If a tile of any other color is drawn, a tally mark is recorded for No. The tile should be replaced in the bag and the bag shaken. This process is repeated ten times. Students should be ready to discuss their results.

During

- Make sure that students are replacing each tile before drawing another tile.
- Are students appropriately recording as they draw tiles?
- Ask students questions about what is occurring with their trials. For example, what do students think when they retrieve the same color tile repeatedly?

After

- Discuss with the class how their respective experiments turned out. Did they turn out the way students expected? With the small number of trials, there will be groups that get rather unexpected results.
- Use results from students' small number of trials to discuss ideas such as how drawing a red tile seven straight times affects the chance of drawing a red tile the next time.

- Make a large tally graph of the data from all of the groups as shown here. Stop and discuss the data at several points as students give you their results. There should be many more No's than Yes's. Here the discussion can help students see that if the experiment is repeated a lot of times, the chances are about as predicted. If students have discussed percents, stopping after data have been collected from 10 students (100 trials) or from 20 students (200 trials) might be useful because the total numbers lend themselves to simple percentage calculations.

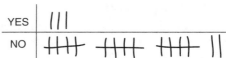

NEXT STEPS

Assessment Notes

- The small-group testing of a design suggests to students that chance is not an absolute predictor in the short run. How do students react to results that are unexpected?
- The group graph may help students understand the difficult concept that chance tends to approach what is expected in the long run. However, this idea involves comparing ratios in the small number of trials with ratios in the large number of trials. For example, the result for 15 trials may be 36 out of 150 total. It will be difficult for students to compare this with 3 out of 10 trials or 43 out of 200.

EXPANDED LESSON 9.24

Toying with Measures

Grade Level: Sixth to eighth grades.

Mathematics Goals

To develop an understanding of how characteristics of a data set (e.g., distribution of data, outliers) affect the mean, median, and mode.

Thinking About the Students

Students know how to find the mean, median, and mode of a data set.

Materials and Preparation

- Prepare a transparency of "Toy Purchases" (Blackline Master 72) to use in the "before" portion of the lesson.
- Provide a copy of the "Toying with Measures" worksheet (Blackline Master 73) for each student.

LESSON

Toy purchases—72

Toying with measures—73

Before

Begin with a simpler version of the task:

- Give the students the following data set: 3, 3, 3, 3, 3. Ask them to determine the mean, median, and mode. After verifying that the mean, median, and mode for this set is 3, ask the students to predict what, if any, changes in these statistics would occur if the number 15 was added to the set. Elicit students' ideas and rationales, asking others to comment on or question the ideas.
- Students should be able to compute the new statistics mentally. Clearly, the median and mode for this new data set remain unchanged. The mean changes from 3 to 5. For each of these statistics, discuss why changes occurred or did not occur.

The Task

- On the transparency of "Toying with Measures," show students the six toys that they have purchased and their prices. Have students calculate the mean, median, and mode for this data set and share those values to ensure that all students have found the correct values.
- The task is to make a series of changes to this original data set of six prices. For each change, first predict—*without computation*—the mean, median, and mode for the new data set and give a reason for the predictions. Do this for each change. Second, compute the actual statistics for the changed set and compare these to the predictions.

  Each of the following changes to the data set are made to the original set of six toy prices:
  1. You decide to buy a seventh toy that costs $20.
  2. You return the $1 toy to the store (leaving only five toys).
  3. By buying six toys the store gives you a free toy.
  4. You decide to buy a second doll for $12.
  5. Make a change you think will be interesting.

Establish Expectations

- Students first record their predictions on the "Toying with Measures" worksheet of the new mean, median, and mode along with their reason for the prediction for each of the five changes. Be sure students understand that each change is to the original set of six toys. The fifth change is one that they think might make an interesting change in the statistics.
- After sharing predictions and reasons with a partner, students should calculate the statistics and compare those with their predictions. If a prediction is very different from the calculation, they should try to find an error in their reasoning.

During

- Listen to individual students' predictions and justifications for those predictions. Is there evidence in students' explanations of their understanding the meaning of the different statistics?
- How are students incorporating the free toy into the set? Do they believe it will affect the mean, median, and mode? (The free toy adds a data point of $0. The mean and median will change.)
- Be sure students do not change their predictions after doing the calculations.
- For a challenge, ask the following question: Suppose that one new toy is added that increases the mean from $6 to $7. How much does the new toy cost?

After

- Have students share their predictions and reasoning and discuss how their predictions compared with the actual statistics.
- Discuss what effect outliers (data that are much greater or smaller than the rest of the data in the set) seem to have on the mean, median, and mode and which statistic(s) are affected more by an outlier.
- Based on their findings, which measure of central tendency do they think would be a better representation of a data set that contains one or more outliers? Students should realize that the mean is significantly affected by extreme values, especially for small sets of data.
- Discuss the fact that these have been very small data sets. How would similar changes affect the mean and median if there were about 100 items in the data set?

NEXT STEPS

Assessment Notes

- How are students using current values for mean, median, and mode to make predictions? Are their predictions reasonable?
- Do students seem dependent on procedures to determine mean, median, and mode?

10 Mathematics Tasks

10.1 The Find!

Grades: PreK–2

Math: To develop efficient counting strategies, such as counting by two or fives.

Task: "I was looking in the closet and found this box of (some countable objects such as beans, connecting cubes, etc.). How many do you think there are? Can you help me count them?"

Expectation: Learners will be given a set of counters (20 to 30 for Kindergartners, up to 100 for second graders). In pairs or individually, learners will be asked to state how many there are and how they know. They should draw how they grouped and counted their objects on the recording sheet. Learners will be asked to explain how to communicate that number to others (orally, written, symbolically).

The Find!

Name: _____

Use this space to show how many counters you have in your closet. You can use pictures, words, or numerals.

10.2 Odd or Even?

Grades: 1–3

Math: Students will be able to explain properties of odd and even numbers.

Task: Is the sum of two consecutive numbers odd or even? How do you know? Write an explanation.

Expectation: This activity provides an opportunity to use counters to model the pairing concept of even numbers (as well as the "pairing with one left out" concept of odd numbers). Through this kind of modeling, students may see the concept of consecutive number sums and may even be able to represent it symbolically or pictorially, or be able to describe it in words. Students may work in pairs to discuss the problem but should submit an individual write up. Students will justify their responses.

Odd or Even?

Name: _____

Is the sum of two consecutive numbers odd or even? How do you know? Complete the table below.

First addend	Second addend	Sum

Are the sums odd or even? Do you think the sums will always be that way? Write an explanation for how you know.

10.3 Factor Quest

Grades: 4–6

Math: Students will create rectangular arrays of a number in order to determine its factors.

Task: How many different rectangular arrangements of a given number of tiles can you make?

Expectation: Using several numbers that have a relatively large number of factors (e.g., 24, 36), students will attempt to build rectangular arrays that have the given number. You can also have different groups/pairs of students with different numbers and have them share their resulting rectangles with the class. Students should write multiplication sentences for each rectangle they make and then list the factors of the selected number. Students can use color tiles or grid paper to model or illustrate the rectangles. Questions you may ask include: Is a 4 by 9 and 9 by 4 the same rectangle? What is the relationship between the rectangles you are building and the factors of the number? How many factors does [your number] have? What numbers will have very few factors? Will there always be an even number of factors?

Factor Quest

Name: _____

Use the grid here to record rectangles that have an area of _____. Label each arrangement with a multiplication sentence.

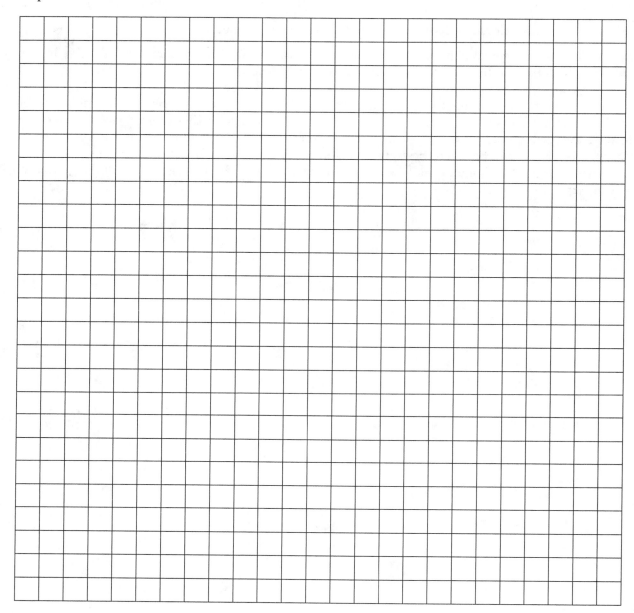

1. Factors for _____: _____

2. What is the relationship between your rectangles and your factors?

10.4 Interference

Grades: 5–7

Math: Students will determine of the least common multiple of two numbers embedded in a context.

Task: Two artificial satellites are in orbits that pass directly over your school. When they are both directly over your school, they cause interference with your school's telecommunication reception. One satellite makes one revolution around the earth every 25 hours; the other makes one revolution around the earth every 20 hours. At 8:00 A.M. on December 3 they were both directly over your school. When (date and time) will both be directly over your school again?

Expectation: Students will work in pairs to discuss the problem but must submit an individual write up. Students will explain their solution process. Students may create tables, draw pictures, or use a calculator to help them in their solution process.

You might need to consider discussing the meaning of orbit. Encourage the construction of a table to examine the relationships. Students may struggle with the "passage of time" (i.e., 24 hours in a day). Stimulate discussion around the idea that the time elapsed from the start time to each time a satellite is over the school is a multiple of the number of hours of the orbit. A possible writing assessment could be a letter to the school board explaining when they can anticipate telecommunication interference.

Interference

Name: _____

Two artificial satellites are in orbits that pass directly over your school. When they are both directly over your school, they cause interference with your school's telecommunication reception. One satellite makes one revolution around the earth every 20 hours; the other makes one revolution around the earth every 25 hours. At 8:00 A.M. on December 3 they were both directly over your school. When (date and time) will both be directly over your school again?

Explain your answer in the space below.

If you were planning the revolution times of two satellites, what would be two compatible options so that they would not interfere very often? Explain.

10.5 Target Number

Grades: 6–8 (this is easily modified for younger students by lowering the number of dice used and the operations involved)

Math: Students will flexibly use operations with whole numbers to reach a desired result. Students will be able to explain the impact of an operation.

Task: Roll seven number cubes (two the same color, the rest a different color). For the two number cubes of the same color, multiply the value on one of them by ten, then add that amount to the other number cube. This becomes your target number. For example, if the dice show 2 and 6, the target number could be 62 or 26. The values on the remaining five number cubes are then to be combined using each once and any mathematical operation known to you (including using some as exponents) to come as close as possible to the target number.

Expectation: Students can work in small groups and each try to see who can come the closest. Students will justify their expressions and write them. For each combination, students should record the expression and check for accuracy in both computation and order of operations notation. For a students result to be considered correct, it must be recorded accurately. Students in the group can check the written answer using calculators. Each target number can be approached from a variety of interesting and mathematically legitimate ways. In fact, there may be several different expressions for the same target number. The opportunity for students to hear others give their expressions and to compare them to their own provides ample opportunity to deepen their number and operation senses.

Target Number

Name: _____

Work in groups of three or four. Use seven number cubes. Mark two of them (or ensure they are the same color). Roll those two. Multiply the value showing on one of them by ten and add it to the value showing on the other. This becomes your target number. Record this number on the chart below. Roll the other five number cubes. Use the values on the five cubes, each only once, to write an expression that when solved is a number as close as possible to the target number (you might even hit the target number!). Record your expression in the chart below. If you find a second expression that is as close or closer, or someone in your group does, record it as your second expression.

Target Number	My Expression	My Result	Second expression (as close or closer than my result)	Second Result

10.6 Fraction Find

Grades: 4–7

Math: Given two fractions, students will be able to find fraction that are between them. Students will justify that given any two fractions, there is always another one in between.

Task: Find a fraction that is between $\frac{5}{8}$ and $\frac{3}{4}$. How do you know you are right? How many different ways of explaining this can you find?

Expectation: Students are to find out that there are many fractions between these two fractions and in fact, given any two fractions, they can find one in between. This task may need to be scaffolded. You might begin with a warm-up that has a context and uses easier fractions. For example, if a person was walking around a track and had passed the $\frac{1}{2}$-mile mark but had not yet reached the ¾-mile mark, at what distance could they possibly be? Explain to students that they should all be able to find one rational number between $\frac{5}{8}$ and $\frac{3}{4}$, but challenge them to find more than one. Encourage the use of manipulatives and sketches. During the sharing of results, students should notice that there are many answers. Ask students to decide how many fractions are between $\frac{5}{8}$ and $\frac{3}{4}$.

Fraction Find

Find a fraction that is between $\frac{5}{8}$ and $\frac{3}{4}$. How do you know you are right? Illustrate or explain how you found the fraction here.

How many different fractions can you find that are between $\frac{5}{8}$ and $\frac{3}{4}$?

Record all the fractions that you and your partner find below, with an illustration or explanation of how you found it.

10.7 Illustrating Ratios

Grades: 4–5

Math: Students will complete a ratio table and a graph. Students will use tables and graphs to analyze a proportional situation.

Task: Monique works for a company that makes Doohickeys. Her company has one machine that can make a certain number of Doohickeys per minute. Monique observed the machine and collected data to see how many Doohickeys were made in 1 minute. An order for 72 Doohickeys came in from AB textbook publishers. She needs to predict how long it will take to make the 72 Doohickeys. From the data provided, can you help her make her prediction? How long will it take to make 100 Doohickeys?

Expectation: Students will complete the ratio table and graph the data. Question prompts should be created to help students see patterns in the table, in the graph, and between the two. They will also use these data to make a prediction. They will write a letter to the AB textbook publisher explaining how long it will take to complete their order and how they know it will take that long. There is an opportunity to ask many "what if" questions here to deepen students' understanding of ratios (e.g., what if the Doohickey machine were faster? How would the table change? How would the graph change?).

Illustrating Ratios

Name: _____

Monique works for a company that makes Doohickeys. Her company has one machine that can make a certain number of Doohickeys per minute. Monique observed the machine and collected data to see how many Doohickeys were made after each minute, as shown in the following table. An order for 72 Doohickeys came in from AB textbook publishers. She needs to predict how long it will take to make the 72 Doohickeys. From the data provided, can you help her make her prediction? How long would it take to make 100 Doohickeys?

Minutes	4			16	22	28	34
Doohickeys			27	36			

Graph your results here. Label the axes.

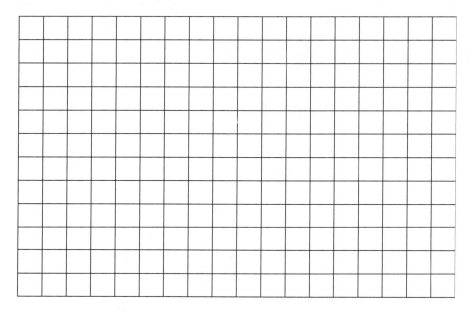

How long will it take to make 72 Doohickeys? How do you know?

How long will it take to make 100 Doohickeys? How do you know?

Write a letter to AB textbook publishers explaining how long it will take to make their 72 Doohickeys and how you know. Use proper letter writing style.

10.8 Building Bridges

(Adapted from MSEB Assessment prototype)

Grades: 3–5

Math: Students will find patterns in analyzing geometric growing patterns. Students will describe in words the general rule for a geometric growing pattern.

Task: We are bridge builders trying to determine the amount of material we need to construct our bridges. If we define a bridge span as (shown in step 1), then how many uprights and how many cross pieces do we need to build an X (any number) span bridge?

Expectation: Working individually, students will construct bridges of different span lengths for each type of bridge presented. Students will determine a relationship to figure out how many pieces they need to build any bridge length. Students will record their solutions on a recording sheet. It may be helpful for students to record their data in a four-column table, with the step number in the left column, number of uprights, number of cross pieces, and number of total pieces. It will be important for the teacher to ask questions that help students connect what is happening in the model and what is recorded on the table. This activity is easily adaptable to easier growing patterns or more difficult growing patterns. In addition, although this task calls for the use of Cuisenaire rods, similar tasks can be created using any material (e.g., Unifix cubes, pattern blocks, color tiles). In fact, after completing experiences like this one, students can design their own growing patterns.

Building Bridges

Name: _____

Using Cuisenaire rods, construct step 1 and step 2 of a bridge like this one:

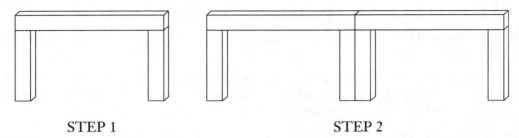

STEP 1   STEP 2

Choose one color (length) for the upright pieces. Choose a different color (length) to be used for the cross piece.

Now, using this type of span, build a 3 step bridge.

1. How many uprights did you need?
2. How many cross pieces did you need?
3. How long (in centimeters) is your bridge?
4. How many pieces did you need altogether?

Build a 5 step bridge.

1. How many uprights did you need?
2. How many cross pieces did you need?
3. How long (in centimeters) is your bridge?
4. How many pieces did you need altogether?

Without building a 9 step bridge, predict the following.

1. How many uprights would you need? How do you know?
2. How many cross pieces would you need? How do you know?
3. How long (in centimeters) will your bridge be? How do you know?
4. How many pieces would you need altogether?

Write a rule (in words) for figuring out the total number of each type of rod you would need to build a bridge if you knew how many steps the bridge had.

_____

_____

10.9 Compensation Decision

Grades: 7–8

Math: Students will compare linear and exponential growth in a context.

Task: Jocelyn wanted to make some extra money. Her father offered to pay her for odd jobs around the home for a week and gave her a choice of two options. The first option was that her father would pay her $1.25 for the week. The second option was that her father would pay her in the following manner for a week: on Monday he would give his daughter $0.01, on Tuesday $0.02, on Wednesday $0.04, and so on through Sunday. What would you tell Jocelyn to do, so she can earn the greatest amount?

Expectation: Students will create tables and graphs for each of these compensation packages. They can use the tables and/or the graph to determine an equation. They will analyze their representations to justify which compensation plan is better. Discussion should focus students' attention to where they can find this information across the representations. Have groups present how they solved their problem. Ask students to consider adaptations to this problem, for example, what if the options expanded for a month? What if one amount was to change?

Compensation Decision

Name: _____

Jocelyn wanted to make some extra money. Her father offered to pay her for odd jobs around the home for a week and gave her a choice of two options. The first option was that her father would pay her $1.25 for the week. The second option was that her father would pay her in the following manner for a week: on Monday he would give his daughter $0.01, on Tuesday $0.02, on Wednesday $0.04, and so on through Sunday. What would you tell Jocelyn to do, so she can earn the greatest amount?

Use this space to solve this problem. You can draw pictures or write number sentences to help you. Be sure to explain how you know that your solution is the one that will earn Jocelyn the greatest amount!

10.10 Solving the Mystery

Grades: 6–8

Math: Students will use variables to illustrate equivalencies in symbolic expressions and equations.

Task: Your older sister attempts to impress you with an old number trick. It goes like this: Think of a number, double it, and add nine. Then add your original number to it and divide by three. Now add four and subtract your original number. The result, she says, is seven. How does this work? Can you prove that this is not magic, but algebra in action?

Expectation: Present the trick to the students initially as an opportunity to do some mental mathematics. Ask them whether they think it will work all the time. Can they prove it? Students should be using variables as a tool for exploring this number trick. If they start by trying out various numbers, it will help them to see that they can plug in a variable instead of a number to see why it works. Algebra is a formal symbolic language for mathematics. Students in this task have an opportunity to discover the power of algebra as a communication tool. Being able to express the relationship either in symbols or in pictures lays a nice foundation for future algebraic concepts.

Ask students to explain how they used variables to discover how the trick works. Challenge them to make up a number trick on their own.

Solving the Mystery

Name: _____

Your older sister attempts to impress you with an old number trick. It goes like this:

1. Choose a number.
2. Double it.
3. Add nine.
4. Add your original number.
5. Divide by three.
6. Add four.
7. Subtract your original number.
8. Your result is seven.

Did it work? Does it work every time? How do you know? Prove that this is not magic, but algebra in action.

10.11 Cover All

Grades: 3–5

Math: Students will explain strategies for finding how many square tiles cover a rectangle region. Students will explain how to use repeated addition and/or multiplication to find areas of rectangles.

Task: How many square tiles (1 inch by 1 inch) are needed to cover the rectangle on this page?

Expectation: Students may want to cut out their tile, and even use more than one tile. This is a good way to support their initial exploration, but limit the number of tiles so that they begin to see other ways to find area (other than covering the entire surface). As with any measurement task, it is a good practice to ask students first to estimate how many they think will cover the surface. Students may work in pairs to discuss the problem, but each must submit an individual write up. Students may verify their estimates using real tiles. Students will explain their solution process. If possible, students can extend this activity to finding areas of other rectangles or rectangular shapes in the classroom.

Cover All

Name: _____

For a mosaic project in art, you and your friend are trying to determine how many tiles of this size will cover the area below. How many tiles do you think will cover the page? How do you know? Explain your answer in the space below.

Explain how you figured out the number of tiles.

_____

_____

_____

_____

11 Balanced Assessment Tasks

The following tasks and supporting materials were developed by the project Balanced Assessment for the Mathematics Curriculum and published in a series of assessment packages by Dale Seymour Publications, 1999.* Further information about additional packages may be obtained from the publisher. Further information about additional tasks and supporting instructional and professional development materials may be obtained from the Balanced Assessment–Mathematics Assessment Resource Service Web site at www.educ.msu.edu/mars.

These tasks and rubrics are offered as an example of how problem-based tasks can be used to determine student understanding. The tasks themselves have been field tested with students in public schools whose responses have been examined to develop the included rubrics. These rubrics are holistic in nature and are intended to help the reader recognize the importance of identifying the core mathematics content and looking for evidence of understanding by describing elements of performance.

Each task also has a completed sample solution.

The first two tasks are designed for elementary level students and can each be modified to address specific needs. The last task is designed for middle school students and can also be modified.

*Tasks adapted from *Balanced Assessment for the Mathematics Curriculum, Elementary Grades Assessment Packages 1 and 2*, © 1999 by the Regents of the University of California. Published by Pearson Education, Inc., publishing as Dale Seymour Publications, an imprint of the Pearson Learning Group. Used by permission.

11.1 Magic Age Rings

Grades: 3–6

Math: Use simple mathematical functions. Explore and discuss the importance of order of operations and the relationship of addition, subtraction, multiplication, and division. Combine various arithmetic operations to solve complex problems.

Task: This task asks students to imagine they are wearing magic rings that change their age. A blue ring doubles one's age, a green ring adds five years, and a yellow ring takes two years away from one's age. Students calculate the effects of wearing different rings and answer questions about this imaginary situation.

You may wish to extend this task by using some of the ideas that follow.

- Make up your own question about these magic rings. Work out the answer. Ask someone else to answer your question.
- Are there any ages that are impossible to produce with the rings?
- Invent different types of rings that also change your age. What would be the most useful set of rings to have?

Investigate what happens when you put two rings in a different order (blue first, then green, or green first, then blue). For which combinations of rings does order matter? Are there combinations in which order doesn't make any difference? Why is this?

Expectation: Most fourth graders should be able to tackle the mathematics of this task. It assumes that students have had prior opportunities to explore the ways addition, subtraction, multiplication, and division relate to each other. The task also assumes that students have some understanding of the significance of order of operations and that they know the meaning of doubling a quantity. Students may discuss the task in pairs, but each student should complete an individual written response.

Magic Age Rings

Name: _____

You are ten years old and as a birthday present you have been given three boxes of magic rings.

BLUE RINGS

Caution — Only wear on the small finger of your left hand

THIS RING DOUBLES YOUR AGE

GREEN RINGS

Caution — Only wear on the small finger of your left hand

THIS RING ADDS 5 YEARS TO YOUR AGE

YELLOW RINGS

Caution — Only wear on the small finger of your left hand

THIS RING TAKES 2 YEARS AWAY FROM YOUR AGE

With great care you slip one of the green rings onto the little finger of your left hand. At once you start to grow and, within seconds, the magic has worked—you are 15 years old. Discuss this with your partner. What does it mean to "double" your age?

1. Complete the table.

Imagine that you are . . .	Rings you wear	Age you become	Number sentences to explain this
10 years old	Green	15	10 + 5 = 15
10 years old	Blue		
10 years old	Yellow		
10 years old	Green and then blue	30	10 + 5 = 15 15 + 15 = 30
10 years old	Green and then yellow	13	10 + 5 = 15 15 − 2 = 13
10 years old	Green and another green		
10 years old	Yellow and then blue		
10 years old	Yellow and another yellow		

2. Use your imagination. Choose to be any age and wear any combination of rings. Complete the table.

Imagine that you are . . .	Rings you wear	Age you become	Number sentences to explain this

3. Latosha is 11 years old. She puts on three blue rings. How old is she now? Explain your answer.

4. Margaux is 10 years old but she wants to be 18. What rings should she put on to change her age to 18 years? Explain your answer.

5. Lloyd is 9 years old. He has a blue ring and a green ring. He wants to wear both rings. Will it make any difference to his age which ring he puts on first? Explain your answer.

6. Jessica is wearing a yellow ring and she tells you she is 13 years old. She takes off the yellow ring and she is back to her real age. What is her real age? Explain your answer.

7. Rashad is wearing three rings and is 12 years old. First he takes off a yellow ring, then a blue ring, and finally a green ring. He is back to his real age. How old is he? Explain your answer.

Magic Age Rings: Sample Solution

1.

Imagine that you are . . .	Rings you wear	Age you become	Number sentences to explain this*
10 years old	Green	15	10 + 5 = 15
10 years old	Blue	**20**	**10 + 10 = 20**
10 years old	Yellow	8	**10 − 2 = 8**
10 years old	Green and then blue	30	10 + 5 = 15, 15 + 15 = 30
10 years old	Green and then yellow	13	10 + 5 = 15, 15 − 2 = 13
10 years old	Green and another green	**20**	**10 + 5 = 15, 15 + 5 = 20**
10 years old	Yellow and then blue	**16**	**10 − 2 = 8, 8 + 8 = 16**
10 years old	Yellow and another yellow	**6**	**10 − 2 = 8, 8 − 2 = 6**

*Other number sentences may also be correct. For example, doubling may be shown as "× 2."

2. There is no reason students should not complete this table with examples that use three or more rings—for example, "Blue, then green, then yellow."
3. Latosha will be 88 years old. $11 \times 2 = 22$, $22 \times 2 = 44$, $44 \times 2 = 88$
4. Margaux could put on a blue ring and then a yellow ring. $10 \times 2 = 20$, $20 - 2 = 18$. Or she could put on two green rings and then a yellow ring. $10 + 5 = 15$, $15 + 5 = 20$, $20 - 2 = 18$. There are other solutions.
5. It does make a difference which ring Lloyd puts on first. If he puts on the blue ring first, his age becomes 23 years. $9 \times 2 = 18$, $18 + 5 = 23$. But if he puts on the green ring first, he becomes 28 years old. $9 + 5 = 14$, $14 \times 2 = 28$.
6. Jessica's real age is 15 years. A yellow ring takes 2 years off your age. So removing a yellow ring will do the opposite. It will make Jessica two years older. $13 + 2 = 15$
7. Rashad's real age is 2 years. $12 + 2 = 14$, $14 \div 2 = 7$, $7 - 5 = 2$. This last question is difficult as it really demands some understanding of inverse operations.

Rubric
Characterizing Performance

This section offers a characterization of student responses and provides indications of the ways the students were successful or unsuccessful in engaging with and completing the task. The descriptions are keyed to the Core Elements of Performance. Our global descriptions of student work range from "The student needs significant instruction" to "The student's work meets the essential demands of the task." The characterization of student responses for this task is based on these Core Elements of Performance:

1. Apply simple functions in a problem-solving situation.
2. Use combinations of various arithmetic operations to solve problems.
3. Demonstrate understanding of what effect reversing the order of operations has on a problem.
4. Use doubling and an understanding of inverse operations to solve complex problems.
5. Explain how answers are decided.

Descriptions of Student Work

The student needs significant instruction. These papers show evidence of some limited success in one or two of the core elements of performance, most commonly in the first and second.

The student needs some instruction. These papers provide evidence of ability in the first two core elements, both in the tables and in some of the problems. There may be some limited evidence of performance in the last three core elements: this evidence, however, is weak and inconsistent. This level of work will show the ability to apply simple functions and to combine various arithmetic operations not just in the table but also in some of the problems 3 through 7. Generally, there will not be evidence of an ability to work with inverse operations, or to double numbers correctly or consistently. The paper will not provide evidence of understanding the importance of order of operations. Explanations will be limited and/or weak.

The student's work needs to be revised. There will be evidence of ability to perform in at least four out of five of the core elements of performance. There may be some inconsistency in one or two core elements (for example, the response may correctly show doubling in the table, but incorrectly solve problem 3, or correctly solve problem 5, but make a mistake in order of operations in the table). The answers may be all correct, but missing any explanation.

The student's work meets the essential demands of the task.
There will be no mistakes (or only very minor mistakes) in the tables. Problems 3 through 7 will fully demonstrate ability in all five core elements of performance. There may be an error in one of the elements of performance; however, that element will be correctly demonstrated elsewhere (for example, many otherwise very strong responses will make a mistake on problem 7).

11.2 Grocery Store

Grades: 5–8

Math: Reason using ratio and proportion. Reason algebraically. Generalize symbolically.

Task: This task asks students to consider the planning of a layout for a new grocery store. Students answer questions using scale models of shopping carts to solve problems related to the store's floor plan.

Expectation: It is assumed that students have had experience with ratio and proportion and with generalizing linear situations symbolically. Students may discuss the task in pairs, but then complete an individual written response.

This task places numerous demands on students. They must successfully move back and forth between the real world and scale model and use proportional reasoning, but they must also know when not to rely on proportional reasoning alone. For example, students are often tempted to measure the 12 nested carts and use this information to answer question 3 (length of 20 nested carts) and question 4 (number of carts that fit in a 10-meter space) by reasoning proportionally. The results they obtain will be off but not by much. However, this type of reasoning shows a lack of attention to the first cart, which is a constant term—a central idea in linear functions, and an idea students must account for in question 4 in order to produce a generalization that accurately represents the relationships in the situation.

Nevertheless, a purely proportional approach that ignores the constant term would not prove detrimental in the real world of shopping carts, especially when dealing with large numbers. As you increase the number of shopping carts, the relative effect of the greater length of the first cart (when compared to the stick-out length of each cart) decreases.

The task also involves issues of measurement. The questions do not indicate to students the level of accuracy required. Some students use rough measurements of the scale model while others strive for as much accuracy as possible. All reasonable responses are accepted.

Grocery Store

Name: _____

Rasheed is planning the layout for a new grocery store. He found the diagram below in a supply catalog. It shows a drawing of a single shopping cart and a drawing of 12 shopping carts that are "nested" together. (The drawings are $\frac{1}{24}$th of the real size.)

length

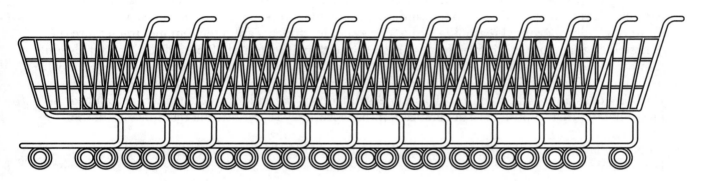

Rasheed has several questions:

1. What is the length of a real shopping cart?

2. When the real carts are nested, how much does each cart stick out beyond the next one in the line?

3. What would be the total length of a row of 20 real nested carts?

4. What rule or formula could I use to find the length of a row of real nested carts for any (n) number of carts?

5. How many real nested carts could fit in a space 10 meters long?

Write a letter to Rasheed that answers his questions.

- For each question, explain your answer so that he can understand it and use it to make decisions about the store.
- To explain question 4, you may want to draw and label a diagram that tells what each part of your formula represents.

Grocery Store: Sample Solution

The following is a sample solution using centimeters. Students may also use inch measurements, although this will require conversion to metric for the last question.

Dear Rasheed,

Here are answers to your questions. I hope they will help you in planning your store. Good luck!

My answer to question 1: The length of a real shopping cart is 96 cm, or .96 m. The scale model of a single shopping cart measures 4 cm. Since the scale is 1 to 24, multiply by 24 to get the real length: 4 cm × 24 = 96 cm.

My answer to question 2: Each cart sticks out beyond the next one in line approximately 26.4 cm or about .26 m. In the scale model of the nested carts, I measured the distance between the handles on the first and second shopping carts and got about 1.1 cm (although it looks like it's a little more than that). You could measure in other ways too—by the grills, between the last two carts, and so on. Anyway, it comes out roughly the same. Then I multiplied by 24 to get the real length: 1.1 cm × 24 = 26.4 cm.

My answer to question 3: The total length of 20 nested carts is approximately 5.98 m. In any row of nested carts, the first cart will take up 96 cm. Each additional cart will add 26.4 cm to the total length. Since you need the length of 20 carts, I added the length of one cart and 19 stick outs to get 96 cm + (19 × 26.4) = 597.6 cm, or about 5.98 m.

My answer to question 4: If L is the total length in centimeters of n nested carts, then the total length of n nested carts is $L = 96 + 26.4(n - 1)$, which can be written as $L = 26.4n + 69.6$. I got this formula in a way similar to finding the answer to your last question. The 96 is for the length of the first cart. After the first cart, there are $n - 1$ carts sticking out. So I multiplied the number of "stick outs" ($n - 1$) by the length of each "stick out" (26.4) and added it all to the length of the first cart (96) giving me $L = 96 + 26.4(n - 1)$. Remember that this formula gives length in centimeters.

My answer to question 5: About 35 carts could fit in a space 10 meters long. I got this answer by using the above formula and letting $L = 10$ m. Since the formula finds length in centimeters, I let $L = 1000$ cm. Plugging in I got $1000 - 26.4n + 69.6$. I solved for n: $n = 35.24$. Since you can't have parts of shopping carts, I rounded this number down to 35.

I hope that these answers help you to make decisions about your store.

Sincerely,
A. Student

Rubric

Characterizing Performance

This section offers a characterization of student responses and provides indications of the ways the students were successful or unsuccessful in engaging with and completing the task. The descriptions are keyed to the Core Elements of Performance. Our global descriptions of student work range from "The student needs significant instruction" to "The student's work meets the essential demands of the task."

The characterization of student responses for this task is based on these Core Elements of Performance:

1. Reason using ratio and proportion and successfully move back and forth between a real work situation and a scale model to determine the lengths of shopping carts
2. Use algebraic reasoning to solve for an unknown and to generalize a linear relationship symbolically
3. Communicate mathematical reasoning

Descriptions of Student Work

The student needs significant instruction. Student may answer some questions correctly (either in the letter to Rasheed or beside the question) but does not successfully find an unknown (as in questions 3 and 5) or formulate a symbolic generalization (as in question 4).

The student needs some instruction. Student successfully finds an unknown (questions 3 and 5) but does not demonstrate an understanding of how to arrive at a general formula.

The student's work needs to be revised. Student successfully finds the unknown (questions 3 and 5) and shows an understanding of how to generalize the situation, but fails to arrive at a completely correct formula.

The student's work meets the essential demands of the task. Student successfully finds the unknown and arrives at a correct generalization of the situation. Minor errors that do not distort the reasonableness of solutions are permitted.

11.3 Bolts and Nuts!

Grades: 3–6 (can be modified to address what you know about your students)

Math: Take pairs of measurements in a practical situation. Make simple ratio calculations.

Task: Students estimate, measure, and calculate the number of turns made to the nut and the distance it moves. Calculations bring in simple ideas of ratio, which pupils of this age will normally find quite challenging.

Expectation: Students should have met the idea of ratio in a practical context. They should be familiar with measurements in millimeters and meters. Students may discuss the task in pairs, but each student should complete an individual written response.

Bolts and Nuts!

Name: _____

Work with a partner on this problem.

You should have a nut, a bolt, a ruler, and a calculator.

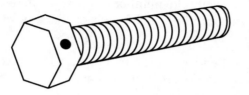

Fix the nut onto the bolt.

Turn the nut so that it moves along the bolt.

1. How many complete turns will move the nut 25 mm along the bolt?

   First make a guess.

   Your guess: _____ turns move the nut 25 mm.

   Your partner's guess: _____ turns move the nut 25 mm.

   Talk to your partner about how you will answer this question. You will need to measure 25 mm with the ruler. There are some marks on the nut and bolt that may help you count the turns.

   Your answer: _____ turns move the nut 25 mm.

   Your partner's answer: _____ turns move the nut 25 mm.

   Do you agree? If not, who has the right answer?

Field Experience Guide: Resources for Teachers of Elementary and Middle School Mathematics © Allyn and Bacon 2007

Now try to answer the following questions *without touching the nut and bolt.*

2. How many times would you have to turn the nut to move it 50 mm? _____

3. Complete this table.

Distance the Nut Moves	Number of Turns
25 mm	
50 mm	
100 mm	
200 mm	
1 meter	

←Write in your answer from the previous page.

←Write in your answer from the last question.

←Figure this out.

←Figure this out.

←Figure this out.

To answer these you will need to imagine a bolt that is longer than the one you are using. The 1-meter bolt would be giant-sized because 1 meter = 1000 mm.

4. How far would the nut move if you turned it 50 complete turns? Explain how you figured this out:

_____

_____

_____

_____

Bolts and Nuts! Sample Solution

1. It takes 20 turns to move the nut 25 mm.
2. You'd have to turn the nut about 40 times to move it 50 mm
3.

Distance the Nut Moves	Number of Turns
25 mm	About 20
50 mm	About 40
100 mm	About 80
200 mm	About 160
1 m	About 800

4. If 1 meter or 1000 mm takes about 800 turns, then 125 mm takes about 100 turns. Therefore, 50 turns would move the nut about 62 mm.

Rubric

Characterizing Performance

This section offers a characterization of student responses and provides indications of the ways in which the students were successful or unsuccessful in engaging with and completing the task. The descriptions are keyed to the Core Elements of Performance. Our global descriptions of student work range from "The student needs significant instruction" to "The student's work meets the essential demands of the task."

The characterization of student responses for this task is based on these Core Elements of Performance:

1. Take pairs of measurements in a practical situation
2. Make simple ratio calculations

Descriptions of Student Work

The student needs significant instruction. These papers show, at most, an attempt to make the estimates or measurements

The student needs some instruction. An attempt has been made to make the estimates and measurements. The table has been at least partially completed, but there is a poor understanding of proportion.

The student's work needs to be revised. Measurements have been correctly made within the generous margin of error (± 4 turns). The table has been partially completed with most figures in proportion.

The student's work meets the essential demands of the task. Measurements have been correctly made within the generous margin of error (±4 turns). The student may have indicated somewhere on the response that figures are "rough," "approximate," or "estimated." The student can handle simple ratio calculations as indicated either by the table completed with all figures in proportion, or by a consistent answer to the final question.

part **III**

Blackline Masters

The reproducible Blackline Masters featured in this section can be used for making instructional materials to support activities. They are also available at the Companion Web site (www.ablongman.com/ vandewalle6e).

Suggestions for Use and Construction of Materials

Card Stock Materials

A good way to have many materials made quickly and easily for students is to have them duplicated on card stock at a photocopy store. Card stock is a heavy paper that comes in a variety of colors. It is also called *cover stock* or *index stock*. The price is about twice that of paper.

Card stock can be laminated and then cut into smaller pieces, if desired. The laminate adheres very well. Laminate first, and then cut into pieces afterward. Otherwise you will need to cut each piece twice.

Materials are best kept in plastic bags with zip-type closures. Freezer bags are recommended for durability. Punch a hole near the top of the bag so that you do not store air. Lots of small bags can be stuffed into the largest bags. You can always see what you have stored in the bags.

The following list is a suggestion for materials that can be made from card stock using the masters in this section. Quantity suggestions are also given.

Dot Cards

One complete set of cards will serve four to six children. Duplicate each set in a different color so that mixed sets can be separated easily. Laminate and then cut with a paper cutter.

Five-Frames and Ten-Frames

Five-frames and ten-frames are best duplicated on light-colored card stock. Do not laminate; if you do, the mats will curl and counters will slide around.

10 × 10 Multiplication Array

Make one per student in any color. Lamination is suggested. Provide each student with an L-shaped piece of tagboard.

Base-Ten Pieces (Centimeter Grid)

Use the grid (number 11) to make a master as directed. Run copies on white card stock. One sheet will make 4 hundreds and 10 tens or 4 hundreds and a lot of ones. Mount the printed card stock on white poster board using either a dry-mount press or permanent spray adhesive. (Spray adhesive can be purchased in art supply stores. It is very effective but messy to handle.) Cut into pieces with a paper cutter. For the tens and ones pieces, it is recommended that you mount the index stock onto *mount board* or *illustration board*, also available in art supply stores. This material is thicker and will make the pieces easier to handle. It is recommended that you *not* laminate the base-ten pieces. A kit consisting of 10 hundreds, 30 tens, and 30 ones is adequate for each student or pair of students.

Little Ten-Frames

There are two masters for these materials. One has full ten-frames and the other has 1 to 9 dots, including two with 5 dots. Copy the 1-to-9 master on one color of card stock and the full ten-frames on another. Cut off most of the excess stock (do not trim) and then laminate. Cut into little ten-frames. Each set consists of 20 pieces: 10 full ten-frames and 10 of the 1-to-9 pieces, including 2 fives. Make a set for each child.

Place-Value Mat (with Ten-Frames)

Mats can be duplicated on any pastel card stock. It is recommended that you not laminate these because they tend to curl and counters slide around too much. Make one for every child.

Circular Fraction Pieces

First make three copies of each page of the master. Cut the disks apart and tape onto blank pages with three of the same type on a page. You will then have a separate master for each size with three full circles per master. Duplicate each master on a different color card stock. Laminate and then cut the circles out. A kit for one or two students should have two circles of each size piece.

Hundredths Disk

These disks can be made on paper but are much more satisfying on card stock. Duplicate the master on two contrasting colors. Laminate and cut the circles and also the slot on the dotted line. Make a set for each student. It's easy and worthwhile.

Tangrams and Mosaic Puzzle

Both tangrams and the Mosaic Puzzle should be copied on card stock. For younger children, the card stock should first be mounted on poster board to make the pieces a bit thicker and easier to put together in puzzles. You will want one set of each per student.

Woozle Cards

Copy the Woozle Card master on white or off-white card stock. You need two copies per set. Before laminating, color one set one color and the other a different color. An easy way to color the cards is to make one pass around the inside of each Woozle, leaving the rest of the creature white. If you color the entire Woozle, the dots may not show up. Make one set for every four students.

Transparencies and Overhead Models

A copy of any page can be made into a transparency with a photocopier. Alternatively, the PDF files can be printed directly onto transparency masters (use the appropriate transparency film for your printer). This method will avoid the minor distortions and blurring that sometimes occur with photocopying.

Some masters make fine transparency mats to use for demonstration purposes on the overhead. The 10 × 10 array, the blank hundreds board, and the large geoboard are examples. The five-frame and ten-frame work well with counters. The place-value mat can be used with strips and squares or with counters and cups directly on the overhead. The missing-part blank and the record blanks for the four algorithms are pages that you may wish to use as write-on transparencies.

A transparency of the 10,000 grid is the easiest way there is to show 10,000 or to model four-place decimal numbers.

A transparency of the degrees and wedges page is the very best way to illustrate what a degree is and also to help explain protractors.

All of the line and dot grids are useful to have available as transparencies. You may find it a good idea to make several copies of each and keep them in a folder where you can get to them easily.

For the Woozle Cards, dot cards, little ten-frames, and assorted shapes, make a reduction of the master on a photocopy machine. Then make transparencies of the small cards, cut them apart, and use them on the overhead.

2 more plus 2	2 more plus 2	1 more plus 1
2 less minus 2	1 less minus 1	1 more plus 1
2 less minus 2	1 less minus 1	zero 0

More-or-less cards — 1

0	1	2	3
4	5	6	7
8	9	10	

Number cards—2

Field Experience Guide: Resources for Teachers of Elementary and Middle School Mathematics © Allyn and Bacon 2007

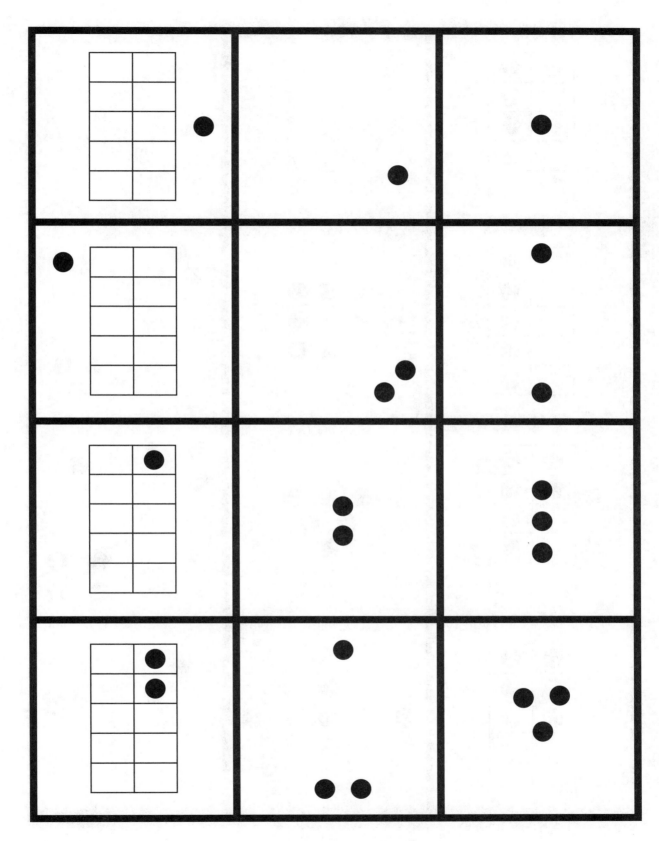

Dot cards—3

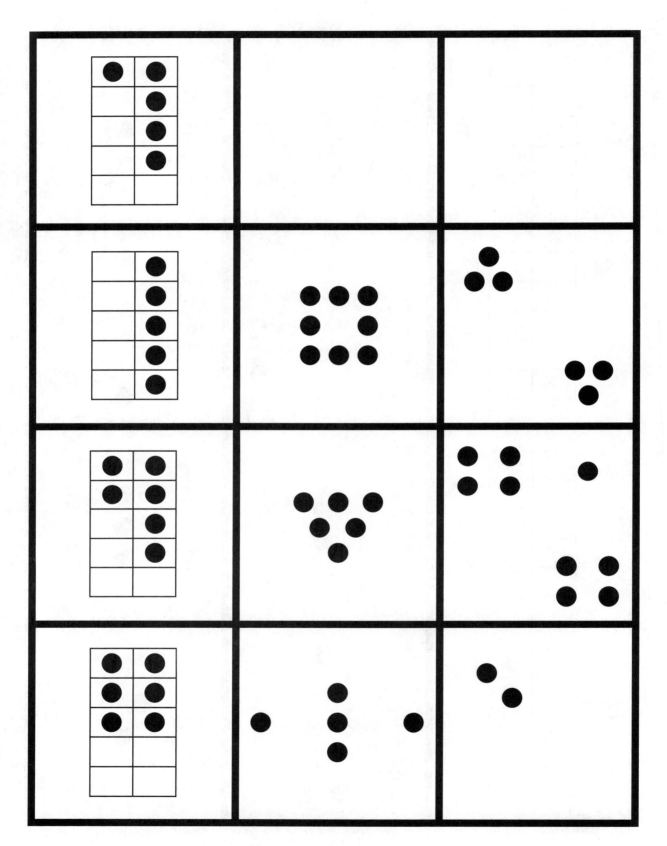

Dot cards—4

Field Experience Guide: Resources for Teachers of Elementary and Middle School Mathematics © Allyn and Bacon 2007

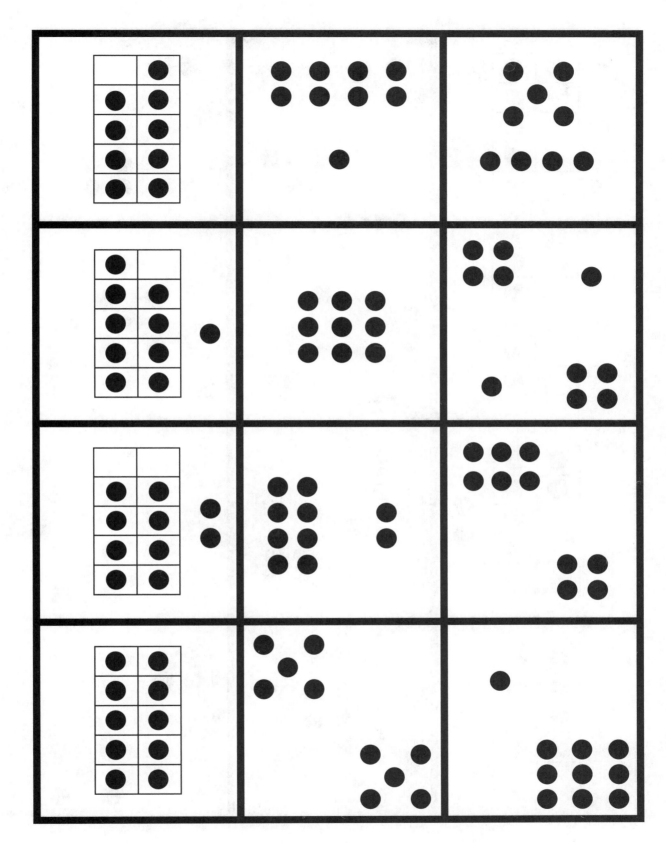

Dot cards—5

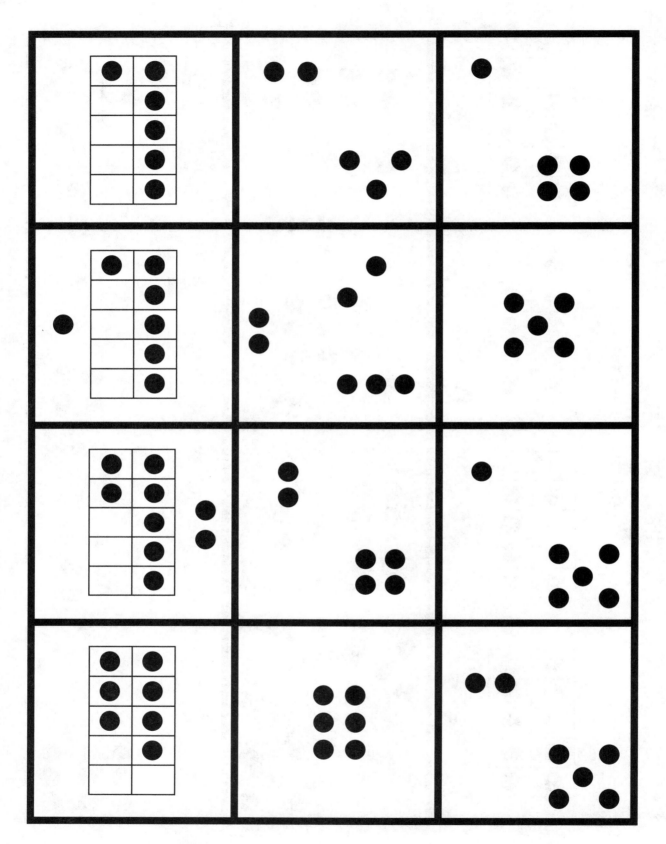

Dot cards—6

Field Experience Guide: Resources for Teachers of Elementary and Middle School Mathematics © Allyn and Bacon 2007

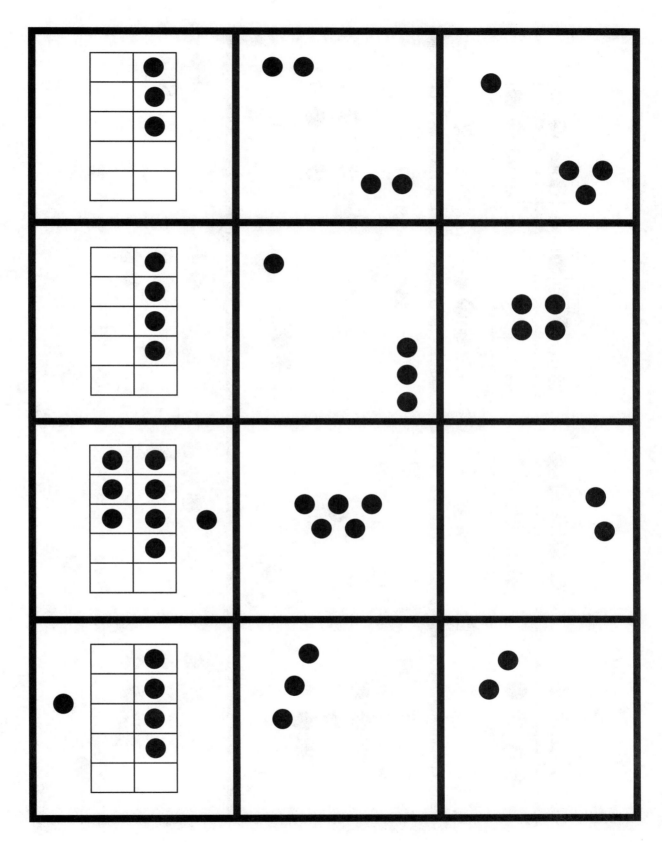

Dot cards—7

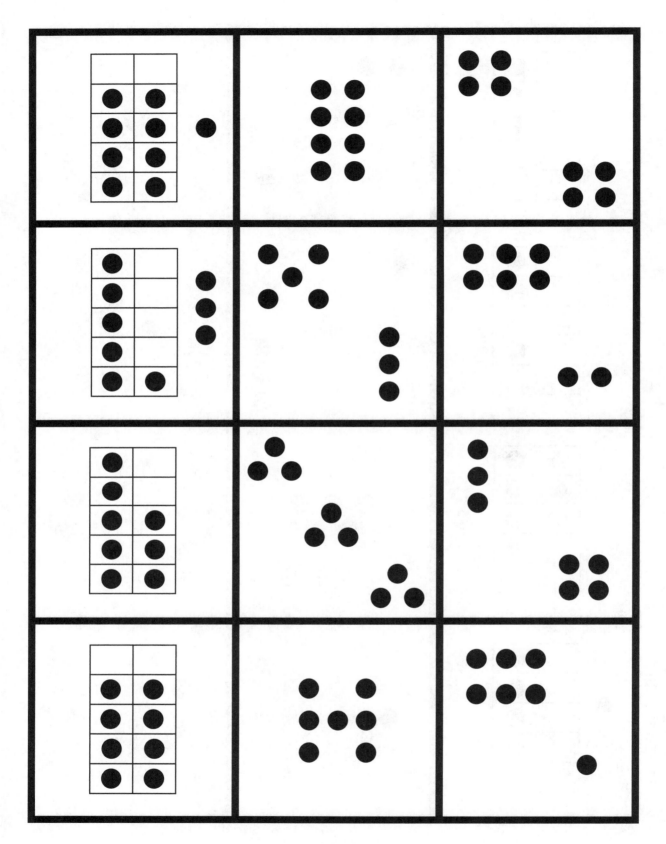

Dot cards—8

Field Experience Guide: Resources for Teachers of Elementary and Middle School Mathematics © Allyn and Bacon 2007

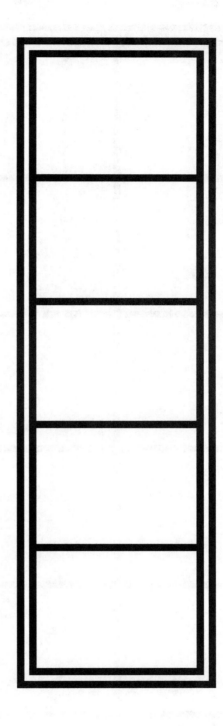

Five-frame—9

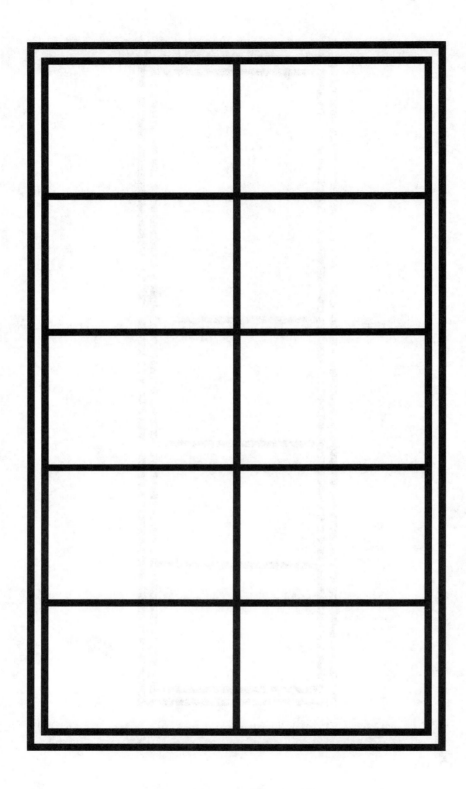

Ten-frame— 10

Field Experience Guide: Resources for Teachers of Elementary and Middle School Mathematics © Allyn and Bacon 2007

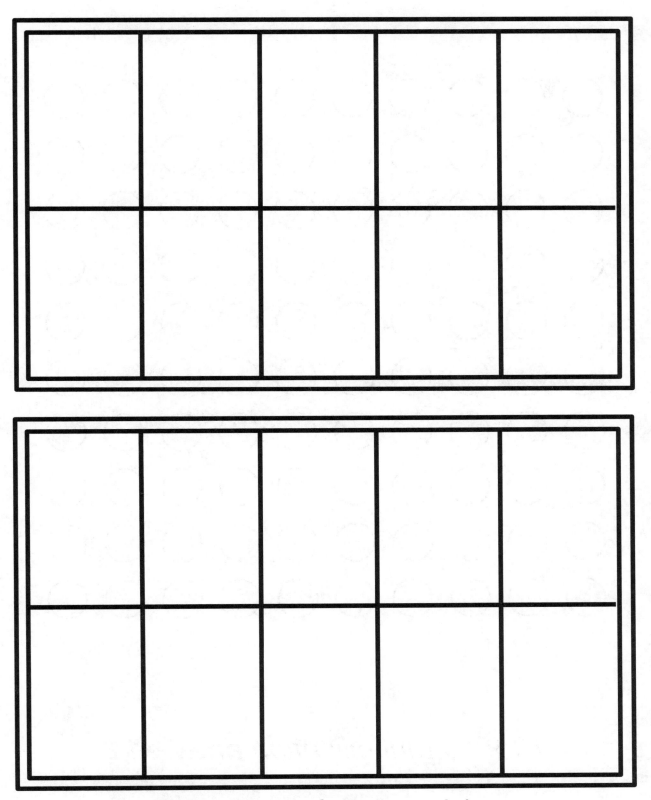

Double ten-frame—11

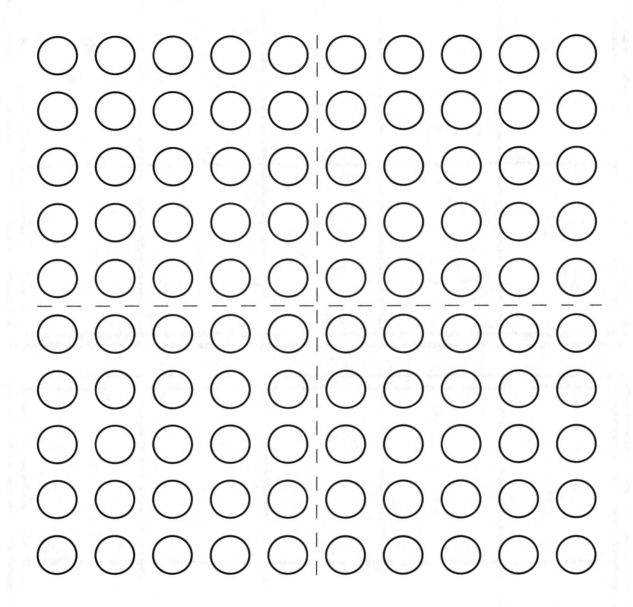

10 × 10 multiplication array—12

Field Experience Guide: Resources for Teachers of Elementary and Middle School Mathematics © Allyn and Bacon 2007

Missing-part blanks—13

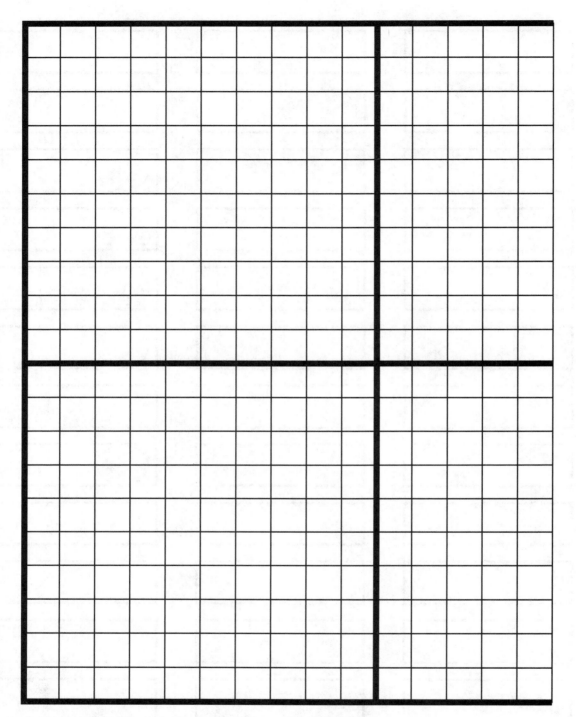

1. Make two copies of this page. Cut out the grid from each copy.
2. Overlap the two grids, and tape onto a blank sheet to form a 20-by-25-cm grid with 4 complete hundreds squares and 2 rows of 5 tens each.
3. Use this as a master to make copies on card stock.

Base-ten materials grid—14

Little ten-frames—15

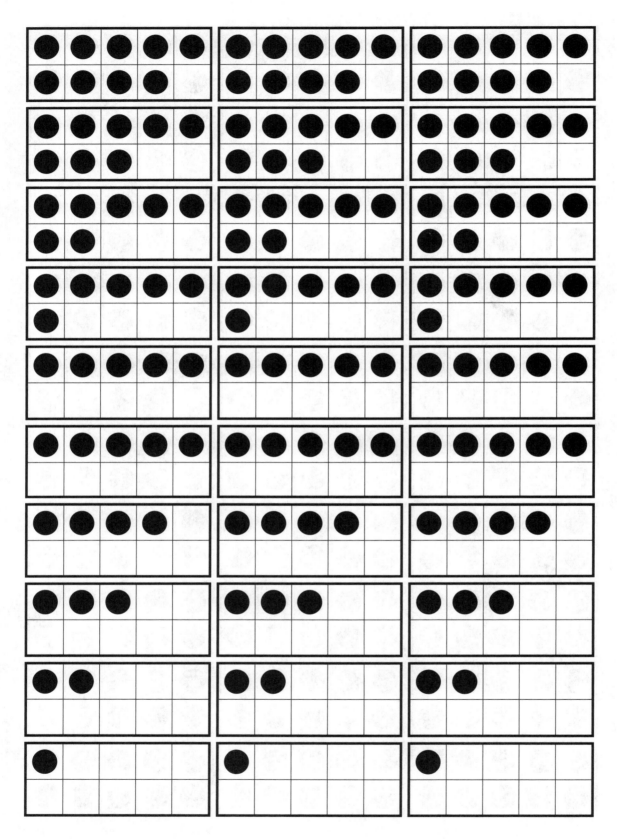

Little ten-frames—16

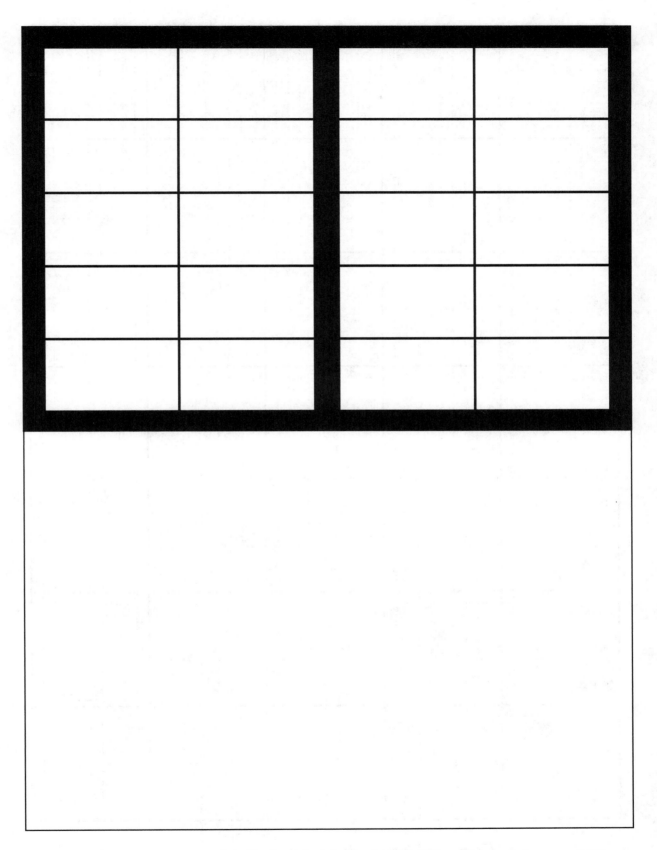

Place-value mat (with ten-frames)—17

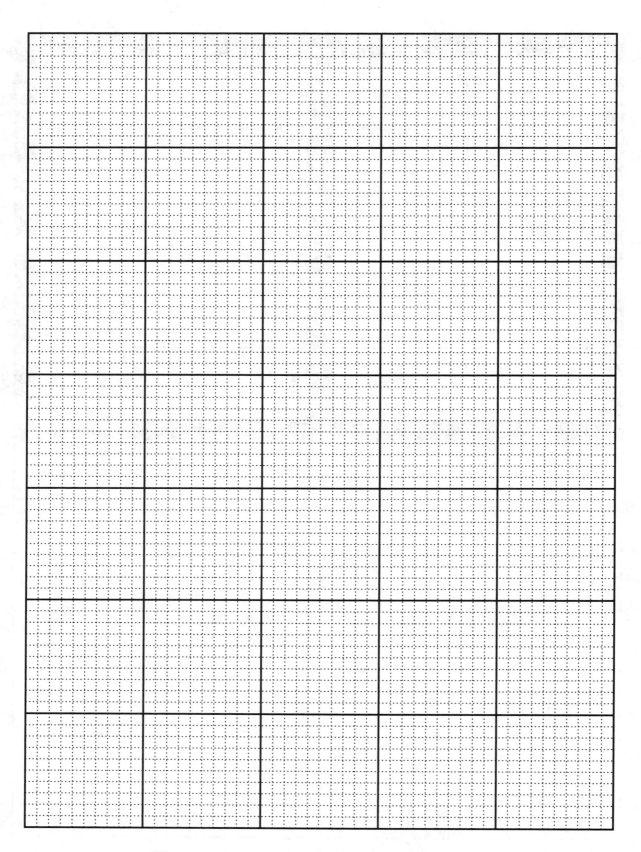

Base-ten grid paper—18

Field Experience Guide: Resources for Teachers of Elementary and Middle School Mathematics © Allyn and Bacon 2007

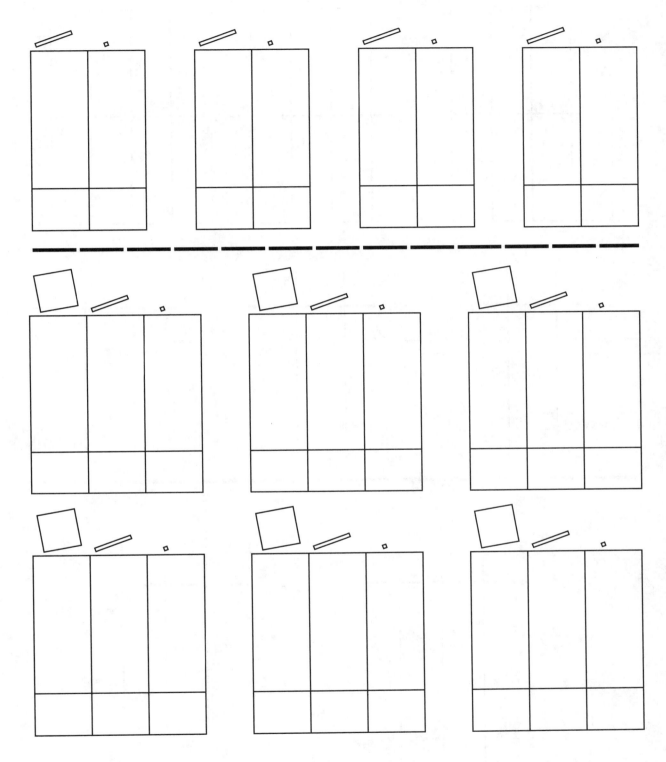

Addition and subtraction record blanks—19

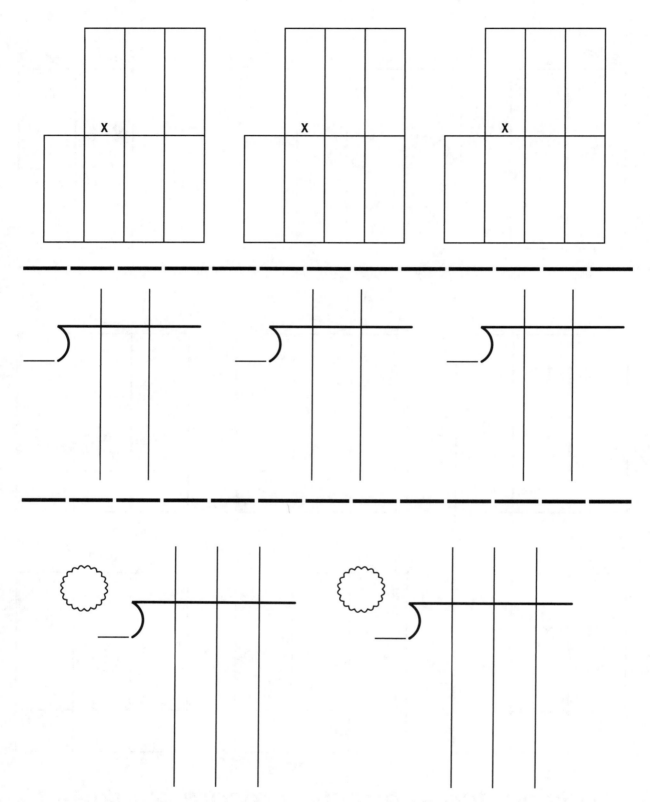

Multiplication and division record blanks—20

Field Experience Guide: Resources for Teachers of Elementary and Middle School Mathematics © Allyn and Bacon 2007

Blank hundreds chart (10 × 10 square)—21

1	2	3	4	5	6	7	8	9	10
11	12	13	14	15	16	17	18	19	20
21	22	23	24	25	26	27	28	29	30
31	32	33	34	35	36	37	38	39	40
41	42	43	44	45	46	47	48	49	50
51	52	53	54	55	56	57	58	59	60
61	62	63	64	65	66	67	68	69	70
71	72	73	74	75	76	77	78	79	80
81	82	83	84	85	86	87	88	89	90
91	92	93	94	95	96	97	98	99	100

Hundreds chart—22

1	2	3	4	5	6	7	8	9	10
11	12	13	14	15	16	17	18	19	20
21	22	23	24	25	26	27	28	29	30
31	32	33	34	35	36	37	38	39	40
41	42	43	44	45	46	47	48	49	50
51	52	53	54	55	56	57	58	59	60
61	62	63	64	65	66	67	68	69	70
71	72	73	74	75	76	77	78	79	80
81	82	83	84	85	86	87	88	89	90
91	92	93	94	95	96	97	98	99	100

1	2	3	4	5	6	7	8	9	10
11	12	13	14	15	16	17	18	19	20
21	22	23	24	25	26	27	28	29	30
31	32	33	34	35	36	37	38	39	40
41	42	43	44	45	46	47	48	49	50
51	52	53	54	55	56	57	58	59	60
61	62	63	64	65	66	67	68	69	70
71	72	73	74	75	76	77	78	79	80
81	82	83	84	85	86	87	88	89	90
91	92	93	94	95	96	97	98	99	100

1	2	3	4	5	6	7	8	9	10
11	12	13	14	15	16	17	18	19	20
21	22	23	24	25	26	27	28	29	30
31	32	33	34	35	36	37	38	39	40
41	42	43	44	45	46	47	48	49	50
51	52	53	54	55	56	57	58	59	60
61	62	63	64	65	66	67	68	69	70
71	72	73	74	75	76	77	78	79	80
81	82	83	84	85	86	87	88	89	90
91	92	93	94	95	96	97	98	99	100

1	2	3	4	5	6	7	8	9	10
11	12	13	14	15	16	17	18	19	20
21	22	23	24	25	26	27	28	29	30
31	32	33	34	35	36	37	38	39	40
41	42	43	44	45	46	47	48	49	50
51	52	53	54	55	56	57	58	59	60
61	62	63	64	65	66	67	68	69	70
71	72	73	74	75	76	77	78	79	80
81	82	83	84	85	86	87	88	89	90
91	92	93	94	95	96	97	98	99	100

Four small hundreds charts—23

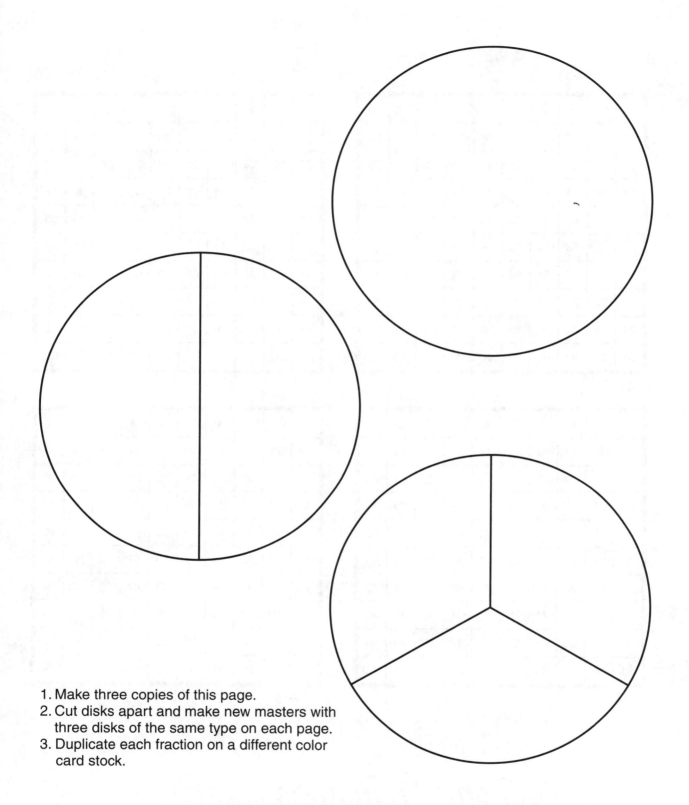

1. Make three copies of this page.
2. Cut disks apart and make new masters with three disks of the same type on each page.
3. Duplicate each fraction on a different color card stock.

Circular fraction pieces—24

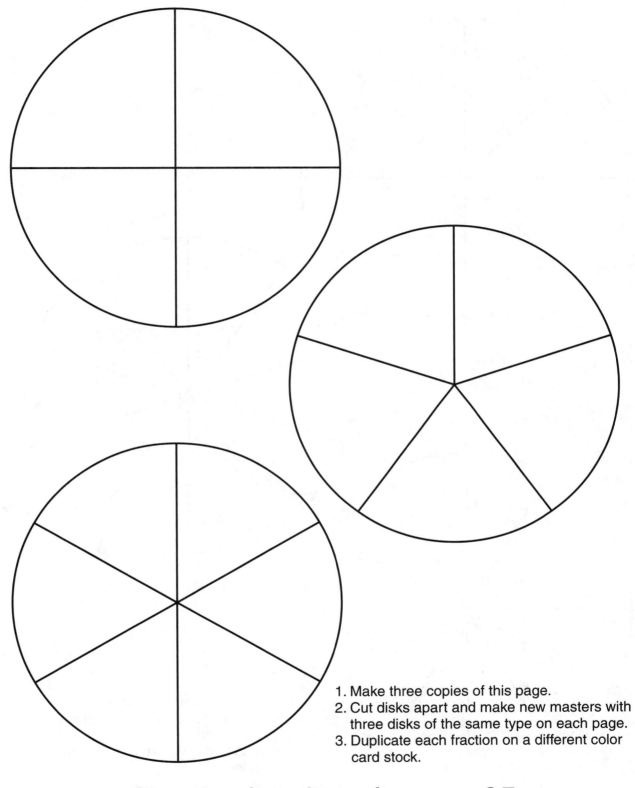

1. Make three copies of this page.
2. Cut disks apart and make new masters with three disks of the same type on each page.
3. Duplicate each fraction on a different color card stock.

Circular fraction pieces—25

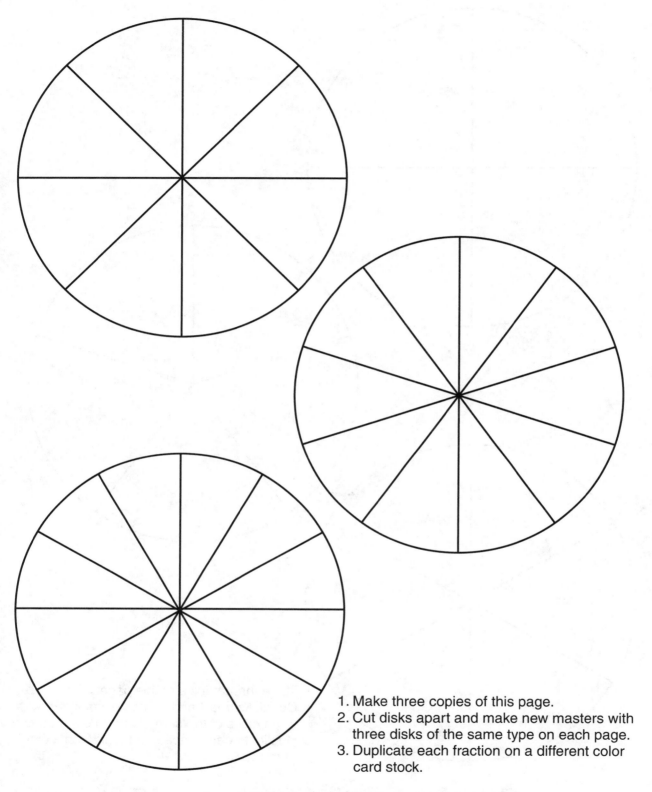

1. Make three copies of this page.
2. Cut disks apart and make new masters with three disks of the same type on each page.
3. Duplicate each fraction on a different color card stock.

Circular fraction pieces—26

Field Experience Guide: Resources for Teachers of Elementary and Middle School Mathematics © Allyn and Bacon 2007

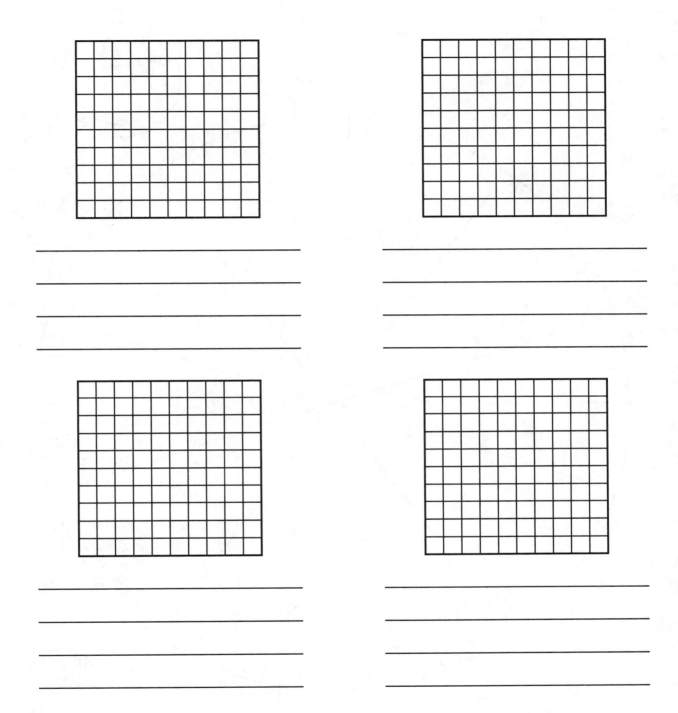

10 × 10 grids—27

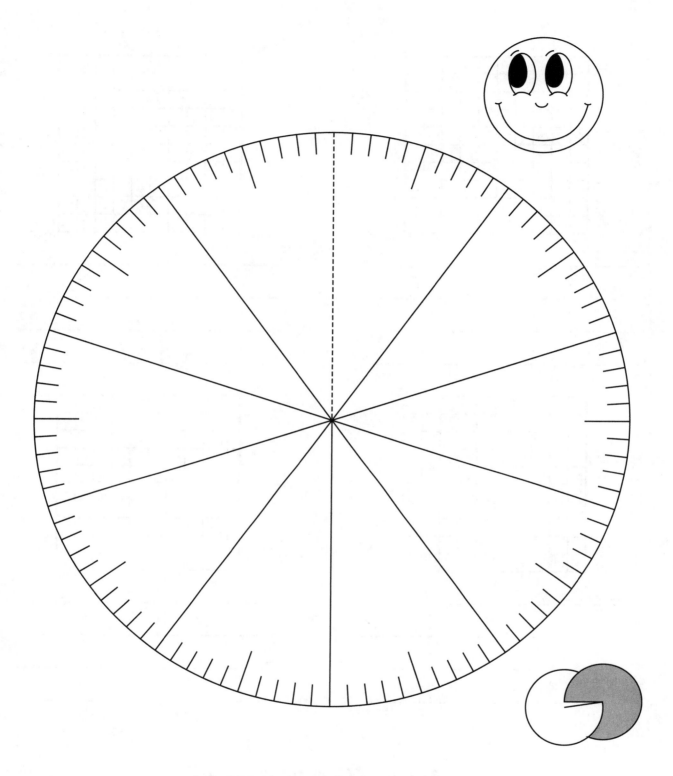

Hundredths disk—28

Field Experience Guide: Resources for Teachers of Elementary and Middle School Mathematics © Allyn and Bacon 2007

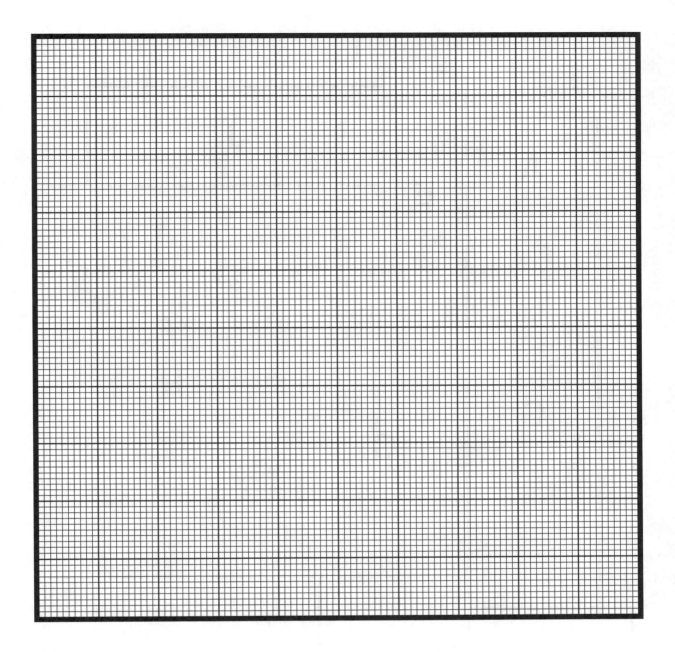

10,000 grid—29

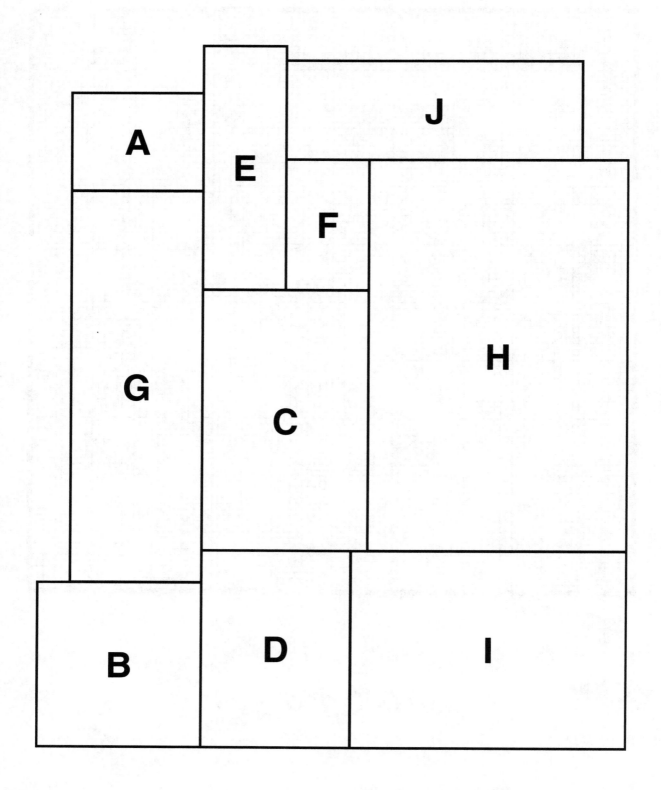

Look-alike rectangles—30

Field Experience Guide: Resources for Teachers of Elementary and Middle School Mathematics © Allyn and Bacon 2007

Look-Alike Rectangles
Three Groups and an Odd Ball

Rectangles Group 1 (Letter of rect.)	Measures in cm		Ratio of sides Short/Long
	Long side	Short side	

Rectangles Group 2 (Letter of rect.)	Measures in cm		Ratio of sides Short/Long
	Long side	Short side	

Rectangles Group 3 (Letter of rect.)	Measures in cm		Ratio of sides Short/Long
	Long side	Short side	

Odd Ball (Letter of rect.)	Measures in cm		Ratio of sides Short/Long
	Long side	Short side	

Look-alike rectangles recording sheet—31

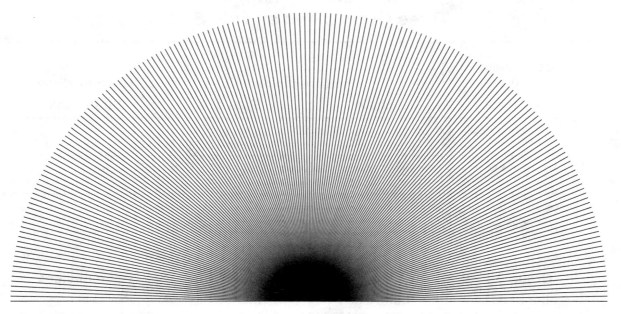

180 Degrees

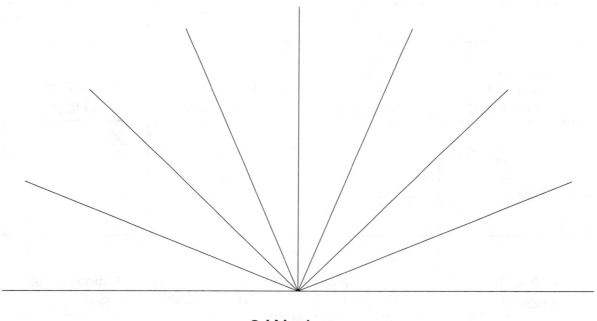

8 Wedges

Degrees and wedges—32

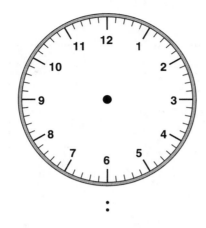

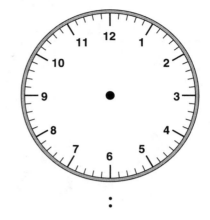

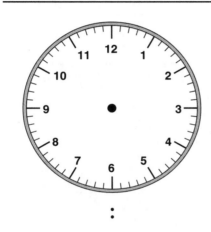

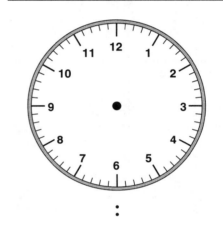

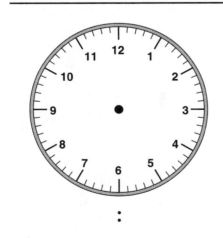

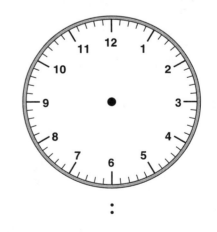

Clock faces—33

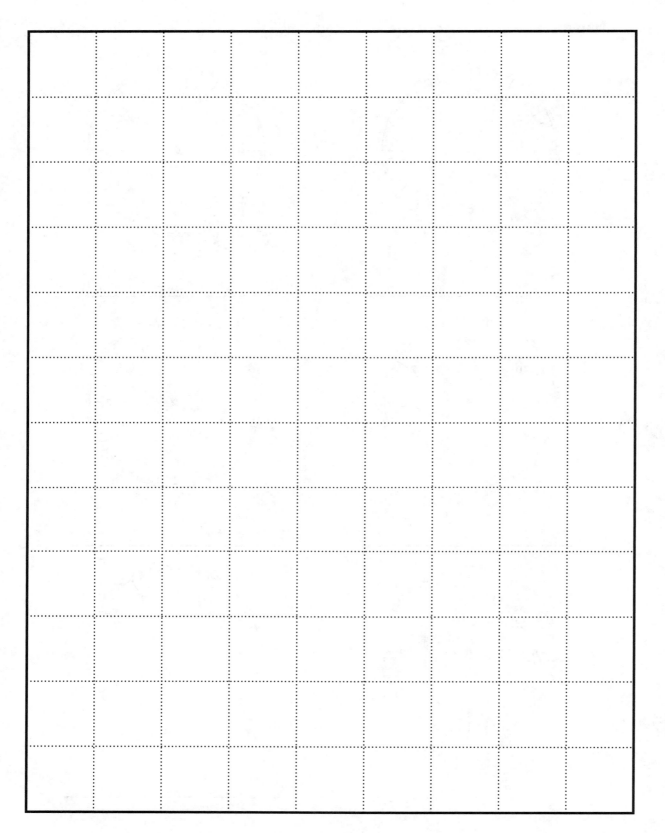

2-cm square grid—34

Field Experience Guide: Resources for Teachers of Elementary and Middle School Mathematics © Allyn and Bacon 2007

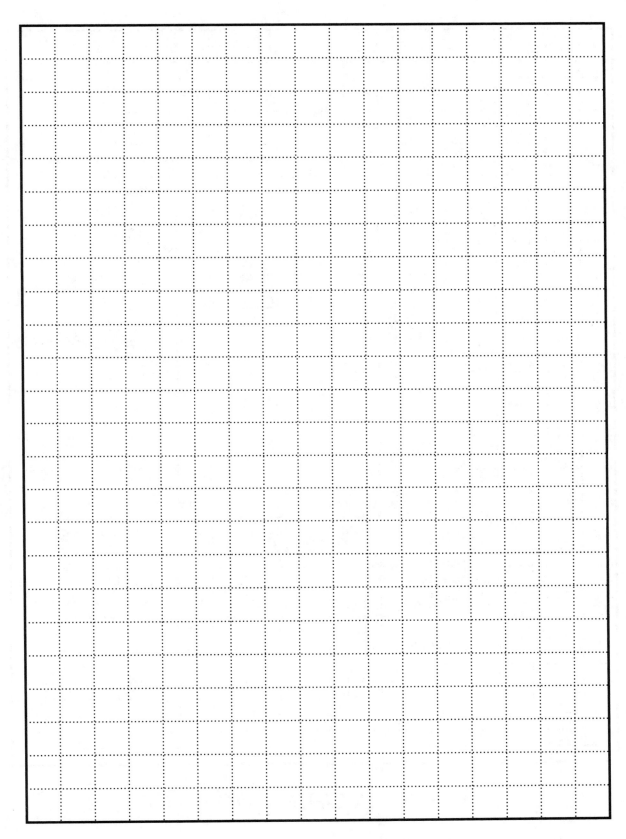

1-cm square grid—35

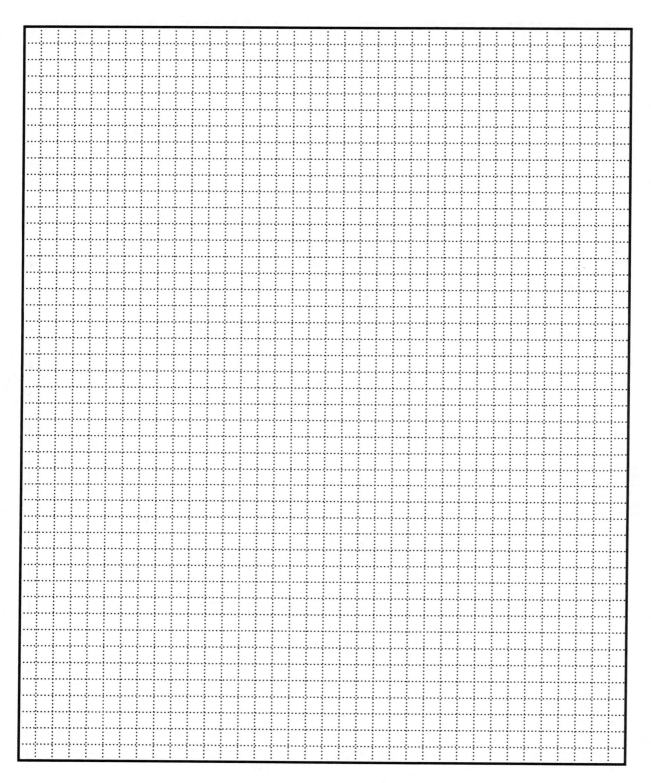

0.5-cm square grid—36

Field Experience Guide: Resources for Teachers of Elementary and Middle School Mathematics © Allyn and Bacon 2007

1-cm square dot grid—37

2-cm isometric grid—38

Field Experience Guide: Resources for Teachers of Elementary and Middle School Mathematics © Allyn and Bacon 2007

1-cm isometric dot grid—39

1-cm square/diagonal grid—40

Field Experience Guide: Resources for Teachers of Elementary and Middle School Mathematics © Allyn and Bacon 2007

Assorted shapes—41

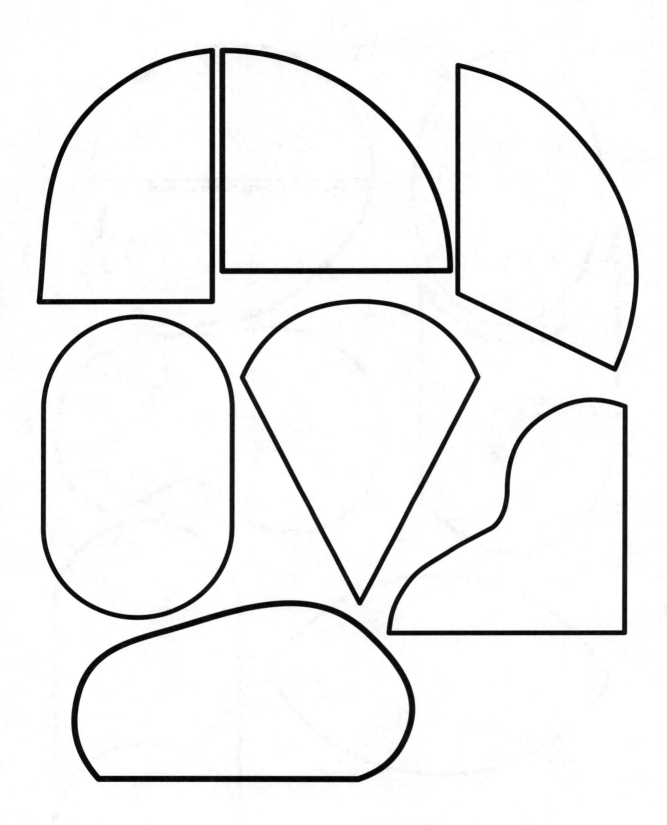

Assorted shapes—42

Field Experience Guide: Resources for Teachers of Elementary and Middle School Mathematics © Allyn and Bacon 2007

Assorted shapes—43

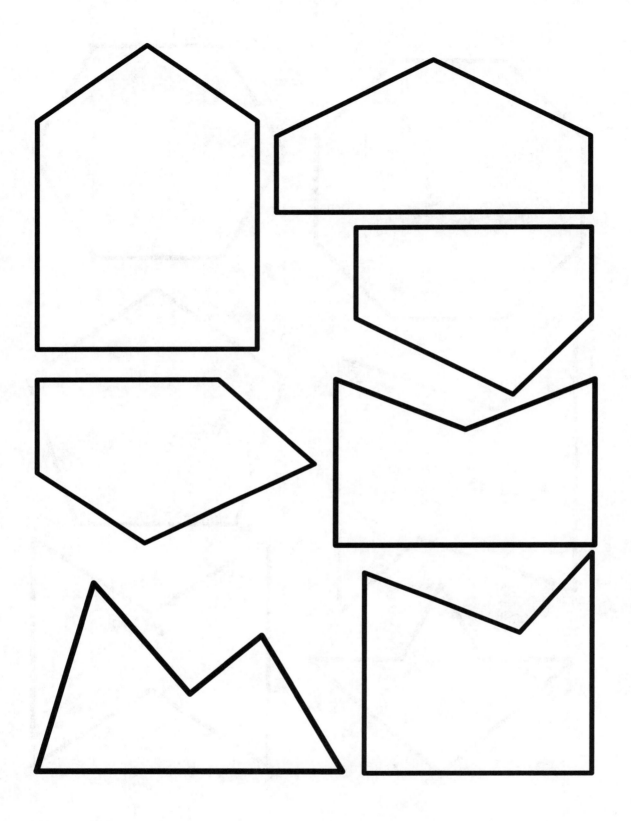

Assorted shapes—44

Field Experience Guide: Resources for Teachers of Elementary and Middle School Mathematics © Allyn and Bacon 2007

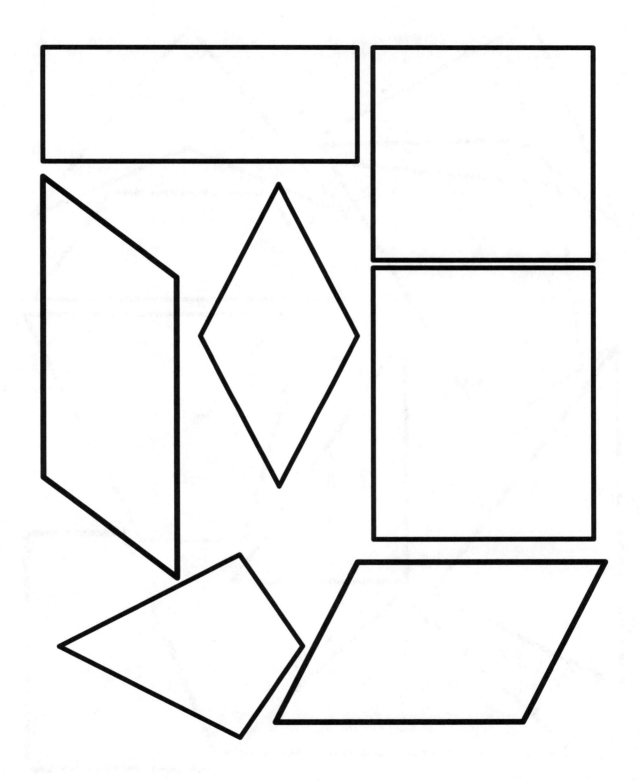

Assorted shapes—45

Assorted shapes—46

Assorted shapes—47

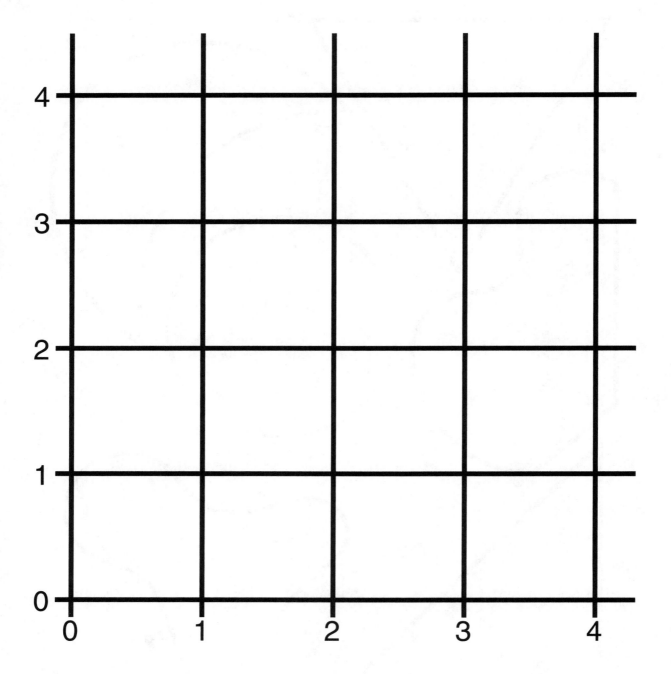

Coordinate grid —48

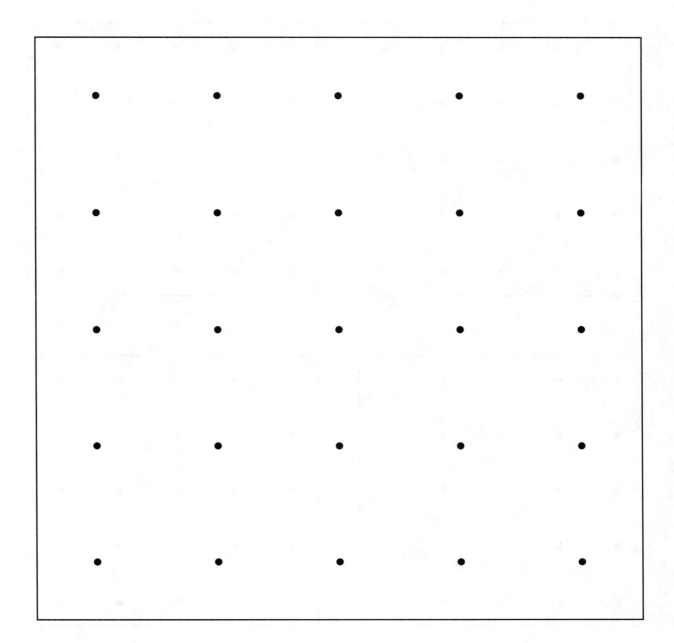

Geoboard pattern—49

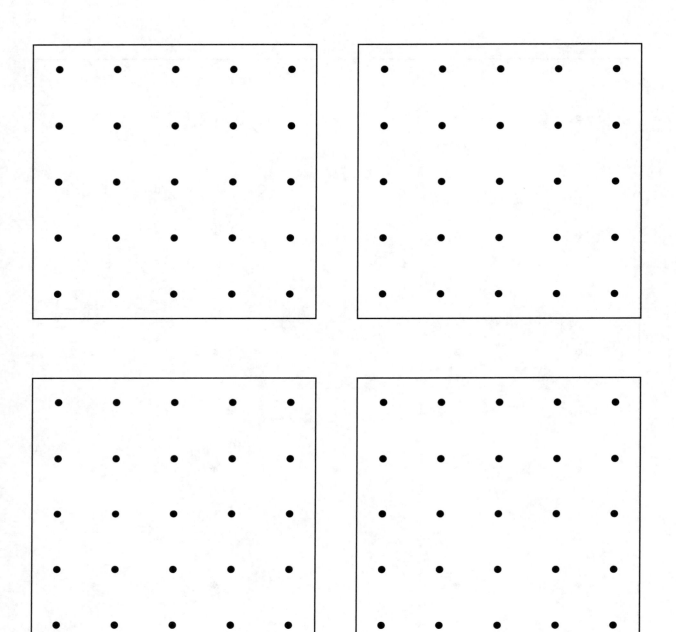

Geoboard recording sheets—50

Field Experience Guide: Resources for Teachers of Elementary and Middle School Mathematics © Allyn and Bacon 2007

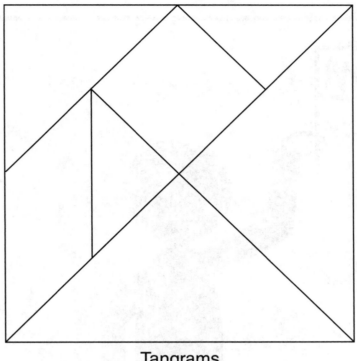

Tangrams

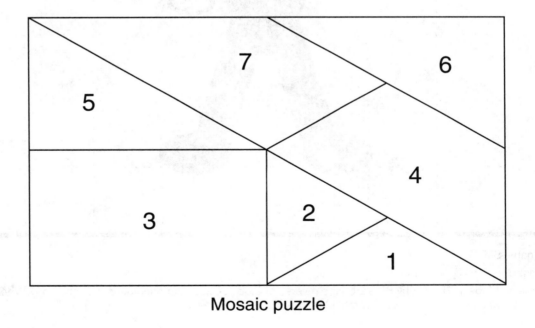

Mosaic puzzle

Tangrams and Mosaic Puzzle—51

Motion man—Side 1

Directions:

Make copies of Side 1. Then copy Side 2 on the reverse of Side 1. Check the orientation with one copy. When done correctly the two sides will match up when held to the light.

Motion Man—52

Motion man—Side 2
(See directions on Side 1.)

Motion Man—53

Parallelograms

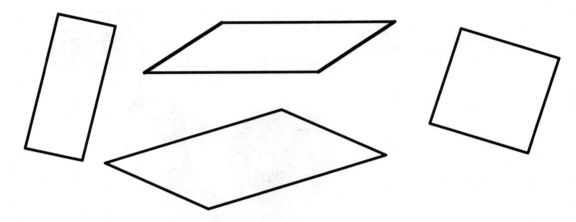

Properties of sides:

Properties of angles:

Properties of diagonals:

    Note: Diagonals are perpendicular or not
                 Bisected by the other or not
                 Congruent or not

Properties of symmetry (line and point):

Property lists for quadrilaterals—54

Rhombuses

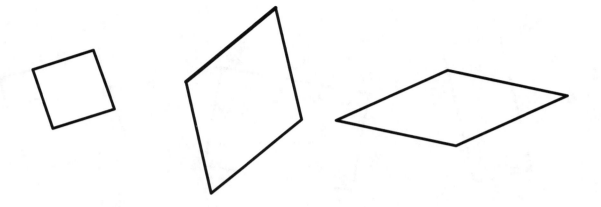

Properties of sides:

Properties of angles:

Properties of diagonals:
  Note: Diagonals are perpendicular or not
         Bisected by the other or not
         Congruent or not

Properties of symmetry (line and point):

Property lists for quadrilaterals—55

Rectangles

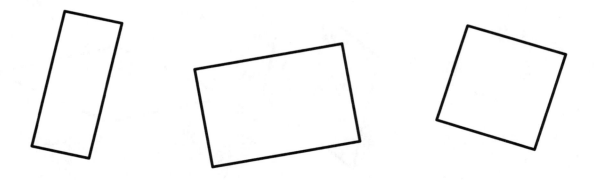

Properties of sides:

Properties of angles:

Properties of diagonals:
    Note: Diagonals are perpendicular or not
                Bisected by the other or not
                Congruent or not

Properties of symmetry (line and point):

Property lists for quadrilaterals—56

Squares

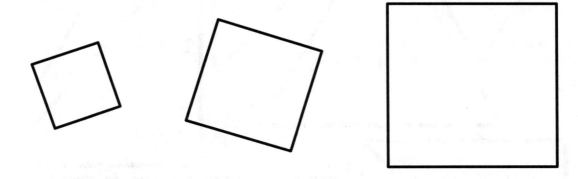

Properties of sides:

Properties of angles:

Properties of diagonals:
  Note: Diagonals are perpendicular or not
       Bisected by the other or not
       Congruent or not

Properties of symmetry (line and point):

Property lists for quadrilaterals—57

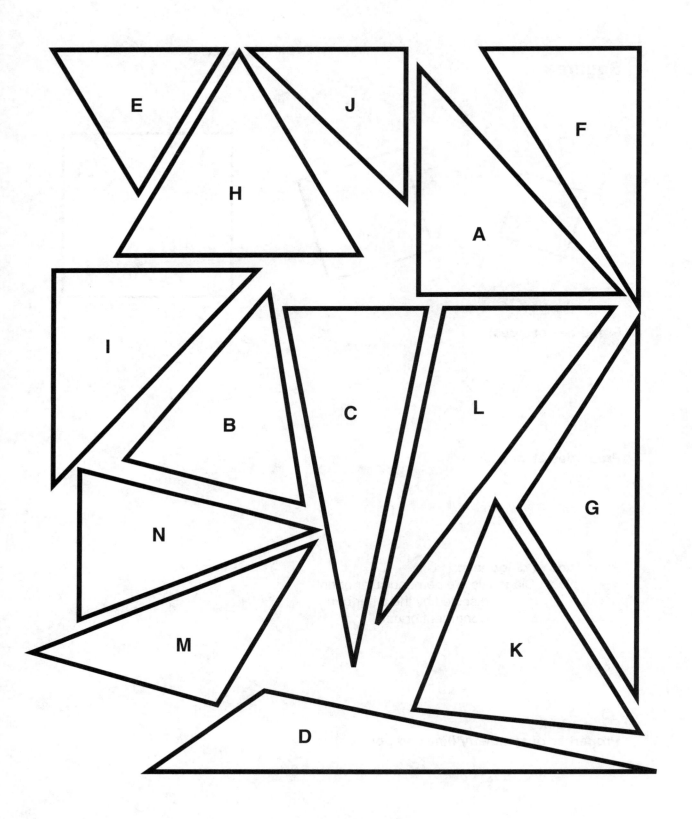

Assorted triangles—58

Woozle Cards—59

Name _____

2 More Than

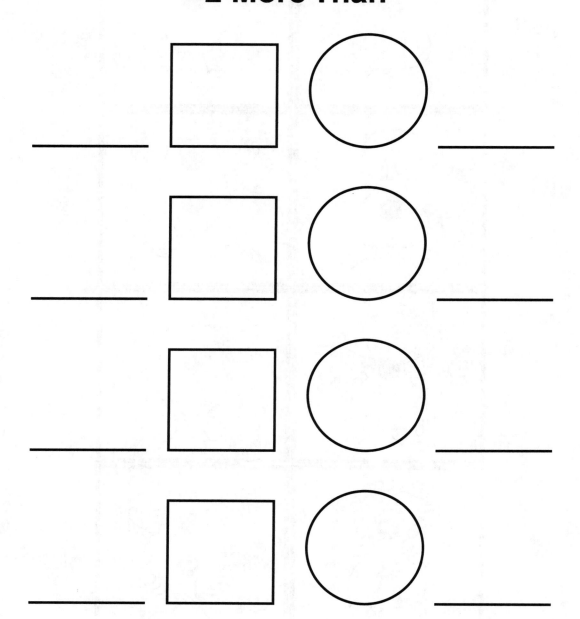

2 more than — 60

Field Experience Guide: Resources for Teachers of Elementary and Middle School Mathematics © Allyn and Bacon 2007

2 Less Than

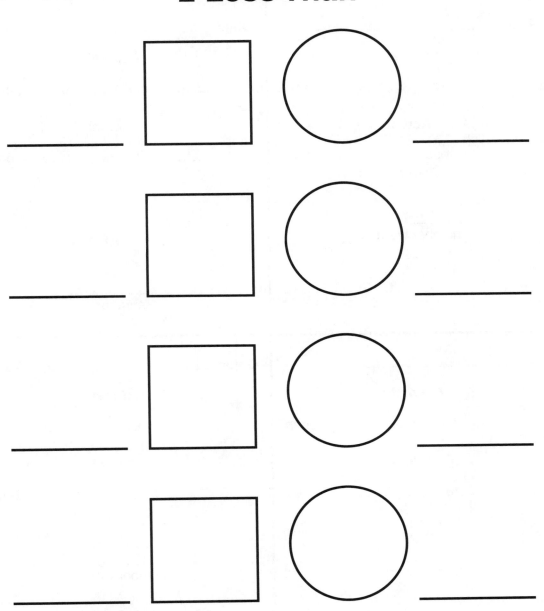

2 less than — 61

How Long?

Object...	**Object**...
Estimate	**Estimate**
.... tens ....ones	.... tens ....ones
Actual	**Actual**
.... tens ....ones	.... tens ....ones
....	....
number word	number word
....	....
number	number
Object...	**Object**...
Estimate	**Estimate**
.... tens ....ones	.... tens ....ones
Actual	**Actual**
.... tens ....ones	.... tens ....ones
....	....
number word	number word
....	....
number	number

How long?—62

Name _____

Fraction Names

Find fraction names for each shaded region. Explain how you saw each name you found.

1.

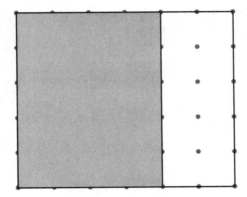

2.

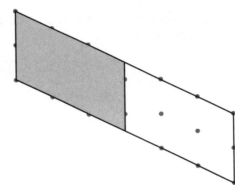

3.

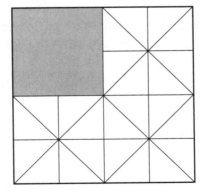

Fraction names—63

Name _____

Solve these problems. Use words and drawings to explain how you got your answer.

1. You have 3/4 of a pizza left. If you give 1/3 of the leftover pizza to your brother, how much of a whole pizza will your brother get?

2. Someone ate 1/10 of the cake, leaving only 9/10. If you eat 2/3 of the cake that is left, how much of a whole cake will you have eaten?

3. Gloria used 2 1/2 tubes of blue paint to paint the sky in her picture. Each tube holds 4/5 ounce of paint. How many ounces of blue paint did Gloria use?

64

It's a Matter of Rates

1. Terry can run 4 laps in 12 minutes. Susan can run 3 laps in 9 minutes. Who is the faster runner?

2. Jack and Jill were picking strawberries at the Pick Your Own Berry Patch. Jack "sampled" 5 berries every 25 minutes. Jill ate 3 berries every 10 minutes. If they both pick at about the same speed, who will bring home more berries?

3. Some of the hens in Farmer Brown's chicken farm lay brown eggs and the others lay white eggs. Farmer Brown noticed that in the large hen house he collected about 4 brown eggs for every 10 white ones. In the smaller hen house the ratio of brown to white was 1 to 3. In which hen house do the hens lay more brown eggs?

4. The Talks-a-Lot Phone Company charges 70¢ for every 15 minutes. Reaching Out Phone Company charges $1.00 for 20 minutes. Which company is offering the cheaper rate?

It's a matter of rates—65

Windows

Name _____

Step	1	2	3	4	5	6	7		20
No. of stiks	4	7	10						

Describe the pattern you see in the drawing:

_____
_____
_____
_____

Describe the pattern you see in the table:

_____
_____
_____
_____

Describe how you can find the number of sticks in the 20th step:

_____
_____
_____
_____
_____
_____

Windows—66

Predict How Many

Name _____

Step	1	2	3	4	5	6	7	8	9	...	20
No. of stiks	2	6	12	20						...	

Describe the pattern you see in the drawing:

_____
_____
_____
_____

Describe the pattern you see in the table:

_____
_____
_____
_____

Describe how you can find the number of sticks in the 20th step:

_____
_____
_____
_____
_____
_____

Predict how many—67

Create a Journey Story

If possible, create a story about a journey that the graph could represent.
If not possible, explain.

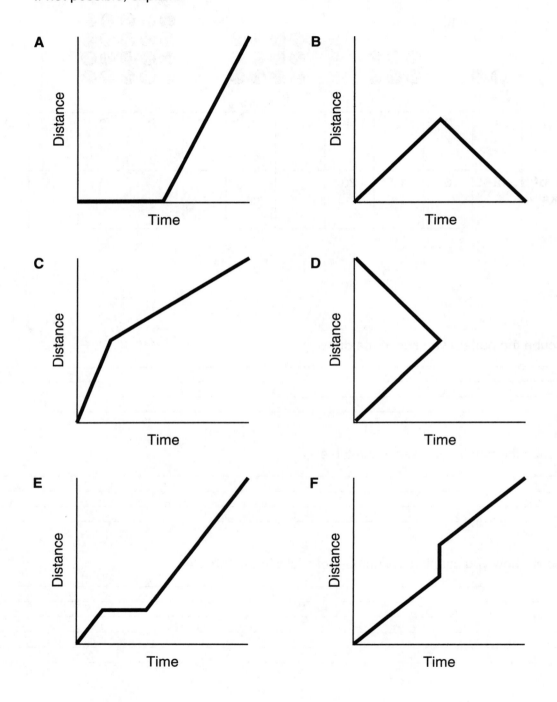

Create a journey story—68

Name _____

Name _____

Crooked Paths

Circle the longer path. If they are the same, circle both.

How we decided: (Draw pictures)

Crooked paths—69

Rectangles made with 36 tiles

Rectangle Dimensions	Area	Perimeter

Rectangles made with 36 tiles—70

Name_____

Properties of Quadrilateral Diagonals

Name of Quadrilateral	Congruent Diagonals		Diagonals Bisected			Intersection of Diagonals	
	Yes	No	Both	One	Neither	Perpendicular	Not

Properties of quadrilateral diagonals—71

Toy Purchases

Toy purchases—72

Field Experience Guide: Resources for Teachers of Elementary and Middle School Mathematics © Allyn and Bacon 2007

Toying with Measures

Name _____

	Mean	Median	Mode
Original Set of 6			

Make predictions based on these change. Give reasons for your predictions.

Add a $20 toy			
Reasons			
Return the $1 toy			
Reasons			
Get a free toy			
Reasons			
Buy a second $12 toy			
Reasons			
Your change:			
Reasons			

Calculate the actual statistics for each of the changes.

Add a $20 toy			
Return the $1 toy			
Get a free toy			
Buy a second $12 toy			
Your change:			

Toying with measures—73